Authentic Assessment and Evaluation Approaches and Practices in a Digital Era

Global Education in the 21st Century Series

Series Editor

Tasos Barkatsas (RMIT *University, Australia*)

Editorial Board

Amanda Berry (*Monash University, Australia*)
Andrea Chester (RMIT *University, Australia*)
Anthony Clarke (*University of British Columbia, Canada*)
Yuksel Dede (*Gazi University, Turkey*)
Vasilis Gialamas (*National and Kapodistrian University of Athens, Greece*)
Kathy Jordan (RMIT *University, Australia*)
Peter Kelly (RMIT *University, Australia*)
Huk Yuen Law (*The Chinese University of Hong Kong*)
Patricia McLaughlin (RMIT *University, Australia*)
Juanjo Mena (*University of Salamanca, Spain*)
Wee Tiong Seah (*The University of Melbourne, Australia*)
Dianne Siemon (RMIT *University, Australia*)
Robert Strathdee (*Victoria University, Australia*)
Ngai Ying Wong (*The Education University of Hong Kong, Hong Kong*)
Qiaoping Zhang (*The Education University of Hong Kong, Hong Kong*)

VOLUME 5

The titles published in this series are listed at *brill.com/gecs*

Authentic Assessment and Evaluation Approaches and Practices in a Digital Era

A Kaleidoscope of Perspectives

Edited by

Tasos Barkatsas and Tricia McLaughlin

BRILL

LEIDEN | BOSTON

All chapters in this book have undergone peer review.

The Library of Congress Cataloging-in-Publication Data is available online at http://catalog.loc.gov

Typeface for the Latin, Greek, and Cyrillic scripts: "Brill". See and download: brill.com/brill-typeface.

ISSN 2542-9728
ISBN 978-90-04-50155-3 (paperback)
ISBN 978-90-04-50156-0 (hardback)
ISBN 978-90-04-50157-7 (e-book)

Copyright 2021 by Koninklijke Brill NV, Leiden, The Netherlands.
Koninklijke Brill NV incorporates the imprints Brill, Brill Nijhoff, Brill Hotei, Brill Schöningh, Brill Fink, Brill mentis, Vandenhoeck & Ruprecht, Böhlau Verlag and V&R Unipress.
All rights reserved. No part of this publication may be reproduced, translated, stored in a retrieval system, or transmitted in any form or by any means, electronic, mechanical, photocopying, recording or otherwise, without prior written permission from the publisher. Requests for re-use and/or translations must be addressed to Koninklijke Brill NV via brill.com or copyright.com.

This book is printed on acid-free paper and produced in a sustainable manner.

Contents

Preface   IX
Acknowledgements   XIII
List of Figures and Tables   XIV
Notes on Contributors   XVII

PART 1
Authentic Assessment and Evaluation Approaches and Practices in Tertiary Education

1 Can a Standards-Based Assessment of Teaching Be Authentic?   3
   Rebecca Cooper and Michelle Ludecke

2 Authentic Assessment in STEM Education: An Integrative Review of Research   24
   Hazel Tan and Gillian Kidman

3 Virtual Simulation in ITE: Technology Driven Authentic Assessment and Moderation of Practice   53
   Zara Ersozlu, Susan Ledger and Linda Hobbs

4 Authentic Assessment to Promote Active Online Learning and Critical Reflection   69
   Greg Oates and Paul Denny

5 A Holistic Review of Authentic Assessment in Mathematics Education   95
   Qiaoping Zhang, Xiaolei Zhang and Jiabo Liu

6 A Model for Developing Preservice Mathematics Teachers' Mathematical Language Skills in the Context of Authentic Assessment   116
   Fatma Nur Aktaş, Pınar Akyıldız and Yüksel Dede

7 Embedding Authentic Assessment in a Capstone Research Course in a Teacher Education Degree 142
Tricia McLaughlin, Kathy Littlewood, Belinda Kennedy and Tasos Barkatsas

8 Making It Happen: A Case Study of Authentic Assessment for Learning in a Final Year Capstone Course 162
Gráinne Ryan and Dallas Wingrove

PART 2
Authentic Assessment Approaches and Practices in Primary and Secondary Education

9 Using Learning Trajectory-Based Ratio Curriculum and Diagnostic Assessments for Promoting Learner-Centred Instruction 187
Jere Confrey, Meetal Shah and Michael Belcher

10 Removing the Teacher 'Blind Spot': Developing a Comprehensive Online Place Value Assessment Tool for Year 3–6 Teachers 217
Angela Rogers

11 How Much Do They Know about 3D Objects: Using Authentic Assessment to Inform Teaching Practice 240
Rebecca Seah and Marj Horne

12 Humanising Mathematics Education through Authentic Assessment: The Story of Sarah 262
Huk-Yuen Law

13 Translanguaging Pedagogies for Multilingual Learner Assessment 285
Naomi Wilks-Smith

PART 3
Educational Evaluation Approaches and Practices

14 Teacher Performance Evaluation Approach from a Brazilian Perspective: A Literature Review 315
Fabiano Pereira dos Santos, Ivan Fortunato and Juanjo Mena

15 A Systemic Approach to Authentic Evaluation in Education: The Case of Mathematics Teaching Effectiveness in Tertiary Engineering Education   329
    Katerina Kasimatis, Andreas Moutsios-Rentzos and Fragkiskos Kalavasis

16 Parents' Views on the Authentic Evaluation of Students in the Experimental Schools of Greece   350
    Antonios Bouras and Anastasia Papadopoulou

17 Authentic Evaluation and Authentic Leadership in Education: Two Converging Concepts in the Case of School Principals   367
    Chrysoula Arcoudis, Anastasia Papadopoulou and Athina Chalkiadaki

Index   387

Preface

This work, Authentic Assessment, is the fifth book in the series Global Education in the 21st Century by Series Editor Tasos Barkatsas. In this book a number of international academics explore the concept of authentic assessment as it applies in both tertiary and school education.

In its broadest definition authentic assessment is the measurement of intellectual accomplishments that are worthwhile, significant, and meaningful. But as the contributors to this work illustrate, authentic assessment is an important pedagogical structure. It is a concept more closely defined as an umbrella term that seeks to immerse learners in environments where they can gain highly practical, lifelong learning skills.

Authentic assessment has been on the educational agenda for a number of years. The term 'authentic assessment' was first coined by Wiggins (1989) in school contexts. He noted that authentic tasks replicate real-world challenges and standards of performance that experts or professionals (e.g., mathematicians, scientists and teachers) typically face in the field.

A number of authors have since aligned authentic assessment with performance assessment. Shepard (2000) noted that authentic tasks are often performance-based, and include complex and ill-structured problems that are well aligned with the rigorous and higher-order learning objectives in a reformed vision of curriculum.

In reality all authentic assessments are performance assessments because they require students to construct extended responses, to perform on something, or to produce a product. Both process and product are crucial to authentic assessments, and hence formative assessments—open questioning, descriptive feedback, self- and peer assessments etc., all play an important part in the process of authentic assessments.

Koh (2017) notes that authentic tasks assess not only students' authentic performance or work, but also their dispositions such as persistence in solving messy and complex problems, positive habits of mind, growth mindset, resilience and grit, and self-directed learning. For teachers authentic assessment enables the provision of descriptive feedback, self- and peer assessment using criteria and standards as in the form of holistic or analytic rubrics. This is well illustrated by Rogers (Chapter 10) when she explores a Comprehensive Online Place Value Assessment Tool for Year 3–6 Teachers. Her work identifies the advantages of reflection and feedback in the learning process.

If the purpose of authentic assessment is to provide students with ample opportunity to engage in authentic tasks so as to develop, use, and extend their knowledge, higher-order thinking, and other 21st-century competencies, then

Cooper and Ludecke (Chapter 1) perfectly illustrate this opportunity. Their work examines an enforced standards-based assessment of practice, concluding that in spite of the rigidity of the imposed teacher practice standards, students were able to negotiate the standards to make links to "real teaching" and match the imposed standards work to the authenticity of the profession. They write of the shift in understanding of the assessment tool from an 'assignment' to an authentic representation of 'real teaching'. They point to the opportunities for aspirational learning that arise from using the authentic assessment tasks as a negotiation rather than as a prescription.

In a similar manner Tan and Kidman (Chapter 2) examine authentic assessment as activities engaging students in authentic inquiry processes involving higher order thinking skills relating to the real world. They present an integrative review of how authentic assessment is understood, and investigated, in STEM education research. By reviewing the empirical studies that focus on authentic assessment in STEM education and analyzing how the conflation of authentic assessment terms are conceptualized in terms of its constituent components in STEM education, they provide an insight into how authentic assessment can strengthen STEM learning and teaching.

Gulikers, Bastiaens, and Kirschner (2004) defined authentic assessment as assessment that require students to use the competence, or a combination of knowledge, skills and behaviors that should be applied in their professional life situations. Ersozlu, Ledger and Hobbs (Chapter 3) argue that authentic assessment aligns well with the functionalities of a virtual learning environment in their chapter about virtual simulation in Initial Teacher Education (ITE). Their findings indicate that Virtual simulations are designed to imitate experiences that professionals face in their every-day work life and thus offer unique learning environments capable of providing opportunities for authentic assessment tasks within initial teacher education programs.

This virtual online approach to authentic assessment is also evident in Oates and Denny's explanation of PeerWise (Chapter 4). Through a range of measurements, their analysis identified that students experienced meaningful shifts in their Pedagogical Content Knowledge (PCK) of mathematics resulting from peer-feedback and facilitated by the online interactions provided by the PeerWise platform.

In addition to relating to the future profession and real-world contexts, there is evidence that authentic assessment allows the learner to extrapolate the lessons learnt through such assessment to their own understanding of the world (Lloyd & Davidson, 2005). Law (Chapter 12) also explores how we can address this issue of allowing learners to extrapolate from lessons learnt when describing the humanising of mathematics education. His study reinstates the advocacy of humanising mathematics through the designing of authentic assessment for learning mathematics itself in view of the learners' struggling over the dominant accountability assessment discourse.

A number of researchers have noted that authentic assessment is a strong measure of a student's skills and knowledge as it relates to specific contexts and is often related to future work skills (Lloyd & Davidson, 2005). This potential for capstone courses at university to be used as sites for future work skills is illustrated in chapters by McLaughlin, Littlewood, Kennedy and Barkatsas (Chapter 7) and in the work of Ryan and Wingrove (Chapter 8). Both groups of authors conclude that authentic learning and assessment is undeniably critical to effective capstone course design and teaching, whilst describing different discipline contexts, the importance of assessments that were were situated within a socially constructed model requiring participation in a community of peers, that allowed for reflective pedagogy; and that allowed for feedback and evaluation from other practising professionals was explicit.

Boud and Falchikov (2006) defined the concept of authentic assessment as assessment that meets academic standards and prepares students for future learning in work and life. But the adaptation of authentic assessment in mathematics is problematic. Both Zhang, Zhang and Liu (Chapter 5) and Aktas, Akyildiz and Dede (Chapter 6) approach this discussion from different viewpoints, but both conclude that whilst traditional mathematics education isolates content knowledge from real-life situations and focuses mainly on tedious and repetitive problem solving, authenticity and authentic assessments play an important role in allowing mathematics to be applied to real life.

Authentic assessments also have the capacity to capture students' dispositions such as positive habits of mind, growth mindset, persistence in solving complex problems, resilience and grit, and self-directed learning. The use of scoring criteria and human judgments are two of the essential components of authentic assessments (Wiggins, 1989).

This is well illustrated by Kasimatis, Moutsios-Rentzos and Kalavasis (Chapter 16) who introduce a systemic approach to authentic assessment in tertiary engineering education. Through a process of systemic reflections, they describe how the subjects in their study observe, reflect and act upon a system that explicitly includes themselves, thus being authentic for the system. This approach supports the educational unit to develop an attitude of mindful participation with a community around matters of shared concern.

In Chapter 15 Fabiano Pereira dos Santos, Ivan Fortunato and Juanjo Mena provide a literature review of teacher performance evaluation approach from Brazilian perspective.

Bouras and Papadopoulou (Chapter 16) provide an insight into the investigation, recording and capture of the views of parents whose children attend Pilot and Experimental schools in Greece. They examine the contribution and effectiveness of authentic evaluation as well as the achievement of educational goals, as they are formulated in the curricula.

The final chapter in this work by Arcoudis, Papadopoulou and Chalkiadaki (Chapter 17) examines the paradigm of authentic assessment and evaluation in authentic leadership with regards to school principals. The study highlights the relationship between authentic leadership and authentic evaluation by outlining the characteristics of authentic leadership and describing some of the tools, methods and approaches of authentic assessment that could be incorporated in school principal selection and evaluation procedures when designing a policy for authentic leadership in education.

These chapters and the totality of this book illustrate how authentic assessment is an effective measure of intellectual achievement or ability as it requires the demonstration of deep understanding, higher-order thinking and complex problem solving through the performance of rich and exemplary authentic tasks.

If nothing else, this book underlines the value of authentic assessment as a powerful tool for assessing students' 21st-century competencies in the context of global educational reforms.

References

Boud, D., & Falchikov, N. (2006). Aligning assessment with long-term learning. *Assessment & Evaluation in Higher Education, 31*(4), 399–413.

Gulikers, J. T., Bastiaens, T. J., & Kirschner, P. A. (2004). A five-dimensional framework for authentic assessment. *Educational Technology Research and Development, 52*(3), 67.

Koh, K. H. (2017). Authentic assessment. In *Oxford research encyclopedia of education*.

Lloyd, D., & Davidson, P. (2005). Task-based integrated-skills assessment. In D. Lloyd, P. Davidson, & C. Coombe (Eds.), *The fundamentals of language assessment: A practical guide for teachers in the Gulf* (pp. 157–166). TESOL Arabia.

Shepard, L. A. (2000). The role of assessment in a learning culture. *Educational Researcher, 29*(7), 4–14.

Wiggins, G. (1989). A true test: Toward more authentic and equitable assessment. *Phi Delta Kappan, 70*(9), 703–713.

Acknowledgements

The Editors and the Series Editor would like to extend a warm and heartfelt thanks to all the authors and reviewers who have so kindly donated their time and their excellent work. We have a great network of academics with extensive experience in their respective fields. It was a joy to work with all of you and your contribution to this book has been invaluable, especially as this work was produced during the COVID-19 pandemic.

Figures and Tables

Figures

1.1 A model of children's learning and development through participation in institutional practice, where different perspectives are depicted: a societal, and institutional, and an individual perspective (Hedegaard et al., 2008, p. 10). 11
1.2 Adaptation of Hedegaard's model. 12
1.3 PSTs self-nominated categories, n = 111. 15
2.1 Flow diagram for the search and selection of literature process. 29
2.2 Reasons for social learning. 42
4.1 Sample *PeerWise* Statistics from a 2020 student (ESP125, UTAS). 79
4.2 Question identified by peer as having ineffective distractors (ESP125, 2018). 84
4.3 Example question showing nested and confused conceptual testing (ESP125, 2018). 85
5.1 The procedure of searching literature. 99
6.1 Procedures of the teaching experiment. 123
6.2 Participant's model. 129
6.3 Using different representations. 130
6.4 Using correct models for fractions. 130
6.5 An example for posters. 131
6.6 Assessment process via authentic assessment tools. 133
6.7 A model for digital communication authentic assessment strategies in mathematical language skills. 135
9.1 Observable characteristics of learner-centred instruction (Confrey & Shah, 2021). 190
9.2 Math-Mapper 6–8's student report display. 191
9.3 Math-Mapper 6–8's teacher report, heatmap display. 192
9.4 Schedule of instruction and corresponding diagnostic assessments. 197
9.5 Pre-test and post-test score distributions of percentage correct on items for cluster 4, "Finding Key Ratio Relationships", and cluster 5, "Comparing Ratios and Solving for Missing Values in Proportions" (for students who took pre-test and post-test). 199
9.6 Average gain scores (post-test – pre-test score) by cluster and group. Error bars represent standard errors. 200
9.7 Pre- and post-test comparisons, by sections, for Cluster 4 and Cluster 5. 200
9.8 (a, b, and c) Compound bar diagrams for constructs in Cluster 4. (d) and (e) Compound bar diagrams for constructs in Cluster 5. Orange and blue represent proportion incorrect and correct, respectively. 202

FIGURES AND TABLES

9.9   L4 item (for non-unit base ratios, finds unit ratio using equipartitioning or fair sharing).   203
9.10 Item for L5 ("Given any non-unit ratio $(a:b)$, finds both unit ratios using division ($\frac{a}{b}:1$ and $1:\frac{b}{a}$) and uses in context").   203
9.11 Strategy one teacher used to show students how to find unit ratios.   206
9.12 Example showing the potential complexity of a procedural approach to finding unit ratios.   207
9.13 Model for learner-centred instruction.   210
9.14 Framework for LT-based data-driven decision making (LT-DDDM) (from Confrey & Shah, 2021).   211
9.15 The agile curriculum framework, leveraging two-cycle feedback (from Confrey et al., 2018, p. 161).   212
10.1 PVAT-O item using the drag and drop feature.   224
11.1 The geometric thinking model.   245
11.2 The dog's perspective task (GPERS) and marking rubric.   248
11.3 Students' bird eye views of objects showing all components.   252
11.4 Students' representation of the dog's perspective.   253
11.5 A correct justification with incorrect drawing of the dog's perspective.   253
11.6 Excerpt from the variable map for geometric reasoning for GPERS.   254
12.1 The left picture shows Sarah's world of circle and the right sees how Sarah used her own way of tailoring circle.   274
12.2 Sarah's "perfect circle".   275
15.1 Mathematics teaching effectiveness as an emergent phenomenon in a learning organisation: multiple, multileveled lived realities.   334
16.1 Box plot of B2 responses.   355
16.2 Box plot of B3 responses.   359
16.3 Bar chart of relative frequencies of parental responses.   359
16.4 Box plot of B10 responses.   362

Tables

2.1 Authentic assessment frameworks.   30
2.2 The sequence of dimensions in the STEM authentic assessment model.   31
2.3 Assessment methods reported in STEM education papers reviewed.   33
2.4 Terms relating to integration.   39
2.5 Specified design processes.   40
4.1 Criteria for evaluating Assessment Task 2 (ESP125, UTAS).   82
4.2 Examples of guidelines and marks for authoring questions in Assessment Task 2 (ESP125, UTAS).   82

4.3	Examples of guidelines and marks for feedback and reflection in Assessment Task 2 (ESP125, UTAS).	83
5.1	Criteria for judging the authentic intellectual quality of assessment tasks.	106
6.1	Sample data analysis.	126
8.1	Sample quantitative student survey.	167
8.2	Capstone course assessment outline.	173
8.3	CES additional Likert scale statement responses from 145 students which have been mapped to Rule's four authentic principles.	175
8.4	CES responses from 116 students that map to Rule's four authentic principles.	175
8.5	CES responses from 116 students produced 236 individual comments that map to Rule's four authentic principles.	177
8.6	Course Experience Survey (CES).	179
9.1	LT-levels for constructs in the *Finding Key Ratio Relationships* cluster	194
9.2	LT-levels for constructs in *Comparing Ratios and Solving for Missing Values in Proportions* cluster.	195
9.3	Overview of curriculum aligned to MM6-8's ratio clusters.	196
9.4	Data sources used to investigate components of the research questions.	198
11.1	Overall results expressed as percentages for the perspective task GPERS.	250
11.2	Percentage breakdown for GPERS1, 2, and 3 according to year level.	251
12.1	A retrospective time-scaled map of the research process.	270
13.1	Overview of examples of practice.	303
14.1	Paper inventory about teacher evaluation.	319
15.1	Learning mathematics and studying in ASPETE: the students' lived complexity (based on Kasimatis et al., 2020, 2021).	341
16.1	Mean values and standards deviations of parents' answers.	356
16.2	Mean values and standard deviations of parents' responses.	358
16.3	Frequencies of parents' views on school segregation.	360
16.4	Mean values and standard deviations of parents' responses.	361
16.5	Distribution of frequencies and relevant frequencies of parents' responses.	362
16.6	Distribution of frequencies and relevant frequencies of parents' responses.	363

Notes on Contributors

Fatma Nur Aktaş
is a doctor of mathematics education department at Kahramanmaras Sutcu Imam University, Turkey. Her research interest includes mathematical language, teachers training, mathematical values, value and valuing in education, mathematics education for the blind students and District students with visual impairment, inclusive classroom, learning trajectory, and algebraic thinking.

Pınar Akyıldız
is a doctor at the Department of Mathematics Education, Bartın University, Turkey. Her research interests are the affective domain (beliefs, values, and attitudes) in mathematics education, instructional explanations of mathematics teachers, teaching of mathematics concepts (statistics and linear algebra), mathematical language, and teacher education (mathematics).

Chrysoula Arcoudis
has completed studies and postgraduate studies in Education and Languages in Sydney, Australia. She has served as senior policy and curriculum officer at the NSW Department of School Education on the implementation of languages education strategic policies. She has served twice as adviser on intercultural education at the Greek Ministry of Education and has since 1997 held the position of academic and scientific adviser at the Centre for Intercultural Studies at the University of Athens working closely with schools in change culture implementation. Between 2017 and 2020, she was seconded as national expert on Roma inclusion to the Council of Europe.

Anastasios (Tasos) Barkatsas
is a Senior Academic in Mathematics, Statistics and STEM Education, a Quantitative Data Analyst and the STEM Research Project/Research Group Team Leader in the School of Education, RMIT University, Australia. Dr Barkatsas has taught mathematics education, assessment and evaluation and research methodology courses at undergraduate and postgraduate levels. Dr Barkatsas has published more than 140 refereed journal articles, chapters, books and conference papers and he has been a Chief Investigator in numerous competitive research grants in Australia and Europe, totalling more than $3,000,000. Dr Barkatsas is a Principal Research Fellow (Honorary) of the Hellenic Educational Evaluation Society, the Series Editor of the Brill Education Series "Global Education in the 21st Century" and an editorial board member in a number of international research journals.

Michael Belcher

is a research associate in the College of Education at North Carolina State University in Raleigh, North Carolina, USA.

Antonios Bouras

studied at the Pedagogical Department of Primary Education of the National and Kapodistrian University of Athens, Greece. He completed his postgraduate studies in Applied Statistics at the Department of Statistics of the Athens University of Economics and Business and his PhD in Evaluation at the Pedagogical Department of Primary Education of the National and Kapodistrian University of Athens. He is a member of the teaching staff of the Pedagogical Department of Secondary Education of the National and Kapodistrian University of Athens. He teaches the courses of School Pedagogy, Assessment and Educational Research. His research work has been published in Greek and international scientific journals and focuses on the issues of Educational Project Evaluation.

Athina Chalkiadaki

is a teacher, Doctor of Education, University of Crete, Greece, with a Master in Educational Evaluation. From 1991 until today, she has been working as a teacher in private and public schools. During the school years 2016–2020 she served as Principal of a School Unit in Primary Education. Since September 2020, she has been seconded to the Quality Assurance Authority of Primary and Secondary Education (Authority for Quality Assurance in Primary and Secondary Education of Greece). She is a member of the Audit Committee of the Hellenic Evaluation Company. She has coordinated and organized innovative educational programs in culture, environmental education and health education in the primary schools she has served. She has conducted research and participated as a speaker in conferences with presentations in the areas of educational policy, evaluation of educational work and textbooks, student self-assessment and innovative teaching methods.

Jere Confrey

is a Distinguished Professor of Mathematics Education, Emerita at North Carolina State University and the President of The Math Door. Her research focuses on articulating empirically-based learning trajectories and designing diagnostic formative assessments to deliver data on student progress digitally to students and teachers. She is an American Educational Research Foundation Research Fellow and won an Innovator of the Year award at her University. She has authored multiple software products including Math-Mapper, Function

Probe, Function Finder, etc., received multiple federal and foundation grants, and published widely. Her teaching experience extends K-16.

Rebecca Cooper

is a Senior Lecturer in the Faculty of Education, Monash University, Australia. Her research is focused on teacher knowledge development considering how science teachers and science teacher educators develop knowledge throughout their career. Her research on science teachers' pedagogical content knowledge, includes considering how teachers practiced can be developed and articulated, especially the practice of highly accomplished teachers. Rebecca is a board member of the Australasian Science Education Research Association and a panel chair for initial teacher education course accreditation for the Victorian Institute of Teaching and Australian Institute for School Leadership.

Yüksel Dede

is a faculty member at the Department of Mathematics Education, Gazi University, Turkey. He worked at Berlin Freie University in Germany with Alexander von Humboldt [AvH] Scholarship and Scientific and Technological Research Council of Turkey [TUBITAK] scholarship respectively. He has worked as a director, expert or consultant in projects supported by various public institutions in Turkey (TUBITAK, Governorships, Governorates, Provincial Directorates of National Education) and abroad (AvH-Germany, Monash University, Australia). Also he is on the board of editors and editors in many refereed national and international journals. There are numerous articles, book chapters, translation book chapters and conference proceedings published nationally and internationally. His research interests include teaching of mathematics concepts (e.g. algebra teaching), teacher education (mathematics), affective domain in mathematics education (values, motivation, and beliefs etc.), mathematical modeling, international comparative studies, research methods and application of advanced statistical techniques in mathematics education

Paul Denny

is an Associate Professor in Computer Science at the University of Auckland, New Zealand. His research interests include developing and evaluating tools for supporting collaborative learning, particularly involving student-generated resources, and exploring how students engage within these environments. Dr Denny has been recognized for contributions to teaching both nationally and internationally, receiving New Zealand's National Tertiary Teaching Excellence Award (2009), the Computing Research and Education Association of Australasia Award for Outstanding Contributions to Teaching (2010), and the QS Reimagine Education Gold Award for ICT Tools for Learning and Teaching (2018) as well as the Overall Award (2018).

Zara Ersozlu
is a specialist in Mathematics and Statistics Education. Zara has broad international and national experience in research and teaching in primary and secondary mathematics and statistics. Her research focuses on psychology of maths (self-regulation, anxiety); assessment in mathematics; MEA and problem solving; virtual simulation; effectiveness of teacher education; educational big data and learning analytics; research methodology.

Ivan Fortunato
holds a Ph.D. in Human Development and Technologies (2018) and a Ph.D. in Geography (2014) both from the Universidade Estadual de São Paulo (UNESP). Ivan is a tenured professor at the Instituto Federal de São Paulo (IFSP) campus, Itapetininga, Brasil.

Linda Hobbs
is a science and STEM educator. Her research focuses on teaching out-of-field, STEM and science education, and she works with schools and teachers in a range of capacities through professional development, student programs and research.

Marj Horne
is an Adjunct Professor of Mathematics Education at The Australian Catholic University, Australia and an experienced teacher of mathematics at all levels from Early Childhood through to University. She was an active researcher on the Early Numeracy Research Project, Contemporary Teaching and Learning of Mathematics Project, and the Family School Partnerships project. Marj is currently engaged in the *Reframing Mathematical Futures II* project where her particular interests and expertise are in the development of evidence-based learning frameworks for Algebraic and Geometrical Reasoning and the corresponding teaching advice and activities to support targeted teaching in those areas.

Fragkiskos Kalavasis
is a mathematician, Professor of didactics of mathematics and educational engineering at the University of the Aegean Sea, Rhodes, Greece, Associate Researcher at Larequoi, Center for research in management, Université Paris-Saclay, UVSQ, Versailles, France and vice-president of the Hellenic Society of Mathematics. His work emphasizes the interactions between representations and understanding of mathematics and how this variety of interactions can be integrated into an interdisciplinary pedagogical design for reflective construc-

tivist learning. From this point of view, his research is linked in the systemic approach of the complexity of learning organizations (individual, collective and structural) and the management models of the school system.

Katerina Kasimatis
is a Professor in the Department of Education, School of Pedagogical and Technological Education (ASPAITE), in the field of Theory, Practice and Assessment of Teaching. She teaches "Educational Evaluation", "Teaching Methodology", "Didactics", "Teaching Practice Sessions" to undergraduate and graduate students, students of the Annual Pedagogical Training Program (EPPAIK), newly appointed and experienced teachers, as well as in training seminars for administrators of Education. She is the Scientific Director of EPPAIK, Head of "Teaching Practice Sessions", Chairperson and member of evaluation committees of Scientific and Laboratory Associates of EPPAIK (in twelve cities all over Greece). Katerina has worked as the Scientific Director of Training Programs (1995–2009). She has published in international journals, books and peer-reviewed proceedings of international and Greek conferences. Katerina is the author of *Modern Educational Evaluation Forms with the use of ICT* (Kallipos, 2015) and has edited two books in the field of "Teaching Methodology" and "Educational Evaluation".

Belinda Kennedy
is a lecturer in the College STEM and School of Education at RMIT University, Australia. Belinda completed a Ph.D. in Science (Biology) at the University of Technology, Sydney Australia. Belinda has broad teaching experience in the Biological Sciences and has completed a number of STEM teaching initiatives for on-campus and off campus programs for students at year all levels. Her educational research studies in STEM have provided her with a clear understanding of the needs of industry and future students in STEM-related areas.

Gillian Kidman
is an Associate Professor of Science Education at Monash University. Dr Kidman has an international reputation in STEM teaching and curriculum design recognised by University, State and National awards. She was a Writer and Senior Advisor of the Australian Curriculum: Science, and Australian Curriculum: Biology. Gillian is particularly interested in inquiry forms of teaching and learning and the potential inquiry has for the integration of science with other disciplines – the development of STEM. Her work in the area of disciplinarity and educational inquiry provides a fertile ground for the exploration of inquiry-based learning, teaching and skill acquisition in STEM.

Huk-Yuen Law

is an Adjunct Assistant Professor at The Chinese University of Hong Kong (CUHK). He obtained his Ph.D. in mathematics education from University of East Anglia. Dr Law taught secondary school mathematics for 23 years. Then, he taught mathematics pedagogy courses for both pre-service and in-service teachers, and also taught action research for post-graduate as well as undergraduate education students at CUHK. His research interests include mathematics teacher education, action research in education, authentic assessment, mentoring in education, communication in the teaching and learning of mathematics, and values in mathematics education.

Susan Ledger

is Professor and Dean of Education at the University of Newcastle, Australia. Professor Ledger is an advocate for the teaching profession and committed to exploring education policies and practices relating to teaching and preparing to teach diverse students and diverse contexts. Susan has a broad experiential base in rural, remote and international school settings and university contexts. Her recent endeavours focus on the affordances of simulation to prepare graduate teachers.

Kathy Littlewood

is a teacher, lecturer, early career researcher, writer and learner who has been fortunate to work across many educational sectors including secondary schools, vocational training, and higher education. Most recently, she has been working in the School of Education at RMIT University Australia, as Program Manager and teacher in the Master of Teaching Practice (Primary and Secondary) programs. Kathy's wide range of experiences in the field has allowed her to see, develop and use authentic assessment practices first-hand in different contexts.

Jiabo Liu

is currently a Research Assistant of the Department of Mathematics and Information Technology at the Education University of Hong Kong. Jiabo obtained her Master's degree in 2020. Her research interest is mainly in mathematics education and teacher education.

Michelle Ludecke

is a Lecturer in the Faculty of Education at Monash University, Australia. Her research explores key issues concerning transitions in teaching. These issues include the increase of 'testing teachers' in their transition to beginning teaching, the impact of increasing casualisation on the teaching profession, retention of beginning teachers upon entering the profession, mentoring in the teaching profession, the formation and transformation of teachers' professional identity, and the embodiment of teaching practices. Her work in Initial Teacher Education includes preparing graduate teachers for the transition to in-service teaching and teachers' ongoing professional learning and identity transformation.

Tricia McLaughlin

is a nationally recognised scholar in lifelong learning and pathways. She has extensive experience in the development of these practices in workplaces and educational settings. Tricia is an active researcher and has been the recipient of many national research grants in the scholarship of learning and teaching and related areas. She has received a number of university and national teaching awards. Her research publications, including seven books, span lifelong learning, pathways and scholarship. Tricia is particularly interested in the delivery of learning and most recently has explored the significance of 21CC skills and STEM in changing educational landscapes.

Juanjo Mena

(PhD) is Associate Professor and head of the department of Education in the University of Salamanca (Spain). He is currently an affiliate professor at the Center for the Study of Teacher Education at the University of British Columbia (Canada) and research collaborator in Kazan Federal University (Russia). He is the Treasurer of the International Study Association on Teachers and Teaching (ISATT). His research interests are focused on the analysis of the teaching practice, mentoring and the practicum, Teacher Education and ICT.

Andreas Moutsios-Rentzos

is an Assistant Professor in the Department of Pedagogy and Primary Education of the National and Kapodistrian University of Athens (Ph.D. in Mathematics Education, University of Warwick, UK). He is an elected member of the International Commission for the Study and Improvement of Mathematics Teaching (CIEAEM) and an elected member of the Board of Directors of the Greek Association for Research in Mathematics Education (ENEDIM). His published work appears in international scientific journals, conference proceedings, edited volumes etc. His research interests focus on mathematical argumentation, reasoning and proving, as well as on the interactions of multiple aspects of the complex, interdisciplinary mathematical teaching-learning phenomena.

Greg Oates

is a Senior Lecturer in Mathematics Education at the University of Tasmania, Launceston, Australia, where he teaches pre-service teachers in primary and secondary mathematics, and professional development for school and tertiary mathematics instructors. Greg is a cheerleader for mathematics and has taught mathematics at all levels from middle through to senior secondary school, and undergraduate calculus, linear algebra, and mathematics education. His research interests include the integration of technology into mathematics curricula, and the use of technology for active student-centred learning and assessment to promote peer-interaction in mathematics.

Anastasia Papadopoulou

is a philologist and holds a PhD in Educational Evaluation from the National and Kapodistrian University of Athens. Dr Papadopoulou is a graduate of the Postgraduate Studies Master's Program "Theory, Practice and Evaluation of the Educational Project", National and Kapodistrian University of Athens and she currently works as a Research Associate in the program and in the Open University of Greece. Dr Anastasia Papadopoulou was a member (2012–2015) of the Quality Assurance Unit (QAU) of the National and Kapodistrian University of Athens. She has been a secretary-general of the Hellenic Association for Educational Assessment since 2015. She has organized, participated and attended numerous seminars and conferences on educational evaluation and assessment.

Angela Rogers

taught in Australian Primary Schools for 10 years and has a passion for improving the teaching and learning of Mathematics. Over her teaching career, she has undertaken roles such as a Numeracy Co-ordinator, Numeracy Coach and Numeracy Intervention specialist teacher. In 2014 she completed her Ph.D. in Mathematics Education at RMIT. Her research focused on the teaching and learning of whole number place value in Years 2–6. Angela currently lectures part-time at RMIT University, Australia and enjoys linking research and practice in her work with parents, teachers and leaders.

Gráinne Ryan

is an Industry Fellow and Lecturer in Construction Management at RMIT University. Prior to this appointment in 2016, Gráinne spent ten years working in site-based construction management both in Australia and internationally. Gráinne has been recognised with a national award in the UK for her Best Practice in Site Management. Gráinne's diverse and specialised construction and contract management experience across the many facets of site construction management and contract management, always underpinned by industry best practice approaches, enables her to successfully teach across a breadth of construction management courses. Here she creates authentic, student centred learning experiences, which successfully integrate learning and work.

Fabiano Pereira dos Santos
holds a Master's degree in Education from the Universidade Federal de São Carlos, campus Sorocaba. He works as a Pedagogical Technician at the Secretaria da Educação do Estado de São Paulo and a teacher at the Faculdades Integradas de Itapetininga (FKB).

Rebecca Seah
is a lecturer in mathematics education at RMIT University, Australia. She has extensive teaching experience in special and mathematics education in early childhood, special, secondary, and higher education. She has authored several refereed articles, and book chapters. She was part of the research team in the Reframing Mathematical Futures II project (2014–2018) where she worked with 32 secondary schools nationally to develop an evidenced based teaching and learning framework for mathematical reasoning in the middle years. Her research interests include children's development of geometric and measurement concepts, design-based classroom research and numeracy, and numeracy and students with special needs.

Meetal Shah
is the outreach director for The Math Door. She is interested in validation of classroom-based diagnostic assessments, learning sciences, and geometry. Before joining The Math Door, Meetal worked as a postdoctoral scholar at North Carolina State University under Dr Confrey's supervision. Previously, Meetal had taught high school mathematics in Sydney, Australia and the mathematics methods course at the University of New South Wales. Meetal has received her Ph.D. in mathematics education from North Carolina State University.

Hazel Tan
is an academic at Monash University and part of the Mathematics, Science and Technology Academic Community. Her areas of research and teaching interest are secondary mathematics education, STEM education, and international comparative studies. Her research methodological expertise is in quantitative and mixed methods and her work on Facebook as a recruitment tool for research has gained academic interest. Hazel is also involved in international STEM education projects, teacher education, and research.

Naomi Wilks-Smith

is a Lecturer in the School of Education at RMIT University in Melbourne, Australia. With an extensive career as an educator, she is particularly passionate about language education, innovative approaches for second language learning, embracing learners' languages, and linguistic and culturally inclusive practices. Naomi's work involves the integrated scholarship of research and education practice and often includes industry partners in schools as well as cross-School, external and international collaborations. Naomi strives for educational impact through research translation and research value creation and has been awarded grants for her work.

Dallas Wingrove

has over 20 years of experience in Academic Development. As an academic developer she has collaborated with educators across diverse disciplines, providing learning and teaching leadership to co-design and teach curriculum that is learner centred and underpinned by good practice principles in tertiary educational practice. She is currently undertaking a Ph.D. which theorises and contributes knowledge of how to foster developmental learning about teaching through peer observation. This research contributes knowledge as to how peer observation as praxis can foster developmental learning and enhance the quality of tertiary teaching.

Qiaoping Zhang

is currently an Assistant Professor in the Department of Mathematics and Information Technology at the Education University of Hong Kong (EdUHK). Before joining EdUHK, he worked at Hubei University, East China Normal University, and the Chinese University of Hong Kong. He obtained his Ph.D. from the Chinese University of Hong Kong in 2010. His research interests are mainly on affect in mathematics education, mathematics teacher education and students' mathematical problem solving.

Xiaolei Zhang

holds a Ph.D. in Education (CUHK) and is Associate Professor at Tianjin University. Xiaolei served as post-doctoral fellow at Tsinghua University. Courses taught include qualitative research method in education, comparative education. Research areas focus on teacher learning and professional development, teacher leadership, curriculum and instruction, and educational reform. Her recent work have been published in *Teachers and Teaching, Professional Development in Education, Journal of Education for Teaching*.

PART 1

Authentic Assessment and Evaluation Approaches and Practices in Tertiary Education

∴

CHAPTER 1

Can a Standards-Based Assessment of Teaching Be Authentic?

Rebecca Cooper and Michelle Ludecke

Abstract

A teaching performance assessment (TPA) is a tool used to assess the practical skills and knowledge of all pre-service teachers (PSTs) who complete an undergraduate or postgraduate initial teacher education (ITE) qualification in Australia. The task is an opportunity for PSTs to showcase their growth during their ITE. However, this is not always realised given the tight structure of the TPA. There is little room for PSTs to respond in aspirational ways when the task is being assessed against a minimum standard. In this chapter, we (authors) share our story; two teacher educators surprised by the autonomy demonstrated by PSTs during a disruptive semester, and report our thinking about authenticity in assessment related to the TPA.

For this qualitative study, data were collected from a select group of PSTs as TPA work samples and transcribed interviews. The data was analysed with a view to exploring how we navigated the spaces between society, institution and individuals. Our findings indicate that when provided greater latitude in what they were able to draw on for their TPA, PSTs rose to the challenge and presented work that was far more authentic example of their knowledge and skills, while still adhering to the requirements of the TPA. The research has inspired further questions for us about what a space for aspirational PSTs who are ready to show more sophisticated thinking about their practice might look like, and how that space might be created given the constraints of the TPA.

Keywords

authentic assessment – teaching performance assessment – graduate standards – initial teacher education

1. Introduction

> Authenticity is a collection of choices that we have to make every day. It's about the choice to show up and be real. The choice to be honest. The choice to let our true selves be seen. (Brown, 2010, p. 49)

To put it mildly, 2020 was a challenging year. With the disruption caused by COVID-19, the world was thrown into chaos and a need for rapid change was obvious and at times overwhelming. However, with all this challenge and change, also came many opportunities to look at things differently and perhaps see and embrace the possibilities. This chapter is the story of two teacher educators and their pre-service teachers (PSTs) who seized the opportunity to think in new ways about a large and often unwieldy piece of assessment, the teaching performance assessment, commonly referred to as the TPA.

The two teacher educators (and authors of this chapter) were surprised and delighted by the autonomy demonstrated by PSTs in the middle of a disruptive semester in relation to their approach and completion of the TPA, and decided to investigate further. This chapter will explore ideas around authentic assessment related to the TPA, the decisions that we made during the semester that led to changes and opportunities for greater authenticity in the TPA and finally, what the authors learned about authenticity in assessment related to the TPA.

2. Context

A teaching performance assessment (TPA) is a tool used to assess the practical skills and knowledge of all pre-service teachers who complete an undergraduate or postgraduate initial teacher education (ITE) qualification in Australia. Pre-service teachers collect evidence of practice to complete a TPA during the final year of their ITE program. The TPA is assessed by ITE providers and is a requirement for graduation (Australian Institute for Teaching and School Leadership [AITSL], 2020b). TPAs (the actual task set and rubrics used for assessment) from ITE providers are accredited by AITSL through their relevant State registration and course accreditation body – in our case the Victorian Institute of Teaching (VIT).

In the final semester of their ITE, PSTs undertake a TPA unit designed to assist them to demonstrate their readiness to make the transition to in-service teaching. In Australia, this means demonstrating their ability to practice at a Graduate Standard level (Australian Institute for Teaching and School

Leadership [AITSL], 2020a). The unit runs alongside a 15-day placement where PSTs collate data from a short learning sequence to discuss, analyse and reflect on in order to demonstrate their ability to meet the Australian Professional Standards for Teaching (APST) at a graduate level. This unit is specifically designed to allow PSTs to demonstrate their competency against all 37 Standards. In addition, we created a layer of authenticity in making explicit connections to Victorian Government School selection criteria in both the delivery (within modules and a separate module) and in some of the terminology used in the TPA Guidebook and rubric.

The unit usually consists of six, 3 hour workshops that are facilitated by academic staff from the university. Students are in classes of approximately 30 students and during their workshops they have the opportunity to explore a nominated section of the TPA through collegiate activities, and make connections between the TPA and writing responses to selection criteria for jobs in Victorian educational settings. The assessment for the unit is entirely bound up in the TPA. In designing a TPA we not only had to address the specific criteria for accreditation with AITSL but also ensure the assessment was aligned with University policy. AITSL requires a TPA to be aligned with "concepts of authentic assessment" (AITSL, 2021). The TPA is a key mechanism by which programs can demonstrate pre-service teachers' impact on student learning (Program Standard 1.3). Our TPA was assessed by AITSL for evidence of content validity, construct validity, standard setting, and evidence of moderation and assessor training. Specifically, AITSL requires that a TPA be situated in a classroom environment, must be a requirement of successful completion of the program and must be completed during the final year. Where possible it should be included in the final professional experience placement or internship, prior to graduation. The TPA must have the following features:

- be a reflection of classroom teaching practice including the elements of planning, teaching, assessing and reflecting
- be a valid assessment that clearly assesses the content of the Graduate Teacher Standards
- have clear, measurable and justifiable achievement criteria that discriminate between meeting and not meeting the Graduate Teacher Standards
- be a reliable assessment in which there are appropriate processes in place for ensuring consistent scoring between assessors
- include moderation processes that support consistent decision making against the achievement criteria.

University policy states that assessment in coursework:

- must have clearly defined marking criteria, consistent with the University grade descriptors
- text-based assignments must be submitted electronically and the submission facility must use a similarity-detection system
- must include at least two major assessment tasks (i.e. tasks worth at least 20 per cent of the total unit assessment) and no task worth more than 60 per cent of the total unit assessment

Due to COVID-19, this unit was offered wholly online with staff meeting their groups for workshops six times. Further, the teaching team made four videos that were offered to PSTs as supporting resources. The videos were discussions that the staff had about specific aspects of the TPA and provided PSTs with insights into how they could approach their TPA under the new and challenging conditions they were faced with.

The primary challenge was the reduction in number of placement days PSTs were required to undertake in order to course complete, due to COVID-19 related statewide school closures. The number of days were reduced from 60 to 45, meaning most PSTs in the unit had their final placement cancelled. As such, most PSTs were in a position to complete their TPA on a previous placement; which may have been completed up to 12 months prior to putting their TPA together. PSTs without the required 45 days were placed with schools and mentor teachers receptive to having a PST during home-based/online/distance learning.

3 Literature Review

3.1 *Authentic Assessment*

Working in initial teacher education (ITE), assessment plays a substantial role both in what we teach our PSTs and how we come to know them and support their learning. When we say assessment, we are talking about any activities undertaken by teachers and their students that provide information that can be used to tailor teaching and learning activities (Black & Wiliam, 1998). We view assessment as an opportunity of getting to know our students. This means we are well positioned to support PSTs and their progress through this unit, which is just one part of their ITE course.

Extending the idea of assessment, authentic assessment refers to any activities that are "conducted through 'real world' tasks requiring students to demonstrate their knowledge and skills in meaningful contexts" (Swaffield, 2011, p. 434). In the case of ITE, the context is predominantly schools and classrooms and the 'real world' is inhabited by students, other teachers and members of the broader educational community. As far back as Wiggins (1993) the notion of authentic assessment has been understood as any activity that must be "engaging and worthy … The tasks are either replicas of or analogous to the kinds of problems faced by … professionals in the field" (p. 229). In the case of the TPA, where PSTs are expected to plan for learning, teach a sequence of lessons, assess student understanding, provide feedback and then reflect on the entire process, the authenticity of this task looks strong. And yet, we wondered if there was room to enhance the authenticity of the TPA? Swaffield (2011) suggests that "authentic assessment is essentially summative, even though the involvement of a real task means that there are opportunities for the student to learn whilst undertaking the assessment" (p. 434). It is this space of learning, here PSTs are able to engage in quality reflective discussions with their mentors about their own learning as students of teaching, and about the learning of the students they are teaching while in a school context, that we believe is so valuable. This learning is usually something we strongly advocate in our workshops and even while our students were on placement. But, then COVID-19 hit, and the shape of placement was altered which in turn meant that the opportunities for this learning while undertaking needed to be rethought, along with the process of completing the TPA itself.

In teaching our students about assessment, we agree with the early work of Black and Wiliam (1998) that there are some essential elements that should be considered, "the quality of teacher/ pupil interactions, the stimulus and help for pupils to take active responsibility for their own learning, the particular help needed to move pupils out of the trap of "low achievement", and the development of the habits necessary for all students to become lifelong learners" (p. 8). Having said this, these are also elements that we consider when writing assessment tasks for PSTs and when supporting their learning about teaching. Thus, in altering the TPA to adapt to the rapid changes brought on by COVID-19, we needed to consider ways of continuing (or even enhancing) the authenticity of the task, through supporting interactions between PSTs and their mentor teachers, inspiring PSTs to take active responsibility for their own learning, identifying specific areas where PSTs needed further support and then finding a way to provide an assessment that was timely and appropriate, instilling a sense of professional learning as an ongoing part of transitioning to teaching and being a professional teacher.

3.2 *Authentic Assessment and Teaching Performance*

Since the turn of the century teacher education programs have been using authentic assessments of teaching, including cases, portfolios, and problem-based inquiries or action research, as a way to support teacher learning for the new challenges of readiness for teaching in the 21st century (Darling-Hammond & Snyder, 2000). This form of 'contextualised' teaching and learning emphasises that authentic learning is shaped by the contexts in which they occur. Thus, authentic assessment of teachers' learning includes:

1. Assessments that sample the actual knowledge, skills, and dispositions desired of teachers as they are used in teaching and learning contexts, rather than relying on more remote proxies.
2. Assessments which require the integration of multiple kinds of knowledge and skill as they are used in practice.
3. Multiple sources of evidence that are collected over time and in diverse contexts.
4. Assessment evidence that is evaluated by individuals with relevant expertise against criteria that matter for performance in the field (Darling-Hammond & Snyder, 2000, p. 524).

In considering these points, it is worth highlighting the importance of context. Authenticity in assessment is heightened when context is considered. Teachers' ability to understand their practice within specific contexts "distinguishes professional practice from an apprenticeship model in which novices aim to copy the skills of a veteran practitioner, as though they will be applicable in all contexts" (Darling-Hammond & Snyder, 2000, p. 528).

Within this period, we have also seen a move back towards a technical view of effective teaching connected with the growth of a "market-oriented political and cultural order" (Connell, 2009, p. 217) from which an *audit culture* emerged. We continue to witness a push for national testing, league tables and the creation of teacher registration institutions. "The lists of competencies for teachers also lists auditable performances … [which] can become the whole rationale of a teacher education programme" (Connell, 2009, p. 218). In the Australian context, these neoliberal discourses have emphasised teacher professional standards as a means of "guaranteeing quality and holding teachers and teacher educators accountable" (Allard et al., 2014, p. 426). Currently, entry to the teaching profession in Australia is regulated by state agencies that still use input models to make decisions about teacher registration and readiness to teach. In negotiating these spaces teacher educators have some autonomy to develop authentic assessment of teacher readiness which requires preservice teachers to be *explicit* about their thinking and decision making (Allard et al., 2014, p. 428) in planning for teaching, enacting inclusive practices, engaging learners, effectively managing the learning environment, and reflecting on teaching in order to refine for future practice. We recognise that the development of any authentic assessment of teachers is not without its problems. While the inherent problems of a market agenda problematise the positioning of preservice teachers as professional learners in light of pressures for compliance and standardization (Paugh et al., 2018), there is room for negotiation between policy and practice in the development and delivery of authentic assessment of teachers in ITE.

3.3 Notions of Classroom Ready, But Where Is the Classroom and What Does It Look Like?

Often policies or standards emerge, in part from societal thought, in this case, that teachers are not meeting the expected societal standard, so we need something to assess them. The (Teacher Education Ministerial Advisory Group [TEMAG], 2014) wrote a report that made several suggestions for improving teacher education, that included the notion of classroom ready stating that "Australian parents, students and communities must be confident that all initial teacher education graduates have been rigorously assessed and found to be ready for the classroom" (p. XI). It was then suggested that classroom readiness could be demonstrated by "Pre-service teachers building a Portfolio of Evidence throughout their initial teacher education program" (p. VII). This portfolio of evidence, curated by a PSTs to demonstrate their classroom readiness, is what we now call the TPA.

During the COVID-19 pandemic, the notion of classroom ready was disrupted in several ways. Online teaching meant that the classroom became a virtual shared space and that parents often played a more significant role in working with their children to support their learning at home. So, what do parents (and society) think of teachers/teaching now? What does classroom readiness really mean? And, what does this mean for the TPA as an authentic assessment task for PSTs to demonstrate their classroom readiness?

3.4 Examples of TPAs as Authentic Assessment

Variations of the TPA are used around the world including Performance Assessment for California Teachers (PACT) later modified and expanded as the edTPA which can be used in the USA. In Europe, many countries have adopted the use of e-portfolios for PSTs to demonstrate their teaching competency. Many of these portfolios are used to show achievement of national standards for the purpose of teacher registration. A similar portfolio tool is also used in Singapore to assess PSTs' achievement against the national teacher competency framework.

In Australia, the TPA has been implemented in all ITE courses and is a requirement for accreditation of all ITE courses (Teacher Education Ministerial

Advisory Group [TEMAG], 2014). When developing their TPA, ITE providers were able to join a consortium (groups of providers who worked together to develop a TPA) or develop their own. All TPAs are subject to a rigorous review process, to ensure national consistency, where it is reviewed by the relevant regulatory authority, and then by an expert advisory group. The TPA as a tool is required to be an authentic assessment of PSTs' practice, however AITSL are, at present, vague on what they define as authentic assessment, and are more focused on the validity and reliability of the TPA as a tool for assessing pre-service teacher readiness (AITSL, 2021). Despite the lack of specifics, Australia's TPAs, like those worldwide, remain founded in portfolio-based assessment based on demonstrating professional knowledge, practice and engagement, developed during practical teaching experiences in educational settings.

By asking PSTs to submit a structured portfolio, we use multiple measures to assess if they have addressed the standards. Designed as a two part 4000-word written discussion, analysis and reflection, the TPA is based on nine key artefacts, plus a mapping of how and where the TPA submission meets the Graduate APSTs. Authenticity in this instance focuses on real world connections, where the learner is required to make judgements, use higher order thinking and place some value on the task in an authentic manner. As designers, we wanted learners to practice real teaching work in a micro way, as a representation of their readiness for broader practices. The sections and related artefacts include:

Part 1: 2000-word commentary plus
    Context Section:
        Artefact 1: School/center overview
        Artefact 2: Learner group overview
    Planning Section:
        Artefact 3: Learning Sequence as planned
    Teaching Section:
        Artefact 4: One Learning Experience – the immediate annotations & self-reflection you did on your lesson plan after teaching
        Artefact 5: Feedback from your Mentor on the same Learning Experience selected for Artefact 4 (use university template)

Part 2: 2000-word commentary plus
    Assessing Section:
        Artefact 6: Learning Group assessment data
        Artefact 7: Representation showing impact of teaching

Artefact 8: Focus student's work sample annotated for moderation

Artefact 9: Feedback to student

Reflecting Section:

Artefact 10: Evidence against the Australian Professional Standards for Teachers – Graduate Level descriptors

4   Framing the Research

During our experience of teaching and adjusting the TPA in an environment of disruption, as the COVID-19 pandemic influenced shifts in policy, we recognised our altered practices had an impact on our PSTs as individuals. This recognition led us to explore the literature to find a framework that would help explain the situation and the links between influencing aspects in the way it actually happened. It was a novel situation that required a novel approach. As we searched for an anchor to help us describe what we did in the situation, backward mapping was an appropriate strategy to find firm ground from which to survey the situation. In other words, to better appreciate the PSTs perspective on the authenticity of the TPA during a disruptive semester, we felt it was important to consider things piece by piece, starting with the cause

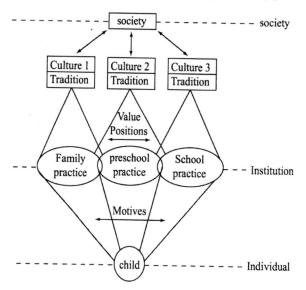

FIGURE 1.1   A model of children's learning and development through participation in institutional practice, where different perspectives are depicted: a societal, and institutional, and an individual perspective (Hedegaard et al., 2008, p. 10)

of the disruption, our response to the disruption and then the PSTs' response to our response. Thus, we sought a model that would support us to look at the links between these pieces.

The work of Hedegaard (Hedegaard, 2018, 2021; Hedegaard et al., 2008), although originally developed to understand children's learning and development, highlights the relationship between "the society, the practice and the person" (2008, p. 10). Situated in a societal and cultural perspective, Hedegaard's model highlights important concepts to describe children's development, that we believe also apply to our PSTs. Similar to Hedegaard's (2008) description of children's development, we view PSTs' development through institutions that contribute to Teacher Education, and we acknowledge that PSTs' development is connected to a view of what constitutes 'good teaching and learning practice' which varies across institutions and those who teach in them. A PST's development can also be connected to a change in social situation that may come about due to a change in institutional practices.

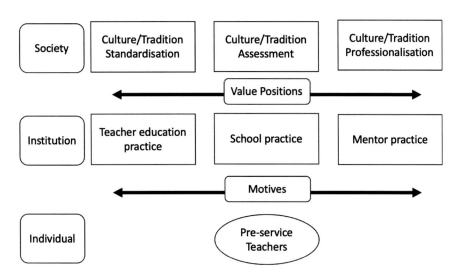

FIGURE 1.2   Adaptation of Hedegaard's model

A PST's development can be considered as a qualitative change in their motives and competencies. Hedegaard et al. (2008) suggest that motives relate to what matters to a person, and their particular orientation, situated within an activity setting and is related to their intentional activity. For example, a PST's motive may be orientated towards completing their TPA so they can graduate their ITE course, thus the intentional activity is completing their TPA. Value positions are formed based on an individual's worldview but are shaped by society, often with shared understandings being developed by individuals in communities. For instance, a PST's apprenticeship of observation (Lortie, 1975, 2002, 2005) as a student in a school and their experiences at university shape their understanding of what 'good' university learning and assignments look like.

Further, Hedegaard's model also considers the influence of multiple cultures and traditions that also generate a broad range of ideas around what 'quality teaching' looks like. For us as teacher educators, our practice is often based on the tricky act of balancing the reality of institution, society and the individual. Our practices are mediated by cultures and traditions of the AITSL Teacher Standards, teacher accreditation by the Commonwealth and the States/Territories, ongoing assessment of teachers and teaching, and the continued professionalization of teachers through institutional registration and compliance with a standardized code of conduct and ethics.

We also place our PSTs on professional experience in numerous schools, each with their own cultures and traditions. Thus, our PSTs develop a broad range of motives and values positions that inspire and also generate a broad range of ideas of what 'classroom ready' looks like. Yet, much of this was disrupted in 2020.

The work of Hedegaard et al. (2008) allows for this disruption by drawing on Vygotsky's conception of crises,

> The first part of Vygotsky's description of crises in a child's social situation [is] deconstruction ... What is important here is the deconstruction and reconstruction of the social situation, where we note that the child's competence and motives for development are allowed to proceed. (p. 25)

Our role as teacher educators was to deconstruct and reconstruct the TPA for both us, and the students. Considering Figures 1.1 and 1.2, we situate ourselves in this model as the negotiators between policies and the effect on individuals at a personal level, and in a sense, we are the resultant practices at the institutional level. The model is useful in respect to considering the authenticity of the TPA as a consequence of the deconstruction and reconstruction of the TPA as it brings together societal influences and policy (in this case COVID-19 and the AITSL standards for demonstrating classroom readiness), with institutional practices (in this case the swift adaptation of the TPA as an authentic assessment) and the individual's perspective (in this case, PSTs perspectives on the authenticity of the TPA). This leads to the research questions that framed this chapter,

1. How did we navigate the spaces between society, institution and individuals as we altered the TPA for greater authenticity during the COVID-19 pandemic?

2. How authentic was the TPA as an assessment for demonstrating classroom readiness from the pre-service teachers' perspectives?

5 Method

For this qualitative study, data were collected from 111 PSTs who completed anonymous Student Evaluation of Teaching and Units (SETU) including qualitative responses, our own teaching materials, observations and discussions, and focused data from seven consenting PSTs who allowed us to analyse their TPA work samples and participated in semi-structured interviews which were recorded and transcribed. Interviews were held at a mutually convenient time and were completed via zoom; most had a duration of 30 minutes. As observations were made within the context of disruption, we found the need to dig deeper and went back to work samples and PSTs for further interrogation and elaboration. Data were analysed with a view to exploring how we navigated the spaces between society, institution, and individuals and how PSTs viewed the authenticity of the TPA as an assessment for demonstrating their classroom readiness. Thus, the processes we used to draw conclusions from our data had several layers. Firstly, we considered the TPA work samples to look for examples of where PSTs had made what we saw as 'authentic commentary'. Secondly, we considered the interview data looking for emergent themes, particularly those related to the authenticity of the TPA as an assessment task, and then arranged this data in light of these themes. Finally, these data were considered using Hedegaard's (2008) model as a framework to draw out the influence of shift in society and policy, that influenced changes in practice at the institutional level, which in turn influence the PSTs as individuals in terms of their response to the TPA.

6 Findings and Discussion: Negotiations and Negotiating

Negotiations are ongoing, tailored, between experts and stakeholders, and involve listening and acting. Our negotiations focused on understanding the value positions of the PSTs, what matters to them, and their particular orientation. Our understandings were situated within the nested settings of PSTs completing their TPA within the context of the pandemic, and related to their intentional activities of completing their course and gaining employment.

6.1 *Negotiating Tutor Facilitations*
At the institutional level, we needed to negotiate by deconstructing and reconstructing the delivery of the unit and the assessment task in order to provide

PSTs with a secure base from which to complete their TPA and course. To do so, in the early weeks of the semester we surveyed the 111 PSTs asking them about their status with regards to placement and whether it was completed, disrupted or postponed. We then asked whether PSTs felt they had enough data from a previous placement on which to base their TPA.

GOT	Got what you need n = 26
DIS	Disrupted learning sequence n = 42
No LS	Never started learning sequence, but started placement n = 25
PNS	Placement never started n = 13
-	No response n = 5

FIGURE 1.3   PSTs self-nominated categories, n = 111

We then conducted intensive workshops with PSTs in small differentiated groups based on the categories in Figure 1.3. Qualitative SETU data showed us that this teaching strategy was valued.

> The small groups that we were placed into for our tutorial, ended up being a fantastic improvisation based on placement challenges caused by COVID-19. It was so much more effective to have one hour of our tutor's time in a small grouping of students who were at a similar phase in our TPA development, than 3 hours of diluted tutor time in a whole class. This group helped one another and I learnt practical lessons about Vygotsky's ZPD in participating in this sort of peer learning. (SETU QE7)

The anecdotal evidence at the time showed us that we were on the right track in facilitating PSTs to understand their TPA at a policy, institutional and personal level. The main teaching focus became assisting PSTs to understand the importance of quality discussion, analysis and reflection of their artefacts, rather than presenting polished work. For example, Ani told us that her tutor "made us feel really safe to share whatever we have ... her comments (feedback) made me aware that I didn't have to have a perfect response". The tutors also spent a lot of workshop time with the GOT and DIS groups making connections between PSTs' teaching artefacts and their future professional practices. These efforts to increase authenticity through real world examples were recognised in qualitative SETU comments such as: "I found this unit very practical and now feel that I have a piece that not only fulfills the requirements of the assessment but can be used as a valuable resource for my teaching portfolio" (SETU QE2).

6.2 *Negotiating Understandings of Teaching Practice*

As a result of the differentiated facilitation of tutorials throughout the semester, we felt many PSTs were able to present a richer understanding of their practice. The societal disruptions faced throughout the semester resulted in a deeper understanding among PSTs of the importance of flexibility in their practice. Kim's response is indicative of many others in the group who contest the notion of 'perfect' practice:

> … my lesson plan did not go to plan! I ended up having to do one lesson twice and then another one … I'd say that is authentic because that's what teaching is, apparently! … I was worried that the work needed to be perfect.

The disruptions caused by the pandemic were reflected in PSTs' discussion of disruptions in their practice. Charlie felt the disruptions revealed some authenticity in the task by being able to reflect on "everyday types of teaching: who are your kids, what do you need to do to teach them, what does it look like in the classroom [and] what happens if something doesn't go to plan?" The additional layer of 'what happens?' when disruptions are experienced was not seen in PSTs' responses from previous years to the extent that we saw in 2020. This developmental trajectory is borne from the social situation of development which indicates that the PSTs personality and social environment are in a dynamic relation.

This shift in understanding of the TPA from an 'assignment' to an authentic representation of 'real teaching' was evident in a range of TPAs, as represented here in Ani's TPA.

> One aspect of personal growth is that I have come to terms with the notion that teaching is in nature messy and problematic. I used to think of teaching as a checklist of what to do and the pursuit of best solutions, but now I believe the desire for teaching to be a positive experience is itself a negative experience, which is as misleading as an apprenticeship of observation assuming "anyone can teach" (Lortie, 1975, p. 62, as cited in Churchill et al., 2011). Paradoxically, the acceptance of teaching as unpredictable and filled with "competing demands" (Loughran, 2010, p. 13) is a positive experience.

The challenges being faced contributed to a more authentic assessment in that the PSTs responses to the assessment task changed from seeking the familiar 'predictable' responses to a more personalised and tailored approach.

This was in part due to the teaching team instruction where there was constant reassurance that 'there is no wrong answer, only limited reflection' and making real-world connections such as to the process of writing job applications.

It is worth noting that the point in time that we gathered the data also shaped the responses. The PSTs interviewed had been working in schools or distanced from their course for three months. Their current practices shaped their perception of the task, and the authenticity of the TPA in relation to their 'present'. An example of this is in the timing of the assessment in relation to when PSTs begin to enter the teaching workforce. The practice tradition of the university and the focus this brings on academic excellence is exchanged for the practice traditions of the teaching profession. A PST's motive hierarchy changes over time because they appropriate new motives and also because practice changes. When a motive becomes a "leading motive the activity connected with this is the most meaningful activity" (Hedegaard et al., 2008).

6.3 *Negotiating Understanding of Context*

PSTs' understanding of context and how it shapes teaching and learning was heightened within the TPA. The intentional orientation or motives of the individuals, as seen in the responses below show the PSTs readiness to discuss the ways their practice was shaped by disruptions within the teaching context:

> Arya: In this new setting, my focus was relaxed in certain areas but heightened in other areas. For example, students' safety no longer required active management as they were not physically present, but at the same time, delivering instructions required more clarity and supporting emotional regulation required more attention.
>
> Drew: The planned sequence was modified throughout this period, with lessons and tasks adapted to meet the demands of the rapidly shifting classroom landscape.
>
> Kim: Attending students' learning was disrupted as anxieties were high ... In response, [we] ran lengthy (30 minutes plus) discussions at the beginning of each day to provide information to students about COVID-19 and promote mental wellbeing.

As part of demonstrating their understanding of how context shapes teaching, we recognised a notable shift in the value PSTs placed on specific teaching strategies when discussed in the TPA.

> Kim: I came to appreciate the value of Think-Pair-Share and Turn-and-Talk as collaborative learning techniques. I ... found it particularly effective in the context of Placement School. As Sampsel (2013) argues, students who are experiencing high anxiety, such as Placement Class during the COVID-19 pandemic, appreciate the comfort and confidence of answering questions in a small group.
>
> Charlie: I found the process of co-teaching the sequence enhanced my capacity to collaboratively engage with colleagues and heightened my reflective capabilities.
>
> Arya: To make my lessons more suitable for online learning, I [shifted] to a more teacher-centred style of delivery, capitalizing on the features of the video conferencing platform to enhance the learning experience, and choosing digital teaching resources to engage my students. ... While it may have seemed counterintuitive, as the modern education narrative favors a learner-centred approach, in this particular context, it allowed my students to undergo a smooth learning experience where information was delivered efficiently under the time and context constraints. Despite shifting to a teacher-centred style of learning, I still allocated time for open-ended discussion where students could share their responses.

While there was a high level of understanding demonstrated within their TPA, most of those interviewed did not recognise the connection between the institutional level context of the school in shaping their teaching. Rather, the dominant factor discussed was the societal level. This could be in part due to moving to online/remote/past teaching where the physical context of the school was removed and replaced with the virtual or distanced teaching context.

It was evident to us that university practices shaped PSTs motives for which context they selected to base their TPA on. Fifteen PSTs stated mid-way through the semester that they would complete their TPA on a previous placement, with many citing the uncertainty of waiting for a deferred placement as too stressful. Many more vacillated between waiting for a deferred placement to begin, and basing their TPA on a previous placement. Time was the determining factor in finalizing the decision, with many waiting until close to the end of the semester before finally deciding. Six withdrew from the unit without penalty. As depicted in Figure 2, the majority of PSTs placements were problematic in relation to completing their TPA. Despite this, many like Sonja who fell in the GOT and DIS (~62%) were "prepared for the TPA before placement, and so got most data before school closure". Those in the NO LS group, who had been allocated a placement and who had a few days on site before school closure, were supported to base their TPA on a previous placement. In these instances, most stated that, like Charlie, they 'needed to have an understanding of TPA before placement" in order to benefit fully. These PSTs felt disadvantaged at the institutional level. While they felt able to produce an authentic representation of real teaching they felt less able to produce an assignment worthy of a high grade.

6.4 Negotiating our Understanding of Authentic Assessment

Throughout the semester, we worked as negotiators in a constant process of back and forth. Our negotiations were instigated by society, and took place between institutions and individuals. At the societal level our academic practices were shaped by the cultures or traditions of policy in regards to teacher standards, assessment and readiness within the context of the COVID-19 pandemic. At the institutional level the performative university culture and what it means for students to achieve a high grade shaped the negotiations we undertook in deconstructing and reconstructing the TPA for PSTs to make it achievable under the societal conditions. The negotiation between the performative culture of assessing 'classroom ready' teachers within the university's grading policy, and preparing graduate teachers for their prospective practice helped us make decisions about the assessment task that we hoped PSTs would view as authentic. Ultimately though, PSTs' engagements and motives have to be seen in relation to the traditional practices of the institution and the activities they generate for themselves. An authentic assessment of teacher readiness means the participants need to get something out of the task for themselves. The authenticity resides in the connection the task created at the institutional level and the level of value the PST places on their success in the task. They wanted both an authentic task and a good grade; which is where our roles as negotiators lay, in trying to give them the opportunity to access both.

We came to this research with the benefit of a perspective of the TPA over time. We have been working in the transition from pre-service to in-service teaching over many years prior to the initiation of the TPA at different tertiary institutions, have been heavily involved in TPA development and refinement, and have extensive knowledge of AITSL accreditation perspectives. Now, with the perspective of the TPA in the context of a global pandemic, we undertook negotiations at policy and institutional levels with what PSTs needed in this specific context. This constant back and forth process in order to move forward with an authentic assessment came from building connections to job selection criteria, listening to the PSTs and negotiating by assimilating new understandings. For example, the change in policy landscape with regards to the reduction in number of placement days that PSTs were now required to graduate coincided with limited access to placements. This resulted in negotiation of university assessment policy and accreditation requirements at the institutional level, which shaped our motives to make the assessment authentic for the individual.

However, there are some instances where our understanding of context overrides what PSTs feel they would have found more authentic in their TPA as an assessment of their teaching readiness. We found that when asked about the structure of the TPA, PSTs spoke about the TPA as an assignment in their qualitative SETU feedback, citing workload management and feedback as areas valued.

> SETU QE10: I liked being able to submit the whole document in one go, but it is nerve wracking not knowing if you're on track.

> SETU Q13: I understand the original plan was to break the TPA into two sections to get marked, but due to COVID19 the situation was different. It was quite stressful knowing that all 100% of the marks depended on that one document.

When interviewed after completing their course the discourse around the TPA shifted to valuing the tool as a foundation for job applications, or as a precursor to their Victorian Institute of Teaching (VIT) Application for Full Registration. Kim credits the TPA as

> the reason I have a job. I wrote my TPA ... as a solid draft, then wrote my [response to selection criteria] off my draft ... That got me an interview ... and I used the framework of the TPA for my portfolio ... all my artefacts went in ... I showed them the artefacts and talked about them ... and I got the job so they must have liked it!

Charlie made the connection between the TPA and the VIT task:

> I can see some overlap between that and the TPA. The most authentic parts are the structure ..., teaching, assessment and rethinking what assessment is, and formative assessment to determine where your learners are at, reflection ...

There were also some comments about the challenge in maximizing placement time against the requirements of the TPA with Kim regretting being

… so focused on my TPA … I should have focused more on teaching. I should have spent two weeks of placement teaching and then done my TPA stuff in my last week.

Most PSTs stated that more practice in schools would have enhanced authenticity overall. In addition, and as a result of completing their course in the midst of a pandemic, many cited soft skills such as drive and passion for teaching, social skills, to be able to advocate for students, the ability to collaborate with other teachers, kindness, the ability to 'roll with it sometimes – pick your battles', and a willingness to learn as the essential skills required to become a graduate teacher.

7 Conclusion

Hedegaard (2008) has provided a model to support our discussion of our navigation and negotiation of the spaces between society (in this case dominated by the COVID-19 pandemic), institution (changes in policy) and individuals (our PSTs completing a TPA) to enhance the authenticity of the assessment. The data highlighted for us that the negotiation was ongoing and that as the front-line negotiators we were faced with a barrage of shifting and competing priorities such as policy shifts, university expectations and PSTs' motives, goals and values. Thinking back to the Brown (2010) quote at the beginning of this chapter, *Authenticity is a collection of choices that we have to make every day …* it could be said that the decisions we made as we rode out each twist and turn of the TPA during the COVID-19 pandemic had an influence on the task's authenticity. In fact, we were the ones who had to choose "… to show up and be real … honest. (and) let our true selves be seen" as we negotiated the spaces between society, institutions and individuals. The flow-on effects are the decisions that the PSTs made based on the decisions we made. An authentic assessment is possible in the TPA if more is done to empower PSTs to make good choices about what is authentic to/for them.

The data shows that PSTs who were able to make links and see the authenticity of the TPA after time had passed (in interviews months after the conclusion of the course) or by placing the work in a different context (using aspects of TPA for job applications or as part of a portfolio). Thus, is the idiosyncratic nature of authentic assessment: Authentic for whom? Authentic to what? Authentic at what time? Linking to Hedegaard, motives and goals play a role here in thinking about why PSTs might want to produce an authentic TPA and what the outcome of having an authentic TPA might be. We also view this as connected with our role of navigating and negotiating the spaces between society, institution and individual; we could tell the PSTs all about the value of an authentic TPA but if it is not aligned with their motives and goals it is unlikely to hold any meaning for them.

The research has inspired further questions for us about what a space for aspirational PSTs who are ready to show more sophisticated thinking about their practice might look like, and how that space might be created given the constraints of the TPA.

References

AITSL. (2021). *TPA fact sheet*. https://www.aitsl.edu.au/deliver-ite-programs/teaching-performance-assessment

Allard, A. C., Mayer, D., & Moss, J. (2014, September 1). Authentically assessing graduate teaching: Outside and beyond neo-liberal constructs. *The Australian Educational Researcher, 41*(4), 425–443. https://doi.org/10.1007/s13384-013-0140-x

Australian Institute for Teaching and School Leadership [AITSL]. (2020a). *Australian professional standards for teachers*. Retrieved November 12, 2020, from https://www.aitsl.edu.au/teach/standards

Australian Institute for Teaching and School Leadership [AITSL]. (2020b). *Teaching performance assessments: An overview for schools*. Retrieved November 12, 2020 from https://www.aitsl.edu.au/deliver-ite-programs/teaching-performance-assessment/teaching-performance-assessments-an-overview-for-schools#:~:text=It%20is%20assessed%20by%20ITE,%2C%20teaching%2C%20assessing%20and%20reflecting

Black, P., & Wiliam, D. (1998). Inside the black box. *Phi Delta Kappan, 2*, 139–148.

Brown, B. (2010). *The gifts of imperfection*. Hazelden Publishing.

Churchill, R., Ferguson, P., Johnson, S. G. N. F., Keddie, A., Letts, W., Mackay, J., McGill, M., Moss, J., Nagel, M. C., Nicholson, P., & Vick, M. (2011). *Teaching: Making a difference*. John Wiley and Sons.

Connell, R. (2009, September 17). Good teachers on dangerous ground: Towards a new view of teacher quality and professionalism. *Critical Studies in Education, 50*(3), 213–229. https://doi.org/10.1080/17508480902998421

Darling-Hammond, L., & Snyder, J. (2000, July 1). Authentic assessment of teaching in context. *Teaching and Teacher Education, 16*(5), 523–545. https://doi.org/10.1016/S0742-051X(00)00015-9

Hedegaard, M. (Ed.). (2018). *Children's creative modelling of conflict resolutions in everyday life: Family life as a site of learning and development*. Information Age Publishing Inc.

Hedegaard, M. (2021). Analysing children's learning and development in everyday settings from a cultural-historical wholeness approach. *Mind, Culture, and Activity, 19*, 127–138. https://doi.org/10.1080/10749039.2012.665560

Hedegaard, M., Fleer, M., Bang, J., & Hviid, P. (Eds.). (2008). *A cultural-historical theory of children's development*. Open University Press.

Lortie, D. C. (1975). *Schoolteacher: A sociological study* (1st ed.). University of Chicago Press.

Lortie, D. C. (2002). *Schoolteacher: A sociological study* (2nd ed.). University of Chicago Press.

Lortie, D. C. (2005). Unfinished work: Reflections on schoolteacher. In A. Lieberman (Ed.), *The roots of educational change, international handbook of educational change* (pp. 133–150). Springer Netherlands. https://doi.org/10.1007/1-4020-4451-8

Loughran, J. (2010). *What expert teachers do: Enhancing professional knowledge for classroom practice*. Allen & Unwin.

Paugh, P., Wendell, K. B., Power, C., & Gilbert, M. (2018, April 3). 'It's not that easy to solve': edTPA and preservice teacher learning. *Teaching Education, 29*(2), 147–164. https://doi.org/10.1080/10476210.2017.1369025

Swaffield, S. (2011). Getting to the heart of authentic Assessment for Learning. *Assessment in Education: Principles, Policy & Practice, 18*, 433–449. https://doi.org/10.1080/0969594X.2011.58

Teacher Education Ministerial Advisory Group [TEMAG]. (2014). *Action now: Classroom ready teachers*. T. A. Government.

Wiggins, G. (1993). *Assessing student performance*. Jossey-Bass.

CHAPTER 2

Authentic Assessment in STEM Education

An Integrative Review of Research

Hazel Tan and Gillian Kidman

Abstract

Authenticity is the cornerstone of STEM (Science, Technology, Engineering, and Mathematics) education activities and pedagogies. In this chapter, we extend this to contend that authentic assessment is the cornerstone of STEM education assessment. Although authentic assessment is an ill-defined concept with a conflation of terms, we adopt the definition of authentic assessment as activities engaging students in authentic inquiry processes involving higher order thinking skills relating to the real world. STEM education also experiences a conflation of terminology around its name and meaning. Some see STEM education as the sum of four silos, but to others it is transdisciplinary, emphasizing the connections between disciplines. This raises the dilemma of how to assess STEM education. This integrative review focuses on the literature (empirical studies, professional practice and theoretical papers) that considers authentic assessment in STEM education and analyses how authentic assessment is defined and conceptualized in terms of constituent components in STEM education.

Keywords

authentic assessment – STEM education – integrative review – complexity of task – real world – social learning

1 Introduction

1.1 Ill-Defined Concepts: Authentic Assessment and STEM Education

Both Authentic Assessment and STEM (Science, Technology, Engineering and Mathematics) are ill-defined concepts and terms found in the literature concerning education and educational research alike. These ill-defined terms are problematic around the interpretation of educational policy intent, and indeed for the interpretation of research results. Loosely defined constructs can lead to misleading conclusions, with communication and database searching implications, as we will highlight in this chapter. For example, the terms authentic assessment and performance assessment – the literature provides a multitude of different meanings resulting in researchers adopting varying interpretations for their research. A further complication occurs when authors fail to define their interpretation of the concept causing misunderstandings and communication problems within the field. For example, Brandt (1998), Newmann (1998), Terwilliger (1988), and Wiggins (1998) debated a conflation of terms (authentic assessment, direct assessment, alternative assessment, performance assessment) that still seems to persist in today's research literature.

In relation to STEM Education, the "acronym has become ubiquitous in the 21st century, with little need to remind readers that it refers to the disciplines of Science, Technology, Engineering and Mathematics" (MacDonald et al., 2019, p. 75). Ritz and Fan (2015) reported on a 20-nation survey of the international STEM agenda, and found varying beliefs as to what STEM is, or should be. "The concept of STEM can and does produce different educational meanings and structures in its use and implementation. Internationally, one approach does not meet the needs of all populations" (Ritz & Fan, 2015, p. 430). The differences arise from the relationships between the four disciplines where Science and Mathematics are emphasized, and the role of Technology and Engineering remains vague. Consider also the addition of other subject areas and literacies, and the below conflation of acronyms adds further confusion to the lack of a STEM definition:

- 'STEAM' where the 'A' is for the Arts (English, 2017) to include design thinking, aesthetics and social construction of STEM products and services, but 'A' might also be Agriculture (Sami et al., 2020) to include contextual competencies,
- 'STREAM' where the 'R' is for Reading and wRiting (Paige et al., 2019) to include literacy and critical thinking and creativity,
- STEMM where the additional 'M' includes Medicine (Root-Bernstein, 2018) to include clinical humanitarian thinking and empathy in particular, and
- steM as we found in our review, where only the M is capitalized to emphasize a mathematics focus (Stohlmann, 2020).

Further research is needed to end this conflation of terms pertaining to authentic assessment and STEM Education, and to define and evaluate the concepts. In this chapter, we aim to identify and use the existing conflation of terms to review the empirical research studies that report on the use of authentic assessment (and other common names for this form of assessment) and STEM Education (and other common names for this form of educational reform). In this chapter, we will use the terms authentic assessment and STEM education, however, we will maintain the integrity of the papers we cite by maintaining the choice of terms selected by individual authors.

1.2 Linking These Ill-Defined Concepts: Authentic Assessment and STEM Education

In considering the nature of authentic assessment, we adopt the definition of authentic assessment as described by Frey et al. (2012) as "a classroom assessment task that involves the student deeply, both in terms of cognitive complexity and intrinsic interest, and are meant to develop or evaluate skills and abilities that have value beyond the assessment itself" (p. 14). A goal of authentic assessment is then to blend the teaching, learning, and assessment into one, For example, in English literature, students may participate in a class discussion having pre-read and synthesized set material (Ferguson, 2019). In this case, the assessment is then a written task involving a critical analysis of the text. This is quite different from assessment in the Sciences where there may be fixed-answer questions, multiple-choice questions, and perhaps an essay emphasizing factual knowledge that collectively fail, according to Ferguson, to indicate long-term student learning. For many students, their individual STEM subjects rely on standardized testing, yet it is becoming more widely recognized that students studying these subjects should be able to contextualize and apply the accumulated facts that they commit to memory during authentic problem-solving activities. We believe that by viewing STEM Education as a multi or transdisciplinary approach to learning, students can integrate knowledge from the individual STEM subjects using inquiry-based practices with authentic real-world issues. This approach is known as integrative STEM, "where teaching and learning concentrate on and derive from the liminal and relational 'inter-spaces' between disciplines, can open up a transdisciplinary space – a transformative space that is at once oriented between, across and beyond all disciplines" (MacDonald et al., 2019, pp. 76–77). This integration assists in eliminating disciplinary hierarchies, and thus the bias towards preferred disciplinary assessment practices.

How then to assess integrated STEM education is largely absent in the STEM education policy documents and STEM education research (Paige et al., 2019). Whist many education authorities have a STEM Education policy; most schools have not progressed beyond traditional subjects and traditional assessments. Gao, Li, Shen, and Sun (2020) undertook a review of the literature relating to the assessment of interdisciplinary STEM education. They found that most assessments relate to monodisciplinary knowledge and affect, as well as transdisciplinary affective domains such as interest, confidence, and self-efficacy relating to STEM education and careers. However, Gao et al. did not delve into the nature of assessment in terms of its authenticity.

We contend that authentic assessment is the cornerstone of STEM education assessment since there is a general agreement that authenticity is the cornerstone of STEM education activities and pedagogies (Hallström & Schönborn, 2019). This chapter presents an integrative review of how authentic assessment is understood, and investigated, in STEM education research. We review empirical studies that focus on authentic assessment in STEM education and analyze how the conflation of authentic assessment terms are conceptualized in terms of its constituent components in STEM education.

2   Method

We follow the methodology described by Toronto and Remington (2020) to conduct an integrative review of how authentic assessment is understood and investigated in STEM education research. The integrative review method has been used by researchers to critique and synthesize empirical studies to provide a comprehensive understanding of a specific phenomenon (Toronto & Remington, 2020; Perignat & Katz-Buonincontro, 2019). This method has been used in various educational contexts such as STEAM education research and practices (Perignat & Katz-Buonincontro, 2019), in-class activities in science classrooms (Arthurs & Kreager, 2017), and methods of argument analysis and assessment (Rapanta et al., 2013). The literature reviewed in this study comprised of empirical studies (qualitative, quantitative and mixed methods studies), professional journal papers (informing STEM assessment practices), and theoretical (STEM education models and frameworks) publications. The selection and review of papers were driven by the research questions:
– What authentic assessment practices are being used in STEM education?
– How is authentic assessment being understood and described by the STEM education academic community?

Following the formulation of the purpose and review questions, a search was conducted with the keywords "STEM education" and any of the following terms: "authentic assessment", "authenticity", "authentic", "performance assessment", "performance based assessment", "assessment for learning", "alternative assessment", or "direct assessment". The use of "STEM education" rather than just "STEM" is to exclude the STEM cell studies and be more specific in the search focus. STEAM and STREAM acronyms were excluded as we were interested in the central core of STEM education and not the authentic assessment influences of additional subject areas.

The databases ProQuest Education and Google Scholar (title search) were employed for the searches, as well as 14 identified STEM education journals: *African Journal of Research in Mathematics, Science and Technology Education*; *Canadian Journal of Science, Mathematics, and Technology Education*; *Eurasia Journal of Mathematics, Science and Technology Education*; *European Journal of STEM Education*; *International Journal of Mathematical Education in Science and Technology*; *International Journal of Mathematics, Science and Technology*; *International Journal of STEM Education*; *Journal for STEM Education Research*; *Journal of Research in STEM Education*; *Journal of STEM Education*; *Journal of STEM Outreach*; *Journal of STEM Teacher Education*; *The STEAM Journal*; and *Review of Science, Mathematics, and ICT Education*. These journals were selected from the list of 45 STEM education journals reviewed by Lin et al. (2020) that explicitly included science, mathematics and technology in their titles.

The search was conducted from 1st to 31st January 2021 and included 2020 papers. A total of 311 publications were identified initially, and their titles and abstracts screened for relevance. For journals with zero results from the searches, a manual search was conducted with "STEM education". Duplicates were then removed, followed by careful reading of the articles for relevance to STEM education and authentic assessment, as well as quality (as determined by impact factor, SNIP or H-index rankings). Finally, 49 publications were included in the analysis. Figure 2.1 shows the inclusion and exclusion process as described in the Preferred Reporting Items for Systematic Reviews and Meta-Analysis (PRISMA) guidelines (Moher et al., 2009).

In our coding and analysis, our 'reading' of each paper was two-fold. Firstly, papers were read with a particular focus on the literature review and goals of the paper to ensure the paper's relevancy to our needs in terms of STEM and authentic assessment. Secondly, each paper was 'read' with a particular focus on the results, discussion, conclusion sections of each paper to ensure coding reflected the research being reported upon, and not the research being reviewed.

3 Analysis and Synthesis

Our goal for this chapter is to advance our existing knowledge of authentic assessment in STEM education through an integrative review of the scholarly literature, and propose directions for future research and practices. However,

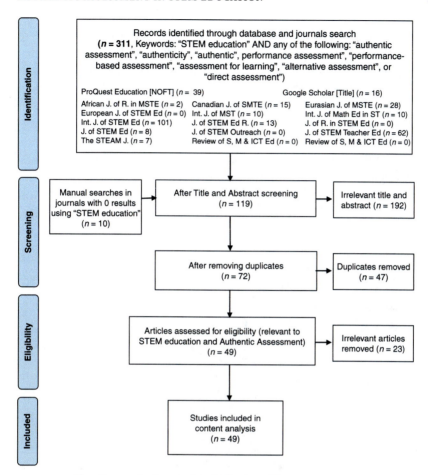

FIGURE 2.1   Flow diagram for the search and selection of literature process

our systematic search of scholarly literature only located six papers explicitly considering both STEM education and authentic assessment. The 43 remaining papers all offered explicit discussions of STEM, STEAM, or steM, and implicit discussions conflating the terms of authentic assessment, alternative assessment, performance-based assessment, as well as formative assessment and integrative STEM assessment.

Our 'two-fold reading' revealed that assessment in STEM seems to be in transition. Conventional summative assessment and/or high-stakes assessment in the Sciences is giving way to an expanded, integrative STEM assessment model that emphasizes content *and* skills that include literacies, competencies and character qualities. This integrative assessment treats the learner not just as a receptacle for facts, but as a thinker and knowledge generator, an empathizer, a designer, and importantly, a collaborator. The integrative STEM assessment, identified in this chapter and book as *authentic assessment*, appreciates the complexity of our world, which gives rise to the need for emergent assessment practices. Our analysis of the scholarly literature pertaining to authentic assessment revealed strong evidence of terminology conflation. We sought theoretical frameworks for authentic assessment to guide our analysis of authentic assessment in STEM education – see Table 2.1. We wanted our STEM analysis to be guided by authentic assessment research theories and literature.

Ashford-Rowe et al. (2014) and Gulikers et al. (2004) are widely cited frameworks originally exploring multimedia and nursing contexts through computer-based learning packages. However, for our purposes, we required a framework that also considered the hands-on aspects commonly used in STEM education. Since we were unable to locate such a framework, we selected the Deutscher

TABLE 2.1 Authentic assessment frameworks

Logic assessment model (Deutscher et al., 2018)	8 Critical elements of authentic assessment (Ashford-Rowe et al., 2014)	Five-dimensional framework (Gulikers et al., 2004)
Authentic modes of assessment		Assessment result or form
Relevant item-sampling	Measure a real world test of ability	
Complexity of task	Degree of challenge of constructing or producing meaning/knowledge Transfer of knowledge beyond a single content area The use of active critical reflection	Complex task integrating knowledge, skills, attitudes
Staged embedding of tasks	Fidelity of the environment and tools	Physical context, time and resources Assessment criteria based on professional practice
Process-orientation	Producing a successful performance or product	
Social embedding	Opportunity for feedback, discussion Collaboration – communication and teamwork skills	Social context and collaboration

et al. (2018) vocational education and training (VET) *Logic Assessment Model* and its associated evaluative framing for variable guidance. Since the majority of the research reported in this current chapter also informs, but not explicitly, the nature of STEM curriculum design in conjunction with assessment practices, we required a framework that identifies this connectedness.

Both Gulikers et al. (2004) and Deutscher et al. (2018) advocate the connection of curriculum design criteria with the assessment design process, thus further indicating their potential to guide our integrative review. Table 2.2 provides an explanation of six dimensions (based on an amalgamation of all elements in the three frameworks considered in Table 2.1) against which we coded the 49 scholarly papers.

The six theoretical dimensions presented in Table 2.2, when sequenced in the order noted in Table 2.2, advocate for a curriculum and assessment coupling that supports real-world ideas in the classroom. This coupling is achieved through problem-based activities that emulate project-based experiences as a form of instruction guiding and assessing the integration of STEM concepts.

TABLE 2.2 The sequence of dimensions in the STEM authentic assessment model

Dimensions	Explanation
Assessment methods	The strategies of assessment, such as single or multiple assessment methods, which is used for formative and/or summative assessment (Deutscher et al., 2018; Gulikers et al., 2004).
Relevance to curriculum and real-life context	The tension between relating the assessment to the curriculum as well as to the real-life context (Deutscher et al., 2018; Ashford-Rowe et al., 2014).
Complexity of task	The types of emphasis in the complexity of the task, such as metacognition, problem solving, higher order thinking (Deutscher et al., 2018; Ashford-Rowe et al., 2014).
STEM integrative thinking	The nature of what is integrated: disciplines, content, or competencies and character qualities (Deutscher et al., 2018; Ashford-Rowe et al., 2014; Gulikers et al., 2004).
Design process emphasis	The sequencing of activities in and between tasks (Deutscher et al., 2018; Ashford-Rowe et al., 2014).
Social learning	The social interaction pertaining to the task and/or assessment (Deutscher et al., 2018; Ashford-Rowe et al., 2014; Gulikers et al., 2004).

Such a sequence may lead to student learning as consideration is given to what is taught in STEM, and to how it is taught, as well as a consideration to the 'what and how' of the associated assessment.

3.1 Assessment Methods

'Assessment method' refers to the way in which students' learning is assessed, including the type or format of assessment such as a portfolio or multiple-choice questions, as well as its associated structure such as rubrics or scoring correct answers and feedback (Gao et al., 2020). This could be a single method using one assessment tool or multiple methods using more than one assessment tool. In the 49 articles reviewed, there were seven papers in which one assessment tool was reported. There were four papers where one assessment method was used summatively, such as a teacher-generated worksheet to record student results and conclusions of investigation (Davis et al., 2020), using rubrics to assess student work (Stehle & Peters-Burton, 2019), survey assessing students' statistical techniques and explanations (Dierdorp et al., 2014), and a 20 multiple-choice question test with meaningful distractors (Wind et al., 2019). In these studies, students' learning product rather than learning process was assessed. Comparatively, there were three out of the seven studies that assessed formative learning using a single method. These were: student notebooks as they conduct their investigations, assessed with performance metrics rubrics (Ernst & Glennie, 2015; Potter et al., 2017) and adaptive computer-based performance assessment where an intelligent tutoring system provides intelligent instructions in real-time during a simulation (Skinner et al., 2018).

Thirty-one papers reported the multiple methods of assessment, out of which 24 papers described the multiple methods to be questionnaires, portfolio, performance assessment, peer and self assessment, written evidence of process and product, tests, classroom observations and student interviews (see Table 2.3). Generally, the STEM projects and programs included methods to assess the formative learning process as well as the summative product. It was also interesting that Weldeana and Sbhatu (2017) included punctuality and attendance as part of the criteria for assessment. In two other papers, only summative methods were employed, which included students' oral presentations and final reports (Campbell & Jobling, 2014; Czaplinski et al., 2019). One paper out of the 31 reported on multiple methods that the researchers, rather than the teacher, use to assess students' engineering design process and performance (Lin et al., 2018). Rubrics were provided in some of the papers, such as rubrics for creativity, innovation and presentations (Kitagawa et al., 2018), a qualitative literacy value rubric (Gray et al., 2017), a game design rubric (Tucker-Raymond et al., 2019), a Co-Measure rubric to assess student collaboration (Herro et al.,

TABLE 2.3   Assessment methods reported in STEM education papers reviewed

Methods	Papers
Questionnaires	Pre-post Metacognitive activity inventory[a] (Anwari et al., 2015); Peffer & Ramezani (2019); Tsai et al. (2018); Watson et al. (2020)
Portfolio	School-based science lessons (Anwari et al., 2015); students perceived portfolio as an appropriate assessment method (Das, 2020); Opperman (2016); project proposals (Singer et al. 2020); Design portfolios (Strimel et al., 2017); portfolio assignment (Weldeana & Sbhatu, 2017)
Performance assessment using rubrics	Asunda (2018); Das (2020); Fahrer et al. (2011); Kinner & Lord (2018); presentation of a prototype (Ludwig et al., 2017); Newton et al. (2018); Opperman (2016); Septiani & Rustaman (2017); Singer et al. (2020); Skurikhina et al. (2018); pictures of design prototypes (Strimel et al., 2017); communication, punctuality and attendance (Weldeana & Sbhatu, 2017)
Peer assessment	Peer critique of research questions (Bielik & Yarden, 2016); Das (2020); Kinner & Lord (2018); teams and individuals provide peer feedback (Mallet, 2008); group critiques that are multi-modal [oral, written, online] (Tucker-Raymond et al., 2019)
Self assessment	Students do not trust themselves and their peers to self-assess (Das, 2020); Kinner & Lord (2018); teacher-led reflection (Skurikhina et al., 2018)
Technology-based strategies	Discussion forum and blogs (Das, 2020); computer simulation and learning analytics (Peffer & Ramezani, 2019); online learning activities (Mallet, 2008)
Written evidence of the learning process	Illustrating iteration progression as students reach as a solution, assessed using rubrics (Asunda, 2018); evidence of idea generation strategies and prototype of design solution (Kelley & Wicklein, 2009); notebooks and design plans, explanations, calculations, and reflections (Kitagawa et al., 2018); weekly journals (Ludwig et al., 2017); weekly activities (Mallet, 2008); regular short answer questions (Singer et al., 2020); summary making, reflective activities, journal writing (Weldeana & Sbhatu, 2017)

(cont.)

TABLE 2.3 Assessment methods reported in STEM education papers reviewed (*cont.*)

Methods	Papers
Written product	Students' research questions (Bielik & Yarden, 2016); academic essays (Das, 2020); written work samples (Gray et al., 2017); journal reflections, exit slips, storyboarding (Guezy et al. 2016); research reports (Kinner & Lord, 2018); persuasive letters to local community officials (Kitagawa et al., 2018); workbooks (Watson et al., 2020)
Tests	Cognitive assessment using multiple-choice questions (Fahrer et al., 2011); test on science process skills (Septiani & Rustaman, 2017); pre-post tests of STEM knowledge (Tsai et al., 2018); midterm test with feedback and final examination (Mallet, 2008)
Classroom observations	Co-Measure rubrics to assess student collaboration (Herro et al., 2017); student interactions (Kitagawa et al., 2018); using observation rubrics (Opperman, 2016); observation sheets (Septiani & Rustaman, 2017); groupwork (Weldeana & Sbhatu, 2017)
Group and individual assessment	Group submit a research report, individual submit abstract (Kinner & Lord, 2018)
Presentations	Kitagawa et al. (2018); Ludwig et al. (2017); presentation to the client (Singer et al., 2020); Tsai et al. (2018)
Student interviews	Kitagawa et al. (2018); Peffer & Ramezani (2019); Tsai et al. (2018)
Quizzes, homework assignments	Newton et al. (2018); weekly assignments (Tsai et al., 2018)
Teacher questioning	Skurikhina et al. (2018); Watson et al. (2020)

a Details are given when there are differences within each method and/or details of the method were described by the authors.

2017), and a STEM integrated thinking and application ability index and an imagination index (Tsai et al., 2018). Guiding questions were provided for peer critique to scaffold students' thinking and interactions (Tucker-Raymond et al., 2019). Strimel et al. (2017) proposed an approach towards grading students' work using an adaptive comparative judgement method where their works are compared, one pair at a time, and ranked through multiple comparisons.

Researchers call for a decrease in the role of assessment so that students "form an understanding that evaluation as such is not important, the main things are the knowledge, skills, skill sets and experience they receive" (Skurikhina et al., 2018, p. 7). This was stipulated in four papers (Bosman & Chelberg, 2019; Davidson & Simms, 2017; Franklin et al., 2018; Kelley et al., 2010) out of the 31, where there were no formal assessment methods mentioned. In these papers, there were no explicit mention of grades, rubrics, or measurement of students' learning, but feedback, self-assessment, self-reflection, observations and anecdotal evidence of learning were highlighted instead.

Eleven out of 49 papers did not explicitly mention any assessment methods. In these papers, assessment methods were assumed to be embedded into the instructions and that authentic assessment methods were advocated. For example, the use of the five E inquiry instruction model (Engage, Explore, Explain, Evaluate, and Elaborate) or its variant (Bosman et al., 2018; Brand, 2020; Duschl & Bybee, 2014), performance-based learning (Ernst, Glennie, & Li, 2017; Iwuanyawu, 2020; Radziwill et al., 2015), problem-based learning (Asunda, 2014; Lamberg & Trzynadlowski, 2015), modelling activities (Hallström & Schönborn, 2019; Stohlmann, 2020), work-integrated learning (Young et al., 2019). In these papers, the instructional and learning processes were described in relation to the integration of STEM education but details about how students' authentic learning was assessed were not evident.

There were two papers in which researchers compared authentic or performance-based assessment methods with traditional assessment (Das, 2020; Fahrer et al., 2011). Das (2020) compared civil engineering students' perceptions of conventional and alternative assessment methods, and found that students' perceptions about the appropriateness of conventional and alternative assessment methods were mixed. He concluded that a mix of conventional and alternative methods might be useful and effective in assessing students' cognitive learning and attainment. Similarly, Fahrer et al. (2011) compared engineering students' performance assessment (solving a 3D model problem) and cognitive assessment (68-item multiple choice test) scores and found that there were no significant differences between them.

In studies that examined STEM units and projects, researchers found that assessment practices were generally inadequately described by teachers. For example, in analyzing 20 STEM units, Guezy et al. (2016) found that generally, teachers did not include sufficient information about the performance and formative assessments to determine if they align closely with the learning objectives and goals. Several units did not provide any specific information about assessment strategies or were vague, such as "teacher checks student progress as they are working on the activity" or "teacher will check group planning sheets for completeness and errors" (p. 21). In their analysis of assessment practices for engineering design projects in secondary schools, Kelley and Wicklein (2009) also found that there were not many assessment strategies used by technology teachers. The more frequently used strategies were "develop prototype model of final design solution" and "work on a design team worked as a functional inter-disciplinary unit", "provide evidence of idea generation strategies" and the least used strategies "use mathematics models to optimize, describe and/or predict results" " and "properly record design information in an engineer's notebook" (Kelley & Wicklein, 2009, pp. 16–17).

We also found this phenomenon in the papers reviewed; researchers have not adequately detailed assessment practices. For example, in describing undergraduate Geoscience projects, Kinner and Lord (2018) hinted at forms of assessment. They said that

> we use exercises, assessment rubrics, and explicit discussions to develop student knowledge in topics such as collaborative work, research questions, experimental design, data analysis, writing, and presentations .... In addition to whole-group assignments, individuals complete peer evaluations and self-assessments, and submit a research product. For example, the group may be required to submit a research report, whereas all individuals must submit an abstract. Exams can also be tools to assess individual learning. (p. 51)

but did not elaborate on the details about the assignments, or peer and self-assessments. In another example, how the "tangible deliverables" and other "gradable materials" mentioned by Ludwig et al. (2017, p. 6) were assessed had not been detailed. Newton et al. (2018) described the use of in-class critiques for sketching evaluation and feedback delivery, of the type frequently used in design and architecture courses, but did not provide more details about these assessment practices. In Opperman's (2016) discussion of maker-space as a strategy for STEAM education, the performance assessment rubrics was mentioned as "one of the preferred ways that educators in maker classrooms opt to assess learning outcomes by observing the ways that students apply knowledge and skills during maker tasks" (p. 4). However, there were no specific examples of rubrics described. This lack of adequate detail in the papers relating to authentic learning and assessment in STEM education is of concern.

3.2 Relevance to Curriculum and Real-Life Contexts

For authentic learning and assessment, researchers stress a high level of fidelity of the assessment tasks to resemble real-life contexts and professional practice (Deutscher & Winther, 2018; Gulikers et al., 2004). There is a tension within STEM education that authentic learning should, on one hand, attend to the traditional school science, technology, engineering, and/or mathematics curricula, and on the other hand, focus on real-life contexts. As such, STEM learning activities in the papers were found to fall into three categories:

1. *School-based activities* (12 papers) which are hands-on activities involving physical objects, such as laboratory experiments (Gray et al., 2017), sketching performance assessment (Netwon et al., 2018), or creating robots to run a maze (Skurikhina et al., 2018). In these settings, the school curriculum or coursework was strongly aligned with the constructivist learning tasks.

2. *Simulated real-life* (27 papers) in which students in classrooms investigate a real-world problem that is meaningful and relevant. This could also include computer-based simulations (Peffer & Ramezani, 2019; Skinner et al., 2018), real-world problem scenarios in the classrooms (Stehle & Peters-Burton, 2019), ill-structured problems based on real-world contexts (Iwuanyawu, 2020). There is a spectrum from using real-life materials in creating artworks (Radzwill et al., 2015), to framing the projects in real-life contexts (e.g., Opperman, 2016), or carrying out an investigation (e.g., measuring and drawing the shadow of students' house in Potter et al., 2017). In these settings, there was a balance between STEM curricular relevance and relevant, representative, and meaningful real-world practices and tasks.

3. *Real-life contexts* (7 papers) in which real-world industry, work and/or community are engaged in authentic learning, such as conducting research at a hydrological station (Kinner & Lord, 2018), partnership with a theatre to create a performance (Davidson & Simms, 2017), work-integrated learning (Czaplinski et al., 2019; Young et al., 2019), and a field trip to the local recycling centre and engaging community in discussions about recycling (Kitagawa et al., 2018).

There were three other papers (Asunda, 2014; Herro et al., 2017; Kelley & Wicklein, 2009) where simulated real-life or real-life contexts were hinted at in authentic or problem-based learning.

3.3 Complexity of Task

Deutscher and Winther (2018), in the context of vocational education and training, highlighted that authentic assessment tasks can focus on a range of cognitive levels that "should represent the complexity of a real work surrounding which usually contains a certain (domain-specific) amount of complex tasks"

(p. 5). In the context of STEM education, the complexity of the task should represent how scientists, engineers, mathematicians, technology experts and STEM professionals work in the real world. In the publications reviewed, the tasks included design-based challenges, problem-solving, modelling, inquiry, investigation, research, performance-based learning, and usually involved aspects of social learning (see later section). At times, these terms were used with overlaps, for example, Ernst and Glennie (2015) described performance tasks, each with "a stated challenge requiring four student application activity phases involving research and investigation brainstorming, exploration, and reflection" (p. 29).

In design-based challenges, students may define their own problems (Bosman et al., 2018) or work on a teacher-defined task (e.g., finding sustainable alternatives to local landfill issues, Kelley et al., 2010), or work with the community (Campbell & Jobling, 2014). Students generally conduct research, collect data and information, analyse and develop a prototype solution, and evaluate the prototype. In scientific investigation tasks, students design and conduct experiments to investigate real-world phenomena, such as flammability and water resistance of fabrics (Davis et al., 2020), and climate change (Franklin et al., 2018). In modelling activities, students conduct an inquiry about a phenomenon and create a scientific, mathematical or computational model for analysis and prediction. For example, Czaplinski et al. (2019) described applied and computational mathematics projects relating to groundwater aquifers in Australia, Dierdorp et al. (2014) highlighted professional practices of a sports physiologist, an official at the public works and a water management facility, and data analyst at a meteorological institute. The different forms of representation of the models can also include 3D modelling in engineering (Fahrer et al., 2011) or designing and investigating bridges using 3D printing technologies (Lin et al., 2018). Hallström and Schönborn (2019) highlighted that the ability for students to switch between different representations of a particular model can improve their learning relating to STEM concepts and practices.

Several of the publications referred to the science and engineering practices in the *Next Generation Science Standards* (NGSS) developed by the U.S. government (Asunda, 2018; Brand, 2020; Duschl & Bybee, 2014; Ernst et al., 2017; Guezy et al., 2016; Kitagawa et al., 2018; Peffer & Ramezani, 2019; Potter et al., 2017; Stehle & Peters-Burton, 2019; Strimel et al., 2017; Tucker-Raymond et al., 2019; Wind et al., 2019). These practices are: asking questions and defining problems, developing and using models, planning and carrying out investigations, analyzing and interpreting data, using mathematics and computational thinking, constructing explanations and designing solutions, engaging in argument from evidence, and obtaining, evaluating, and communicating information (NGSS, 2013). Similar practices are involved in modelling and inquiry tasks.

Overall, the authentic learning tasks reported in the publications indicate that there is a high level of complexity of the authentic learning and assessment tasks, which relate to real-world design and modelling, problem solving, and investigations. Certain terms were associated more with different disciplines, such as engineering design, scientific investigations, and mathematical and computational modelling. The intricacies of the STEM integration and design process are discussed in the next sections.

3.4   STEM *Integrative Thinking*

The papers in this integrative review use a variety of terms to describe what is being integrated (see Table 2.4). Clearly, the term integrate/ion is the most widely used in relation to STEM assessment. Guezy et al. (2016) identify STEM assessment tasks capture both content and skill practices, to which Iwuanyanwu (2020) adds that integration occurs because the student is able to retrieve prior knowledge.

In terms of assessing integrated content, science and engineering are the most prevalent with science being the preferred integrative knowledge base (Czaplinski et al., 2019). Das (2020) identifies mathematics as the integrative knowledge base for urban planning problems *if* mathematics is used creatively. Both Dierdorp et al. (2014) and Watson et al. (2020) identify statistics as

TABLE 2.4   Terms relating to integration

Terms	Papers
Combine	Anwari et al. (2015)
Integrate	Asunda (2014, 2018); Brand (2020); Campbell & Jobling (2014); Czaplinski et al. (2019); Das (2020); Davidson & Simms (2017); Davis (2020), Dierdorp et al. (2014); Guzey et al. (2016); Hallström & Schönborn (2019); Iwuanyanwu (2020); Kelley et al. (2009, 2010); Lamberg & Trzynadlowski (2015); Lin et al. (2018); Ludwig et al. (2017); Radziwill et al. (2015); Skinner et al. (2018); Stehle & Peters-Burton (2019); Stohlmann (2020); Tsai et al. (2018); Tucker-Raymond et al. (2019); Weldeana & Sbhatu (2017); Young et al. (2019)
Blend	Asunda (2014)
Infused	Asunda (2018)
Fused practices	Duschl & Bybee (2014)
Intersecting concepts	Guezy et al. (2016)

a natural integrator of science and mathematics, however, Stohlmann (2020) warns that the inclusion of mathematics needs to be age-appropriate to the student. In terms of integrated skills, the 21st Century skills relating to competencies and character qualities seem to be favoured. Specific skills from the technology domain assess technical skills (Newton et al., 2018; Fahrer et al., 2011; Lin et al., 2018; Ludwig et al., 2017) like using CAD or 3D printers.

3.5 Design Process Emphasis

As discovered for the STEM integrated thinking dimension, a variety of terms were found in the papers. This particular dimension was interested in the sequencing of activities that the student undertook, both in and between tasks. Five papers made mention of assessing the 'design process' (Bielik et al., 2016; Campbell & Jobling, 2014; Kelley et al., 2009; Kitagawa et al., 2018; Ludwig et al., 2017), with a further three papers discussing 'logical steps'. A further five publications each used a different term to draw attention to the process the students undertake in completing a STEM task: scaffold instructions, procedures, iterative process, sequences, systematic approach, yet the terms go unexplained. Table 2.5 present the explained sequences of eight papers.

Ernst et al. (2015, 2017) and Young et al. (2019) specify the design process as a sequence of steps that they name as either activity phases or action research. The remaining authors simply present the sequence in the process. When we align the steps in the sequences, we see that most studies begin the design process with understanding or research pertaining to the task. Franklin et al.

TABLE 2.5 Specified design processes

Paper	*Sequence named* and/or sequence
Ernst et al. (2015, 2017)	*Activity phases* – research & investigation, brainstorming, exploration, reflection
Franklin et al. (2018)	Experimentation, reflection, metacognition
Gray et al. (2017)	Interpretation, representation, calculation analysis, assumptions, communication
Kitagawa et al. (2018)	Ask, imagine, plan, create, improve
Lin et al. (2018)	Problem scoping, developing solution, project realisation
Sthele et al. (2019)	Identify the problem, pose a solution, test solution, share with the client
Young et al. (2019)	*Action research* – plan, act, observe, reflect, plan, repeat

(2018) use formative assessment, reflection and self-correction throughout their 2-week summer program that is divided into three distinct components: experimentation, reflection, metacognition. One would assume there is time allocated to understanding the climate change curriculum on offer, but the authors do not specify this. Gray et al. (2017) and Stehle and Peters-Burton (2019) seem to be the only authors to use a design process sequence that concludes with some form of communication.

3.6   Social Learning

There appear to be different priorities concerning why social learning is included in the assessment of STEM. The research literature base for social learning identifies knowledge, attitudes, and skills as "associated with children's success in school and with a wide range of concurrent and later life outcomes" (McKown, 2019). McKown advocates the use of the *Collaborative for Academic Social and Emotional Learning* (CASEL) model for exploring social learning due to its ubiquity and influence. CASEL identifies five broad areas of interest:
- self-awareness
- social awareness
- self-management
- relationship skills
- responsible decision-making

Social learning outcomes in STEM education, as evidenced in our review of the 49 papers, are increasingly becoming a focus of standards, programs, and classroom practices – alongside academic competencies.

Figure 2.2 presents the nature of social learning in our 49 papers. Based upon the terms used by the authors of the papers, we found nine reasons for the inclusion of social learning as a component of STEM authentic assessment. Each reason was either explicitly defined, or described in sufficient detail to code into a 'reason' category. For discussion purposes, we group the reasons into three categories based upon the CASEL model: Self-Awareness and Self-Management, Self-Awareness and Relationship Skills, and Responsible Decision Making.

Self-Awareness and Self-Management consist of active critical self-reflection. Five papers included the notion of assessing self-reflection in STEM education. In a study of self-assessment and perceived STEM learning gains in undergraduate students, Kinner and Lord (2018) found that frequent feedback from professors and peers initiates a reflective response in the learner, advancing as individuals and as a group. The learners are accountable for their own learning

FIGURE 2.2   Reasons for social learning

as well as the group's learning. The social learning in Kinner and Lord's study requires self and group learning strategies prompted by self-reflection. Ludwig et al. (2017) used Strengths-Based Leadership to assist students to identify their strengths in relation to personal behavior and performance in MakerSpace and multidisciplinary teamwork settings. A key finding was students reporting a deepening understanding of their own disciplinary interests through inter-professional teamwork. This involved identity growth and the development of empathy and innovative ways to approach and solve problems. Asunda (2014) informs us that the essence of STEM Education involves systems thinking, situated learning theory, constructivism, and goal orientation theory. It is in the goal orientation theory that we find self-directed learning strategies and the need for the student to be actively engaged in their own learning. Stehle and Peters-Burton (2019) discuss this self-directed learning in relation to 21st Century skills and self-regulation. Self-regulation guides the students' individual connections, reflections, and revisions between knowledge construction and real world problem solving. Stehle and Peters-Burton (2019) stress that 'time' is essential for students to develop the ability to monitor and reflect on their progress. 'Time' implies opportunities beyond individual lessons, and in the geometry case study presented by Weldeana and Sbhatu (2017), the 'Portfolio of Evidence' provides a mechanism that engages students in reflective practices and focuses on the provision of feedback with constructive comments and future directions. Over time, the portfolio of evidence improved self-reflection, critical thinking, learning responsibility, and multiple intelligences.

Social-Awareness and Relationship Skills was the most assessed social learning category in STEM education. Figure 2.2 indicates 34 papers provide discussions relating to social-awareness and relationship skills, adopting four competencies: collaboration, communication, interpersonal respectfulness, and peer critique. This category requires developing the ability to understand differing perspectives, and to be able to empathise with others. Building relationships is critical to social learning as it can differentiate 'working in a group' or 'working as a group'. Anwari et al. (2015) used the quality of student responses on worksheets as an indicator of the quality of social learning and relationships skills. They concluded that the poor level of worksheet completion represented poor group attitudes, and that not all students were capable of working together in a group. If a group is not capable of an adequate discussion, is not collaborating and communicating, then this can influence their cognition and progress. The Das (2020) study discussed the notion of group projects leading to deep learning, however, some students take advantage of the other group members and do not contribute significantly – they take advantage of others in the group. This was contra to the findings of Bosman and Chelberg (2019) who reported that embedded assessment of group dynamics results in students working in relaxed and mutually supportive ways where the focus was on learning and interpersonal respectfulness. Peer critique provided formative feedback on attitudes as well as outputs. Bielik et al. (2016) included peer-critique to engage students in collaborative discussions and critiquing of research question construction. Peer-critiquing success is assessed via a comparison between questions written in peer-critique lessons and pre-lesson questions written in a questionnaire. Collaboration is typically seen in our papers in the form of group or teamwork embedded in a problem solving process. The advantages of collaboration are attributed to a more effective division of labor, the generation of solutions from group members with differing background interests, knowledge, and experience. Solution quality is enhanced by the inclusion and development of ideas of the group collective. Communication was seen to be related to collaboration as together they provide opportunities to verbalize and elaborate upon one's own ideas, and to resolve discrepancies with peers, thus facilitating critical thinking (Herro et al., 2017). Herro et al. provide a much needed description of the assessment of collaboration in STEAM activities. Their 'Co-Measure' rubric focuses on assessing collaborative problem solving, and assists teachers to identify collaborative skills specific to STEAM activities.

Responsible Decision Making highlights the need for behaviors that positively influence decision making during STEM activities. Lamberg and Trzynadlowski (2015) allude to behavior problems influencing engagement, Kinner and Lord (2018) identify both individual and group behavior accountability, and Stehle and Peters-Burton (2019) identify a need for building trust amongst group members. Appropriate behavior, accountability and trust are all necessary components of group work, and when present, the group members enjoy a learning environment where learning is promoted, knowledge is constructed, ideas generated, and creativity abounds. Duschl and Bybee (2014) informed us of assessment for learning practices where the learner's thinking becomes visible.

4   Discussion and Conclusion

Most of the 49 papers we reviewed are not specific in terms of researching authentic assessment in STEM education. However, the papers included authentic learning and assessment practices in some form. In this review, we found that a variety of authentic assessment methods and practices are used in STEM education. These methods are associated with authentic learning contexts and tasks, which relate to either individual disciplines (e.g., Science, Mathematics, Technology, Engineering) or an integrated STEM curriculum. Assessment methods are both formative (students' learning process) and summative (students' learning products). In addition, several papers consider the assessment of 21st Century skills as a form of authentic assessment. However, only a few papers provided a detailed description of their assessment practices in this area.

There is a range of fidelity of the assessment tasks to the real-life contexts. Three categories emerged, which are school-based activities, simulated real-life investigations and real-life projects. In some cases, authors were not explicit in their writing about the fidelity of their assessment tasks. This is also reflected in the complexity of tasks. In general, there is a high level of complexity in the types of assessment tasks reported. However, some authors report the use of problem-based, inquiry and/or modelling tasks, yet, these are rarely defined.

Of the papers reviewed, there are two broad ideas of what is being integrated within STEM education that is being assessed. One is content knowledge, such as science or mathematics, whereas the other is skills, such as 21st Century skills or creativity. Interestingly, statistics is considered as an integrator to support students' integration of mathematics and science disciplines. Additionally, the majority of the reviewed papers did not highlight the assessment of the design process. Fewer than half of the papers mentioned a design process, with a minority of these actually outlining the steps of the design process being assessed.

The publications that considered social learning in their STEM assessment discussions included reflective practices. These practices require students to express their learning and progress explicitly in terms of their likes and dislikes, areas of strength, and areas needing improvement. All claimed to develop 21st Century skills and a STEM or professional identity. It is difficult to assess individual 21st Century skills. Therefore, in STEM education assessment, 21st Century skills are assessed in conjunction with other competencies and character qualities.

5 Recommendations for Research

Research is needed to define what authentic assessment means for STEM education, to address and establish a shared meaning for the authentic assessment practices in integrated STEM education. This shared meaning can be explored by answering these questions:

- What assessment methods are used? Our research revealed a lack of content or process assessment methods, and a lack of research reporting on the rubrics used in the assessments.
- How relevant are the tasks to the integrated STEM curriculum and the real-life contexts? Our research revealed simulated real-life tasks are favoured. There is room for the exploration of school-based tasks and how these are assessed to reflect real-life contexts.
- How are the complexity required in the authentic tasks being assessed? Our research revealed high complexity tasks. Further research is needed relating to the relationships in assessing the inquiry process and the modelling process.
- What STEM disciplines are integrated and how that is being assessed? Our research revealed both content and skill practices are assessed. Further exploration is needed in relation to the creative integrative practices of mathematics.
- How are the design process and social learning being assessed? Our research revealed scant research of the design process. Further, the links between content knowledge and the design process have not been explored, and this needs addressing. Our review revealed social learning is a key characteristic of STEM education where the assessment of social awareness and relationships are favoured. Further research is needed relating to responsible and shared decision making leading to creativity.

We suggest that in authentic STEM education, researchers need to make explicit not only the learning tasks but also the assessment methods and tools.

Authentic learning is performance-based, project-based, problem-based learning, and we need to provide these opportunities in STEM education. Thus, we advocate that more authentic STEM education research studies need to be conducted within primary and secondary classroom learning contexts.

6 Recommendations for Practice

Researchers and teachers in STEM education have not adequately addressed authentic assessment practices. We believe that authentic learning and assessment can strengthen STEM teaching and learning. Thus, to reiterate our recommendations in the previous section, more authentic STEM education research studies are needed to inform classroom practices. The same set of questions above can be used to guide teacher professional development programs. Teachers are struggling to undertake meaningful assessments in STEM, so professional development is needed around the potential of authentic learning and assessment as valid practices of STEM education. A third of the papers (16 out of 49) are found to be at the tertiary or adult level, and four papers are on informal out-of-school contexts. Therefore, insights around authentic assessment, drawn from all age groups and educational contexts, need to be aggregated to guide our STEM education practices into the future.

References

Note: * denotes that the paper is included in the integrative review.

*Anwari, I., Yamada, S., Unno, M., Saito, T., Rahma S., Mutakinati, L., & Kumano, Y. (2015). Implementation of authentic learning and assessment through STEM education: Approach to improve students' metacognitive skills. *K-12 STEM Education, 1*(3), 123–136. https://doi.org/10.14456/k12stemed.2015.24

Arthurs, L. A., & Kreager, B. Z. (2017). An integrative review of in-class activities that enable active learning in college science classroom settings. *International Journal of Science Education, 39*(15), 2073–2091. https://doi.org/10.1080/09500693.2017.1363925

Ashford-Rowe, K., Herrington, J., & Brown, C. (2014). Establishing the critical elements that determine authentic assessment. *Assessment and Evaluation in Higher Education, 39*(2), 205–222. http://dx.doi.org/10.1080/02602938.2013.819566.

*Asunda, P. (2014). A conceptual framework for STEM integration into curriculum through career and technical education, *Journal of STEM Teacher Education, 49*(1), 3–15. https://doi.org/10.30707/JSTE49 .1Asunda

*Asunda, P. A. (2018). Infusing computer science in engineering and technology education: An integrated STEM perspective. *Journal of Technology Studies, 44*(1), 2–12. http://dx.doi.org.ezproxy.lib.monash.edu.au/10.21061/jots.v44i1.a.1

*Bielik, T., & Yarden, A. (2016). Promoting the asking of research questions in a high-school biotechnology inquiry-oriented program, *International Journal of STEM Education, 3*(1), 1–13. https://doi.org/10.1186/s40594-016-0048-x

*Bosman, L. B., & Chelberg, K. A. (2019). Integrating context and authenticity to increase pre-college engagement through the STEM academy for renewable energy education. *International Journal of Pedagogical Innovations, 7*(2), 17–29. http://dx-doi.org/10.12785/ijcnt/070102

*Bosman, L. B., O'Brien, S., Shanta, S., & Strimel, G. J. (2018). Validating the value proposition of engineering design problems through quantitative analysis. *Technology and Engineering Teacher, 78*(2), 32–37. https://www.iteea.org/Publications/Journals/TET/TETOct2018/139128.aspx

*Brand, B. R. (2020). Integrating science and engineering practices outcomes from a collaborative professional development. *International Journal of STEM Education, 7*(13), 1–13. https://doi.org/10.1186/s40594-020-00210-x

Brandt, R. (1998). Research news and comment: An exchange of views on "Semantics, psychometrics, and assessment reform: A close look at 'authentic' assessments". *Educational Researcher, 27*(6), 20. https://doi.org/10.3102/0013189X027006020A

*Campbell, C., & Jobling, W. (2014). STEM education: Authentic projects which embrace an integrated approach. *Australasian Journal of Technology Education, 1*, 29–38. http://dx.doi.org/10.15663/ajte.v1i1.14

*Czaplinski, I., Turner, I. W., Helmstedt, K., Corry, P., & Mallet, D. G. (2019). Industry-based, transdisciplinary, complex problems as realistic settings for applying the M in STEM. *International Journal of Mathematical Education in Science and Technology.* https://doi.org/10.1080/0020739X.2019.1692932

*Das, D. K. (2020). Civil engineering students' perceptions of conventional and alternative assessment methods. *African Journal of Research in Mathematics, Science and Technology Education, 24*(1), 116–128. https://doi.org/10.1080/18117295.2020.1738102

*Davidson, C. D., & Simms, W. (2017). Science theatre as STEAM: A case study of "save it now". *The STEAM Journal, 3*(1), Article 14. https://doi.org/10.5642/steam.20170301.14

*Davis, J. P., Du, J., Tang, J.-H., Qiao, L., Liu, Y.-Q., & Chiang, F.-K. (2020). Uniformity, harmony, and emotional energy in a Chinese STEM classroom. *International Journal of STEM Education, 7*(44). https://doi.org/10.1186/s40594-020-00232-5

Deutscher, V., & Winther, E. (2018). A conceptual framework for authentic competence assessment in VET: A logic design model. In S. McGrath et al. (Eds.), *Handbook of vocational education and training: Developments in the changing world of work* (pp. 1–14). Springer International Publishing. https://doi.org/10.1007/978-3-319-49789-1_80-1

*Dierdorp, A., Bakker, A., van Maanen, J. A., & Eijkelhof, H. M. C. (2014). Meaningful statistics in professional practices as a bridge between mathematics and science: An evaluation of a design research project. *International Journal of STEM Education, 1*(9). https://doi.org/10.1186/s40594-014-0009-1

*Duschl, R. A., & Bybee, R. W. (2014). Planning and carrying out investigations: An entry to learning and to teacher professional development around NGSS science and engineering practices. *International Journal of STEM Education, 1*(12). doi: 10.1186/s40594-014-0012-6

English, L. D. (2017). Advancing elementary and middle school STEM education. *International Journal of Science and Mathematics Education, 15*(1), 5–24. http://dx.doi.org/10.1007/s10763-017-9802-x

*Ernst, J. V., & Glennie, E. (2015). Redesigned high schools for transformed STEM learning: Performance assessment pilot outcome. *Journal of STEM Education, 16*(4), 27–35. https://jstem.org/jstem/index.php/JSTEM/issue/view/129

*Ernst, J. V., Glennie, E., & Li, S. (2017). Performance-based task assessment of higher-order proficiencies in redesigned STEM high schools. *Contemporary Issues in Education Research, 10*(1), 13–32. http://dx.doi.org/10.19030/cier.v10i1.9877

*Fahrer, N. E., Ernst, J. V., Branoff, T. J., & Clark, A. C. (2011). Performance and cognitive assessment in 3-D modeling. *Journal of STEM Teacher Education, 48*(1), 68–95. https://ir.library.illinoisstate.edu/jste/vol48/iss1/

Frey, B. B., Schmitt, V. L., & Allen, J. P. (2012). Defining authentic classroom assessment. *Practical Assessment, Research, and Evaluation, 17*(2), 1–18. https://doi.org/10.7275/sxbs-0829

Ferguson, J. S. (2019). *Using authentic assessment in information literacy programs.* Rowman & Littlefield.

*Franklin, S. V., Hane, E., Kustusch, M. B., Ptak, C., & Sayre, E. C. (2018). Improving retention through metacognition: A program for deaf/hard-of-hearing and first-generation STEM college students. *Journal of College Science Teaching, 48*(2), 21–27. https://www-jstor-org/stable/26616264

Gao, X., Li, P., Shen, J., & Sun H. (2020). Reviewing assessment of student learning in interdisciplinary STEM education. *International Journal of STEM Education, 7*(24). https://doi.org/10.1186/s40594-020-00225-4

*Gray, J. S., Brown, M. A., & Connolly, J. P. (2017). Examining construct validity of the quantitative literacy VALUE rubric in college-level STEM assignments. *Research & Practice in Assessment, 12*(Summer), 20–31. https://www.rpajournal.com/archive/

*Guezy, S. S., Moore, T. J., & Harwell, M. (2016). Building up STEM: An analysis of teacher-developed engineering design-based STEM integration curricular materials. *Journal of Pre-College Engineering Education Research (J-PEER), 6*(1), 11–29. https://doi.org/10.7771/2157-9288.1129

Gulikers, J. T., Bastiaens, T. J., & Kirschner, P. A. (2004). A five-dimensional framework for authentic assessment. *Educational Technology Research and Development, 52*(3), 67–86. https://doi-org/10.1007/BF02504676

*Hallström, J., & Schönborn, K. J. (2019). Models and modelling for authentic STEM education: Reinforcing the argument. *International Journal of STEM Education, 6*(22). https://doi.org/10.1186/s40594-019-0178-z

*Herro, D., Quigley, C., Andrews, J., & Delacruz, G. (2017). Co-measure: developing an assessment for student collaboration in STEAM activities. *International Journal of STEM Education, 4*(26), 1–10. https://doi.org/10.1186/s40594-017-0094-z

*Kelley, T. R., Brenner, D. C., & Pieper, J. T. (2010). Two approaches to engineering design: Observations in sTEm education. *Journal of STEM Teacher Education, 47*(2), 5–40. https://doi.org/10.30707/JSTE47.2Kelley

*Kelley, T. R., & Wicklein, R. C. (2009). Examination of assessment practices for engineering design projects in secondary education (second in a three part series). *Journal of STEM Teacher Education, 46*(2), 6–25. https://ir.library.illinoisstate.edu/jste/vol46/iss2/4

*Kinner, D., & Lord, M. (2018). Student-perceived gains in collaborative, course-based undergraduate research experiences in the Geosciences. *Journal of College Science Teaching, 48*(2), 48–58. https://www-jstor-org/stable/26616270

*Kitagawa, L., Pombo, E., & Davis, T. (2018). Plastic pollution. *Science and Children, 55*(7), 38–45. https://doi.org/10.2505/4/sc18_055_07_38

*Lamberg, T., & Trzynadlowski, N. (2015). How STEM academy teachers conceptualize and implement STEM education. *Journal of Research in STEM Education, 1*(1), 45–58. https://doi.org/10.51355/jstem.2015.8

*Lin, K.-Y., Hsiao, H.-S., Chang, Y.-S., Chien, Y.-H., & Wu, Y.-T. (2018). The effectiveness of using 3D printing technology in STEM project-based learning activities. *EURASIA Journal of Mathematics, Science and Technology Education, 14*(12), em1633. https://doi.org/10.29333/ejmste/97189

Lin, Y., Wang, K., Xiao, Y., & Froyd, J. E. (2020). Research and trends in STEM education: A systematic review of journal publications. *International Journal of STEM Education, 7*(11). https://doi.org/10.1186/s40594-020-00207-6

*Ludwig, P. M., Nagel, J. K., & Lewis, E. J. (2017). Student learning outcomes from a pilot medical interventions course with nursing, engineering, and biology undergraduate students. *International Journal of STEM Education, 4*(1). https://doi.org/10.1186/s40594-017-0095-y

MacDonald, A., Hunter, J., Wise, K., & Fraser, S. (2019). STEM and STEAM and the spaces between: An overview of education agendas pertaining to 'disciplinarity' across three Australian states. *Journal of Research in STEM Education, 5*(1), 75–92. https://doi.org/10.51355/jstem.2019.64

*Mallet, D. G. (2008). Asynchronous online collaboration as a flexible learning activity and an authentic assessment method in an undergraduate mathematics course. *Eurasia Journal of Mathematics, Science & Technology Education, 4*(2), 143–151. https://doi.org/10.12973/ejmste/75314

McKown, C. (2019). Challenges and opportunities in the applied assessment of student social and emotional learning. *Educational Psychologist, 54*(3), 205–221, https://doi.org/10.1080/00461520.2019.1614446

Moher, D., Liberati, A., Tetzlaff, J., Altman, D. G., The PRISMA Group. (2009). Preferred reporting items for systematic reviews and meta-analyses: The PRISMA statement. *PLoS Med, 6*(7), e1000097. https://doi.org/10.1371/journal.pmed1000097

Newmann, F. M. (1998). Research news and comment: An exchange of views on "semantics, psychometrics, and assessment reform: A close look at 'authentic' assessments". *Educational Researcher, 27*(6), 19–20. https://doi.org/10.3102/0013189X027006019

*Newton, S., Alemdar, M., Hilton, E., Linsey, J., & Fu, F. (2018). Incorporating industrial design pedagogy into a mechanical engineering graphics course: A Discipline-Based Education Research (DBER) approach. *International Journal of STEM Education, 5*(29). https://doi.org/10.1186/s40594-018-0122-7

Next Generation Science Standards (NGSS). (2013). *Appendix F: Science and engineering practices in the NGSS*. https://www.nextgenscience.org/get-to-know

*Opperman, A. (2016). Maker education: The STEAM playground. *The STEAM Journal, 2*(2), Article 4. https://doi.org/10.5642/steam.20160202.04

Paige, K., O'Keeffe, L., Geer, R., Macgregor, D., & Panizzon, D. (2019). Using artefacts to articulate teachers' perceptions of STEM. *Teaching Science, 65*(1), 48–54. https://search.informit.org/doi/abs/10.3316/aeipt.222771

*Peffer, M. E., & Ramezani, N. (2019). Assessing epistemological beliefs of experts and novices via practices in authentic science inquiry. *International Journal of STEM Education, 6*(3). https://doi.org/10.1186/s40594-018-0157-9

Perignat, E., & Katz-Buonincontro, J. (2019). STEAM in practice and research: An integrative review. *Thinking Skills and Creativity, 31*, 31–43. https://doi.org/10.1016/j.tsc.2018.10.002

*Potter, B. S., Ernst, J. V., & Glennie, E. J. (2017). Performance-based assessment in the secondary STEM classroom. *Technology and Engineering Teacher, 76*(6), 18–22. https://www.iteea.org/Publications/Journals/TET/TETMar17.aspx

*Radziwill, N. M., Benton, M. C., & Moellers, C. (2015). From STEM to STEAM: Reframing what it means to learn. *The STEAM Journal, 2*(1), Article 3. https://doi.org/10.5642/steam.20150201.3

Rapanta, C., Garcia-Mila, M., & Gilabert, S. (2013). What is meant by argumentative competence? An integrative review of methods of analysis and assessment in education. *Review of Educational Research, 83*(4), 483–520. https://doi.org/10.3102/0034654313487606

Ritz, J. M., & Fan, S.-C. (2015). STEM and technology education: International state-of-the-art. *International Journal of Design Education, 25*(4), 429–451. https://doi.org/10.1007/s10798-014-9290-z

Root-Bernstein, R. (2018). STEMM education should get "HACD". *Science, 361*(6397), 22–23. https://doi.org/10.1126/science.aat8566

Rule, A. C. (2006). The components of authentic learning. *Journal of Authentic Learning, 3*(1), 1–10. http://hdl.handle.net/1951/35263

Sami, J., Sinclair, K., Stein, Z., & Medsker, L. (2020). Data science outreach educational program for high school students focused in agriculture. *Journal of STEM Education, 21*(1), 18–25. https://www.jstem.org/jstem/index.php/JSTEM/article/view/2405

*Septiani, A., & Rustaman, N. Y. (2017). Implementation of performance assessment in STEM (Science, Technology, Engineering, Mathematics) education to detect science process skill. *Journal of Physics: Conference Series, 812*, 012052. https://doi.org/10.1088/1742-6596/812/1/012052

*Singer, A., Montgomery, G., & Schmoll, S. (2020). How to foster the formation of STEM identity: Studying diversity in an authentic learning environment. *International Journal of STEM Education, 7*(57). https://doi.org/10.1186/s40594-020-00254-z

*Skinner, A., Diller, D., Kumar, R., Cannon-Bowers, J., Smith, R., Tanaka, A., Julian, D., & Perez, R. (2018). Development and application of a multi-modal task analysis to support intelligent tutoring of complex skills. *International Journal of STEM Education, 5*(14). https://doi.org/10.1186/s40594-018-0108-5

*Skurikhina, J. A., Valeeva, R. A., Khodakova, N. P., & Maystrovich, E. V. (2018). Forming research competence and engineering thinking of school students by means of educational robotics. *EURASIA Journal of Mathematics, Science and Technology Education, 14*(12), em1639. https://doi.org/10.29333/ejmste/97827

*Stehle, S. M., & Peters-Burton, E. E. (2019). Developing student 21st Century skills in selected exemplary inclusive STEM high schools. *International Journal of STEM Education, 6*(39). https://doi.org/10.1186/s40594-019-0192-1

*Stohlmann, M. (2020). STEM integration for high school mathematics teachers. *Journal of Research in STEM Education, 6*(1), 52–63. https://j-stem.net/index.php/jstem/article/view/71/63

*Strimel, G. J., Bartholomew, S. R., Jackson, A., Grubbs, M., & Bates, D. G. M. (2017, June 25–28). *Evaluating freshman engineering design projects using adaptive comparative judgement* [Paper presentation]. American Society for Engineering Education Annual Conference & Exposition. https://www.asee.org/public/conferences/78/papers/17703/view

Task Force Report, S. T. E. M. (2014). *Innovate: A blueprint for science, technology, engineering, and mathematics in California public education.* Californians Dedicated to Education Foundation. https://www.cde.ca.gov/pd/ca/sc/documents/innovate.pdf

Terwilliger, J. (1998). Research news and comment: Rejoinder: Response to Wiggins and Newmann. *Educational Researcher, 27*(6), 22–23. https://doi.org/10.3102/0013189X027006022

Toronto, C. E., & Remington, R. (2020). *A step-by-step guide to conducting an integrative review.* Springer.

*Tsai, H.-Y., Chung, C.-C., & Lou, S.-J. (2018). Construction and development of iSTEM learning model. *EURASIA Journal of Mathematics, Science and Technology Education, 14*(1), 15–32. https://doi.org/10.12973/ejmste/78019

*Tucker-Raymond, E., Puttick, G., Cassidy, M., Harteveld, C., & Troiano, G. M. (2019). "I broke your game!" Critique among middle schoolers designing computer games about climate change. *International Journal of STEM Education, 6*(41). https://doi.org/10.1186/s40594-019-0194-z

*Watson, J., Fitzallen, N., English, L., & Wright, S. (2020). Introducing statistical variation in Year 3 in a STEM context: Manufacturing licorice. *International Journal of Mathematical Education in Science and Technology, 51*(3), 354–387. https://doi.org/10.1080/0020739X.2018.1562117

*Weldeana, H. N., & Sbhatu, D. B. (2017). Portfolio of evidence: An assessment tool in promoting geometry achievement among teacher education college students. *EURASIA Journal of Mathematics Science and Technology Education, 13*(6), 1981–2004. https://doi.org/10.12973/eurasia.2017.01210a

Wiggins, G. (1998). Research news and comment: An exchange of views on "Semantics, psychometrics, and assessment reform: A close look at 'authentic' assessments". *Educational Researcher, 27*(6), 20–22. https://doi.org/10.3102/0013189X027006020A

*Wind, S. A., Alemdar, M., Lingle, J. A., Moore, R., & Asilkalkan, A. (2019). Exploring student understanding of the engineering design process using distractor analysis. *International Journal of STEM Education, 6*(4). https://doi.org/10.1186/s40594-018-0156-x

*Young, K., Palmer, S., Binek, C., Tolson, M., & Campbell, M. (2019). Assessment-led reform: Creating a sustainable culture for on and off campus WIL. *Journal of Teaching and Learning for Graduate Employability, 10*(1), 73–87. https://doi.org/10.21153/jtlge2019vol10no1art784

CHAPTER 3

Virtual Simulation in ITE

Technology Driven Authentic Assessment and Moderation of Practice

Zara Ersozlu, Susan Ledger and Linda Hobbs

Abstract

Authentic and performance assessments are recurrent terms in teacher education. However, their definitions and applications differ. Simulated learning environments have the capacity to address both assessment types. Assessing practicum performance has traditionally been limited to real life experiences in diverse school contexts, in diverse classroom settings, and assessed by a diverse range of mentors and assessors (Ledger & Fischetti, 2020). Virtual simulation offers a technological solution to prepare preservice teachers for these diverse contexts and moderate individual practices and performances within a controlled learning environment to mitigate the contextual differences outlined. Authentic simulated assessment tasks can be designed to replicate placement contexts, improve the self-efficacy of future teachers and in turn improve student performance. Pedagogies of practices (Grossman et al., 2009) provides a framework for analysing simulation as an authentic assessment tool for assessing student preparedness for practicum and performance moderation. This chapter builds on a conceptual review of literature in which the principles of authentic assessment and the features of teaching simulations will be outlined. We argue that a simulated learning environment is beneficial for addressing both authentic and performance assessments for preservice teachers and recommend strategies on how these principles can be applied within a initial teacher education using the lenses of five dimensions of authenticity.

Keywords

authentic assessment – performance assessment – virtual simulations – teacher education

1   Introduction

Effectively assessing preservice teachers' knowledge, skills and capabilities are important aspects of teacher education (Teacher Education Ministerial Advisory Group, 2014). Assessment provides opportunities for preservice teachers to improve their skills and be successful in their professional life. Typically, preservice teachers are assessed on their teaching ability during practicums. The assessment process provides feedback on teaching and learning performance and engagement. On practicums assessment is used as a diagnostic and reflective approach to improve educational practice and student learning. The introduction of virtual simulation tools provides further opportunities to practice and rehearse the art and science of teaching outside of practicum. Many discipline areas such as health (Weeks et al., 2019; Schuwirth & van der Vleuten, 2003), business and marketing (Vos, 2015; Nelly & Tucker, 2012), and gamification (Wood et al., 2013) have outlined how virtual simulations are beneficial for assessment purposes for performance and authentic assessment within their fields. The emerging field of virtual simulations in education has focused on the training and skill development aspect of simulation rather than the use of an assessment tool (Pankowski & Walker, 2016; Ledger, Ersozlu & Fischetti, 2019; Dieker et al., 2014; Straub et al., 2014). There is limited research focusing on the assessment aspect of virtual simulations in teacher education with most focusing on physical engagement such as body gesture and eye movement during the use of virtual simulations (Barmaki, 2016; Rappa et al., 2019), and preparatory experiences for professional placement (Ledger, Ersozlu & Fischetti, 2019). This study addresses this identified gap.

Preservice teachers are expected to gain and improve necessary skills and knowledge through a series of professional placements where they refine and develop their knowledge and practice their teaching skills in a real-life context. These experiences are without doubt invaluable but are complex components of an initial teacher education degree. The logistics and planning for practicums require a great deal of attention to detail and are at times not cost-effective or equitable. However, they are necessary in terms of accreditation and knowledge transfer. Simulation allows student teachers to practice and rehearse their skills in an authentic context that replicates a practicum and real-life experience. These experiences promote the authenticity of assessment by providing some level of resemblance to a real-life situation (Nelly & Tucker, 2012).

Virtual simulation can be a highly useful tool to improve the authenticity of assessment activities. Although using virtual simulations and games as an assessment tool is a well-known concept (Ingram & Jackson, 2004), it is still not fully developed as an area of research (Wood et al., 2013). It is even less researched within the context of initial teacher education programs (Ledger & Fischetti, 2020). We would like to explore here the full potential of virtual simulations as authentic assessment tools in ITE. The purpose of this chapter is to discuss whether virtual simulations can be used as an authentic assessment tool in education. To explore authentic assessment and the affordances of virtual classrooms, the research question underpinning this study is:

> *How do we know if advanced technology environments such as virtual simulations can be effectively used as an authentic assessment tool for pre service teachers?*

This chapter addresses the gaps in the literature on authentic assessment models in relation to virtual simulations for initial teacher education. It begins with a critique of literature on authentic and performance assessments and the use of virtual simulation in teacher education. The functionality of authentic assessment in virtual simulation environment is then discussed. Specifically, we argue that authentic assessment aligns well with the functionalities of a virtual learning environment for preservice teachers.

2   Authentic vs Performance Assessment

Authentic and performance assessment concepts are longstanding approaches to assessment (Gulikers, Bastiaens & Kirschner, 2004; Newman, 1997). Their definitions are ubiquitous partly because they are understood from different discipline perspectives. The diversity in definitions create difficulty in shared understanding of the real meaning between researchers and educators. They are also commonly used interchangeably, giving the same meaning to both assessment types. To distinguish between these concepts, Meyer (1992) provides two different cases to represent each assessment type. In the first case students are given a writing assignment, (writing as a process instructional model). Students participate in a standardised series of activities to produce their writing samples and the teacher guides them through the assessment with limited teacher direction. In the second case (writing as a process stage), students develop their papers under non standardized conditions in a way that represents the ongoing work of the student for the year. Each student has a conference with their teacher to determine which paper from their portfolio to submit for assessment purposes. Meyer (1992) defined the first case as *performance assessment* since students were asked to achieve a set of actions to be assessed within a prescribed context. However, the second case was considered as performance assessment because the portfolio includes examples of student performances as well as authentic assessment. Performance is assessed in a context where students make personal decisions about how and what they present. The second example replicates a real-life writing experience and is more similar to a real-life experience.

According to Meyer (1992) performance assessment addresses student achievement on a specific set of procedures to be evaluated while authentic assessment addresses the context itself where the student performs. Authentic assessment not only provides a real-life environment but also gives students control of their work. All authentic assessments are performance assessments while not all performance assessments are authentic (Gulikers, Bastiaens & Kirschner, 2004).

For some researchers, 'authentic assessment should replicate meaningful performances in real world contexts and should provide real life tasks with multiple solutions to students' (Khaira & Yambo, 2005). Others believe that students should be 'proficient at performing the tasks which replicate real world challenges' because they are most likely to encounter similar situations when they graduate (Mueller, 2006). Some others suggest the main difference between performance and authentic assessment is the degree of fidelity. Authentic assessment places more importance on high level of fidelity, whereas performance assessment does not need to include any degree of fidelity (Okey, 1996). This paper considers the notion of fidelity in assessment through an active implementation lens which focuses on how well the performance assessment is being implemented as intended (US Dept Ed, 2011).

Similarly, Gulikers, Bastiaens and Kirschner (2004) define authentic assessment as requiring that 'students to use the same competencies attributes and capabilities, or combinations of knowledge, skills, and attitudes that they need to apply in the criterion situation in professional life' (p. 69). Authentic assessment allows educators to evaluate students' knowledge and abilities as well as how they use those skills and knowledges in a real-life context to solve real life problems. These contexts introduce students to scenarios and interactions that are likely to occur within the daily lifecycle of a workplace.

In this chapter, we draw from Gulikers, Bastiaens and Kirschner's (2004) interpretation of authentic assessment to better determine how authentic assessment can be used effectively in initial teacher assessment using virtual simulation environments. Biggs, (1996), Resnick (1987), Wiggings (1993), concluded that: (a) authentic assessment should be aligned to authentic instruction to help student learning; (b) students should achieve relevant attributes and capabilities through authentic assessment task; and (c) authenticity is subjective. Gulikers, Bastiaens and Kirschner (2004) built on this premise to develop five dimensions to determine the varying degree of authenticity of an assessment. Their dimenisons are summarized below:

Task: There should be some semblance between the criteria of the authentic task and the complexity of the tasks and the level of ownership of the tasks as professionals face in their work life. This includes how knowledge, skills, and attitudes are integrated, its complexity, and its ownership. Ultimately students should find meaning and relevance in the task.

Physical Context: There should be semblance between physical environment simulated by the task and the real workplace environment, both literally and figuratively. Fidelity of such an environment can be maintained particularly well by computer simulations that reproduce certain aspects of the physical environment of the workplace.

Social Context: There should be semblance between the social relationships/processes that exist in the real professional environment and the opportunities created in the authentic assessment for this type of interaction. For example, where group work is a feature of the real workplace then the assessment should be designed to allow collaboration; similarly, individual work can be simulated through designs that focus on individual attributes and capabilities.

Assessment Result or Form: Performance should be the basis on which assessment is judged and this performance should resemble the competences that a student might exhibit in a real-life situation. Students should have multiple opportunities through tests and tasks to demonstrate these attributes and capabilities and be allowed to defend the authenticity of their work.

Criteria and Standards: There should be semblance between the criteria they will be judged by in their workplace and the criterion-referenced judgement applied in their assignment. The criteria and standards should be explicitly stated so that students are aware of how their performance through a series of assessment tasks will be judged.

In summary, authentic assessment is promoted as being useful for producing graduates equipped with the knowledge and skills that they will encounter in the workforce. We argue that authentic assessment should be use widely and alongside standardised tests to better prepare work-ready graduates from initial teacher education. Virtual simulations provide one way of embedding authentic assessment in initial teacher education and is discussed next.

3   Virtual Reality Simulations (VRS) in Initial Teacher Education

The use of virtual simulations (VS) has increased rapidly over the last decade (Dede, 2017). As an assessment mechanism, simulated learning environments, immersive environments and artificial intelligence are being used in several different discipline areas including teacher education. VRs are interactive tools which allow learners to be immersed within a simulated environment replicating real-life like experiences both psychologically and physically. VR has been categorised in a range of ways. Burdea and Coiffet (2003) characterise VR in three ways: immersion, interaction and imagination. Immersive learning experiences include 'actional' immersion, symbolic/narrative immersion (Dede, Jacobson & Richardson, 2017), sensory immersion (Jacobson et al., 2015) and social immersion (Hartanto et al., 2014). Psychological immersion is achieved when a range of these immersion factors are embedded in the design features.

The psychological benefit of immersion relates to VRs ability to enhance motivation and learning (Dede, 2009). VRs increase intrinsic motivation for mastering complex knowledge and skills, particularly if the assessment task is designed within a reflective practice cycle or action learning cycle such as plan, act, reflect or plan, teach, assess process (Ledger & Fischetti, 2020). Interaction refers to VR being capable of detecting and responding to user signals, which may, for example be through direct control of virtual objects. Imagination refers to the fact that VR is a new approach and enables people to learn the world and imagine objects not existing in the real world, thereby 'increasing perceptual and rational knowledge, deepening understanding of concepts, and triggering new associations" (Liu et al., 2017, p. 109). Liu et al., however, indicate that research has yet to show that VR technology facilitates user creativity.

Like Burdeah and Coiffett (2003), Sherman and Craig (2003) describe four elements of virtual reality but speak to it in terms of a process consisting of a virtual world, immersion, sensory feedback and interactivity. They attempt to capture the interrelated components that provide the overall learning experience of VR engagement. First, the virtual world is created by a series of rules and relationships between the elements of the system that provides life-like environments. Second, they consider immersion as the feeling of involvement and being in the moment experience of users. Third, the sensory feedback produced by system elements provides data about user's actions during the simulation. Finally, there is interactivity in terms of reflection and perception of the user's actions and response to the experience.

In comparison, the focus of Liu et al.'s (2017) categorisation of VR is on learning. They suggest four types of VR use in educational contexts: observational learning, operational learning, social learning and academic research. Although not mutually exclusive the four types are inherent in simulated learning environments. The learning theories used in the design and development of simulated learning environments typically centre on constructivism. Virtual reality offers a platform suitable for instructional strategies aligned with situated learning, experimental learning and collaborative learning processes (Liu et al., 2017). Autonomous learning or self-directed/self-regulated learning theories are also embedded in VR contexts (Zimmerman, 1994). Additionally, cognitive load theory (Sweller, 2004), is realized within VR practices. The cognitive load processing imposed on working memory during human activities can also be addressed in simulated environments.

The learning theories inherent in VR-situated learning environments suggest the suitability of simulated classrooms as a tool to prepare pre-service and in-service teachers for a range of diverse classroom contexts. VR has immense potential for positive educational outcomes within teacher education environments as it uses immersive practices, interactive engagement and triggers imagination, and is a promising tool for improving individualized instruction (Dalgarno & Lee, 2010).

New technologies provide another opportunity to categorise VR in terms of users – single or multi. Single-user mixed reality virtual environments such as the synchronous learning environment of *TeachlivE* (Dieker et al., 2014), *Teacher Talk Game* (Simiosys, 2014), *The Cook School District* simulation,[1] *Teacher Work Sample Methodology* (Girod & Girod, 2006), single user environments such as *Simschool* (Gibson, 2011) focusing on diverse learners and classroom strategies, and *Classroom SIM* (Aha!, Process Ing, 2012) focusing on discipline strategies. Many studies highlight the benefits and affordances of these new technologies. *SimSchool*, for example, has been shown to be a useful educational tool for teaching practice (Badiee and Kaufman 2014; Gibson and Halverson 2004). *SimSchool* simulation has been shown to be more successful in increasing a sense of self-efficacy than traditional teaching experience (Christensen et al., 2011).

Multi-user environments such as *TeacherSim, Active World* and *Second Life* also provide life-like experiences for students to interact with their peers in a collaborative environment and with other experts. Ferry, Kervin, Cambourne, Turbill, Puglisi, Jonassen et al. (2004) evaluated ClassSim with preservice teachers and found that the simulation was successfully suited to preservice teachers' critical thinking abilities and provided engaging, complex situations during their teaching sessions.

Another simulation, *Classroom teacher training 3D* simulation for teacher training (Aten Inc, 2015) enabled preservice teachers to develop their decision-making skills in a life-like simulated environment based on problems encountered in a real-life context. Preservice teachers were seen to practice expert opinions on their decisions. Kognito Interactive (2012) produced a simulation named *At Risk for Middle and High School Educators*, which focused on high and middle school students who were experiencing distress in the classroom.

Kognito interactive (2012) also created the *Step In! Speak Up!* program to educate teachers to support LGBTQ youth and to prevent bullying behaviours. *VirtualPREX* is another simulation created by Gregory, Dalgarno, Crisp, Reiners, Masters, Drehe and Knox (2013) for preservice teachers' professional development (http://www.virtualprex.com). It was created in *Second Life* virtual simulation, which allows the participants to present themselves in an environment as a teacher. They can also practice teaching skills with their classmates who are pretending to be school students in a virtual environment (Gregory, 2014). *Teacher Talk Game* is a similar simulation created by Simiosy (2014) that uses mixed reality virtual puppetry approach to allow teachers to practice with five students controlled remotely by an actor who role plays as a student. The puppetry method allows a professional actor (interactor) to combine puppetry functionalities and sound morphing equipment to control avatars that model the specific behaviour of students through avatars in pre-created learning scenarios. The teacher can just see the screen with students, and the actor can see both screens with students and the screen shows the teachers' actions. The actor is also connected to a motion sensor that provides non-verbal communication between students and teacher. Similarly, *TeachlivE* (TLE) is a mix of a real and artificial intelligence that creates a life-like environment which uses prepared classroom scenarios controlled by a trained interactor. The *TeachlivE* program is different to other simulations regarding computing, realisation and artificial intelligence aspects due to the human in the loop interactor process.

Each of these virtual simulation environments have specific components that enable effective interaction between users and the components of the system within meaningful learning experiences. Aldrich (2004) suggests that two aspects of VR environments impact efficacy: content type referring to linear (sequential content), systems (system interactions) cyclical (mastery); and delivery types as simulation (real-life scenarios), game (entertainment) and pedagogical (productive learning). The fidelity of these interactions rest on how each component works together to create a successful educational experience.

Virtual Simulations, no matter how they are categorised, show affordances and benefits to preparing students for performance and authentic assessment. They are not only useful in providing rich learning content and scenario-based environments that emulate real life contexts, they also help students reflect on their practice in ways that promote productive learning pedagogies.

In the next section we will discuss how well authentic assessment aligns with the characteristics of VR and mixed reality learning simulations and whether they can be effectively used in initial teacher education as not only a learning tool but also an authentic assessment tool.

4   Using Virtual Simulations as Authentic Assessment Tools

Assessment aspects of virtual simulations are emerging, but its potential has not been fully investigated (Wood et al., 2013), particularly within teacher education. In this section we discuss the process of simulation as a learning tool as outlined by Sherman and Craig (2003): *a virtual world, immersion, sensory feedback* and *interactivity*. We then link the process of simulation to the context of authentic assessment elements suggested by Gulikers, Bastiaens & Kirschner (2004): *task, physical context, social context, assessment result* and *criteria and standards*. We aim to highlight the usefulness of combining the two conceptual elements, VR and authentic assessments, or more pragmatically VR as an authentic assessment tool.

The four elements outlined in Sherman and Craig's (2003) simulation process captures the learning that takes place in VR. *A virtual world* allows students to perform in a real-life like environment influencing the *task, physical and social context*. Students are engaged in similar tasks professionals face in their everyday work life. They are able to rehearse their skills by interacting with avatars and elements of the system. Scenario based interactions are representative of the social context in which they may find themselves interacting with in the future, such as students, parents or colleagues (Ledger & Fischetti, 2020).

Immersion allows students to have a real sense of involvement during the simulation. The synchronous nature of the human in the loop simulation gives the sense of being in the moment in a real environment. The physical and social assessment task is facilitated through the functionality of the simulated context. The authentic assessment afforded through simulated interactions improves critical thinking skills as they immerse themselves into interactions they have to respond to and/or problem-solve (Simon & Gregg, 1993).

Sensory feedback provides opportunity for self-assessment during the simulated interactions. The immediacy of synchronous responses from the avatars provide authentic feedback loops similar to those experienced working with real students. For example, if the assessment task is based on student management, the avatars (controlled by human in the look interactors) will provide direct responses to the dialogic engagement and behaviour presented. In this way, *interactivity* function is supported by *assessment results*.

Interactivity relates to the clearly defined *criteria and standards* students are being judged. Each interaction is judged against performance levels, capabilities, improvement and engagement that might be expected in real school-based interactions.

Aldrich's (2004) criteria for a productive virtual simulation experience match Sherman and Craig's (2003) elements, however concern is expressed in terms of feedback. Aldrich (2004) argues that the authentic assessment tool used during a simulation does not guarantee students will improve performance based on the assessment type. Moreover, Aldrich (2004) suggests that an additional human element needs to be included in the simulated process. They call on the need for a lecturer/tutor/teacher to scaffold the learning process before, during and after simulation. This approach matches the *assessment result* in authentic assessment from the point of students defending the authenticity of their work and believing that they have been successful.

5 Linking VRS to the Context of Authentic Assessment Elements

Through investigating both authentic assessments and VR simulations, we conclude that mixed reality simulations are appropriate platforms and learning environments in which authentic assessments are generated. We integrate Sherman and Craig's (2003) simulation framework above with Gulikers, Bastiaens and Kirschner (2004) categories of authentic assessment to justify our claim:

1. *Task:* An authentic task resembles the criterion task with respect to the integration of knowledge, skills, and attitudes, its complexity, and its ownership. The simulation addresses this by replicating the context in which these tasks are completed?
2. *Physical Context:* physical environment should resemble the real workplace environment both literally and figuratively. New technologies continue to improve this aspect. Current human in the loop simulations allow synchronous interactions and transform backdrops to resemble real contexts.
3. *Social Context:* authentic assessment should include social relationship and processes that are exist in real life environment such as collaboration. Simulation offers opportunities for collaborative planning, teaching, assessment and feedback loops.
4. *Assessment Result or Form:* An authentic assessment result should be a result of a performance that students can generate in real life and this performance should allow to demonstrate the underlying competences.

Teaching attributes and capabilities can be targeted in a simulated learning environment.

Virtual simulations have been widely used to improve meaningful learning experiences in higher education. The meaningful learning experiences leads into meaningful learning outcomes since learners can use their existing attributes and capabilities to restructure their learning and skills (Zhao & Ye, 2012). Virtual simulations can also provide preservice teachers with a tool for reflecting on their learning. Reflection is also an important aspect of authentic learning and assessment (Lombardi, 2007) and a process that engages students in meaningful experiences (Boud, Keogh & Walker, 1985). By reflecting on their experiences preservice teachers can see what worked and what did not work during their interactions and create strategies to overcome weaknesses, which also triggers metacognitive thinking skills (Rule, 2006; Kramarski, Mevarech & Arami, 2002). Thinking about their thinking, preservice teachers gain another important skill that can help them in their real-life experience.

6 Conclusion

In this chapter, we have sought to explore how a simulated learning environment is beneficial for addressing both authentic and performance assessments for preservice teachers. We have discussed the function and application of authentic assessment in teaching simulations elements (Alrdich, 2004; Sherman & Craig, 2003) using the five dimensions of authenticity (Gulikers, Bastiaens & Kirschner, 2004). This allows us to identify how simulation elements are appropriate and support authentic assessment to provide valuable feedback on preservice teacher's attributes and capabilities and moreover, learning as professionals. Based on our discussion, we conclude that mixed reality simulations are appropriate platforms and learning environments to use authentic assessments. Some suggestions are provided for inclusion of simulations into authentic assessment activities.

Virtual simulations are designed to imitate experiences that professionals face in their every-day work life. Virtual simulations offer unique learning environments capable of providing opportunities for developing authentic assessment tasks within initial teacher education programs. Typically, preservice teachers integrate and further develop their knowledge and skills through application in real world practice during professional practicums (Ruben, 1999; Ledger & Fischetti, 2020). This process takes much time and effort and comparability between experiences cannot be guaranteed. Simulations provide an alternative to preparing student teachers for practicums, they offer ITE programs a controlled learning environment that captures and moderates performance across cohorts.

Research is showing that there are many advantages of using virtual simulations as an authentic assessment tool (Ingram & Jackson, 2004). New technologies will continue to be refined, thus narrowing the gap between reality and the virtual world. The presence of avatars in simulations has been found to motivate participants and improve their self-efficacy (Jarmon et al., 2009). Virtual simulations are an effective tool in providing students an opportunity to be actively engaged in their own self-assessment, which is an important feature of authentic assessment (Falchikov & Boud, 1989; Rolheiser & Ross, 2001).

7 Limitations of the Study

This study is limited by the concepts used with no experimental validation for these claims made other than theorisations from the literature. The main purpose of this research was to discuss the elements of simulations to explore the best use of authentic assessment designs which does not cover the all kinds of simulations and technological tools fully in the context of performance and authentic assessment. Our aim was to develop a framework that can be used to trial and explore how intersecting elements of virtual simulations impact on authentic assessment results and hence preservice teachers' experiences and learning.

Note

1 See http://cook.wou.edu

References

Aldrich, C. (2004). *Simulations and the future of learning*. Pfeiffer.
Aten Intelligent Educational Systems Inc. (2015). *Classroom teacher training 3D simulation*. Aten, Inc. http://www.a10ed.com/explore/professional-development/classroom-teacher-training-3d-simulation
Badiee, F., Kaufman, D. (2014). Effectiveness of an online simulation for teacher education. *Journal of Technology and Teacher Education, 22*, 167–186.

Biggs, J. (1996). Enhancing teaching through constructive alignment. *Higher Education, 32,* 347–364.

Burdea, G. C., & Coiffet, P. (2003). *Virtual reality technology* (2nd ed.). Wiley Interscience.

Boud, D., Keogh, R., & Walker, D. (Eds.). (1985). *Reflection: Turning experience into learning.* Routledge.

Christensen, R., Knezek, G., Tyler-Wood, T., & Gibson, D. (2011). SimSchool: An online dynamic simulator for enhancing teacher preparation. *International Journal of Learning Technology, 6*(2), 201–219.

Dede, C. (2009). Immersive interfaces for engagement and learning. *Science, 323,* 66–69.

Dede, C., Jacobson, J., & Richards, J. (2017). *Virtual, augmented, and mixed realities in education.* Springer.

Dalgarno, B., & Lee, M. J. W. (2010). What are the learning affordances of 3D virtual environments? *British Journal of Educational Technology, 40*(1), 10:32.

Dieker, L. A., Rodriguez, J., Lignugaris-Kraft, B., Hynes, M. & Hughes, C. (2014). The potential of simulated environments in teacher education: Current and future possibilities. Teacher Education and Special Education. *The Journal of the Teacher Education Division of the Council for Exceptional Children, 37,* 21–33. doi:10.1177/08884064135126

Dieker, L. A., Straub, C., Hughes, C., Hynes, M. C., & Hardin, S. E. (2014). Virtual environments can take us virtually anywhere. *Educational Leadership, 71*(8), 54–58.

Ferry, B., Kervin, L, Cambourne, B., Turbill, J., Puglisi, S., Jonassen D., & Hedberg, J. (2004). Online classroom simulation: The 'next wave' for pre-service teacher education? In R. Atkinson, C. McBeath, D. Jonas-Dwyer, & R. Phillips (Eds.), *Beyond the comfort zone: Proceedings of the 21st ASCILITE Conference* (pp. 294–302). http://www.ascilite.org.au/conferences/perth04/procs/ferry.html

Falchikov, N., & Boud, D. (1989). Student self-assessment in higher education: A meta-analysis. *Review of Educational Research, 59*(4), 395–430. doi:10.3102/00346543059004395

Gibson, D., Christensen, R., Tyler-Wood, T., & Knezek, G. (2011). SimSchool: Enhancing teacher preparation through simulated classrooms. In M. Koehler & P. Mishra (Eds.), *Proceedings of society for information technology & teacher education international conference 2011* (pp. 1504–1510). AACE.

Gibson, D., & Halverson, B. (2004). SimSchool: Preparing tomorrow's teachers to improve student results. In R. Ferdig, C. Crawford, R. Carlsen, N. Davis, J. Price, R. Weber, & D. A. Willis (Eds.), *Proceedings of the society for information technology & teacher education annual conference 2004* (pp. 3318–3321). AACE.

Girod, M., & Girod, G. (2006). Exploring the efficacy of the Cook School district simulation. *Journal of Teacher Education, 57*(5), 481–497. http://dx.doi.org/10.1177/0022487106293742

Gregory, S. (2014). Taking the distance out of learning for students through a virtual world. In A. Hebbel-Seeger, T. Reiners, & D. Schäffer (Eds.), *Synthetic worlds: Emerging technologies in education and economics* (Vol. 33, pp. 205–231). Springer Science+Business Media.

Gregory, S., Dalgarno, B., Crisp, G., Reiners, T., Masters, Y., Dreher, H., & Knox, V. (2013). *VirtualPREX: Innovative assessment using a 3D virtual world with pre-service teachers*. Office for Learning and Teaching.

Grossman, P., Compton, C., Igra., Ronfeldt, M., Shanan, E., & Williamson, P. (2009). Teaching practice: A cross professional perspective. *Teachers College Record, 111*(9), 2055–2100. http://www.tcrecord.org.contentID15018

Gulikers, J., Bastiaens, T., & Kirschner, P. (2004). A five-dimensional framework for authentic assessment. *Educational Technology Research and Development, 52*(3), 67–85.

Hartanto, D., Kampmann, I. L., Morina, N., Emmelkamp, P. G. M., Neerincx, M. A., & Brinkman, W.-P. (2014). Controlling social stress in virtual reality environments. *PLoS ONE, 9*(3), e92804. doi:10.1371/journal.pone.0092804

Jacobson, J., Renard, M., Lugrin, J.-L., & Cavazza, M. (2005). The CaveUT system: Immersive entertainment based on a game engine. *ACM International Conference Proceeding Series, 265*, 184–187. doi:10.1145/1178477.1178503

Jarmon, L., Traphagan, T., Mayrath, M., & Trivedi, A. (2009). Virtual world teaching, experiential learning, and assessment: An interdisciplinary communication course in Second Life. *Computers & Education*. doi:10.1016/j.compedu.2009.01.010

Khaira, H. G., & Yambo, D. (2005, June). *The practicality of authentic assessment*. Paper presented at The First International Conference on Enhancing Teaching and Learning through Assessment.

Kognito Interactive. (2012). *At-risk for high school educators*. http://www.kognito.com/products/highschool/research/

Kramarski, B., Mevarech, Z. R., & Arami, M. (2002). The effects of metacognitive instruction solving mathematical authentic tasks. *Educational Studies in Mathematics, 49*(2), 225e250.

Lombardi, M. M. (2007). Authentic learning for the 21st century: An overview. In D. G. Oblinger (Ed.), *Educause learning initiative: Advancing learning through IT innovation* (pp. 1–12). Educause Learning.

Ledger, S., Ersozlu, Z., & Fischetti, J. (2019). Preservice teachers' confidence and preferred teaching strategies using TeachLivE™ virtual learning environment: A two-step cluster analysis. *Eurasia Journal of Mathematics, Science and Technology Education, 15*(3), 1–17. doi:10.29333/ejmste/102621

Ledger, S., & Fischetti, J. (2020). Micro-teaching 2.0: Technology as the classroom. *Australasian Journal of Educational Technology, 36*(1), 37–54. https://doi.org/10.14742/ajet.4561

Liu, D., Bhagat, K. K., Gao, Y., Change, T.-W. & Huang, R. (2017). The potentials and trends of virtual realisty in education. In D. Liu, C. Dede, R. Huang, & J. Richards (Eds.), *Virtual augmented, and mixed realities in education* (pp. 105–132). Springer.

Meyer, C. A. (1992). What's the difference between authentic and performance assessment? *Educational Leadership, 49*, 39–40.

Mueller, J. (2006). *Authentic assessment toolbox*. Retrieved January 15, 2021, from http://jonathan.mueller.faculty.noctrl.edu/toolbox/whatisit.htm#looklike

Neely, P., & Tucker, J. (2012). Using business simulations as authentic assessment tools. *American Journal of Business Education (AJBE), 5*. 449. doi:10.19030/ajbe.v5i4.7122

Newmann, F. (1997). Authentic assessment in social studies. In G. Phye (Ed.), *Handbook of classroom assessment* (pp. 359–380). Academic Press.

Pankowski, J., & Walker, J. T. (2016). Using simulation to support novice teachers' classroom management skills: Comparing traditional and alternative certification groups. *JNAAC, 11*(1), 3–20.

Rappa, N. A., Ledger, S., Teo, T., Wong, K. W., Power, B., & Hilliard, B. (2019). The use of eye tracking technology to explore learning and performance within virtual reality and mixed reality settings: A scoping review. *Interactive Learning Environments*. https://doi.org/10.1080/10494820.2019.1702560

Resnick, L. B. (1987). Learning in school and out. *Educational Leadership, 16*(9), 13–20.

Rolheiser, C., & Ross, J. A. (2001). *Student self-evaluation: What research says and what practice shows*. Retrieved March 2, 2021, from http://csimmonds.pbworks.com/w/file/fetch/118283790/Student%20Self%20Evaluation%20What%20Research%20Says%20and%20What%20Practice%20Shows.pdf

Ruben, B. D. (1999). Simulations, games, and experience-based learning: The quest for a new paradigm for teaching and learning. *Simulation & Gaming, 30*(4), 498–505. https://doi.org/10.1177/104687819903000409

Rule, A. C. (2006). The components of authentic learning. *The Journal of Authentic Learning, 3*(1), 1e10.

Schuwirth, L. W. T., & van der Vleuten, C. P. M. (2003). The use of clinical simulations in assessment. *Medical Education, 37*(Suppl. 1), 65–71.

Sherman, W., & Craig, W. (2003). *Understanding virtual reality. Interface, application and design*. Morgan Kaufmann Publishers.

Simiosys. (2014). *Teacher talk game*. http://www.simiosys.com/starclassroom.html

Straub, C., Dieker, L., Hynes, M., & Hughes, C. (2014). *Using virtual rehearsal in TLE TeachLivE™ mixed reality classroom simulator to determine the effects on the performance of mathematics teachers*. 2014 TeachLive National Research Project: Year 1 Findings. University of Central Florida.

Sweller, J. (2004). Instructional design consequences of an analogy between evolution by natural selection and human cognitive architecture. *Instructional Science, 32*(1–2), 9–31.

Teacher Education Ministerial Advisory Group. (2014). *Action now: Classroom ready teachers*. Department of Education. http://www.studentsfirst.gov.au/teacher-education-ministerial-advisory-group

Vos, L. (2014). Marketing simulation games: A review of issues in teaching and learning. *The Marketing Review*. doi:10.1362/146934714X13948909473220

Weeks, K. W., Coben, D., O'Neill, D., Jones, A., Weeks, A., Brown, M., & Pontin, D. (2019). Developing and integrating nursing competence through authentic technology-enhanced clinical simulation education: Pedagogies for reconceptualising the theory-practice gap. *Nurse Education in Practice, 37*, 29–38. https://doi.org/10.1016/j.nepr.2019.04.010

Wiggins, G. P. (1993). *Assessing student performance: Exploring the purpose and limits of testing*. Jossey-Bass/Pfeiffer.

Wood, L. C., Teras, H., Reiners, T., & Gregory, S. (2013). The role of gamification and game-based learning in authentic assessment within virtual environments. In S. Frielick et al. (Eds.), *36th HERDSA annual international conference* (pp. 514–523). Higher Education Research and Development Society of Australasia.

Zhao, D., & Ye, Y. (2012). Using virtual environments simulation to improve construction safety: An application of 3D online-game based training. *Lecture Notes in Electrical Engineering, 172*, 269–277. doi:10.1007/978-3-642-31006-5_33

Zimmerman, B. J. (1994). Dimensions of academic self-regulation: A conceptual framework for education. *Self-Regulation of Learning and Performance: Issues and Educational Applications, 1*, 21–33.

CHAPTER 4

Authentic Assessment to Promote Active Online Learning and Critical Reflection

Greg Oates and Paul Denny

Abstract

COVID-19 necessitated an entirely online approach for many higher education institutions and schools. This in turn provided opportunities to rethink classroom pedagogies and re-examine the ways online and blended courses are offered. Student engagement levels have always fluctuated, but fostering active learning has proved more challenging in the online environment.

It is known that assessment can be a significant driver of student learning. Formative Assessment (or 'assessment for learning') can be used to not only inform students about their learning progress, but authentic practices, embedded in their lessons, can signal value to them with respect to the activity. Thus, formative assessment activities that can be used online and facilitate peer-interaction are increasingly valuable.

This chapter examines an assessment approach in the context of a one-semester online course for pre-service mathematics teachers in Years 7–10 of the Australian curriculum, known as ESP125 Mathematics Pedagogical Content Knowledge Years 6–10. The approach uses the free, web-based tool *PeerWise,* which enables students to work with their peers to construct, share, answer, evaluate, and discuss a repository of assessment questions relevant to their course. The value of this approach in promoting critical reflective practice in pre-service teachers is explored. A survey, which was administered to measure students' perceptions, showed students enjoyed the task and found it a valuable learning experience. In addition, student responses to the questions authored by their peers as part of the online task were examined. The analysis identified that students experienced meaningful shifts in their Pedagogical Content Knowledge (PCK) resulting from peer-feedback and facilitated by the online interactions provided by the *PeerWise* platform.

Keywords

online assessment – collaboration – peer interaction – critical reflection – pre-service mathematics teacher education

1   Introduction

Online learning in a formal sense has been increasing in importance for many years in higher education courses (Harding et al., 2005; Pizzi, 2014). Engelbrecht, Llinares, and Borba (2020) suggest that the internet is transforming the mathematics classroom in both a formal and informal sense at all levels, with the burgeoning range of tools, platforms, and social media sites available to students and teachers alike (Borba et al., 2016). COVID-19 has further necessitated a rapid shift to an entirely online approach for many universities and schools worldwide, and this in turn has provided opportunities to rethink our classroom pedagogies and re-examine the ways we offer our online units (Engelbrecht, Borba et al., 2020; Hardman, 2020). While much of the discussion in this chapter will have applications across all levels of schooling, the principle focus here will be on fostering active learning and collaborative forms of assessment in undergraduate mathematics education, specifically for pre-service teachers.

There have long been questions of how to encourage student engagement and peer interaction in their learning (Bonwell, 1997; Topping, 2007). Student engagement levels have always fluctuated, but fostering active learning has proven more challenging in the online environment (Resta & Laferrière, 2007; Vlachopoulos et al., 2020). Over many years, teaching in many disciplines in higher education has remained largely traditional, with for example, face-to-face lectures still a standard component of most university mathematics courses in many countries (e.g., in Australia and South Africa, Wood & Harding, 2007; in Croatia, Pale, 2013; in New Zealand, Yoon et al., 2014; and the USA, Garrett et al., 2019). This is despite the increasing use of online and blended modes of delivery, other examples of innovative practices, and research suggesting the value of alternative approaches for student learning (Pritchard, 2010; Hardman, 2020).

Assessment in tertiary education has also focused predominantly on conventional summative assessment practices used to measure students' achievement (often referred to as *Assessment of Learning*, e.g., Dixson & Worrel, 2016), such as moderated, closed book tests and examinations, often without the use of technology (Iannone & Simpson, 2011; Oates, 2010). And while technological advances have facilitated better online and remote delivery of courses, and more recently a growth in blended learning and the use of approaches such as flipped classrooms (e.g., Pizzi, 2014; Voigt et al., 2020), online use has remained predominantly traditional (Garrett et al., 2019; Hardman, 2020). For example, many online courses offer pre-recorded traditional-style lectures as a substitute for face-to-face classes, and similarly, while many institutions have continued with live lectures, they have invested in recording these for students unable to attend or studying remotely (Attard et al., 2020; Picardo et al., 2021;

Yoon et al., 2014). Adoption of blended or hybrid learning approaches has been slower than might have been anticipated, despite the sudden change to fully online courses forced on many institutions by the COVID-19 pandemic (Hardman, 2020). The third CHLOE report (Changing Landscape of Online Education, Garrett et al., 2019) found that relatively few institutions in the USA were investing substantially in blended learning, as opposed to more traditional online delivery approaches.

Traditional face-to-face approaches may still have value however, especially when combined with online learning in a hybrid approach. By practicing blended learning, the conveniences of online courses are gained without the loss of face-to-face contact (Harding et al., 2005). Charlton (2006) claims lectures still have value for students in many circumstances; especially for communicating conceptual knowledge, and where there is a significant knowledge gap between lecturer and audience. Prichard (2010) shares this view, observing:

> There is evidence that lectures can be effective in communicating information, modelling reasoning and motivating students. Therefore, when supported appropriately by other activities, lectures provide an effective component of a mathematical education. (p. 609)

With respect to assessment, some formative assessment measures such as quizzes are simple to enact and are common as a means of monitoring progress online. However, there are fewer examples of online assessment used as a means of monitoring and reporting summative achievement, often due to concerns about the robustness and integrity of online tests and take-home exams (Fluck, 2019; Sangwin, 2012). Further to this, other common forms of formative classroom practices (for example questioning, discussion and peer assessment), especially those which involve collaboration between students, have presented challenges in translating to large lecture rooms and the online environment (Engelbrecht & Harding, 2004; Oates, 2016; Oates et al., 2016). Trenholm et al. (2015) conclude that online assessment and the provision of feedback practices are varied and complex:

> ... we found there was not a simple emphasis on summative assessment instruments, nor a concomitant expectation these would always be invigilated. Though richer assessment feedback appears to be emphasized, evidence suggests this feedback may not be primarily directed at advancing student learning. Moreover, we found evidence of a reliance on computer–human interactions (e.g., via computer-assisted assessment systems) and further evidence of a decline in human interactions. (p. 1197)

A common criticism of many of the traditional modes of learning (including assessment) described above is that they are not seen as providing authentic learning experiences for students in the modern context (Hardman, 2020). These traditional modes of learning do not encourage active student learning (Bonwell, 1997), or foster engagement and support collaborative interaction between peers (Engelbrecht & Harding, 2004; 2005; Oates et al., 2016), seen as essential for effective learning in mathematics (Rivers et al., 2017). While Schuetz (2014) notes that the combination of a human teacher with online resources in a blended learning environment can potentially provide an effective way for students to construct learning socially, the asynchronous nature of much online learning presents challenges for facilitating peer interaction, especially with respect to online collaboration and assessment (e.g., Vlachopoulous et al., 2020).

In this chapter, we will initially consider some of the opportunities identified in the literature that currently exist for collaborative assessment online. We will then highlight two such initiatives that have been trialled in pre-service teacher mathematics education courses in the School of Education at the University of Tasmania (UTAS), namely Team-Based Learning (TBL, e.g., Michaelsen et al., 2004; Vlachopoulos et al., 2020); and the online peer-learning tool *PeerWise*[1] developed and supported by the University of Auckland (Denny et al., 2008a). While the effectiveness of *PeerWise* has been extensively studied and documented (e.g., Bottomley & Denny, 2011; Hancock et al., 2018; Hardy et al., 2014; Huang et al., 2021; Singh, 2015; Walsh et al., 2018), there are limited studies which examine the use of *PeerWise* for summative assessment, or for use in teacher professional development. This is especially so at the tertiary level, where no prior work exists involving mathematics education classes. At the secondary level, *PeerWise* has been used to support the development of STEM-teachers (Milner-Bolotin, 2018), while a recent study has examined the use of *PeerWise* for formative and summative assessment purposes in first-year chemistry classes in the UK (Fergus et al., 2021).

We finish by presenting some data and findings to support the effectiveness of *PeerWise* for use in summative assessment, and in promoting critical, reflective practice in pre-service mathematics teachers.

2   Assessment, Technology and Collaboration in Undergraduate Mathematics

Assessment is widely accepted as a key driver in mathematics education and student engagement (Jürges et al., 2012; Sangwin, 2012), and as such is a critical consideration in the design of any online learning program (Engelbrecht

& Harding, 2005; Yerushalmy & Olsher, 2020). Assessment, and in particular the importance of feedback to students, were also noted as a significant theme in studies in tertiary mathematics education reviewed by Coupland et al. (2016). Authentic assessment practices, embedded in their learning, not only inform students about their learning progress, but also signal value to them with respect to the learning activity (Bonwell, 1997; Sangwin, 2012; Sumantri & Satriani, 2016). Further, it has long been understood that collaboration and peer-interaction are significant contributors to effective student learning (Johnson & Johnson, 1996; Rattanatumma & Puncreobutr, 2016). Bonwell (1997), for example, concluded that the case for using active learning in college and university classrooms is both research-based and persuasive. He cites one study which found that:

> ... if a sixty-minute lecture were stopped three times every thirteen to twenty-eight minutes to allow students to compare notes for two minutes, not only was student learning increased in a statistically significant way, but the increase could amount to a differential of two grades depending on the cut-off points. (Ruhl et al., 1987, cited in Bonwell, 1997, p. 73)

Combining assessment with well-designed peer-learning activities can promote active learning, by promoting dialogue, agency and trust (Rivers et al., 2017). Thus, while assessment activities that can be used online to facilitate peer collaboration have become increasingly valuable, the increasing reliance on online environments for delivering assessment tasks presents challenges with respect to student collaboration (Oates, 2016; Resta & Laferrière, 2007). The increasing move to online delivery, and the limited opportunities for effective online assessment, may be one of the reasons assessment featured less predominantly in the latest four-year review of tertiary mathematics education in Australasia (Galligan et al., 2020). This led the authors to conclude that "this is an area where future research efforts could be focused" (Galligan et al., 2020, p. 272). A consistent theme in many studies over the years is the limited opportunities for authentic online assessment, and the need for greater collaboration and interaction in online learning (Borba et al., 2016; Engelbrecht & Harding, 2005). Trenholm et al. (2012) conclude that problems of lecturing in the digital age are clearly complex and further, that online learning may encourage and enable a form of learning that is in conflict with the disciplinary nature of mathematics itself (i.e., encourage rote learning versus conceptual understanding):

> While technology may drive, and be driven by, mathematics pedagogy to the benefit of student learning, we would argue that the nature of

> mathematical thinking needs to drive the adoption and use of technology, and not the reverse. (p. 713)

The largely asynchronous nature of much online learning is generally regarded as one of its key advantages, in that it affords students some autonomy over their learning, such as the flexibility to study at times which are convenient (Borba et al., 2016; Engelbrecht, Llinares, & Borba, 2020). However, this can pose problems for collaboration and assessment, and the quality and mathematical integrity of their learning experiences. For example, there are questions about the levels of engagement and quality of peer-to-peer dialogue in online discussion forums (Parks-Stamm et al., 2017; Staines & Lauchs, 2013), while facilitating and assessing group-work asynchronously presents challenges (Vlachopoulous et al., 2020). A key challenge for students studying remotely, in a self-determined fashion, as well as for instructors in the design of such courses, lies in the question of how to evaluate and compare options, and make informed choices about the learning value, quality and mathematical integrity of the myriad available resources (Borba et al., 2016; Oates, 2016).

There are also questions about the nature and purpose of online assessment, and different issues with synchronous versus asynchronous learning for summative and formative assessment (Sandene et al., 2005; Sangwin, 2012). Summative assessment is sometimes regarded as providing less support for student learning, because it emphasises the student's achievement at the end of the program, and is more commonly associated with evidence of standards and as a gatekeeper to progression in the program (Dixson & Worrel, 2016; Kippers et al., 2018). Jürges et al. (2012), for example, found from their examination of 2003 PISA data in Germany, that central exit exams did little to impact on mathematical literacy, and that teachers actively participating in these central exit exams tend to be more performance oriented. However, as described earlier, summative assessment remains a dominant form of assessment in many university mathematics courses, and developing technology has meant it is becoming progressively easier to adapt it to an online environment, albeit mostly simultaneously in a synchronous manner. Remote proctoring and e-exams are seen by many as a means of achieving effective summative assessment online (Fluck, 2019).

By contrast, formative assessment approaches (*assessment for learning*, e.g., Popham, 2009) are commonly seen as providing better support for both students and teachers to improve performance, by providing immediate information about students' learning progress (Hattie & Timperley, 2007; Kippers et al., 2018; Sumantri & Satriani, 2016). Formative assessment enables teachers to elicit information to adjust their teaching, and teachers and students alike to identify gaps in their learning, through timely feedback seen as critical in the learning process (Hattie & Timperley, 2007; Kippers et al., 2018). Kramarski and Dudai (2009), for example, explored two different group-metacognitive support methods in online mathematical inquiry for ninth grade students in Israel. They found that students who worked collaboratively using the group feedback guidance (GFG) approach designed for their study, consistently outperformed other students in the class who did not receive this level of regular feedback.

As described earlier, many formative, collaborative assessment practices were initially developed for use in the classroom or lecture-room setting (e.g., TBL, think-pair-share; audience response systems, see Hodges, 2017), and instructors have had to find ways of adapting these, or developing new mechanisms, for the online environment (Engelbrecht & Harding, 2004; Sangwin, 2012). One example of this is the use of audience-response systems, which have been used effectively in large lectures to poll students' thinking and promote active learning (e.g., Wood & Shirazi, 2020). Similar polling tools exist online in synchronous environments (for example Zoom[2]), but polling tools in asynchronous environments may be less collaborative. Consider for example H5P,[3] described as "a plugin for existing publishing systems that enables the system to create interactive content like Interactive Videos, Presentations, Games, Quizzes and more". The many quiz options that can be inserted into online resources using H5P are well suited for learning platforms designed for students studying individually online, but lack impetus for collaboration.

Despite the challenges of transferring classroom assessment practices online, there has nevertheless been a growing number of developments for both online summative and formative assessment purposes. There has been, for example, an increasing use of computer-aided assessment systems (CAA), which have been developing beyond the more historically common use of multiple-choice questions or similar fixed responses (e.g., True/False, or Sometimes True/Always True/Never True), to allow for richer entry of complete mathematical arguments, expressions and solutions in the form of algebraic expressions and diagrams. Sangwin (2012) has developed STACK, an advanced CAA system that can randomly generate problems in a structured mathematical way, and analyse the mathematical properties of expressions and arguments entered by the student. It thus has both formative and summative capabilities. For students, it can generate immediate formative feedback, as necessary, which may include mathematical computations of the student's answer. For teachers, it can help the teacher analyse the classes' attempts at one question, or just one student's attempt. Such capabilities lead Sangwin to conclude that "the uptake of CAA will increase, in both informal and self-directed situations and in formative settings. It is highly likely that CAA will become [more widely] used in high-stakes examinations" (Sangwin, 2012, p. 14).

Other studies have also examined CAA use. Yerushalmy and Olsher (2020) developed an automated scoring environment that assessed students' geometric reasoning by creating examples to verify or dispute geometric claims. They found their approach enabled them to "assess students' exploration of the logic of universal [geometric] claims, characterise successful and partial answers, and differentiate between students according to their work" (p. 1033). Herbert et al. (2019) also describe the development of a new formative CAA assessment approach that generates automatically marked mathematics assessments using LaTeX and PDF forms in conjunction with a computer algebra system (e.g., Maple), independent of a Learning Management System (LMS). Their method was implemented in undergraduate mathematics subjects servicing non-mathematics–focused higher education courses. They found that "the method provided the teaching academic with a more efficient way of designing formative mathematics assessments without compromising the effectiveness of the assessment task" (Herbert et al., 2019, p. 153).

Team-Based Learning (TBL) is one example of how a traditionally classroom based synchronous assessment may be successfully adapted to the online environment, in both synchronous and asynchronous formats. TBL is a structured form of small-group learning, which traditionally requires synchronous classroom interaction, at least for the team-based readiness assurance test (TRAT) and task components (Michaelsen et al., 2004). Key features of TBL are that students are accountable for their learning, both individually, and to other members of the group, as well as providing learners with frequent and immediate feedback. A blended TBL model (combining synchronous and asynchronous elements) is reasonably easy to achieve, as demonstrated in the study by Gomez et al. (2010), who placed the pre-readings online, and delivered the individual readiness test (iRAT) asynchronously via an online quiz (a simple and common approach). Students then attended class to complete the TRAT, and begin the task, with some ongoing discussions conducted asynchronously through online forums.

To achieve the peer-interaction and collaboration required by the TRAT and task asynchronously online is more challenging, especially in mathematics where online tools do not always allow for the easy use of syntax or graph sketching. Palsolé and Awalt (2008) described how they achieved this through discussion boards and wikis for the group interactions, in a fully online course, but they do note it takes a lot of work to establish. At UTAS, we have followed a similar approach, but our experience found that an asynchronous approach using discussion boards was less effective and not favoured by the students. Instead, we have found that synchronous, online meetings using web-conferencing and/or social media platforms has been more useful for the TRAT and task. The teams can choose their own time to meet up, and preferred platform (for example *Zoom, FaceTime, WhatsApp*, or the *Collaborate*[4] facility provided by the university through our LMS. Intedashboard[5] is an online platform purposely designed to facilitate both synchronous and asynchronous online TBL. It has been developed by the Duke-NUS Medical School, a collaboration between Duke University (North Carolina, USA), and the National University of Singapore (NUS). The platform was used in an undergraduate course in the Faculty of Medicine and Health Sciences at a large metropolitan university in Australia (Vlachopoulos et al., 2020). While they note that this is a commercial site, and further, that they did not use the asynchronous components in their study, they nevertheless conclude that "their findings present valuable practical implications for academics looking to implement carefully structured collaborative learning methodologies that effectively enhance student engagement, experience and learning along with fostering teamwork and communication skills" (Vlachopoulos et al., 2020, p. 1).

In an alternative approach, Galligan and Hobohm (2013) investigated the use of *screencasts* as an assessment tool for a blended course in undergraduate mathematics education. Their aim was to foster metacognitive and cognitive processes, by encouraging students to reflect on mathematical concepts and how they might teach them (at a year 4 to 9 level). Participants were first asked to create a screencast to explain the concept, and how they might teach it to students to improve understanding, with reference to the Australian Mathematics Curriculum proficiencies.[6] They were then asked to peer-critique other students' screencasts, in tutorials for on-campus students, and using a discussion forum for off-campus students. While the authors suggest scope for refining their approach, they conclude that "students, prompted by assignment marks, were willing to create and evaluate their own, and others' screencasts" (Galligan & Hobohm, 2013, p. 328).

Finally, in this discussion of online assessment developments, we consider *PeerWise* (Denny et al., 2008a), an innovative, purpose built online tool designed to encourage students to interact with their peers, develop their higher order cognitive skills and engage in critical reflection, through the construction and evaluation of multiple-choice questions (MCQs). *PeerWise* enables students to generate their own questions, provide and improve their explanations, and test their understanding by attempting and commenting on others' questions. We will expand on the design and history of *PeerWise* and its use at UTAS next.

3 *PeerWise* Design and History

PeerWise is a free, web-based tool that enables students to work with their peers to construct, share, answer, evaluate, and discuss a repository of assessment questions relevant to their course. The basis of the approach is that students author their own multiple-choice assessment questions which are then made available for their peers to answer for practice. Combining question-generation with self-testing in this way leverages two well-established learning techniques, the generation effect and the retrieval-practice effect (Denny et al., 2017; Kelley et al., 2019). Students are anonymous to one another within the interface of *PeerWise*, a design decision which aims to encourage students to evaluate the quality of content on its merit, rather than through knowing the identity of the author. There is evidence that providing anonymous interfaces in online learning environments can reduce certain kinds of biases when students are rating content and can lead to higher levels of participation overall (Morales-Martinez et al., 2020).

PeerWise was first used in a large (500 students) computer science class at the University of Auckland in 2007 (Denny et al., 2008b). Since that time, *PeerWise* has been used in courses at 2000 universities, schools and technical institutes globally, and hosts more than 5.5 million course-related assessment questions that have been generated by students. In 2018, *PeerWise* won the Gold Award in the "ICT Tools for Teaching and Learning" category as well as the "Overall Award" in the QS Reimagine Education competition (Wharton School of Business, University of Pennsylvania[7]) an international competition attracting nearly 1200 projects from 39 countries.

Denny et al. (2008b) describe several anticipated benefits and theoretical perspectives that informed the development of *PeerWise,* which have been explored and confirmed in multiple studies (see the 111 publications from 2008 to 2021 listed on the *PeerWise* site[8]). Benefits include the creation of a large bank of MCQ's quickly and with little staff effort (students collectively can generate a vastly greater number of questions than is feasible by staff); the explicit focus on learning outcomes and goals brought about by public discussion of the assessment process; the additional understanding needed to choose appropriate distractors and write effective explanations; and the higher-order cognitive skills required to evaluate not only the content of a question, but what makes a particular question more effective than other questions. "The element of peer assessment and provision for feedback moves a student from being merely the recipient of an educational process to being an active partner, creating, assessing and making critical judgements" (Denny et al., 2008b, p. 69).

Theoretical perspectives include the value of drill and practice for developing skills that students get from answering others' questions, such as

remembering, understanding and applying known procedures to new data, identified at the lower end of Bloom's taxonomy (see Anderson & Bloom, 2001); the value of peer-assessment in helping students become independent learners; and the deeper learning that students gain from fully engaging in the process of constructing, using, and evaluating MCQ test items. Rather than just engaging in a superficial level of answering routine questions, students must bring critical analysis skills to bear, in asking questions such as:
- How effective was this question at evaluating one of the learning outcomes?
- What makes the item a good or bad question?
- Were the distractors effective?
- How could the item be improved?

These kinds of questions engage the student in a deeper and richer learning experience (Denny et al., 2008b, p. 72).

Another important design feature of *PeerWise* lies in the use of 'gamification', or the application of gaming elements and game design techniques in non-game-based systems, as a motivational technique. Modern information and communications technologies have facilitated the development and implementation of gamification, and reinforced its suitability in online learning environments that are easily accessible to learners (Singh, 2015). Within *PeerWise*, students can earn badges (basic, standard and elite) for exhibiting effective learning behaviours, such as the use of spaced repetition where students space their practice over an extended period of time. Students can also gain reputation by making contributions that are perceived as useful by others (reputation score), and can earn points for answering questions accurately (answer score). These badges and scores are displayed on a leader board, enabling students to reflect on their progress relative to other students in the course. Prior research has shown that these virtual rewards are influential at modifying student behaviour within *PeerWise* (Denny, 2013), and that there is evidence in favour of a causal relationship between gamification and learning outcomes, mediated by self-testing behaviour (Denny et al., 2018). Figure 4.1 shows an example of the achievements displayed to a student who had

Highest rating of any of your questions
(rated by at least 5 students)

Total number of answers to all
questions you have contributed

3.6700

47

FIGURE 4.1
Sample *PeerWise*
Statistics from
a 2020 student
(ESP125, UTAS)

contributed two questions in a class of 25 pre-service mathematics education students at UTAS.

From the multiple design influences described, we can observe that a key aspect in the design of *PeerWise* is the value of formative assessment and timely feedback for student learning. There is additional value for instructors in the ease of use in setting it up, the motivation for active learning it generates in students, and the establishment of a wide database of MCQ questions that can be used in later assessments, as supported by the following instructor testimonials on the *PeerWise* website:

> PeerWise represents an effective, easy to use tool that instructors can readily appreciate the educational benefits of using.

> Peerwise has catalysed a surge of engagement around my subject. It has provided an outlet for so many different learning approaches: the creative, the critical, the studious, the explainers and the inquisitive. The best rated questions are generally better than what I would get from my academic colleagues; they are related to the syllabus, tested, refined and, above all, they have explanations.

As a formative learning tool, *PeerWise* provides no in-built mechanisms for summative assessment, and thus, few studies have examined such usage in any extensive manner. Denny et al. (2008a) described how they awarded a nominal 2% mark for participation towards the students' final grade in their course (the students were required to develop at least two questions, and answer and rate at least ten questions in the system). Only recently have studies begun to report on the use of *PeerWise* for more extensive measurement of attainment with contributions towards final course grades (e.g., Fergus et al., 2021). We will discuss the way in which we have approached this in our teaching at UTAS next.

4 *PeerWise* Use at UTAS

The case for collaboration in online assessment has been clearly established in preceding discussions, and was thus the rationale underpinning the decision to use *PeerWise* in the teaching and assessment of a one-semester online mathematics education unit (elsewhere commonly known as a course) ESP125 Mathematics Pedagogical Content Knowledge Years 6–10 at UTAS.

> ... by engaging students in the process of designing and appraising assessment questions, we hope to set up partnerships in ways that support students and value their input. (Healey, Flint, & Harrington, 2014, cited in Rivers et al., 2017, p. 2)

ESP125 covers Pedagogical Content Knowledge (PCK) in mathematics (Ball et al., 2008), for pre-service teachers in Years 7–10 of the Australian curriculum. The unit is taught over a 12-week semester, mostly online, although there are weekly tutorials for locally based students. Two of the learning objectives of the unit are to:
- Exemplify the proficiencies, skills, and content knowledge as described in the Australian Curriculum Mathematics with reference to contemporary teaching practices in middle school and secondary mathematics education.
- Design mathematical teaching experiences which provide formative and summative assessment of student learning.

PeerWise is used in the second assessment task, to scaffold student learning of these objectives, through formative feedback, combined with a summative component of assessment, which contributes 36% to their final grade. Students are asked to author two multiple-choice questions on *PeerWise* that would be useful as formative assessment items for school students in a Year 7–10 class, in a mathematical content area of their choice. They are asked to provide one best-answer and three distractor choices (i.e., a standard 4-option multiple choice question), and ensure that each question targets conceptual understanding, rather than being a pure skills-based question.

Next, the students attempt to answer questions published by their fellow students and comment on three of these attempts, using their understanding of PCK to frame their responses. To this point, the task is consistent with the standard, formative use of *PeerWise*, except that marks are also awarded in the summative assessment rubric for appropriately framed comments. The final, wholly summative requirement, is to critically reflect on their two questions, and refine their explanation of these, using what they have learned from their experiences and their peers' feedback. The overall criteria against which the task is judged are shown in Table 4.1, while examples of the guidelines and marks they receive for selected components from the task rubric are shown in Table 4.2 (authoring questions) and Table 4.3 (feedback and comments). Students receive three marks per question they author for each of the three focus areas in Table 4.2, for a total of 18 marks; a further four marks each for commenting on three of their peers' questions (12 marks in total); and three marks

TABLE 4.1   Criteria for evaluating Assessment Task 2 (ESP125, UTAS)

Criterion	Criterion description
Criterion 1	Aligns questions with appropriate year levels and content descriptors from the Australian Mathematics Curriculum
Criterion 2	Undertakes pedagogical analysis and design of mathematical questions, with a clear focus on mathematics and conceptual development
Criterion 3	Demonstrates correct mathematical understandings
Criterion 4	Critically reflects on your learning and responds to feedback
Criterion 5	Engages effectively with peers

TABLE 4.2   Examples of guidelines and marks for authoring questions in Assessment Task 2 (ESP125, UTAS)

Focus area	Guidelines
Content	Are the topics, level of mathematics, notation, and language appropriate for, and appropriately aligned with the selected/stated Curriculum Level and Content area?
Quality	Is the question mathematically correct, is there clearly one best answer and are the distractors distinct and appropriate? Did you adhere to the brief about conceptual understanding or is the question mostly skill-based?
Originality and explanation	Are the underlining ideas and style of question original? Have you included a clear and consistent explanation justifying your question choice?

for the final reflection on each of their own two questions (6 marks total), adding up to the total of 36% they receive for the task overall.

In many ways, the design of the assessment task in ESP125 mirrors the approach taken by Fergus et al. (2021), in the way marks are awarded for question quality, reflection and constructive feedback. However, in our case, less emphasis is placed on the mathematical correctness of the questions themselves (each question only receives 3 marks for this). As discussed earlier, some studies identify mathematical integrity as a key concern of student's self-directed and peer-supported interactions (Borba et al., 2016; Oates, 2016).

TABLE 4.3 Examples of guidelines and marks for feedback and reflection in Assessment Task 2 (ESP125, UTAS)

Focus	Reflective prompt
Commenting on peers' questions	Is the comment appropriate, well written and insightful? Is it helpful to the question writer? Does your response show what you have learnt from attempting the question (e.g., clarity, difficulties; how useful, helpful effective was their explanation?)
Critical reflection on your own question	– What did you learn from other students' attempts and comments about your questions? – What changes if any might you make to your questions and why? – How 'good' and/or effective do you feel your questions are for students' learning?

However, we were less concerned about the effect of this here, as we believed that any potential errors in mathematical accuracy would be detected by the students themselves in their evaluations, which certainly proved to be the case, as witnessed by the following students' observation in reflecting on their learning:

> I was quite nervous when I did my question, I'm not that confident with maths & I was worried I'd make a mistake or write a really bad question ... but my classmates were really kind when they pointed out my mistake. Now I think I am not so scared about making them .... I learned a lot from this process about how mistakes can actually help us learn, it didn't make me feel too stupid ... I will try and get my students to feel its ok too.

One aspect of the task that has proved continually challenging for the students is in designing sufficiently suitable distractors. What they are guided to do is think of solutions that students may feasibly arrive at, or which might be identified as common misconceptions. However, more commonly, at least one of the distractors would be more of an invented error, for which they then could not identify their reasons for choosing it as an effective distractor. Often the distractors are identified in comments by their peers as "easily eliminated" or "non-plausible". One student, who did design a question with effective distractors (one based on incorrect rounding; one based on incorrect process-dividing instead of multiplying; and one on reading/misinterpretation) observed that "I can now see that creating questions with appropriate distraction options will take much more effort than I would have thought before undertaking this unit". The value of the task, and *PeerWise,* in prompting critical reflection about this aspect, may be gauged by the 41 peer comments for the 50 questions submitted by the 2018 semester class that specifically referenced 'distractors'. For one question, a peer commented in support of what they viewed as effective distractors:

> It is obvious that you have put a lot of thought into the 'distractor answers', as you have shown how a student may reach them during the course of their calculation if they had a misconception.

The distractors in another question (as shown in Figure 4.2) were seen as less effective, attracting the following comment:

> For me, the only issue with your question is that it does not provide any real distractors. If students have even the most basic understanding of how to calculate an average, the likelihood they would have to consider all of your possible answers is quite low. In the future, to build on the fantastic context of your question, perhaps think about rewording your question so that you can create possible answers that could be genuine distractors. For example, incorporate an answer that showed the median, or mode instead?

Another aspect that proved difficult for the students in authoring their questions was the notion of what constitutes a *conceptual* question compared to a *skills-based* question. Frequently, the students interpreted this as meaning a difficult question, and this often resulted in questions that while essentially just requiring a skill or procedure to answer, might be overly convoluted and confusing. A common approach to this was to have double-barrelled, or nested questions within the one MCQ, which meant it was difficult to determine what the question was testing, and what use it might ultimately

Question	Cole Hartman is going to play his final season in the NFL. He wants to finish his career with an average of 45 touchdowns thrown per season. In his first six seasons, he has thrown 47, 43, 50, 33, 45 and 30 touchdowns. How many touchdowns does Cole need to throw in his seventh and final season to finish with an average of 45 touchdowns?
A	20
B	42
C	50
D	67

FIGURE 4.2   Question identified by peer as having ineffective distractors (ESP125, 2018)

be in diagnosing a student's understanding or misconceptions. For example, one question had an effective practical context (pre-COVID at least, as it was embedded in international air travel), and was effectively linked to the curriculum level and appropriate content descriptors with a detailed explanation and clear working for the best answer, and an identification of the distractor choices. However, the question was confused in its conceptual focus, with in fact two separate questions embedded in it; one asking about time, and the other about distance (see Figure 4.3, the *B* indicates the student's identified best response).

Question	Barbara currently lives in Hobart and has has won a trip from Singapore Airlines to spend 3 weeks in London, England. Barbara must catch **3 different flights** to attend this trip. The date of her fight flight is 21/08/16. Her first flight, Hobart – Melbourne leaves at **7:15AM** and lands at **8:30AM**. Barbara's second flight from Melbourne – Singapore leaving at **10:30AM** and arriving at **18:25PM** (AEST). Barbara 's final flight leaves at **22: 25PM** and landing at **12:00PM** (AEST). If **Australia** is **AEST+10** time zone, **Singapore** is **SST+8** time zone and **London** is **GMT+0** time zone. What time in **GMT+0** did Barbara land in London? And, how far did she travel if her first flight travelling at 478.40 KM/HR, her second flight travelling at 762. 62KM/HR and the third flight travelled at 801.25KM/HR. **This may help; distance (d) = hours (h) x speed (s).** **Round to the nearest whole number.**
A	4:00AM; 16 921 kilometres
B	2:00AM; 17 519 kilometres
C	4:00AM; 17 519 kilometres
D	2:00AM; 16 921 kilometres

FIGURE 4.3   Example question showing nested and confused conceptual testing (ESP125, 2018)

Comments from peers identified this confusion, with one student observing:

> Hiya, I like that you decided to tackle an interesting topic (e.g., time zones). It is evident you have put real thought into the development of your question. Moreover, your question specifically aligns with the Australian Curriculum and does an excellent job of testing students understanding of duration and time zones. However, in the future to improve the quality of your question, I would encourage you to write your question more succinctly. The most challenging aspect of your question was not the mathematics required to achieve the desired answer. Instead, for me, the most challenging aspect of your question was unpacking the two questions you asked? I would ask two separate questions, one about time, one about distance?

This example, and the authors' overall effort in their detailed explanation and working out for both the correct answer and all of the distractors they provided for the question in Figure 4.3 support the value of the rubric in achieving the aims of the task. See for example their reflective comments on their learning from this:

> One of the crucial things that I learnt after completing my questions was how important it is to have specific content areas from the Australian Maths Curriculum in mind when developing them ... In future, I would start at the beginning and have a clear focus in mind from the curriculum, that way I would have a goal as to where I really wanted the questions to go.

The student scored highly on all aspects of the task, except for the *Quality* component where they lost marks for the nesting of the double curricula foci, and ended with a HD mark overall (High Distinction).

5   Evidence of Critical Reflection

Fergus et al. (2021) provide a detailed analysis of their use of *PeerWise* to engage students in first-year chemistry courses, which included a classification of the question types using a framework based on Bloom's taxonomy (Anderson & Bloom, 2001). Our study to date has not conducted such an exhaustive analysis of the question quality, but we have found clear evidence in our assignment marking to support effective engagement and critical reflection. Engagement levels have remained high, with all students completing the minimum requirements (two questions and three feedback comments each) in the five courses from 2018 to 2020, and while this may be attributed in part to the high summative component (36%), students have also enjoyed the experience, with many students trying out multiple questions authored by other students, well beyond the task requirements (one student in 2018 attempted all 52 of the questions submitted). They also commented favourably on many aspects of the use of *PeerWise*, for example in the following two responses to the 2019 student survey:

> I found *PeerWise* really easy to use and was a very effective site to utilise. The fact that it is anonymous as well makes for a lot better learning opportunities for everyone. I think *Peerwise* should be used in more units as it is a great and different way for students to learn.

> I enjoyed this task as you not only had to construct the question but also needed to explain the working out and how it is possible to achieve the correct answer which was great for learning.

The feedback provided to other students about their questions was somewhat mixed, for example there were some reasonably ineffective comments such as "this is a good question", with no indication of what was meant by "good". Overall, we have found the level of feedback to be encouraging, with some detailed and effective examples of deep critically reflective and helpful feedback, that reflects the development and scaffolding of the students' PCK:

> This question relates to the Year 10 curriculum and would be a good source for formative assessment. It aligns with the understanding and application of algebraic equations, use of formulas and growth & probability skills to help expand knowledge for the learning of mathematics. As well as assessing fluency in accurately using algebraic expressions while using a range of strategies to solve equations using a calculator.
>
> I would improve this question by being really explicit in what I am asking students to do. Wordy questions can sometime be hard to understand, however really brief questions can come off in the same manner and be hard to interpret.

The self-reflection about their own questions and learning tended to be deeper than their feedback to others, perhaps reflecting their personal connection and depth of understanding of their own work, for example:

> After reflection, I am pleased with the mathematical question I have created. My peers and I agreed that the scenario is a real-world maths problem and this makes the mathematics relevant to the students .... To improve the question I could add further instruction to 'show calculations', as this would provide more feedback as to how the answer was derived. There are multiple ways to arrive at a correct solution and the strategy being used could then be identified and alternate methods could be taught.

One aspect, which generated several feedback comments, related to the uneven spread of feedback. We tried directing students to spread their feedback fairly across their peers' questions, but with mixed success:

> I did get some feedback but not as much as I hoped for. The most constructive feedback I received wasn't posted until after Part 2 was due so I couldn't respond to it in time. However, answering and giving feedback on other students' questions was very helpful, and I found I could use this in my own reflections ....

I feel as though I provided in depth responses to others, and they only gave a few sentences to me. I know a guide was provided for feedback, but perhaps make it more strict on the sort of responses they need to provide.

6 Implications and Concluding Thoughts

This chapter has considered the role of assessment in promoting engagement and peer interaction in online learning. We have highlighted key theoretical and practical issues that can influence the success of any assessment activity, especially in differentiating between synchronous and asynchronous access. Further, we have identified several opportunities currently used in online collaborative assessment, most especially TBL and *PeerWise* which are being used in a pre-service mathematics teacher education unit at the University of Tasmania, Australia. Our experiences and findings from the use of *PeerWise* have supported the value of an effective combination of formative and summative peer-assessment in driving student engagement, and the affordances of *PeerWise* in prompting critical reflection and learning.

We found clear evidence of students developing their thinking about PCK, and metacognition, in their online reflections and feedback to others' questions. In addition, students clearly enjoyed their participation in the task, and perceived value in *PeerWise* as an effective tool for their own learning. Comments and feedback from students suggested that key affordances in this respect included the asynchronous assessment, the gamification, and the sense of 'safety' provided by the anonymity of *PeerWise*.

Further work will seek to improve the fair spread of feedback across student questions, and better scaffold them in identifying and constructing effective distractors. We will also look to conduct more in-depth analysis of the question quality, building on the work by Fergus et al. (2021). This should be useful, both in helping to inform and develop our assessment instrument, and as robust evidence for the value of *PeerWise*. Nevertheless, we have collected and presented compelling evidence for the value of intelligently-designed online assessment approaches that facilitate online peer-interaction. This is especially true for asynchronous settings, which are increasingly favoured by online learners. We will continue to develop our use of *PeerWise* and TBL in our pre-service mathematics teacher education units, and explore ways in which other classroom-based collaborative, formative assessment activities may be adapted for online use.

Notes

1. *PeerWise*: https://peerwise.cs.auckland.ac.nz/
2. https://support.zoom.us/hc/en-us/articles/213756303-Polling-for-meetings
3. https://h5p.org/
4. https://www.blackboard.com/teaching-learning/collaboration-web-conferencing/blackboard-collaborate
5. https://www.intedashboard.com/
6. https://www.australiancurriculum.edu.au/resources/mathematics-proficiencies/
7. https://www.reimagine-education.com/winners-2019-2018/
8. https://peerwise.cs.auckland.ac.nz/docs/publications/

References

Anderson, L. W., & Bloom, B. S. (2001). *A taxonomy for learning, teaching, and assessing: A revision of Bloom's taxonomy of educational objectives*. Longman.

Attard, C., Calder, N., Holmes, K., Larkin, K., & Trenholm, S. (2020). Teaching and learning mathematics with digital technologies. In J. Way, C. Attard, J. Anderson, J. Bobis, H. McMaster, & K. Cartwright (Eds.), *Research in mathematics education in Australasia 2016–2019* (pp. 319–347). Springer.

Ball, D. L., Thames, M. H., & Phelps, G. (2008). Content knowledge for teaching: What makes it special? *Journal of Teacher Education, 59*(5), 389–407.

Bonwell, C. C. (1997). Using active learning as assessment in the postsecondary classroom. *The Clearing House, 71*(2), 73–76.

Borba, M. C., Askar, P., Engelbrecht, J., Gadanidis, G., Llinares, S., & Sánchez Aguilar, M. (2016). Blended learning, e-learning and mobile learning in mathematics education. *ZDM Mathematics Education, 48*(5), 589–610.

Bottomley, S., & Denny, P. (2011). A participatory learning approach to biochemistry using student authored and evaluated multiple-choice questions. *Biochemistry and Molecular Biology Education, 39*(5), 352–361. https://doi.org/10.1002/bmb.20526

Charlton, B. G. (2006). Lectures are such an effective teaching method because they exploit evolved human psychology to improve learning. *Medical Hypotheses, 67*(6,) 2006, 1261–1265.

Coupland, M., Dunn, P. K., Galligan, L., Oates, G., & Trenholm, S. (2016). Tertiary mathematics education. In K. Makar, S. Dole, J. Visnovska, M. Goos, A. Bennison, & K. Fry (Eds.), *Research in mathematics education in Australasia 2012–2015*. Springer.

Denny, P. (2013). The effect of virtual achievements on student engagement. In S. Bødker, S. Brewster, P. Baudisch, M. Beaudouin-Lafon, & W. Mackay (Eds.), *Proceedings of the SIGCHI conference on human factors in computing systems* (pp. 763–772). Association for Computing Machinery. https://doi.org/10.1145/2470654.2470763

Denny, P., Hamer, J., Luxton-Reilly, A., & Purchase, H. (2008a). PeerWise: students sharing their multiple choice questions. In R. Lister, M. Caspersen, & M. Clancy (Eds.), *Proceedings of the 4th international workshop on computing education research* (pp. 51–58). ACM. https://doi.org/10.1145/1404520.1404526

Denny, P., Luxton-Reilly, A., & Hamer, J. (2008b). The PeerWise system of student contributed assessment questions. In Simon & M. Hamilton (Eds.), *Proceedings of the 10th conference on Australasian computing education* (Vol. 78, pp. 69–74). Australian Computer Society.

Denny, P., McDonald, F., Empson, R., Kelly, P., & Petersen, A. (2018). Empirical support for a causal relationship between gamification and learning outcomes. In R. Mandryk & M. Hancock (Eds.), *Proceedings of the 2018 CHI conference on human factors in computing systems* (Paper 311, pp. 1–13). Association for Computing Machinery. https://doi.org/10.1145/3173574.3173885

Denny, P., Tempero, E., Garbett, D., & Petersen, A. (2017). Examining a student-generated question activity using random topic assignment. In R. Davoli & M. Goldweber (Eds.), *Proceedings of the 2017 ACM conference on innovation and technology in computer science education* (pp. 146–151). Association for Computing Machinery. https://doi.org/10.1145/3059009.3059033

Dixson, D. D., & Worrell, F. C. (2016). Formative and summative assessment in the classroom. *Theory into Practice, 55*(2), 153–159.

Engelbrecht, J., Borba, M. C., Llinares, S., & Kaiser, G. (2020). Will 2020 be remembered as the year in which education was changed? *ZDM, 52*, 821–824.

Engelbrecht, J., & Harding, A. (2004). Combing online and paper assessment in a web-based course in undergraduate mathematics. *Journal of Computers in Mathematics and Science Teaching, 23*(3), 217–231.

Engelbrecht, J., & Harding, A. (2005). Teaching undergraduate mathematics on the internet. *Educational Studies in Mathematics, 58*(2), 253–276.

Engelbrecht, J., Llinares, S., & Borba, M. C. (2020b). Transformation of the mathematics classroom with the internet. *ZDM, 52*, 825–841.

Fergus, S., Hirani, E., Parkar, N., & Kirton, S. B. (2021). Strategic engagement: Exploring student buy-in across a formative and summative assessment. *AISHE-J: The All Ireland Journal of Teaching & Learning in Higher Education, 13*(1).

Fluck, A. E. (2019). An international review of eExam technologies and impact. *Computers & Education, 132*, 1–15.

Galligan, L., Coupland, M., Dunn, P. K., Martinez, P. H., & Oates, G. (2020). Research into teaching and learning of tertiary mathematics and statistics. In J. Way, C. Attard, J. Anderson, J. Bobis, H. McMaster, & K. Cartwright (Eds.), *Research in mathematics education in Australasia 2016–2019* (pp. 269–292). Springer.

Galligan, L., & Hobohm, C. (2013). Students using digital technologies to produce screencasts that support learning in mathematics. In V. Steinle, L. Ball, & C. Bardini (Eds.), *Mathematics education: Yesterday, today and tomorrow. Proceedings of the*

36th annual conference of the Mathematics Education Research Group of Australasia (pp. 322–329). MERGA.

Garrett, R., Legon, R., & Fredericksen, E. E. (2019). *CHLOE 3 behind the numbers: The changing landscape of online education 2019.* https://www.qualitymatters.org/qa-resources/resource-center/articles-resources/CHLOE-3-report-2019

Gomez, E. A., Dezhi Wu, D., & Passerini, K. (2010). Computer-supported team-based learning: The impact of motivation, enjoyment and team contributions on learning outcomes. *Computers & Education, 55*(1), 378–390.

Hancock, D., Hare, N., Denny, P., & Denyer, G. (2018). Improving large class performance and engagement through student-generated question banks. *Biochemistry and Molecular Biology Education, 46*(4), 306–317. https://doi.org/10.1002/bmb.21119

Harding, A., Kaczynski, D., & Wood, L. (2005). Evaluation of blended learning: analysis of qualitative data. In *Proceedings of the Australian conference on science and mathematics education* (formerly UniServe Science Conference) (Vol. 11, pp. 56–62). https://openjournals.library.sydney.edu.au/index.php/IISME/article/view/6436/7085

Hardman, P. (2020). Universities need strategic investment in learning design. *University World News.* https://www.universityworldnews.com/post.php?story=20200928134607579

Hardy, J., Bates, S., Casey, M., Galloway, K., Galloway, R., Kay, A., Kirsop, P., & McQueen, H. (2014). Student-generated content: Enhancing learning through sharing multiple-choice questions. *International Journal of Science Education, 36*(13), 2180–2194. https://doi.org/10.1080/09500693.2014.916831

Hattie, J., & Timperley, H. (2007). The power of feedback. *Review of Educational Research, 77*(1), 81–112.

Herbert, K., Demskoi, D., & Cullis, K. (2019). Creating mathematics formative assessments using LaTeX, PDF forms and computer algebra. *Australasian Journal of Educational Technology, 35*(5), 153–167.

Hodges, L. C. (2017). Ten research-based steps for effective group work. *IDEA Papers, 65.* https://mdsoar.org/bitstream/handle/11603/17461/PaperIDEA_65.pdf?sequence=1

Huang, A., Hancock, D., Clemson, M., Yeo, G., Harney, D., Denny, P., & Denyer, G. (2021). Selecting student-authored questions for summative assessments. *Research in Learning Technology, 29.* https://doi.org/10.25304/rlt.v29.2517

Iannone, P., & Simpson, A. (2011). The summative assessment diet: How we assess in mathematics degrees. *Teaching Mathematics and its Applications: An International Journal of the IMA, 30*(4), 186–196.

Johnson, D. W., & Johnson, R. T. (1996). Cooperation and the use of technology. In D. Jonassen (Ed.), *Handbook of research for educational communications and technology* (pp. 785–812). MacMillan.

Jürges, H., Schneider, K., Senkbeil, M., & Carstensen, C. H. (2012). Assessment drives learning: The effect of central exit exams on curricular knowledge and mathematical literacy. *Economics of Education Review, 31*(1), 56–65.

Kelley, M., Chapman-Orr, E., Calkins, S., & Lemke, R. (2019). Generation and retrieval practice effects in the classroom using PeerWise. *Teaching of Psychology, 46*(2), 121–126.

Kippers, W. B., Wolterinck, C. H. D., Schildkamp, K., Poortman, C. L., & Visscher, A. J. (2018). Teachers' views on the use of assessment for learning and data-based decision making in classroom practice. *Teaching and Teacher Education, 75*, 199–213.

Kramarski, B., & Dudai, V. (2009). Group-metacognitive support for online inquiry in mathematics with differential self-questioning. *Journal of Educational Computing Research, 40*(4), 377–404.

Michaelsen, L., Knight, A., & Fink, D. (2004). *Team-based learning: A transformative use of small groups in college teaching.* Stylus Publishing.

Milner-Bolotin, M. (2018). Evidence-based research in STEM teacher education: From theory to practice. *Frontiers in Education, 3*(92). https://doi.org/10.3389/feduc.2018.00092

Morales-Martinez, G., Latreille, P., & Denny, P. (2020). Nationality and gender biases in multicultural online learning environments: The effects of anonymity. In R. Bernhaupt & F. Mueller (Eds.), *Proceedings of the 2020 CHI conference on human factors in computing systems* (pp. 1–14). Association for Computing Machinery. https://doi.org/10.1145/3313831.3376283

Oates, G. (2010). Integrated technology in undergraduate mathematics: Issues of assessment. *Electronic Journal of Mathematics and Technology, 4*(2), 162–174.

Oates, G. (2016). Technology in mathematics education: A stocktake & crystal-ball gazing. In W.-C. Yang, D. B. Meade, & K. Khairee (Eds.), *Proceedings of the 21st Asian technology conference in mathematics* (pp. 103–119). Mathematics & Technology, LLC. http://mathandtech.org/

Oates, G., Paterson, P., Reilly, I., & Woods, G. (2016). Seeing things from others' points of view: Collaboration in undergraduate mathematics. *PRIMUS, 26*(3), 206–228.

Pale, P. (2013). Intrinsic deficiencies of lectures as a teaching method. *Collegium Aantropologicum, 37*(2), 551–559.

Palsolé, S., & Awalt, C. (2008). Team-based learning in asynchronous online settings. *New Directions for Teaching and Learning, 116*, 87–95.

Parks-Stamm, E. J., Zafonte, M., & Palenque, S. M. (2017). The effects of instructor participation and class size on student participation in an online class discussion forum. *British Journal of Educational Technology, 48*(6), 1250–1259.

Picardo, V., Denny, P., & Luxton-Reilly, A. (2021). Lecture recordings, viewing habits, and performance in an introductory programming course. In C. Szabo & J. Sheard (Eds.), *Proceedings of the Australasian computing education conference* (pp. 73–79). ACM. https://doi.org/10.1145/3441636.3442307

Pizzi, M. A. (2014). Blended learning pedagogy: The time is now! *Occupational Therapy in Health Care, 28*(3), 333–338.

Popham, W. J. (2009). Assessment literacy for teachers: Faddish or fundamental? *Theory into Practice, 48*(1), 4–11.

Pritchard, D. (2010). Where learning starts? A framework for thinking about lectures in university mathematics. *International Journal of Mathematical Education in Science and Technology, 41*(5), 609–623.

Rattanatumma, T., & Puncreobutr, V. (2016). Assessing the effectiveness of STAD model and problem based learning in mathematics learning achievement and problem solving ability. *Journal of Education and Practice, 7*(12), 194–199.

Resta, P., & Laferrière, T. (2007). Technology in support of collaborative learning. *Educational Psychology Reviews, 19*, 65–83.

Rivers, J., Smith, A. B., Higgins, D., Mills, R., Maier, A. G., & Howitt, S. M. (2017). Asking and answering questions: Partners, peer learning, and participation. *International Journal for Students as Partners, 1*(1), 1–10.

Sandene, B., Horkay, N., Bennett, R. E., Allen, N., Braswell, J., Kaplan, B., & Oranje, A. (2005). *Online assessment in mathematics and writing: Reports from the NAEP technology-based assessment project, research and development series.* NCES 2005–457. National Center for Education Statistics.

Sangwin, C. (2012). Computer aided assessment of mathematics using STACK. In S. J. Cho (Ed.), *Selected regular lectures from the 12th international congress on mathematical education* (pp. 695–713). Springer.

Schuetz, R. (2014). *Self-directed vs. self-determined learning: What's the difference?* https://www.rtschuetz.net/2014/12/self-directed-vs-self-determined.html

Singh, L. (2015). Peerwise: Flexible learning and the contributing student pedagogy. *Journal of Innovation in Psychology, Education and Didactics, 19*(1), 67–90.

Staines, Z., & Lauchs, M. (2013). Students' engagement with Facebook in a university undergraduate policing unit. *Australasian Journal of Educational Technology, 29*(6), 792–805.

Sumantri, M. S., & Satriani, R. (2016). The effect of formative testing and self-directed learning on mathematics learning outcomes. *International Electronic Journal of Elementary Education, 8*(3), 507–524.

Topping, K. J. (2007). Trends in peer learning. *Educational Psychology, 25*(6), 631–645.

Trenholm, S., Alcock, L., & Robinson, C. L. (2012). Mathematics lecturing in the digital age. *International Journal of Mathematical Education in Science and Technology, 43*(6), 703–716.

Trenholm, S., Alcock, L., & Robinson, C. L. (2015). An investigation of assessment and feedback practices in fully asynchronous online undergraduate mathematics courses. *International Journal of Mathematical Education in Science and Technology, 46*(8), 1197–1221.

Vlachopoulos, P., Jan, S. K., & Buckton, R. (2020). A case for team-based learning as an effective collaborative learning methodology in higher education. *College Teaching*. doi:10.1080/87567555.2020.1816889

Voigt, M., Fredriksen, H., & Rasmussen, C. (2020). Leveraging the design heuristics of realistic mathematics education and culturally responsive pedagogy to create a richer flipped classroom calculus curriculum. *ZDM Mathematics Education, 52*, 1051–1062.

Walsh, J., Harris, B., Denny, P., & Smith, P. (2018). Formative student-authored question bank: Perceptions, question quality and association with summative performance. *Postgraduate Medical Journal, 94*(1108), 97–103. https://doi.org/10.1136/postgradmedj-2017-135018

Wood, L. N., & Harding, A. (2007). Can you show you are a good lecturer? *International Journal of Mathematical Education in Science and Technology, 38*(7), 939–947.

Wood, R., & Shirazi, S. (2020). A systematic review of audience response systems for teaching and learning in higher education: The student experience. *Computers & Education*, 103896.

Yerushalmy, M., & Olsher, S. (2020). Online assessment of students' reasoning when solving example-eliciting tasks: Using conjunction and disjunction to increase the power of examples. *ZDM, 52*, 1033–1049.

Yoon, C., Oates, G., & Sneddon, J. (2014). Undergraduate mathematics students' reasons for attending live lectures when recordings are available. *International Journal of Mathematical Education in Science and Technology, 45*(2), 227–240.

CHAPTER 5

A Holistic Review of Authentic Assessment in Mathematics Education

Qiaoping Zhang, Xiaolei Zhang and Jiabo Liu

Abstract

Since the 1990s, when authentic assessment first originated, a key aim has been to overcome the challenges caused by traditional standardised tests. Authentic assessment focuses upon students' real-life performances and promoting their learning. Teachers, however, have been facing considerable challenges when implementing and integrating authentic assessments in classroom teaching and daily evaluations. This study provides an extensive review of the nature of authentic assessment in mathematics education. It discusses its integration into mathematics teaching and learning, and the current context of development in mathematics education. Using relevant keywords such as "authentic assessment" and "authentic task" in a search on the EBSCO host Library, we identified and analysed approximately 70 articles from 1988 to 2020 relating to mathematics education. The findings revealed that, firstly, authentic assessment tools, including cases, portfolios, exhibitions of performance, and problem-based inquiries, facilitate teachers to improve students' learning. Secondly, the complexity of test items in some authentic assessment tasks (such as in PISA) is usually lower than the real-life tasks due to the limitations of time and the contents of assessment questions. Thirdly, three approaches for STEM education, the silo approach, the embedded approach, and the integrated approach, emphasise active learning which echoes the principles of authenticity assessment. Besides, in the e-learning environment, mathematics teachers need to re-design teaching tasks and set some examples for authentic context. The review concludes with a discussion about the role of authentic assessment in promoting students' mathematical competencies, as a basis for further research.

Keywords

authentic assessment – mathematics education – mathematics learning

1 Introduction

In the last century, informed by a traditional cognitive approach, standardised tests were used widely to measure students' mastery of subskills. These tests were designed to address the differences in evaluation results caused by teachers' subjectivity (Hart, 1994). However, the results of these standardised tests did not necessarily reflect students' learning and understanding of the content (Darling-Hammond et al., 1995); there was evidence that they only provided general evaluative information about learning performance (Wilson, 1973). Furthermore, this form of assessment gives limited information about students' learning processes, especially when diagnostic information is not available to instructors (Allsopp et al., 2008). In some cases, students also experience test anxiety when taking high-stakes standardised tests (Althauser & Harter, 2016). Given that the test results might be inaccurate or biased, some alternatives were developed to address these problems, such as performance assessment, outcome-based assessment, and authentic assessment (Hart, 1994).

Authentic assessment is related closely to authentic activities which involve the situated nature of cognition. From the perspective of situated cognition (Anderson, Reder, & Simon, 1996), Brown and colleagues (1989) defined authentic activities as the "ordinary practices of a culture" (p. 34) that are similar to what actual practitioners do. They foster the kinds of problem-solving thinking skills that are important in out-of-school settings. Consequently, the way a person learns a particular set of knowledge and skills, and the situation of learning become fundamental parts of the whole learning process. From the early 1990s, researchers began to emphasise the effect of the learning situation in evaluation. For example, in order to enhance primary school students' mathematical sense-making and computational fluency, Fuson (2004) pointed out that the real-life situations, problem-solving, and calculations need to be integrated into the assessment constantly.

In contrast to the standardised assessment, some teachers found that students responded naturally to authentic assessment because they were not aware that they were taking a 'test'. And students often feel that the authentic 'tests' are easier than the standardised tests (Gao & Grisham-Brown, 2011) because the latter usually have time constraints, and the questions in standardised tests are well-designed. Also, educators realise the importance of letting students transfer the knowledge or skills from previous learning experiences to new contexts in order to resolve meaningful tasks (Bottge, 2001). In at least one study, teachers indicated a willingness to utilise authentic assessment in practical teaching (Gao & Grisham-Brown, 2011) and to use the assessment results to improve students' skills connected to real-life and classroom contexts.

Additionally, Onwuegbuzie (2000) noted that authentic assessment must contain knowledge application in the real-life environment. In this regard, however, it is challenging for instructors to look for authentic and meaningful activities.

There are two aspects relating to the quality of authentic assessment. The authentic context is an imperative factor in designing these forms of activities or tasks. However, this type of assessment cannot necessarily improve students' motivation since authenticity is sometimes not apparent to the learners, which means the task designer has to foresee how students will identify the authenticity of the context and the question, and whether they are capable of understanding these (Vos, 2018). This is an important consideration, because test users' understanding and attitudes towards authentic assessment directly affect the accuracy of their assessment results (Frey et al., 2012).

Another point to note, as explained by Wiggins (1990), is that the validity and reliability of authentic assessment depends upon emphasising and standardising criteria for scoring varied products such as students' performance on worthy intellectual tasks, students' problem-posing and problem-solving ability. Thus, teachers who want to utilise authentic assessment in practical instruction need to develop an accurate understanding of its principles, as well as the ability to design authentic tasks that are both meaningful to students and appropriate for assessment purposes.

The application of authentic assessment in practical instruction poses challenges for both teachers and students. Teachers have reported several factors that can affect their teaching performances, including student characteristics, the amount of time it takes to conduct authentic assessment, class size, and the amount of preparation required for instructional material (Gao & Grisham-Brown, 2011). As well, it can take time and effort for students to adapt to authentic instruction and to become familiar with this new form of assessment (Svinicki, 2004). By reviewing the literature on authentic assessment, this study attempts to provide suggestions for mathematics educators about how to conduct authentic assessment.

2   Method

With the aim of focusing on authentic assessment in mathematics education holistically, we identified full-text articles, using the EBSCO host Library, from 1988 (when the term "authentic" was first used in the assessment area) to 2020. Search terms included "authentic assessment", "authentic intellectual work", "authentic instruction" (Villarroel et al., 2018), and "authentic task" (Murphy et al., 2017) along with "math*". The outcome of the initial search was 113 articles. After removing those with irrelevant words in the article titles, such as "historical", "discourse intonation", and "geographical" (for example, those which were not related explicitly to mathematics education and focused on other subjects), there were 107 articles chosen for the next phase.

We then narrowed the selection to studies focusing on mathematics education and authentic assessment. The selected studies were first checked to ensure whether they actually did focus on mathematics education, especially those in the STEM field. Papers which used 'authentic' as a descriptor but did not actually focus on real-life contexts or assessment were excluded from the review. For example, Swaffield (2011) clarified the meaning of "authentic" as "genuine", but did not associate it with the term "authentic assessment". The frequency of the term 'authentic' and its synonyms was generally low in these articles. Finally, there were around 70 articles retained after two rounds of screening. The screening process is shown in Figure 5.1.

3 The Nature of Authentic Assessment

The term "authentic" was first used formally in the area of assessment, as one of the key characteristics of assessment promoting students' learning by Archibald and Newmann (1988). They believed "worthwhile, significant, and meaningful tasks" to be important for ensuring the validity of an assessment system (Archibald & Newmann, 1988). In many references, the terms "tasks", "problems" and "activities" are used interchangeably to describe authentic tasks. In this paper, we also use them interchangeably. As Wiggins (1990) pointed out, when teachers check students' performances directly on valuable intellectual tasks, the assessment is authentic. In other words, without imitating the use of paper-and-pencil or even computer-drill-and-practice-type tests, authentic assessment is close to the real-life performances based on students' activities. Later, Wiggins (1998) provided six standards for designing problems in authentic assessment:

1. *Is realistic.*
2. *Requires judgment and innovation.*
3. *Asks the student to "do" the subject.*
4. *Replicates or simulates the contexts in which adults are "tested" in the workplace, in civic life, and in personal life.*
5. *Assesses the student's ability to efficiently and effectively use a repertoire of knowledge and skill to negotiate a complex task.*
6. *Allows appropriate opportunities to rehearse, practice, consult resources, and get feedback on and refine performances and produces.*

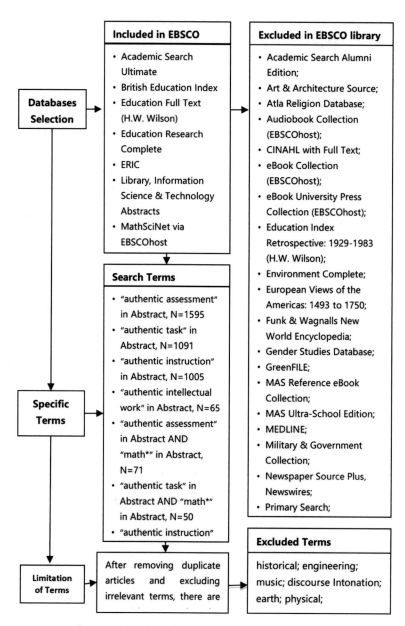

FIGURE 5.1   The procedure of searching literature

Admiraal et al. (2019) recognised three principles for designing an authentic, productive learning environment: (1) realistic, complex task situations; (2) multidisciplinary focus; and (3) social interaction. Herrington and Oliver (2000) identified nine elements from previous literature. Three of these are related to authentic learning: Provide authentic contexts that reflect the way the knowledge will be used in real life; provide authentic activities; provide for authentic assessment of learning within the tasks. In other words, authentic learning contains authentic contexts, authentic tasks (activities), and authentic assessment. Meaningful and realistic contexts (authenticity) are prerequisites for authentic learning and central influences to authentic tasks (activities). There are some factors that are helpful for improving the authenticity of assessment methods, such as some practical assignments and some students-developed tests developed. While, some factors might have negative effects on the authenticity of assessment methods, such as student monitoring system tests or textbook tests (Veldhuis & van den Heuvel-Panhuizen, 2014). Authentic assessment revolves around authentic tasks and measures students' authentic learning abilities through matching them to evaluation criteria.

4   Authentic Assessment in Mathematics Education

Traditional mathematics education isolates content knowledge from real-life situations and focuses mainly on tedious and repetitive problem solving (Kerekes, Diglio, & King, 2009). When learning in this way, students will forget the mathematical knowledge easily, and will not know how to apply it to unfamiliar contexts (Freudenthal, 1971, 1973). Authenticity plays an important role in mathematics education due to the importance of relating it to real-life (Vos, 2018). Authentic mathematics pedagogies can eliminate rote memorisation stereotypes and promote the development of curriculum-based, meaningful, and attractive knowledge (Garrett et al., 2016). According to Wedege's (1999) studies, "real-life contexts" or "meaningful and authentic contexts" are often included in curriculum materials, but this is not necessarily equivalent to Realistic Mathematics Education (RME) (Van Den Heuvel-Panhuizen, 2005). The English translation of RME causes misunderstanding. RME is not the same as real-world mathematics education or authentic mathematics problems (Colignatus, 2014). The Dutch verb "zich REALISEren" means "to image", which means the Dutch adjective "realistisch" has a more general connotation than "realistic", and problems in the real-world or in students' minds are both suitable for RME (Van den Heuvel-Panhuizen, 2005; Van den Heuvel-Panhuizen, & Drijvers, 2014). An example to explain this is an activity in which the students in Grade 1 are asked to decide their own lunch menu to the value of 50 Hong Kong dollars in a supermarket. In an RME activity, the teacher usually prepares some information (ie. some food pictures) related to supermarket and lead students to solve such problems. Students are not physically in the supermarket. However, in authentic assessment activity, the teacher must choose an appropriate situation close to real life, so the students can visit a supermarket and identify the food information themselves.

A possible way to link authentic assessment and mathematics education could be the problem-solving teaching approach proposed by the NCTM in 1989 (NCTM, 1989) and later emphasised in the *Principles and Standards for School Mathematics* (NCTM, 2000; Suurtamm, 2004). Teaching students to solve mathematical problems in different situations can help them not only to construct new mathematical knowledge, but also to make connections between mathematics and other subjects or situations. In addition to the United States, mathematical problem solving is at the core of mathematics learning in other places around the world, such as in the Singapore Mathematics Curriculum Framework (Koh & Chapman, 2018). Instead of rote memorisation, "understanding mathematics" and "student-centred" learning is promoted with the reform in mathematics education since the NCTM documents of the 1980s (Suurtamm, 2004). Koh and Chapman (2018) summarised five essential goals of students' mathematics literacy from the NCTM Standards of 1989, 1991, and 1995:

1. *Becoming a mathematical problem solver*
2. *Learning to reason mathematically*
3. *Learning to communicate mathematically*
4. *Learning to value mathematics*
5. *Becoming confident of one's own ability*

These goals are also core elements in many other countries' mathematics curricula (Zhang, 2017). To meet such goals, as well as the demands in society for employable school leavers, the growth of authentic teaching has led to an increase in the demand for authentic assessment in mathematics (Lajoie, 1995). Some studies have focused on the factors that impact upon its application. Both internal (including student and teacher factors) and external factors have been identified. For example, student factors, including students' characteristics and class sizes, may influence the teacher's ability to conduct effective authentic assessment (Gao & Grisham-Brown, 2011). As well, teacher-related factors can support or be detrimental to ongoing authentic instruction. Internal teacher-related factors include different cognitive interpretations of authentic assessment (Hernández & Brendefur, 2003), the extent and nature of instructional material (Gao & Grisham-Brown, 2011), the quality of instructors and their co-operative working (Dennis & O'Hair, 2010).

The most frequently reported external obstacle is the consumption of additional time (Dennis & O'Hair, 2010; Gao & Grisham-Brown, 2011; Guskey, 1994). Planning and preparing for authentic lessons requires more time and work for instructors (Dennis & O'hair, 2010; Guskey, 1994). It puts more pressure on teachers and hence they can tend to move away from authentic instruction (Gao & Grisham-Brown, 2011). According to Guskey's (1994) studies, more teachers in secondary schools reported time-related obstacles than those in primary school. Guskey suggested that this could be due to content orientation or noticeable differences in their beliefs about authentic assessment. Additionally, other external factors such as outdated professional training as well as limited materials and funding also hinder the use of authentic assessment in schools (Dennis & O'Hair, 2010). Hernández and Brendefur (2003) found most teachers have a relatively shallow understanding of authenticity in mathematics education, tending to confine it to daily life and future occupations. Due to this limited understanding, only a few teachers can extend the authentic classroom beyond superficial connections with real-life contexts, to authentic, critical problem solving (Hernández & Brendefur, 2003). Instructors need a combination of authentic assessment and on-going high-quality vocational training that can facilitate assessment and have a greater chance to bring about benefits for students' learning (Guskey, 1994), thus promoting effective 21st century mathematics classrooms (Mahanin et al., 2017).

As discussed above, in authentic learning, teachers and students often face time deficiencies and a lack of teamwork (Garrett et al., 2016). On the other hand, the lack of time limitations is also one reason why authentic assessment is more popular with students than standard assessment (Onwuegbuzie, 2000). For example, Herrington and Oliver (2000) reported students showing positive attitudes toward authentic assessment because they enjoyed being assessed in realistic contexts; this was even the case for the students who preferred traditional assessment. Even though complex matters and practical learning in authentic tasks may force students to step out of their comfort zones, these real experiences can help them to transfer what they learn into their future professions and improve their abilities to adapt in the workplace (Garrett et al., 2016). There was also some evidence reported in the literature (Herrington & Oliver, 2000) that parents' attitudes towards authentic assessment were generally positive, and some of them found that the content of such assessments were clear and made them feel close when they watched the instruction process (Gao & Grisham-Brown, 2011).

Despite these positive findings, an examination of students' attitudes towards fourteen assessment styles (Onwuegbuzie, 2000) revealed that authentic assessment was not commonly known. This underlines the need to develop the assessment literacy of stakeholders in relation to authentic assessment. Although both teachers and students recognise the value of authentic assessment, to help teachers implement authentic assessment in their teaching, we provided three different perspectives of understanding authentic assessment in mathematics education.

5   Three Approaches to Authentic Assessment in Mathematics Education

5.1   *Authentic Assessment as a Tool*

As an assessment tool, authentic assessment can be carried our during the mathematics learning process. There are many different methods of authentic assessment, such as cases, portfolios, exhibitions of performance, and problem-based inquiries. These have also been identified as tools to enhance students' learning and support teachers in the classroom (Darling-Hammond & Snyder, 2000) at various education levels. Some literature has already identified authentic assessment as a 'tool' to help teachers not only to distinguish children's mathematical competencies but also to enhance them. The findings of these studies provide some recommendations for educators. Gao and Grisham-Brown (2011), Reikerås et al. (2012), and Reikerås et al. (2017) focused on the mathematical skills or competencies of toddlers and collected information and data through authentic assessment tools. Ongoing observation of teachers was used as the instrument in these three studies (Gao & Grisham-Brown, 2011; Reikerås et al., 2012; Reikerås et al., 2017). To ensure the validity of the instrument, Reikerås et al. (2012) and Reikerås et al. (2017) utilised "The Mathematics, the Individual, and the Environment"(MIO) resource as assessment material (Davidsen et al., 2008a; Davidsen et al., 2008b). This consists of six sections: *Counting and series of numbers*; *Enumeration*; *Shape and space*; *Pattern and order*; *Mathematical language*; and *Logical reasoning*. Gao and Grisham-Brown (2011) applied the Assessment, Evaluation, and Programming System, 2nd Edition (AEPS®) (Bricker & Pretti-Frontczak, 2002) and examined it as a concurrent validation tool. These two selection standards (MIO and AEPS®) for examining young children's functional skills in a natural evaluation environment, are close to the "authenticity" of authentic assessment. The former is related to the nature of the evaluation instrument; in other words, the instrument's validity should be tested before use, as suggested by Gao and Grisham-Brown (2011). The latter is related to the toddlers' characteristics, which are relatively fragile in their relationship with adults. Hence, rather than causing them mental or physical harm, the authentic assessment allowed them to fully express themselves in a comfortable environment (Reikerås et al.,

2017). The children's attitudes were positive because they thought the authentic assessment methods were easier than traditional tests (Gao & Grisham-Brown, 2011).

In addition to the pre-school level application, authentic assessment can also be used in higher education to foster students' mathematical abilities. Based on Rhodes' 4P's Model (1961), a theoretical framework to analyse creativity contains of four strands: person, process, press and products, Adams (2020) utilised authentic assessment methods (Three Creativity-Fostering Projects) to develop first-year university students' creativity for relieving their "math anxiety". As a project combining mathematics and arts, the Math Graffiti Art Project provides opportunities for students to design creative artefacts through applying descriptive statistical knowledge. In Adams' study, a table of specific evaluation criteria was given to students so they could realise what they were expected to do. Most students showed positive attitudes toward this authentic assessment project, demonstrating their knowledge creatively and enhancing their course grades in general (Adams, 2020). Similarly, McDonald (2012) asked first-year students in a tertiary educational institution to record their learning information via a portfolio. This provided hands-on authentic learning evidence for these students. It also empowered them because they realised from sharing their work products with colleagues that other people recognised their contributions.

The two authentic assessment tools mentioned above give authority to learners, especially the portfolio assessment which highlights the summative assessment results, and participants' beliefs about the value of the authentic assessment tool (McDonald, 2012). When students felt the task was meaningful and important to them, they would recollect it longer than some traditional items (Adams, 2020). A particular value of the Math Graffiti Art Project is that it can be transferred to a range of grade levels to take the place of high-stakes tests, such as portfolios in K-12 education (Adams, 2020). However, it was noted that time was an issue in both of these studies. The students also did not easily understand the provided rubric (Adams, 2020) in the limited time. students who had little time to engage authentic activities did not benefit from the authentic activities when it came to their final grades (McDonald, 2012). Hence, time factors should be noticed by instructors who want to apply authentic assessment in higher education.

5.2 *Authentic Assessment as a Task*

A situated context is an essential element in designing authentic activities in the classroom. If the learning context is related to daily life in a problem-based learning environment, the instruction and assessment can improve students' mathematical thinking, understanding, and internalisation (Kerekes, Diglio, & King, 2009). Authentic assessment results are consistent with students' learning processes in terms of knowledge, competencies, and transfer. Thus, an authentic assessment can be regarded as a collection of learning tasks. Through these tasks, students' participation is enhanced in the authentic assessment situation (Newmann, 1996). Some assessment tasks allow students to construct knowledge related to real-world contexts, which is more meaningful than using traditional assessment (Koh, 2011).

In cooperative learning environments, as noted by Lowrie (2011), the authentic assessment can be more complicated. It can be difficult for students to build meaningful and authentic comprehension in team situations. Authenticity can be shown through problem-solving combined with individual experiences (Lowrie, 2011). Hernández and Brendefur (2003) found that when students had sufficient opportunities to explain generalisations, classifications, and relationships related to situations, problems or topics, or to defend their ideas, the course was considered more authentic. Hence, emphasising the collaborative situation in authentic assessment is crucial.

Since the task of designing authentic assessment is very complex, another concern is how to examine teachers' assessment literacy through their training. For example, Singapore has been carrying out a series of educational reforms during the 21st century (Koh, 2017). Task design for mathematics authentic assessment is always incorporated into pre-service mathematics teachers' professional development programmes (Koh & Chapman, 2018). To assess these student teachers' understanding and ability to design authentic assessment tasks, Koh and Chapman (2018) summarised the criteria for authentic intellectual quality of assessment tasks developed from Koh's (2011) studies (see Table 5.1 for the criteria list).

5.3 *Authentic Assessment as a Process*

Authentic assessment can also be situated as a learning process in some cases. The Programme for International Student Assessment (PISA), for instance, could be seen as one that uses authentic assessment to test the students' processes during the test. According to the PISA 2000 framework (Schleicher & Tamassia, 2000), authenticity validity has begun to be emphasised in many OECD countries. The authentic situation is also related to students' mathematics literacy in the PISA framework. Mathematical literacy is defined as:

> an individual's capacity to formulate, employ, and interpret mathematics in a variety of contexts. It includes reasoning mathematically and using mathematical concepts, procedures, facts and tools to describe, explain

TABLE 5.1   Criteria for judging the authentic intellectual quality of assessment tasks

Criteria	Examples of indicators
1. *Depth of knowledge*	
Factual knowledge	Recognise mathematical terms; identify objects, patterns, or list properties; recall rules, formulae, algorithms, conventions of number, or symbolic representations
Procedural knowledge	Know how to carry out a set of steps; use a variety of computational procedures and tools
Advanced concepts	Make connections to other mathematical concepts and procedures; explain one or more mathematical relations
2. *Knowledge criticism*	
Presentation of knowledge as a given	Accept or present ideas or information as a fixed body of facts; follow a set of preordained procedures
Comparing and contrasting information	Identify the similarities and differences in observations, data, or theorems; develop heuristics to identify, organise, classify, compare, and contrast data
Critiquing information Knowledge	Comment on different mathematical solutions; make mathematical arguments
3. *Knowledge manipulation*	
Reproduction	Recognise equivalents; perform a set of preordained algorithms; carry out computations
Organisation, interpretation, analysis, evaluation, and synthesis of information	Interpret given mathematical equations, diagrams, tables, graphs, or charts; predict mathematical outcomes from the trends in the data
Application/problem solving	Apply mathematical concepts and procedures to solve non-routine problems
Generation/construction of new knowledge	Come up with new proofs or solutions to a mathematical problem; generate mathematical procedures, strategies, or solutions to new problem situations
Extended communication Making	Elaborate on mathematical reasoning through arguments, prose, diagrams, sketches, drawings, or symbolic representations
Making connections to the real world beyond the classroom	Address a question, issue, concept, or problem that resembles one that they have encountered or are likely to encounter in daily life beyond the classroom

and predict phenomena. It assists individuals to recognise the role that mathematics plays in the world and to make the well-founded judgments and decisions needed by constructive, engaged and reflective citizens. (OECD, 2013)

In this view, mathematical literacy is about meeting needs in real life. However, some open-ended questions in PISA merely require students to answer with a few words or short sentences, which are less complicated than daily life tasks (Koh & Chapman, 2018), which shows that these questions are not actually authentic in nature. To develop students' mathematical literacy, the degree of authenticity of mathematical problems needs to be enhanced.

Mathematical literacy is expressed through using and engaging with mathematics, making informed judgements, and understanding the usefulness of mathematics in relation to real-life demands. Three process skills of mathematical literacy are emphasised in PISA assessments: connection, reproduction and reflection (Shiel, Perkins, Close, & Oldham, 2007, p. 6). In fact, these process skills in mathematical problem solving also reflect the characteristics of authentic assessment.

6 Authentic Assessment in STEM Education

In the most recent two decades, mathematics is included and thought of as the foundation of STEM. STEM education is promoted to solve real-world situations through a design-based problem-solving process (Williams, 2011). Three approaches for STEM education are currently practiced, the silo, embedded, and integrated approaches (Roberts & Cantu, 2012). The main difference among these methods is the content used in STEM. The silo approach refers to isolation instruction between each STEM subject (Dugger, 2010). It emphasises learning knowledge instead of "learning by doing" (Morrison, Bartlett, & Raymond, 2009), which is in contrast to *"Asks the student to 'do' the subject"* (Wiggins, 1998). The embedded approach can be defined broadly as an educational method in which the primary knowledge is acquired by emphasising real-world situations and problem-solving techniques in the social, cultural, and functional context (Chen, 2001). However, the embedded material does not reflect the "evaluated and assessed" standard (Chen, 2001). The integrated approach has identified all individual STEM subjects as a whole (Morrison, Bartlett, & Raymond, 2009). Additionally, this integration starts from a real-life problem (Wang, Moore, Roehrig, & Park, 2011), which is suitable for the "Is realistic" standard (Wiggns, 1998).

Driven by student-centred teaching and catering for different students' learning needs, teachers who plan and construct authentic and interdisciplinary classroom activities should be encouraged; this is also advocated by the 21st-century skills (Mahanin et al., 2017). Tan et al. (2019) noted mathematics tasks would become more complicated when integrated into the STEM framework. By integrating mathematics and science curricula, statistical literacy can be measured by the authentic problems (for example the Farmers' Market Project and School Garden from Tan et al. (2019)). This example assesses the teacher's ability to balance the empowerment and scaffolding provided to improve the statistical problem-solving process (Selmer et al., 2014). In summary, the concept of STEM means to apply the knowledge and skills of science and mathematics, in support of the tools of technology, and to resolve real, systematic, and engineering problems (Cunningham & Kelly, 2017). STEM education suggests the importance of authentic activities in students' classroom learning to enhance their competence. It also provides much richer and more meaningful contexts and materials for teachers to design and conduct authentic assessments, promoting their students' lifelong learning and creativity.

7 Authentic Assessment in Mathematics Education in the E-Learning Era

With the rapid development of information and communication technology (ICT) and its close integration with education, an e-learning approach has been advocated. Students are encouraged to integrate and apply the knowledge and skills of ICT in practical situations to meet the changes in the 21st century. Since PISA 2012, a computer-based assessment for mathematics (CBAM) has been provided optionally for participants (OECD, 2013). Authentic assessment is related closely to the real world and the learning process. The high use of computer competence as a 21st-century mathematics-literacy skill may improve the interaction, authenticity, and engagement of authentic assessment in mathematics (Hoogland & Tout, 2018).

Mathematical literacy explicitly includes the use of mathematical tools, for example, physical and digital equipment, software and calculation devices. Shaffer and Resnick (1999) maintain that new media can create an authentic situation for learning in terms of connectivity, authenticity, and epistemological pluralism. Through informative technologies, communication avoids geographical limitations and changes the quality of the learning experience; at the same time, these technologies provide an authentic environment for assessment (McLoughlin & Luca, 2001). For example, the continuous interaction of personal digital moments in the professional learning community is a fundamental element in which problem-based learning and actual evaluation of that learning can occur (Barber, King, & Buchanan, 2015). Authenticity poses great challenges to teachers' instruction in online learning because, in the digital world, regardless of academic status, teachers must redefine themselves continuously as lifelong learners and set an example for students (Barber, King, & Buchanan, 2015). However, information and computer skills and task re-designing are also challenging for teachers (Barber, King, & Buchanan, 2015).

Instead of using many descriptions to introduce mathematics problems, authentic and video-based learning may alleviate students' difficulties with tests. Generally, in standardised tests, students have to read the long descriptive text, and pick the appropriate answer from the existing options or give their answer through analysing problems (Bottge, 2001). Vos (2018) described these inauthentic word problems as a narrative problem that is artificial, remote from real life, and ending in numbers so that students cannot experience and understand the real applications of mathematics. Another researcher found that when students had difficulties in solving mathematics problems, this was likely to have been because they encountered difficulties with reading the problems (Bottge, 2001). In Bottge's (2001) study, video-based learning could alleviate this problem of students' reading difficulties. Although some young students might have been unwilling to accept the new form of instruction in the early stages of the research, they gradually adapted to the video-based learning and their mathematics performances also improved. Herrington and Oliver (2000) also found that it was necessary to conduct authentic assessment in multimedia as part of the learning environment.

Furthermore, digital tools provide virtual storage space, which solves the problem of actual assessment information storage, and is also convenient for review and use at any time. For example, portfolios provide authentic evidence via gathering evidence to trace students' learning performances (especially for inquiry) and ePortfolios can also address the storage issue (McDonald, 2012). This form of assessment also provides a platform for students to conduct self-reflection (self-assessment) and record the authentic learning experiences. Once collected, this information can be used in holistic assessment (Hubert & Lewis, 2014).

8   Conclusion

With the emergence of competency-based curriculum reforms around the world (OECD, 2018), there is a call for developing and enhancing students' mathematical competencies. Authentic assessment could play a crucial role in achieving this goal. This review has summarised and identified, from the literature, the inherent hindrances to the application of authentic assessment in mathematics teaching. These reasons include student factors (class size and students' characteristics), teacher factors (cognitive deviations about authentic assessment), and external factors (lack of time and funding, and insufficient related professional development training). Many of the relevant recommendations in the literature are related to external factors, such as collaboration among teachers. This can promote their professional competencies and reduce the preparation time needed to conduct authentic assessments. It is also noted that there is a need to combine authentic assessment and on-going high-quality vocational training to assess instructors' adaptability to facilitating authentic assessment in the classroom in order to promote students' mathematics learning (Mahanin et al., 2017). This kind of effort will also alleviate teachers' pressure in conducting authentic assessment to a certain extent.

In mathematics education, students are usually asked to solve lots of word problems, with the aim of developing their calculating ability rather than fostering reasoning, creativity, and realistic problem-solving abilities. They seldom solve real-life questions in authentic settings, which can lead them to believe that mathematics knowledge is only for artificial situations (Vos, 2018). Hence, to design and conduct authentic assessment or activities is to provide more opportunities for students to learn mathematics. Existing research on authentic assessment has focused mainly on students' achievement. How and what they experience during the processes of authentic assessment is underexplored. Future research could pay more attention to student factors in implementing authentic assessment in mathematics teaching and learning. Currently, computer-based mathematical tools are in common use in workplaces. Therefore, developing computer-based authentic assessment might be a new challenge in future education.

Acknowledgement

This study is partially funded by the Education University of Hong Kong FLASS Dean's Research Fund (Ref. FLASS/DRF04629). The content is solely the responsibility of the authors and does not necessarily represent the official views of the university.

References

Adams, M. (2020). Three creativity-fostering projects implemented in a statistics class. *Journal of Humanistic Mathematics*, *10*(2), 484–510. https://doi.org/10.5642/jhummath.202002.22

Admiraal, W., Post, L., Guo, P., Saab, N., Makinen, S., Rainio, O., Vuori, J., Bourgeois, J., Kortuem, G., & Danford, G. (2019). Students as future workers: Cross-border multidisciplinary learning labs in higher education. *International Journal of Technology in Education and Science, 3*(2), 85–94.

Allsopp, D. H., Kyger, M. M., Lovin, L., Gerretson, H., Carson, K. L., & Ray, S. (2008). Mathematics dynamic assessment: Informal assessment that responds to the needs of struggling learners in mathematics. *Teaching Exceptional Children, 40*(3), 6–16.

Althauser, K., & Harter, C. (2016). Math and economics: Implementing authentic instruction in grades K-5. *Journal of Education and Training Studies, 4*(4), 111–122.

Anderson, J. R., Reder, L. M., & Simon, H. A. (1996). Situated learning and education. *Educational Researcher, 25*(4), 5–11.

Archbald, D. A., & Newman, F. M. (1988). *Beyond standardised testing: Assessing authentic academic achievement in secondary schools*. National Association of Secondary School Principals.

Barber, W., King, S., & Buchanan, S. (2015). Problem based learning and authentic assessment in digital pedagogy: Embracing the role of collaborative communities. *Electronic Journal of e-Learning, 13*(2), 59–67.

Bottge, B. A. (2001). Building ramps and hovercrafts – and improving math skills. *Teaching Exceptional Children, 34*(1), 16–23.

Bottge, B. A., & Hasselbring, T. S. (1993). A comparison of two approaches for teaching complex, authentic mathematics problems to adolescents in remedial math classes. *Exceptional Children, 59*(6), 556–566.

Bricker, D., & Pretti-Frontczak, K. (2002). *Assessment, evaluation and programming system for children and infants* (2nd ed.). P.H. Bookers.

Brown, J. S., Collins, A., & Duguid, P. (1989). Situated cognition and the culture of learning. *Educational Researcher, 18*(1), 32–42.

Chen, M. (2001). A potential limitation of embedded-teaching for formal learning. In J. Moore & K. Stenning (Eds.), *Proceedings of the twenty-third annual conference of the cognitive science society* (pp. 194–199). Lawrence Erlbaum Associates.

Colignatus, T. (2014). *Pierre van Hiele, David Tall and Hans Freudenthal: Getting the facts right*. arXiv preprint arXiv:1408.1930.

Cunningham, C. M., & Kelly, G. J. (2017). Epistemic practices of engineering for education. *Science Education, 101*(3), 486–505.

Darling-Hammond, L., Ancess, J., & Falk, B. (1995). *Authentic assessment in action: Studies of schools and students at work*. Teachers College Press.

Darling-Hammond, L., & Snyder, J. (2000). Authentic assessment of teaching in context. *Teaching and Teacher Education, 16*(5–6), 523–545.

Davidsen, H., Løge, I. K., Lunde, O., Reikerås, E., & Dalvang, T. (2008a). *MIO-Matematikken-Individet-Omgivelsene. Observasjonsark* [MIO – The mathematics, the individual and the environment. Registration form]. Aschehoug.

Davidsen, H., Løge, I. K., Lunde, O., Reikerås, E., & Dalvang, T. (2008b). *MIO, Matematikken, Individet og Omgivelsene. Håndbok* [*MIO, the mathematics, the individual and the environment. Handbook*]. Aschehoug.

Dennis, J., & O'hair, M. J. (2010). Overcoming obstacles in using authentic instruction: A comparative case study of high school math & science teachers. *American Secondary Education*, *38*(2), 4–22.

Dugger, W. E. (2010). Evolution of STEM in the United States. In *6th biennial international conference on technology education research*. http://citeseerx.ist.psu.edu/viewdoc/download?doi=10.1.1.476.5804&rep=rep1&type=pdf

Freudenthal, H. (1971). Geometry between the devil and the deep sea. *Educational Studies in Mathematics*, *3*(3–4), 413–435.

Freudenthal, H. (1973). *Mathematics as an educational task*. Reidel.

Frey, B. B., Schmitt, V. L., & Allen, J. P. (2012). Defining authentic classroom assessment. *Practical Assessment, Research, and Evaluation*, *17*(1), 2. https://scholarworks.umass.edu/pare/vol17/iss1/2

Fuson, K. C. (2004). Pre-K to grade 2 goals and standards: Achieving 21st century mastery for all. In D. H. Clements, J. Sarama, & A. M. DiBiase (Eds.), *Engaging young children in mathematics: Standards for early childhood mathematics education* (pp. 105–148). Routledge.

Gao, X., & Grisham-Brown, J. (2011). The use of authentic assessment to report accountability data on young children's language, literacy and pre math competency. *International Education Studies*, *4*(2), 41–53.

Garrett, L., Huang, L., & Charleton, M. C. (2016). A framework for authenticity in the mathematics and statistics classroom. *Mathematics Educator*, *25*(1), 32–55.

Guskey, T. R. (1994). What you assess may not be what you get. *Educational Leadership*, *51*(6), 51–54.

Hart, C., Hammer, S., Collins, P., & Chardon, T. (2011). The real deal: Using authentic assessment to promote student engagement in the first and second years of a regional law program. *Legal Education Review*, *21*(1), 97–121.

Hart, D. (1994). *Authentic assessment: A handbook for educators* (Assessment bookshelf). Addison-Wesley Pub.

Hernández, V., & Brendefur, J. (2003). Developing authentic, integrated, standards-based mathematics curriculum: [More than just] an interdisciplinary collaborative approach. *Journal of Vocational Education Research*, *28*(3), 259–283.

Herrington, J., & Oliver, R. (2000). An instructional design framework for authentic learning environments. *Educational Technology Research & Development*, *48*(3), 23–48. https://doi.org/10.1007/BF02319856

Hoogland, K., & Tout, D. (2018). Computer-based assessment of mathematics into the twenty-first century: Pressures and tensions. *ZDM*, *50*(4), 675–686.

Hubert, D. A., & Lewis, K. J. (2014). A framework for general education assessment: Assessing information literacy and quantitative literacy with ePortfolios. *International Journal of EPortfolio, 4*(1), 61–71.

Kerekes, J., Diglio, M., & King, K. P. (2009). How can teachers enable students to pose and solve problems using contexts within and outside mathematics? *International Forum of Teaching & Studies, 5*(2), 5–10.

Koh, K. (2011) Improving teachers' assessment literacy through professional development. *Teaching Education, 22*(3), 255–276. https://doi.org/10.1080/10476210.2011.593164

Koh, K. H. (2017). Authentic assessment. In *Oxford research encyclopedia of education*. Oxford University Press. https://doi.org/10.1093/acrefore/9780190264093.013.22

Koh, K., & Chapman, O. (2018). Improving teachers' assessment literacy in Singapore mathematics classrooms: Authentic assessment task design. In K. Philipp, T. Leuders, & J. Leuders (Eds.), *Diagnostic competence of mathematics teachers* (pp. 207–221). Springer.

Lajoie, S. P. (1995). A framework for authentic assessment in mathematics. In T. A. Romberg (Ed.), *Reform in school mathematics and authentic assessment* (pp. 19–37). SUNY Press.

Lowrie, T. (2011). "If this was real": Tensions between using genuine artefacts and collaborative learning in mathematics tasks. *Research in Mathematics Education, 13*(1), 1–16. https://doi.org/10.1080/14794802.2011.550707

Mahanin, H. U. H., Shahrill, M., Tan, A., & Mahadi, M. A. (2017). Integrating the use of interdisciplinary learning activity task in creating students' mathematical knowledge. *International Journal of Research in Education and Science, 3*(1), 280–298.

McDonald, B. (2012). Portfolio assessment: Direct from the classroom. *Assessment & Evaluation in Higher Education, 37*(3), 335–347. https://doi.org/10.1080/02602938.2010.534763

McLoughlin, C. E., & Luca, J. (2001). Quality in online delivery: What does it mean for assessment in E-learning environments? In G. Kennedy, M. Keppell, C. McNaught, & T. Petrovic (Eds.), *Meeting at the crossroads. Proceedings of the 18th annual conference of the Australian Society for Computers in Learning in Tertiary Education* (pp. 417–426). Biomedical Multimedia Unit, The University of Melbourne.

Morrison, J., Bartlett, R., & Raymond, V. (2009). STEM as curriculum. *Education Week, 28*(23), 28–31.

Murphy, V., Fox, J., Freeman, S., & Hughes, N. (2017). "Keeping it real": A review of the benefits, challenges and steps towards implementing authentic assessment. *All Ireland Journal of Higher Education, 9*(3), 3233–3235.

National Council of Teachers of Mathematics. (1989). *Curriculum and evaluation standards for school mathematics*. Author.

National Council of Teachers of Mathematics. (2000). *Principles and standards for school mathematics*. Author.

Newmann, F. M. (1996). *Authentic achievement: Restructuring schools for intellectual quality.* Jossey-Bass.

OECD. (2013). *PISA 2012 assessment and analytical framework: Mathematics, reading, science, problem solving and financial literacy.* OECD Publishing.

OECD. (2018). *The future of education and skills: Education 2030.* OECD Publishing.

Onwuegbuzie, A. J. (2000). Attitudes toward statistics assessments. *Assessment & Evaluation in Higher Education, 25*(4), 321–339. https://doi.org/10.1080/713611437

Reikerås, E., Løge, I., & Knivsberg, A.-M. (2012). The mathematical competencies of toddlers expressed in their play and daily life activities in Norwegian kindergartens. *International Journal of Early Childhood, 44*(1), 91–114. https://doi.org/10.1007/s13158-011-0050-x

Reikerås, E., Moser, T., & Tønnessen, F. E. (2017). Mathematical skills and motor life skills in toddlers: Do differences in mathematical skills reflect differences in motor skills? *European Early Childhood Education Research Journal, 25*(1), 72–88. https://doi.org/10.1080/1350293X.2015.1062664

Rhodes, M. (1961). An analysis of creativity. *The Phi Delta Kappan, 42*(7), 305–310.

Roberts, A., & Cantu, D. (2012, June). Applying STEM instructional strategies to design and technology curriculum. In *PATT 26 conference; technology education in the 21st century* (No. 073, pp. 111–118). Linköping University Electronic Press.

Schleicher, A., & Tamassia, C. (2000). *Measuring student knowledge and skills: The PISA 2000 assessment of reading, mathematical and scientific literacy. Education and skills.* OECD Publishing.

Selmer, S., Rye, J., Malone, E., Fernandez, D., & Trebino, K. (2014). What should we grow in our school garden to sell at the farmers' market? Initiating statistical literacy through science and mathematics integration. *Science Activities, 51*(1), 17–32. https://doi.org/10.1080/00368121.2013.860418

Shaffer, D. W., & Resnick, M. (1999). "Thick" authenticity: New media and authentic learning. *Journal of Interactive Learning Research, 10*(2), 195–216.

Shiel, G., Perkins, R., Close, S., & Oldham, E. (2007). *PISA mathematics: A teacher's guide.* Department of Education and Science.

Suurtamm, C. A. (2004). Developing authentic assessment: Case studies of secondary school mathematics teachers' experiences. *Canadian Journal of Science, Mathematics and Technology Education, 4*(4), 497–513.

Svinicki, M. D. (2004). Authentic assessment: Testing in reality. *New Directions for Teaching and Learning, 100,* 23–29.

Swaffield, S. (2011). Getting to the heart of authentic assessment for learning. *Assessment in Education: Principles, Policy & Practice, 18*(4), 433–449.

Tan, V., Nicholas, C., Scribner, J. A., & Francis, D. C. (2019). Enhancing STEM learning through an interdisciplinary, industry-generated project. *Technology and Engineering Teacher, 79*(1), 26–31.

Van den Heuvel-Panhuizen, M. (2005). The role of contexts in assessment problems in mathematics. *For the Learning of Mathematics, 25*(2), 2–23.

Van den Heuvel-Panhuizen, M., & Drijvers, P. (2014). Realistic mathematics education. In S. Lerman (Ed.), *Encyclopedia of mathematics education* (pp. 521–525). Springer.

Veldhuis, M., & van den Heuvel-Panhuizen, M. (2014). Primary school teachers' assessment profiles in mathematics education. *PLoS ONE, 9*(1), 1–11. https://doi.org/10.1371/journal.pone.0086817

Villarroel, V., Bloxham, S., Bruna, D., Bruna, C., & Herrera-Seda, C. (2018). Authentic assessment: Creating a blueprint for course design. *Assessment & Evaluation in Higher Education, 43*(5), 840–854.

Vos, P. (2018). "How real people really need mathematics in the real world" – Authenticity in mathematics education. *Education Sciences, 8*(4), 195.

Wang, H. H., Moore, T. J., Roehrig, G. H., & Park, M. S. (2011). STEM integration: Teacher perceptions and practice. *Journal of Pre-College Engineering Education Research (J-PEER), 1*(2), 2.

Wedege, T. (1999). To know or not to know–mathematics, that is a question of context. *Educational Studies in Mathematics, 39*(1–3), 205–227.

Wiggins, G. (1990). The case for authentic assessment. *Practical Assessment, Research, and Evaluation, 2*(1), 2. https://doi.org/10.7275/ffb1-mm19

Wiggins, G. (1998). *Educative assessment designing assessments to inform and improve student performance* (1st ed.). Jossey-Bass.

Williams, J. (2011). STEM education: Proceed with caution. *Design and Technology Education: An International Journal, 16*(1), 26–35.

Wilson, J. W. (1973). Standardized tests very often measure the wrong things. *The Mathematics Teacher, 66*(4), 295–370.

Zhang, Q. (2017). Mathematical competencies in western mathematics education: Review, comparison and prospect. *Global Education, 46*(3), 29–44.

CHAPTER 6

A Model for Developing Preservice Mathematics Teachers' Mathematical Language Skills in the Context of Authentic Assessment

Fatma Nur Aktaş, Pınar Akyıldız and Yüksel Dede

Abstract

Assessment is an integral part of the learning-teaching process and communication and authentic assessment strategies gain importance in assessments made in the distance education process. This chapter discusses developing a model based on a teaching experiment for improving mathematical language skills with the help of authentic assessment tools in the distance education process. The activities that were enriched and assessed with authentic assessment tools have been designed to reveal and improve language skills based on communication and interaction in the distance education process. Thus, this study examines the role and reflections of authentic assessment tools in the development of mathematical language skills.

Keywords

authentic assessment – mathematical language skills – preservice mathematics teachers – distance education

1 Introduction

The COVID-19 pandemic process has dramatically changed the importance and role of technology use in education due to this process requiring not only educational environments to extend beyond the classroom and school buildings but also teaching practices to change. The most striking of these changes have been the differences in the roles lecturers and learners have in the process and the teaching/learning practices that shape these roles (Mishra & Close, 2020). In this context, lecturers need to apply some significant innovations in their teaching strategies and material preferences in order to increase learners' motivation toward distance education courses (Russell et al., 2009). Similarly, the sources of motivation in distance education practices (Keller, 1997), learners' needs (see Albano, 2012), and the needs and expectations of the processes for assessing learners (see Conrad & Openo, 2018) have also changed. Therefore, increasing interactions in the teaching process (Parker, 1999) and changing assessment strategies (see Conrad & Openo, 2018) are ways to transfer the effectiveness of classrooms to distance education applications. Classroom interactions include the communication processes between lecturer and learners as well as among learners (Moore, 1989), while assessments include formative assessments and alternative assessment strategies (Conrad & Openo, 2018; Hart, 1994). As such, two important criteria can be mentioned for maintaining distance educational practices in mathematics classes: mathematical communication and authentic assessment strategies.

2   Theoretical Perspective

This chapter focuses on the development of pre-service teachers in mathematical language skills and examines the roles of mathematics communication and authentic assessment strategies. Mathematics is basically about meaning. Language is used to express mathematical concepts and the interactions and relationships among them. Each natural language uses its own words to represent mathematics and to signify the worldwide expressions known in mathematics (Lee, 2006). In this context, this chapter will include theoretical frameworks for mathematical language, authentic assessment strategies, and fractions.

2.1   *Mathematical Communication and Mathematical Language*

Communication, one of the process skill standards listed by the National Council of Teachers of Mathematics (NCTM, 2000), refers to the ability to write, speak, explain, and describe mathematical ideas. Communication is also one of the process skills that have been included in Turkish mathematics curricula since 2005; according to the curricula, communication provides important links among visual, graphic, verbal, and symbolic representations of mathematical thoughts and concepts (Ministry of National Education [in Turkish: MEB], 2018). Mathematical communications among students and between a teacher and students are also contributive, reflective, and instructive interactions (see Brendefur & Frykholm, 2000). Brenner's (1998) theory of finite element methods also provides a specific category known as communication in mathematics that considers the effects of mathematical language in communication.

The Oxford English Dictionary (n.d.) defines language as "the system of communication in speech and writing that is used by people of a particular country or area" and "a way of expressing ideas and feelings using movements, symbols, and sound". These definitions build the bridge between one's native tongue and mathematical language because the components of language are semantics and syntax. Syntax replaces notations in mathematical language. Thus, while syntax is the correct spelling (or writing) of mathematical statements using symbolic or verbal components, semantics express the meanings these statements have (Radford, 2002). For example, while $x^2 + y^2 = 1$ is a product of the syntax structure, understanding it as the equation of a circle is a result of the semantic structure of the mathematical language. Goldin and Shteingold (2001) stated syntax as the verbal handling of a structure; as such, the language used is informal and reflects mental images. They stated formal notational structures reflect symbolic mathematical language. Miura (2001) also emphasised informal language to be influenced by one's native language, which causes some differences in representing concepts. For example, Turkish expresses 'one-third', which is used for rational numbers, as 'one over three'.

The grammatical structures of mathematical language are categorised as terms (e.g., $x + 1$), objects (e.g., $\mathbb{Z}$), nouns (e.g., natural number), adjectives (such as isosceles triangle), statements (e.g., $\forall x \in \mathbb{Z}$), definitions, and declarations. Thus, sentence and discourse categories can be said to emphasise the verbal and symbolic structure of mathematical language (see Kamareddine et al., 2004). Because language plays an effective role in mathematical communication, Sfard (2001) considers mathematics to be a discourse. However, a commognitive perspective also stands out here, and cognitive variables such as concept image, concept definition, and misconception are said to gain importance in language use (see Dede & Soybaş, 2011; Tall & Vinner, 1981). In this context, Sfard (2001), focusing on mathematical communication from a holistic perspective, provides a theoretical framework that endorses *using word* for verbal statements, *visual mediators* for visual representations, *routines* for mathematical rules, and *endorsed narrative* for mathematical argumentations in the theory focusing on mathematical communication.

The structures of mathematical language include communications such as the written and verbal representations of symbols, words, graphics, notations, and images, which are forms of mathematical vocabulary (Riccomini et al., 2015). Thus, mathematical representation is carried out by means of these communications. The structures that form mathematical language (e.g., words, symbols, and graphs) fall within the scope of mathematical representation as important components of the mathematical communication process. Thus, the numerical, graphical, verbal, and symbolic representations recommended here are already related to the nature of mathematical language (Matteson, 2006). Therefore, insufficient skills in mathematical representation cause difficulties in understanding mathematical language and in translating between representations (Zhe, 2012). As such, mathematical language development cannot be considered apart from the skills of representation.

2.2 Mathematical Language Skills

Mathematical language is a competence for preservice mathematics teachers not only in mathematics teaching but also in learning mathematics (see Rubio et al., 2011). This is because the related literature has noted mathematical language skill to play an active role in the learning advanced mathematics during undergraduate education (see Ferrari, 2004). Therefore, examining the development of mathematical language used by preservice mathematics teachers in mathematical communication processes and having them acquire mathematical language skills as a competence are important. In this way, Lajoie (1995) touched on the importance of scaffolding or adaptive feedback between lecturers and learners for authentic assessment processes that address mathematical communication because authentic assessments can "provide information on what the learner knows or does not know" (Lajoie, 1995, p. 28), particularly in distance education processes. They are important in assessing preservice teachers' development regarding mathematical language skills. In this context, determining authentic assessment strategies for developing preservice teachers' mathematical language skills has become necessary during distance education. In this regard, the importance of determination of competencies related to the use of mathematical language skills (Drábeková et al., 2018) appears first. Authentic assessment tools suitable for examining the development of these skills in the process (Herrington & Herrington, 1998; Kearney, 2013) emerge next.

2.3 Authentic Assessment and Mathematical Language Skills Development

Assessment in mathematics education is defined as "the process of gathering evidence about a student's knowledge of, ability to use, and disposition toward mathematics and of making inferences from that evidence for a variety of purposes" (see NCTM, 1995, p. 3). Traditionally, mathematics teachers have preferred using paper-and-pencil tests to assess students' mathematics learning. However, more varied information about learners' mathematical competence, skill development, and understanding is needed. The way to do this is through authentic assessment because authentic assessment provides a more comprehensive picture of the learner and provide more authentic information than traditional assessment implementations (Yeo, 2011).

Authentic assessment is defined by many researchers (see Messick, 1994; Wiggins, 1998). In terms of the definition adopted in this chapter, "authentic assessment is based on activities that represent actual progress toward instructional goals and reflect tasks typical of classrooms and requires the integration of language skills" (Pierce & O'Malley, 1992, p. 1). Therefore, two related reasons are found for implementing authentic assessment in mathematics classrooms: authentic assessment reveals at a very concrete level what the curricular objectives are, and it offers lecturers examples of how they can activate learners' thinking and learning (Yeo, 2011). In addition, authentic assessment activities also allow for mathematical communication (Suurtamm, 2004).

Meanwhile, authentic assessment processes aim to associate what learners have learned and to provide feedback to learners about their learning development (Mohanty & Akalamkam, 2012). In this context, Murdoch (1994) drew attention to activity-based tasks, self-development strategies, and interaction with classroom language for mathematical language development in teacher training programs. He also emphasised understanding and academic success to increase when multi-faceted communications are included between the lecturer and learner and among learners in the interactions in distance education. Encouraging critical thinking, providing immediate communication and feedback, and group/individual tasks are important within the scope of interactions (see Flottemesch, 2000). In addition, Gaytan and McEwen (2007) expressed that teachers consider projects, peer-assessment, and self-assessment to be effective measures in online environments.

2.4 Mathematical Language and the Concept of Fractions

Lecturer-learner and learner-content interactions are noteworthy among the interactions in distance education (see Moore, 1989). These interactions are based on learners' understanding and perspectives. Therefore, the concept choice for language use is important in the mathematical communication process. In fact, knowledge plays an important role in the emergence and development of skills (see Albano, 2012). In addition, mathematical content knowledge is related to the mathematical language presented through the content. Thus, teachers should be careful with how they use mathematical language such as definitions, terms, and representations. Teachers should analyse and establish a balance between the correct mathematical language they need and its receptivity (Zhe, 2012). This is because mathematical statements are not a set of rules for understanding symbols but on the contrary are products of mathematical language that consist of reading, writing, and discourse

(Jamison, 2000). However, studies have indicated learners to have a significant gap between their mathematical language and formal definition skills regarding the concept of fractions (see Steffe, 2001).

Fractions include the use of representations and inter-translations, so fractions are one of the topics where mathematical language is most heavily used. In addition, fractions are important because they contain elements suitable for the features in Sfard's theory (2001) and are a sufficient concept for the preparation of suitable environments for the use of authentic assessment tools. Teaching fractions using basic concepts such as full, half, quarter, numerator, denominator, division, allocation, equal parts, smaller, larger, and equal starts in third grade in the United States (see NCTM, 2000) and first grade in Turkey (see MEB, 2018). However, fractions are a subject of which students often have incomplete knowledge, poor understanding, and difficulty learning (Tirosh, 2000; Toluk-Uçar, 2009; Ünver & Bukova Güzel, 2019).

"Children are likely to meet five different meanings of the concept of fraction..." (Orton & Frobisher, 1996, p. 107). These meanings are part-whole, ratio, measure, operator, and division. Namely, the symbol x/y indicates a whole being divided into y parts with x parts present, the ratio of two multiples to each other or of the part to the whole, a measure of x amounts of $1/y$ units, the enlargement or reduction of a geometric figure through an x/y ratio, or a numerical value obtained when x is divided by y. That fractions are a congruence class of integers x and non-zero y in the form of (x, y) should not be forgotten here (Argün et al., 2014).

3 Methodology

3.1 *Teaching Experiment and Design Classroom*

The study's participants are sophomore students at the Primary Mathematics Teaching Program of a State University in Turkey. Moreover, this chapter has been designed as a teaching experiment (see Cobb & Steffe, 1983), because this provides the opportunity to assess using authentic assessments (Hart, 1994) to examine learners' development in the learning process and to reveal learners' thinking processes (Steffe & Thompson, 2000); it also plays a role in revealing learners' mathematical knowledge through the interactions between the researcher and the learners (Cobb & Steffe, 1983). In this context, data have been collected in the "Communication in Mathematics Classes" course, which was designed based on Cognitively Guided Instruction (CGI; Carpenter et al., 2002) due to CGI including instructional decisions, teaching objectives, and student knowledge and assessment components as well as its focus on student learning processes. CGI's features and components provide very suitable environments for revealing learners' mathematical language skills using authentic assessment.

Zhe (2012) emphasised the benefit of designing a program based on the concepts and student knowledge in the model that aims to develop mathematical representation skills built on mathematical language skills. In addition, social interaction, and communication, which is required in the concept development process, also affect language development (Vygotsky, 1994).

3.2 *Procedures*

Turkish studies are found to have examined pre-service and in-service teachers' language skills and indicated certain deficiencies (see Baki & Çelik, 2018; Toluk-Uçar, 2009; Ünver & Bukova Güzel, 2019; Yeşildere, 2007), the results of which show a model for the development of mathematical language skills in teacher training programs to be needed. Therefore, this chapter discusses the nine-week teaching experiment designed for developing mathematical language skills using distance education regarding the concept of fractions. In this vein, the course has been designed according to the participants' performance in their previous classes; their insufficient knowledge of mathematical communication, mathematical language, and concept representations have been taken into consideration. Firstly, mathematical vocabulary such as notations, symbols, and terms (see Riccomini et al., 2015); mathematical concepts; and forms of representation (see Zhe, 2012) were discussed in terms of the mathematical language skills components. In this context, the courses, which meet weekly and focus on written and verbal mathematical language skills (see Aktaş & Argün, 2020; Barwell, 2008; Sfard, 2001; Wessel, 2020), were arranged by considering the basic concepts, symbols, and discourses regarding the concept of fractions (see McGee, 1997; Wessel, 2020; Zhe, 2012). Information about the assessment tools used, and the weekly courses are given in Figure 6.1.

Participants were divided into four groups of eight. These groups were brought together throughout the teaching experiment without changing them for small-group discussions. Participants' preliminary knowledge was first determined through small-group discussion over open-ended questions and vignettes followed by a whole-class discussion. After the discussions, a presentation was made on fractions, their representation types, and their models. A video-vignette was presented in the second- and sixth-week classes, with the homework of writing an assessment report for the next week also being given. All assignments, studies, and quizzes on the assessments and analyses were conducted using both verbal and written mathematical language. Groups

PRESERVICE MATHEMATICS TEACHERS' MATHEMATICAL LANGUAGE SKILLS 123

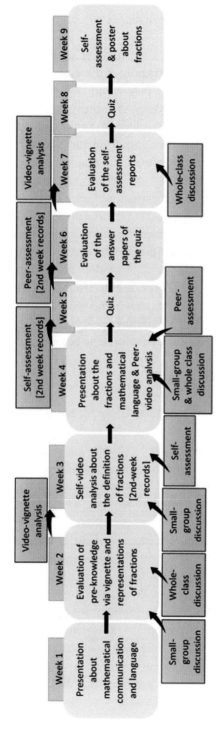

FIGURE 6.1 Procedures of the teaching experiment

watched and discussed their own videos and prepared individual self-assessment reports.

Participants reported their own mathematical language improvements using the self-assessment reports only in the ninth week. They assessed what they had done right and wrong before and after the teaching experiment in these reports. Similarly, they assessed another group that had been identified for peer-assessment. Each open-ended question was shown during the time allocated for it in the fifth-week quiz. This quiz was aimed to determine the written mathematical language level, and questions were limited to the duration of the quiz to check whether mistakes continued to occur by making sudden decisions. The problem situations based on the relationship between different representation types, determination of various types of models, transformations or transitions between representation and models are included in the quiz. The eighth-week quiz had six open-ended questions and lasted 60 minutes. The concept definitions, models, and representation types were expected to be explained in detail, also focused on symbolic representations and transformations between models in this quiz. Written language skills were also measured in the context of problem posing in this quiz. Student prepared individual posters and were asked to provide key points for the use of mathematical language regarding fractions. In addition, a forum was held every week for discussions and questions.

3.3 Authentic Assessment Tools Using the Model

This section contains details of the authentic assessment tools used for the teaching experiment model aimed at improving language skills.

Self-assessment means the students assess themselves individually; the teachers gather evidence from this about students through their self-reviews, self-reflections, and self-reports about their learning in mathematics in the self-assessment (Fan, 2011). Peer-assessment is an arrangement in which individuals assess the learning outcomes or results of their peers (Topping, 1998). These tools were used next for the discussion and writing strategies (a report) in the teaching experiment sessions.

Whole-class and small-class discussions improve communication skills (Dallimore et al., 2008), learning (Bender, 2003), and critical thinking (Garside, 1996). Inter-student interactions that occur during these discussions can enable the formation of mathematical knowledge (NCTM, 1995) as well as lead to enhancing learning and instruction in distance education (Hamann et al., 2012). In addition, the students gave feedback during the discussions on how well they had learned, and this can increase their self-confidence and motivation (Frederick, 1994).

The study in this chapter video-recorded the participants' whole-class and small-class discussions on scenario-based classroom dialogues on mathematical language. These videos have been used as video-vignette. This type of video-vignette has several advantages in qualitative studies, but the most frequently referenced one is the ability to get a deeper understanding of the subject (Barter & Renold, 1999; Hughes, 1998).

Finally, the poster preparations and presentations are important in terms of helping students gain self-learning and discovering new ideas (Fuller, 2000). In this chapter, participants prepared posters expressing their own progress and misunderstanding they had about fractions before and after the training.

3.4 Data Analysis & Trustworthiness

Data analysis has been performed using ongoing and retrospective analyses, as has been suggested in teaching experiment studies (see Cobb & Gravemeijer, 2008). While ongoing analyses were conducted during the teaching and after each class (see Cobb, 1999), retrospective analysis has been carried out to determine the extent to which goals had been achieved after the teaching (see Steffe & Thompson, 2000).

The video recordings have been transcribed in accordance with content analysis criteria, and the documents were analysed in these analyses. The participants' statements and reports have been assessed with subcomponents (i.e., true, false, or mistaken) with a focus on the use of verbal and written mathematical language.

Triangulation was provided through the teaching experiment and the CGI theory for model development using a wide perspective and authentic assessment tools for mathematical language skills. In addition, the researchers encoded the data separately, with the data being confirmed by a participant. Examples from the analyses are given in Table 6.1.

4 Result

This section is presented to assess changes and the role of authentic assessment tools. The results determined typically from the participants are included.

4.1 Determining Participants' Pre-Knowledge

Participants' pre-knowledge was first determined in a small-group discussion and then a whole-class discussion. The participants were observed to have difficulty expressing themselves in the class discussion and more time was needed for them to have equal opportunities.

TABLE 6.1 Sample data analysis

		Verbal language		Written language	
Theme		Category	Example	Category	Example
Ongoing analysis / Using model	Using model	Descriptive language	…the whole is divided into equal parts…	Type of representation	There should have been congruent shapes in the mixed fraction…
Retrospective analysis		Using terms	…I should have said equal parts in the area model…	Using terms in the type of representation	The fraction had to be represented in the area model by the congruent rectangles.

Some of the participants were determined to *not know the definition* of a fraction, to have *difficulty understanding notations*, and to make *mistakes in their discourses* and modeling of the representation types. Participants generally were unable to establish the relationship between fractions' part-whole meaning and notations and did not know the relationship between numerator-denominator and the part-whole meaning. They used statements such as 'rational numbers', 'ratios', and '*a* over *b*' for fractions. They were determined to *not know the terms* fraction bar or whole part regarding mixed numbers. They were also understood to not know the fraction models:

Lecturer: What is a fraction?
A: Something unable to be expressed rationally.
B: Fractions can be expresses as a division. It does not matter if it is rational or irrational.
Lecturer: How does the division happen?
B: There is a line in between.
Lecturer: What do we call that line?
A: It is the proportional the numbers have to each other. The line shows the proportion.

The mistakes in fraction models were identified using *written language*. For example, participants used different geometric shapes for expressing the part of a whole and proper fractions while using the area model for mixed numbers; they did not pay attention to units. These results show that the discourses had arisen from not knowing the conceptual definitions. Therefore, the next sessions focused on mathematical language skills using conceptual definitions and representation types.

4.2 The Self-Assessments Using Video Analysis

Each group watched the video of their own group's small-group discussion in the second week and assessed it in the context of mathematical language. One important result is that the participants paid attention to their own discourse and made corrections. Of course, a peer-assessment also occurred here. However, group members were accepted as supporting these ideas unless they had stated something contrary to their classmates' opinions during the discussion. Therefore, the self-group video analysis was a self-assessment tool in this process.

Participants frequently used *descriptive verbal statements* in the self-assessment such as, "I said line there, I should have said fraction bar". These statements were seen to focus on the discourse of notations as well as the descriptive language. However, common erroneous statements such as "3 over 5" were determined to continue. In addition, the participants were determined to have tried to explain the notations or models with *verbal statements* such as "We should have said given amount over 4, plus [...] to express the sum of three-quarters of a given amount".

The participants were determined to have used the discourses about the model more and to be able to explain the relationship between the numerator and denominator using the relationship between the whole and the part. However, some participants had tried to express or model fractions without using the terms whole or part.

Participants' ability to use *terms based on the relationship between concepts*, to *focus on concept definitions* and *different representations*, and to use mathematical language that includes terms suitable for *the model* was determined to have developed after analysing the self-assessment reports. The following small-group discussion about fraction models is a descriptive example of the categories regarding the concepts of 'interval', 'number lines', and 'area models':

D: For example, (s)he said to divide it into equal intervals. I think (s)he should have said equal parts.
Lecturer: So, can we use the term interval?
D: Maybe we can use the term interval for the number line and the ratio of the parts we selected to all the parts for the area model.

4.3 The Peer-Assessments Using Video Analysis

Each group member analysed the videos of another group from the second week in the context of mathematical language and individually wrote a peer-assessment report. The participants were determined to have paid more attention to using *descriptive language in their verbal statements* and *discourses about notation* and to *using models with correct representation* in these reports. Another important result is that each of these criteria is based on the formal definition of the fraction. The following discussion in which the concepts of rational number, ratio, and fraction are discussed can be given as an example of the increase in the importance of the conceptual definition:

K: I think he thought fractions are rational numbers because rational numbers are written as *a* over *b* where *b* also must be nonzero.

L: Yes, the congruence class formed by a divided by b is a set of fractions.

M: Fractions are mathematical notations and symbols consisting of a numerator, denominator, and fraction bar; they are quantities that can be proportional to each other... where we write the number of parts in the numerator and the whole in the denominator; fractions are the ratio of the numerator to denominator.

L: The concept of *proportional* in the video is wrong. A fraction refers to a ratio.

The participants were more careful in their discourse on fraction notation. They also included descriptive language corrections in their peers' discourse such as "It is correct to say the whole part instead of the whole" or "We should say we divide it into 4 equal parts, not divide by 4". In addition, they noteworthily included discourses such as "Instead of multiplying fourths by 3, it can be counted 3 times instead. We know that the numerator is counted. We get three-fourths", in explaining the relationship between notation and concept. In the example of "(S)He should have worked using the same whole in the simple fraction and the part of a whole part. (S)He should have used a rectangular whole again", they were determined to have started paying attention to the relationship between the whole and its unit parts when using the model.

4.4 Analysis of the Video-Vignette for Verbal and Written Mathematical Language

Participants' reports assessing a teacher's classes on fractions for the use of verbal and written language gave information on their use of mathematical language. This section will comparatively present the data from the reports collected in the second and seventh weeks. Thus, the reflections on the courses made with self-assessment and peer-assessment tools on the development of mathematical language skills can be determined.

The analysis of the first video-vignette determined the participants to have focused on teacher's *terms* chosen for definitions, the discourse on *notation*, and the *model* presenting the part-whole relationship. Participants focused on the teacher's discourse regarding the definition of fraction and stated that the teacher should have arranged her discourses using 'equal parts' instead of parts, 'three-fifths' instead of 3 over 5, integer instead of 'whole part', and the whole in her expressions for dividing a cake into 3 parts.

The second video-vignette analysis is noteworthy in that, aside from the improvements in the participants' language skills, they attached importance to the discourses for each term, model, and notation regarding the concept of fractions. They stated that the discourses should include descriptive language and emphasised the terms, as in the examples "Fraction notation is explained by specifying the fraction bar, numerator, and denominator", and "Dividing the area model into equal parts should be emphasised". In addition, they arranged the division into 3 equal parts in the fraction example represented by the teacher using the area model, as in Figure 6.2.

4.5 *Self- and Peer-Assessments Using Reports*

These reports, in which the participants assessed themselves and their peers in the context of mathematical language by watching their videos from the second week, presented results regarding the development of written mathematical language. The participants were determined to have focused more on *the definition of concepts* and *representation types* in their self-assessments and on the use of *descriptive language* and *types of terms* in their peer-assessments. The reflections of verbal statements on language use were encountered in the reports. For example, they included descriptive language while emphasising the ratio meaning of fractions to avoid any errors that may arise from the same notation. In other words, they emphasised discourses in their reports such as 'a by b' or 'equals (=)'. They were also determined to have included symbolic representations such as the definition of K = {(a, b) ∈ ℤ × ℤ where b ≠ 0}. In addition, they were determined to have paid attention to context while using fractions as a term in a sentence. For example, they were seen to criticise describing a fraction as a number or proportion and to avoid saying

FIGURE 6.2
Participant's model

shape instead of model. They paid attention to using the correct terms, notations, and representations of fractions in their reports.

4.6 Written Mathematical Language Using a Quiz

Quizzes were conducted twice during the teaching experiment. Their development in written language was attempted to be determined in this manner. In addition, timed questions that enabled them to make instant decisions allowed for determining their reflections on the discourses on language use. In the first quiz, most of the participants explained equivalent fractions with *statements based on the discourses* such as "expanding the numerator and denominator" or "because it coincides with the same point on the number line" instead of basing them on models.

In the first quiz, fractions were asked to be written out as statements indicating the amount of ingredients in a recipe. In this question, most of the participants included both fraction notations and models. Similarly, *the types of representations* they included were noteworthily diverse while explaining equivalent fractions, as shown in Figure 6.3.

Participants often preferred *using models* instead of symbolic representations for the solutions to problems; they also frequently used fraction bars for their fraction models. Some participants still used the statement "fraction and a whole" for mixed fractions. Regarding the models, they made *the most mistakes* for the cluster model. However, the participants who determined the correct representations in fraction models were seen to consider areas or circle segments, as shown in Figure 6.4.

In the results of the second quiz, they were seen to *support symbolic representations using models*, to include *terms* and *discourses in descriptive*

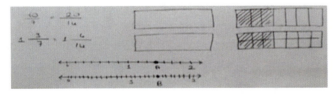

FIGURE 6.3   Using different representations

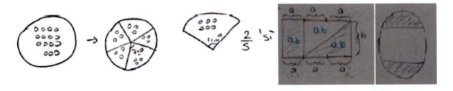

FIGURE 6.4   Using correct models for fractions

language, to emphasise *concept definitions*, and to *pay attention to terms* in this regard. They were seen to use verbal statements such as mixed numbers, half, and quarter correctly by supporting them with notations. They were seen to be more successful regarding sets and area models and to have made no mistakes in modeling multiplication with regard to fractions.

4.7 The Self-Assessments Using Posters

According to these reports, they each prepared a poster consisting of key points on the concept of fractions. The most emphasised key points in these reports and posters were *the formal definition, notation, function,* and *model types* of concept of fractions (see Figure 6.5). These noteworthy also included *discourses*. One participant emphasised mathematical language in his report with the following discourse:

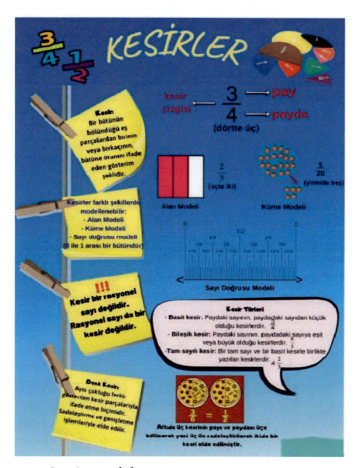

FIGURE 6.5   An example for posters

Because we were constantly saying '*a over b*', I had always read it this way. This phrase was only visualising the part-whole structure of the fraction in my mind. However, fractions also have structures such as measurements, division, operators, and ratios.

5   Discussion

This section examines the role of authentic assessment tools in the development of mathematical language skills and the model that was introduced using these tools in a certain order.

5.1   Role of Assessment Tools for Mathematical Language

Results, discussions, and suggestions are among the effective strategies for determining the concept-focused state of one's mathematical language skills communications (see Brendefur & Frykholm, 2000; Dallimore et al., 2008; Flottemesch, 2000). Therefore, determining pre-knowledge through small-group discussions provided in particular more data than had it been determined using an achievement exam. This is because their discourses on mistakes and misconceptions led to the emergence of different mistakes and misconceptions in other groups. In addition, participants used non-mathematical terms in their statements such as 'proportional' because daily language has on their use of mathematical language. Moreover, their lack of conceptual knowledge led to incomplete statements such as 'the ratio of the part to the whole'. Thus, mathematical language skills, which are influenced by conceptual knowledge (Sfard, 2001; Zhe, 2012) and daily language use (Miura, 2001), can be assessed and improved.

This chapter has basically used self-assessments and peer-assessments. In addition, various tools such as video-based self-assessments and peer-assessments, video-vignettes, and posters have been used. The reports assessing the participants' personal development after the teaching experiment have provided the most comprehensive self-assessment results. These reports allowed them to identify critical points in mathematical language development and provided an opportunity for reflective thinking. In addition, the participants' constructed posters containing the components of the development of mathematical language skills regarding fractions. Thus, the reports and posters are also considered as self-assessment tools (see Figure 6.6). Thus, they learned how to determine the critical points in language development and how to use the assessment tools.

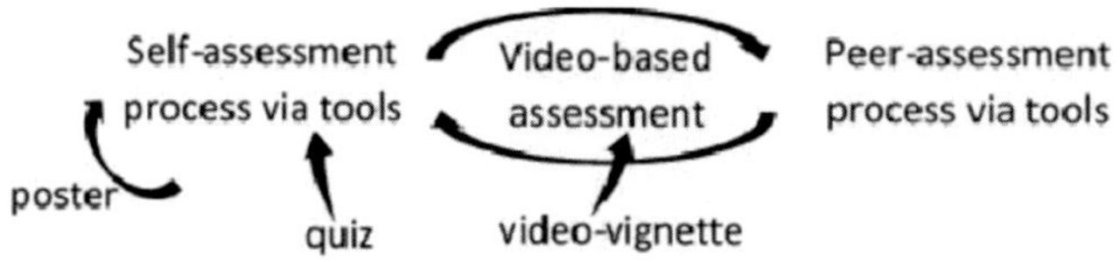

FIGURE 6.6 Assessment process via authentic assessment tools

The video-based assessments were handled in two dimensions: video-vignette and self-video analysis. Based on the analysis reports from the second week, participants were focused more on the use of mathematical language in the vignette than in the self-video analysis. This is because the participants often focused on concept definitions in group discussions. While the discussions did support learning (Bender, 2003) and critical thinking (Garside, 1996), the use of language allowed them to focus on definitions, terms, symbols, and discourses (McGee, 1997; Riccomini et al., 2015; Sfard, 2001). Therefore, the usage of terms and notations rather than discourses was examined. However, the teacher's use of expressions and symbols regarding oral and written language causes attention to be drawn to the vignette because these led the teacher to deeply examine the context addressed in the vignettes (Barter & Renold, 1999).

The self-video analysis allowed participants to notice their mistakes and misconceptions in developing mathematical language skills. In addition, the participants who had wanted to explain their discourse in the video in more detail increased their use of descriptive language. Thus, the discourses on the symbols, terms, and notations were able to be revealed and their misconceptions detected. This made monitoring both their development and progress possible. This assessment tool acted as a bridge among assessment, learning, and skills because, as Fan (2011) advocated, it enables the learner to pay attention to definitions, relationships between concepts, types of representations, and models. Thus, skill development such as defining concepts and using mathematical language based on discourse becomes possible.

Because the peer-video analysis took place after an instructive presentation about fractions, their attention toward definitions, representation types, and models increased. This enabled the participants to focus more on the discourses. The need to give feedback, which arises from the nature of peer-assessment (Topping, 1998), led the learners to assess themselves and their peers in detail. Thus, they discovered the similar and different uses of mathematical language they had with their peers. This enabled them to focus on their deficiencies and misconceptions regarding the conceptual knowledge that appeared in their discourses. As can be seen in Figure 6.6, a cyclical relationship thus arose between the self- and peer-assessment processes using the video-based assessment tools.

The role of the video-based assessment tool should not be thought of as just a discussion on video. Alongside the group discussions in the self- and peer-assessments, individual reports are also an effective assessment tool. Using these reports, the participants both reflect upon their individual opinions and gain a view toward examining the use of language from the perspective of their peers. Therefore, they focus more on conceptual definitions and representation types in their self-video analysis. This is because they question their knowledge regarding concepts. The participants focused more on the use of descriptive language and terminology in the peer-video analyses, as they analysed their peers through their use of language. Consequently, the use of written language based on symbolic language was determined to have improved by using definitions and terminology.

The video-vignettes (see Figure 6.6), which contributed to the video-based assessment process, made participants realise the general importance of discourse and mathematical language in the classroom. Based on the role of video analysis in conceptual understanding (see Barter & Renold, 1999; Hughes, 1998), they understood the use of mathematical language in the teaching process to also depend on concepts, representation types, models, and notations. Therefore, they were able to identify correct and incorrect uses in the vignette by focusing on these components. They were able to decide how a teacher should use concept-oriented mathematical language accordingly.

The most important contribution of the timed quizzes to the development of language skills is the ability to determine the participants' instant decisions and the use of written language. Both are important in the use of mathematical language in the classroom. Teachers are expected to make decisions and support their discourses with writing while teaching. Therefore, this tool is critical for developing language skills. Indeed, the participants included more than one representation type in the quizzes in order to express their opinions better. Thus, the situation regarding different components of mathematical language skills such as notations, models, and statements was able to be determined. This tool additionally contributes to the self-assessment process with the feedback that is given (see Figure 6.6). In this way, it creates an important awareness in the development of language skills. Therefore, the importance of the selected terms, as well as the deficiencies and misconceptions, emerged.

5.2   Model for Mathematical Language Skill Development

A concept-oriented (Sfard, 2001) model based on the strategy of discussion (Dallimore et al., 2008) has been developed using authentic assessment tools

(Yeo, 2011) through this teaching experiment, which was designed to examine mathematical language development inclusive of active-learning and thinking processes. In each component of the model in Figure 6.7, interactive processes based on small-group discussions (see Dallimore et al., 2008) are important; the model is based on the distance education process (see Hamann et al., 2012). Thus, in line with Lajoie's (1995) proposal, a model for skill development based on authentic assessment has been presented.

The model, which started with the discussions on definitions, notations, representation types, and models, continued with the video recordings. Information about the current situation and development of the learner's skills was obtained in this way. In addition, the video-vignettes of a real classroom provided a deep analysis of language skills. The self- and peer-assessment processes using video-based tools allowed their skill development to be monitored and contributed to their skill development by increasing awareness. In an authentic assessment process, feedback should be given at every step after a presentation related to conceptual knowledge and the mathematical language based on that concept (see Lajoie, 1995). Their language use developed this way.

If skill development does not reach the desired level after the self-assessment and poster design, the cycle can be continued by analysing the videos of the group discussions (see Figure 6.7). In addition, emphasising the necessary critical points throughout the process is important. Attention also should be paid to feedback and sharing the results of reports and quizzes. Identifying the source of mistakes and misconceptions is possible in this process. Thus, a teaching sequence based on authentic assessment tasks regarding developing mathematical language skills is proposed in Figure 6.7. This model allows the digital communication of authentic assessment strategies in mathematical language skills to be revealed and the role of these strategies to be examined (see Herrington & Herrington, 1998; Kearney, 2013).

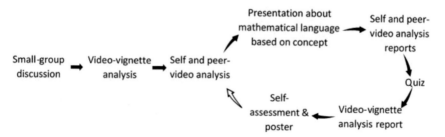

FIGURE 6.7 A model for digital communication authentic assessment strategies in mathematical language skills

6 Moving On

Thus, although no possibility exists for applying one model based on the teaching experiment for every mathematical concept, the components that should be considered in the use of mathematical language can be learned.

The need for arranging something to improve the use of mathematical language based on communication skills in teacher training programs in Turkey (see Toluk-Uçar, 2009; Ünver & Bukova Güzel, 2019; Yeşildere, 2007) has led to the introduction of this model. This model, which has been put forward about the development of mathematical language skills, may be developed by repeating in different cultures and educational policies. In addition, the model can be edited or improved based on the assessment tools in skill development by removing the limitation of the distance learning process. The process can be deepened, and its effects observed by adding self- and peer-assessment tools, as well as other types of tools. Thus, the possibility exists to assess the role of different authentic assessment tools.

This chapter has extensively covered mathematical language skills (see Aktaş & Argün, 2020; Barwell, 2008; Dubinsky, 2000; McGee, 1997; O'Halloran, 2008; Sfard, 2001; Wessel, 2020; Zhe, 2012). The development process of mathematical language skills can be examined in the context of the components under this framework within the discussion of a single theoretical framework. In this way, information about both the order and implementation of assessment tools and concept-oriented detailed language development can be obtained. In situations involving activities with additions, subtractions, multiplications and divisions of fractions, the model can be applied to different mathematical concepts as well. Thus, it will be possible to both include the mathematical language development and to determine the concept-oriented differences.

References

Aktaş, F. N., & Argün, Z. (2020). Examination of mathematical language use of individuals with visual impairment in mathematical communication processes: The role of braille. *Turkish Journal of Computer and Mathematics Education, 11*(1), 128–156.

Albano, G. (2012). A knowledge-skill-competencies e-learning model in mathematics. *RUSC, Universities and Knowledge Society Journal, 9*(1), 306–319.

Argün, Z., Arıkan, A., Bulut, S., & Halıcıoğlu, S. (2014). *Temel matematik kavramların künyesi* [Basic mathematical concepts' tag]. Gazi Kitabevi.

Baki, A., & Çelik, S. (2018). Veri işleme öğrenme alanına yönelik sınıf içindeki söylemlerin matematiksel dil bağlamında incelenmesi. *Turkish Journal of Computer and Mathematics Education, 9*(2), 283–311.

Barter, C., & Renold, E. (1999). The use of vignettes in qualitative research. *Social Research Update (University of Surrey), 25*, 1–6.

Barwell, R. (2008). Discourse, mathematics, and mathematics education. In N. H. Hornberger (Ed.), *Encyclopedia of language and education* (pp. 317–328). Springer.

Bender, T. (2003). *Discussion-based online teaching to enhance student learning*. Stylus.

Brendefur, J., & Frykholm, J. (2000). Promoting mathematical communication in the classroom: Two preservice teachers' conceptions and practices. *Journal of Mathematics Teacher Education, 3*(2), 125–153.

Brenner, M. E. (1998). Development of mathematical communication in problem solving groups by language minority students. *Bilingual Research Journal, 22*(2–4), 149–174.

Carpenter, T. P., Fennema, E., Franke, M. L., Levi, L., & Empson, S. B. (2002). *Cognitively guided instruction: A research-based teacher professional development program for elementary school mathematics*. Wisconsin Center for Education Research. http://www.wcer.wisc.edu/ncisla/publications /index.html

Cobb, P. (1999). Individual and collective mathematical development: The case of statistical data analysis. *Mathematical Thinking and Learning, 1*(1), 5–43. https://doi.org/10.1207/s15327833mtl0101_1

Cobb, P., & Gravemeijer, K. P. E. (2008). Experimenting to support and understand learning process. In A. E. Kelly, R. A. Lesh, & J. Y. Baek (Eds.), *The handbook of design research methods in education: Innovations in science, technology, engineering and mathematics* (pp. 68–95). Lawrence Erlbaum Associates.

Cobb, P., & Steffe L. P. (1983). The constructivist researcher as teacher and model builder. *Journal for Research in Mathematics Education, 14*(2), 83–94.

Conrad, D., & Openo, J. (2018). *Assessment strategies for online learning: Engagement and authenticity*. Athabasca University Press.

Dallimore, E. J., Hertenstein, J. H., & Platt, M. B. (2008). Using discussion pedagogy to enhance oral and written communication skills. *College Teaching, 56*(3), 163–172.

Dede, Y., & Soybas, D. (2011). Preservice mathematics teachers' concept images of polynomials. *Quality & Quantity, 45*(2), 391–402.

Drábeková, J., Pechočiak, T., & Matušek, V. (2018). Mathematical competencies of students entering university studies. Case study of Slovakia. *Mathematics in Education, Research and Applications, 4*(1), 23–30. https://doi.org/10.15414/meraa.2018.04.01.23-30

Dubinsky, E. (2000). Meaning and formalism in mathematics. *International Journal of Computers for Mathematical Learning, 5*(3), 211–240.

Fan L. (2011). Implementing self-assessment to develop reflective teaching and learning in mathematics. In B. Kaur & W. K. Yoong (Eds.), *Assessment in the mathematics classroom: Yearbook 2011* (pp. 275–289). Association of Mathematics Educators.

Ferrari, P. L. (2004). Mathematical language and advanced mathematics learning. In M. Johnsen Hoines & A. Berit Fugelstad (Eds.), *Proceeding of International Group for the Psychology of Mathematics Education XXVII* (Vol. 2, pp. 383–390).

Flottemesch, K. (2000). Building effective interaction in distance education: A review of the literature. *Educational Technology, 40*(3), 46–51.

Frederick, P. J. (1994). Classroom discussions. In K. W. Prichard & R. Mclaran Sawyer (Eds.), *Handbook of college teaching: Theory and applications.* Greenwood Publishing Group.

Fuller, R. (2000). Encouraging self directed learning through poster presentations. In A. Herrmann & M. M. Kulski (Eds.), *Flexible futures in tertiary teaching. Proceedings of the 9th Annual Teaching Learning Forum.* Curtin University of Technology. http://lsn.curtin.edu.au/tlf/tlf2000/fuller.html

Garside, C. (1996). Look who's talking: A comparison of lecture and group discussion teaching strategies in developing critical thinking skills. *Communication Education, 45*(3), 212–227.

Gaytan, J., & McEwen, B. C. (2007). Effective online instructional and assessment strategies. *American Journal of Distance Education, 21*(3), 117–132. https://doi.org/10.1080/08923640701341653

Goldin, G., & Shteingold, N. (2001). Systems of representations and the development of mathematical concepts. In A. A Cuoco (Ed.), *The roles of representation in school mathematics-2001 Yearbook* (pp. 1–23). National Council of Teachers of Mathematics.

Hamann, K., Pollock, P. H., & Wilson, B. M. (2012). Assessing student perceptions of the benefits of discussions in small-group, large-class, and online learning contexts. *College Teaching, 60*(2), 65–75. https://doi.org/10.1080/87567555.2011.633407

Hart, D. (1994). *Authentic assessment.* Addison-Wesley.

Herrington, J., & Herrington, A. (1998). Authentic assessment and multimedia: How university students respond to a model of authentic assessment. *Higher Education Research & Development, 17*(3), 305–322.

Hughes, R. (1998). Considering the vignette technique and its application to a study of drug injecting and HIV risk and safer behaviour. *Sociology of Health and Illness, 20*(3), 381–400.

Jamison, R. E. (2000). Learning the language of mathematics. *Language and Learning across the Disciplines, 4*(1), 45–54.

Kamareddine, F., Maarek, M., & Wells, J. B. (2004). Mathlang: Experience-driven development of a new mathematical language. *Electronic Notes in Theoretical Computer Science, 93*, 138–160.

Kearney, S. (2013). Improving engagement: the use of 'Authentic self-and peer-assessment for learning' to enhance the student learning experience. *Assessment & Evaluation in Higher Education, 38*(7), 875–891.

Keller, J. M. (1997). Motivational design and multimedia: Beyond the novelty effect. *Strategic Human Resource Development Review, 1*(1), 188–203.

Lajoie, S. P. (1995). A framework for authentic assessment in mathematics. In T. A. Romberg (Ed.), *Reform in school mathematics and authentic assessment* (pp. 19–37). State University of New York Press.

Lee, C. (2006). *Language for learning mathematics: assessment for learning in practice.* Open University Press.

Matteson, S. M. (2006). Mathematical literacy and standardized mathematical assessments. *Reading Psychology, 27*(2–3), 205–233. https://doi.org/10.1080/02702710600642491

McGee, V. (1997). How we learn mathematical language. *The Philosophical Review, 106*(1), 35–68.

Messick, S. (1994). The interplay of evidence and consequences in the validation of performance assessments. *Educational Researcher, 23*(2), 13–23.

Ministry of National Education [Milli Eğitim Bakanlığı (MEB)]. (2018). *İlköğretim matematik dersi 5-8. sınıflar öğretim programı* [*Middle school mathematical curriculum for grade 5–8*]. Ankara, Turkey.

Mishra, P., & Close, C. (2020). The value of school. *ECNU Review of Education, 3*(3), 576–583. https://doi.org/10.1177/2096531120926687

Miura, I. T. (2001). The influence of language on mathematical representations. In A. A Cuoco (Ed.), *The roles of representation in school mathematics, 2001 Yearbook* (pp. 53–62). National Council of Teachers of Mathematics.

Mohanty, B. B., & Akalamkam, K. (2012). Reflections on portfolios as means of authentic assessment in a teacher education programme. *The International Journal of Learning, 18*(7), 1–12.

Moore, M. G. (1989). Three types of interaction. *American Journal of Distance Education, 3*(2), 1–6.

Murdoch, G. (1994). Language development provision in teacher training curricula. *ELT Journal, 48*(3), 253–265. https://doi.org/10.1093/elt/48.3.253

National Council of Teachers of Mathematics. (1995). *Assessment standards for school mathematics.* Author.

National Council of Teachers of Mathematics. (2000). *Principles and standards for school mathematics.* Author.

O'Halloran, K. (2008). *Mathematical discourse: Language, symbolism and visual images.* A&C Black.

Orton, S., & Frobisher, L. (1996). *Insights into teaching mathematics.* Cassel.

Oxford Learner Dictionary. (n.d.). Language. In *Oxford learner dictionary*. Retrieved January 1, 2021, from https://www.oxfordlearnersdictionaries.com/definition/english/language?q=language

Parker, A. (1999). Interaction in distance education: The critical conversation. *AACE Journal*, *1*(12), 13–17.

Pierce, L. V., & O'Malley, J. M. (1992). *Performance and portfolio assessment for language minority students* (Program Information Guide Series, Vol. 9). National Clearinghouse for Bilingual Education.

Radford, L. (2002). Algebra as tekhne. Artefacts, symbols and equations in the classroom. *Mediterranean Journal for Research in Mathematics Education*, *1*(1), 31–56.

Riccomini, P. J., Smith, G. W., Hughes, E. M., & Fries, K. M. (2015). The language of mathematics: The importance of teaching and learning mathematical vocabulary. *Reading & Writing Quarterly*, *31*(3), 235–252.

Rubio, N., Font, V., Giménez, J., & Malaspina, U. (2011). Pre-service teachers learning to assess mathematical competencies. In M. Pytlak, T. Rowland, & E. Swoboda (Eds.), *Proceedings of the Seventh Congress of the European Society for Research in Mathematics Education* (pp. 2838–2847). Hal Archives-Ouvertes.

Russell, M., Carey, R., Kleiman, G., & Venable, J. D. (2009). Face-to-face and online professional development for mathematics teachers: A comparative study. *Journal of Asynchronous Learning Networks*, *13*(2), 71–87.

Sfard, A. (2001). There is more to discourse than meets the ears: Looking at thinking as communicating to learn more about mathematical learning. *Educational Studies in Mathematics*, *46*(1–3), 13–57.

Steffe, L. P. (2001). A new hypothesis concerning children's fractional knowledge. *The Journal of Mathematical Behavior*, *20*(3), 267–307. https://doi.org/10.1016/S0732-3123(02)00075-5

Steffe, L. P., & Thompson, P. W. (2000). Teaching experiment methodology: Underlying principles and essential elements. In A. E. Kelly & R. A. Lesh (Eds.), *Handbook of research design in mathematics and science education* (pp. 267–306). Routledge.

Suurtamm, C. A. (2004). Developing authentic assessment: Case studies of secondary school mathematics teachers' experience. *Canadian Journal of Science*, *4*(4), 497–513. http://dx.doi.org/10.1080/14926150409556630

Tall, D. O., & Vinner, S. (1981). Concept image and concept definition in mathematics with particular reference to limits and continuity. *Educational Studies in Mathematics*, *12*(2), 151–169.

Tirosh, D. (2000). Enhancing prospective teachers' knowledge of children's conceptions: The case of division of fractions. *Journal for Research in Mathematics Education*, *31*(1), 5–25.

Toluk-Uçar, Z. (2009). Developing pre-service teachers understanding of fractions through problem posing. *Teaching and Teacher Education*, *25*(1), 166–175. https://doi.org/10.1016/j.tate.2008.08.003

Topping, K. J. (1998). Peer assessment between students in colleges and universities. *Review of Educational Research, 68*(3), 249–276. https://doi.org/10.3102/0034654306800324

Ünver, S. K., & Bukova Güzel, E. (2019). Matematik öğretmeni adaylarının limit öğretimlerindeki matematik dili kullanımları. *Manisa Celal Bayar Üniversitesi Eğitim Fakültesi Dergisi, 7*(1), 12–28.

Vygotsky, L. S. (1994). Extracts from thought and language and mind and society. In B. Stierer & J. Maybin (Eds.), *Language, literacy and learning in educational practice* (pp. 45–58). The Open University.

Wessel, L. (2020). Vocabulary in learning processes towards conceptual understanding of equivalent fractions – specifying students' language demands on the basis of lexical trace analyses. *Mathematics Education Research Journal, 32*(4), 653–681.

Wiggins, G. (1998). Research news and comment: An exchange of views on "Semantics, psychometrics, and assessment reform: A close look at 'authentic' assessments". *Educational Researcher, 27*(6), 20–22.

Yeo, K. K. J. (2011). Implementing alternative assessment in the lower primary mathematics classroom. In B. Kaur & W. K. Yoong (Eds.), *Assessment in the mathematics classroom: Yearbook 2011* (pp. 113–130). Association of Mathematics Educators.

Yeşildere, S. (2007). İlköğretim matematik öğretmen adaylarının matematiksel alan dilini kullanma yeterlikleri. *Boğaziçi Üniversitesi Eğitim Dergisi, 24*(2), 61–70.

Zhe, L. (2012). Survey of primary students' mathematical representation status and study on the teaching model of mathematical representation. *Journal of Mathematics Education, 5*(1), 63–76.

CHAPTER 7

Embedding Authentic Assessment in a Capstone Research Course in a Teacher Education Degree

Tricia McLaughlin, Kathy Littlewood, Belinda Kennedy and Tasos Barkatsas

Abstract

The capstone research course in the Master of Teaching Practice degree at RMIT University is an opportunity for all students to engage in a transformative learning experience based upon student-centred pedagogy. Conducted at the conclusion of the postgraduate degree, the capstone research course allows students to engage in learning through experiential activities and research skills in a comprehensive, intensive project set around key teacher education themes. The course allows students to showcase their knowledge, skills, and abilities in a unique and individualised manner. The assessment is based upon authentic learning principles and aligns with professional teaching capabilities and skills. This chapter outlines the authentic assessments within the Master of Teaching Practice capstone research course in three areas explored by students: international and remote learning; STEM and 21st century learning and cross-disciplinary learning in psychology and education. This chapter demonstrates how assessment was developed around these capstone research course projects in Australian teacher education and the authenticity of such assessment. It illustrates how authentic assessment models were built through collaboration with stakeholders in these areas and differentiated to allow students to develop and display their skills in a unique format. The chapter also provides valuable insights around authentic assessment in capstone research course projects in teacher education and may provide insights for higher education staff regardless of discipline.

Keywords

authentic assessments – teacher education – capstone

1   Introduction

Capstone research courses in teacher education programmes in Australia are generally designed to allow pre-service teaching students opportunities to reflect and synthesise their educational journey, link theory to practice, undertake professional disciplinary research and make real-world connections (Brown & Benson, 2005; Hine, 2013; Jordan et al., 2019). These capstone research courses in teacher education typically result in an end product of a project, case-study analysis, thesis, presentation, report or portfolio for assessment.

Yet whilst there is significant agreement on the need for capstone research courses in teacher education programmes, the disconnect between the research inquiry and actual teaching practice in which graduates will be engaged post-graduation has been highlighted by a number of researchers (Cochran-Smith & Lytle, 1999; Lattimer, 2012; Loughran, 2007; Fulmer & Bodner 2017). This 'disconnect' often means that the capstone experience does not enable the pre-service teacher to develop inquiry, personal growth or reflection skills that will transform their own practice beyond graduation. Even if pre-service teachers pursue a capstone that bridges this disconnect and allows them to develop these skills in their own professional practice, the difficulty for teacher educators is how to assess such skills in an authentic and sustainable way.

Several researchers have noted the challenge of designing authentic assessment that values self-assessment, personal growth and reflection in pre-service teachers' capstone learning (Schlichting & Fox, 2015; Darling-Hammond & Snyder, 2000). How capstone research courses are assessed also indicates to the pre-service teachers how valuable the connection between professional practice and theory is viewed and also how much value is placed upon translational inquiry and reflection skills (Kerrigan & Jhaj, 2007).

This chapter outlines the development of authentic assessments within the Master of Teaching Practice capstone research course in three areas explored by pre-service teachers over a three-year period at RMIT University. The areas examined: international and remote learning; the development of STEM and 21st century learning and cross-disciplinary learning in psychology and education, have been selected to illustrate the flexibility of authentic assessment in capstone research course projects and the relevance of such an assessment in the professional development of graduate teachers. Each of these areas was also a key theme of research by a teacher educator at RMIT University during this period.

Using narrative research, the exploration and description of how authentic assessment was achieved through collaboration with stakeholders in these areas is explained. The differentiation of these assessments to allow pre-service teachers to display their developing professional skills in a unique format is further explained in the detailed description of each area.

2   Authentic Assessment

Authentic assessment is defined as assessment that is contextualised, student-centred and has value for learners beyond the classroom (Boud & Falchikov, 2005; Wiggins, 2006). Authentic assessment relates to activities that enable learners to experience real work-based problems that they may undertake or encounter in their future professional careers. These experiences enable pre-service teachers to take more responsibility for their own learning, while still being supported by their teacher educators. A number of researchers have noted that authentic assessment is a strong measure of a student's skills and knowledge as it relates to specific contexts and is often related to future work skills (Aitken & Pungur, 2005; Lloyd & Davidson, 2005). In addition to relating to the future profession and real-world contexts, there is evidence that authentic assessment allows the learner to extrapolate the lessons learnt through such assessment to their own understanding of the world (Lloyd & Davidson, 2005).

The importance of assessment that requires input, advice, discussion and feedback from others in the same context, such as teaching communities, is also a key feature of authentic assessment. It results in learning that is situated within a socially constructed model requiring participation in a community of others, often peers (Gee, 2001; Sheehy, 2002). In this context, the learner is able to co-construct knowledge through social interaction with others (Aitken & Pungur, 2005). Through this interaction with knowledgeable members of the learning community and the profession, pre-service teachers can learn from and through others while deeply reflecting upon their own learning. Reflective practice is seen as a form of ongoing authentic assessment, which values students' experiences, learning processes, and evidences. It is also viewed in the educational community as a dynamic and socially constructive process. Osterman and Kottkamp (2004) supported the position of reflective practice as dynamic and socially constructive: "reflective practice, while often confused with reflection, is neither a solitary nor a relaxed meditative process, but a challenging, demanding, and often trying process that is most successful as a collaborative effort" (p. 2).

The combination of peer input, advice and professional feedback, combined with reflective practice that in turn will impact upon future practice is the framework for authentic assessment adopted in the Master of Teaching Practice capstone research course at RMIT University.

3   Capstone Research Courses in Teacher Education and Authentic Assessment

Brown and Benson (2005) define a capstone as a culminating performance assessment that allows pre-service teachers to synthesise their learning in order to make meaningful connections that may influence their future performance. Capstone research courses in teacher education programmes in Australia, whilst quite diverse across institutions, are generally designed to allow pre-service teachers students opportunities to reflect and synthesise their educational journey, link theory to practice and make real-world connections (Brown & Benson, 2005). Capstone research course "end-products" are typically a project, case-study analysis, thesis, presentation, or portfolio for assessment. This end product allows teacher educators the opportunity to assess the overall learning of their pre-service teachers, as well as the ability to assess the teacher education program's effectiveness (Berheide, 2007). The impetus and need for such capstone research courses has been noted by a number of researchers (Loughran, 2007; Fulmer & Bodner 2017) who called for teacher education programmes to rethink the nature of research as it relates to practice, and to reassess the role of the teacher in the classroom and in research.

The advantages of a capstone research course in teacher education have been linked to the improvement of both individual practice and overall school/systemic practice; the deeper understanding of one aspect of practice; the discussion of new and topical practice; the building of pedagogical knowledge both for the individual and the profession; the understanding of the profession in issues of equity, social conditions and society; and professional development of the capstone researcher (Zeichner & Noffke, 2001; Yancovic-Allen 2018). In general, it is agreed that capstone research courses provide "refined abilities for connecting educational theory and pedagogical practices to real-world implementation" as well as the knowledge and skills for designing and interpreting research, inquiry and collaboration (White & Forgasz, 2016, p. 38).

Maxwell (2012) has indicated that the strength of using action research and authentic assessment in a pre-service teachers professional programme is that pre-service teachers are creating research-based outcomes to support their own work and at the same time learning the discourse of research-based outcomes that impact upon their understanding of the complexity of their profession and potential ways to improve it. In this way such capstone research course projects can see pre-service teachers contributing to the outcomes of the profession. Graduate teachers are expected by the profession to act as agents of change, becoming innovators in their profession, continually open to growth, inquiry, and research. As a result, monitoring and "testing one's knowledge in the context of the discipline" is fundamental to the foundation of authentic assessment (Wiggins, 2006, p. 41). Yancovic-Allen (2018) has even suggested that capstone research course action research as an avenue of combining teaching and research with authentic assessment approaches, has the potential to foster future improved teaching and an interest in teaching.

Yet whilst the linking of professional or personal growth and "real-world" or authentic teaching practice through a capstone research course is often an intended outcome in the inclusion of capstone research courses in teacher education degrees, this linkage may not always be achieved. Sanford and Hopper (2010) noted that "too often teacher education capstone programs promote fragmentation, maintenance of a theory-practice divide, and research that does not connect to the real world of schooling" (p. 90). This failure to connect capstone research with authentic professional practice has also been accredited to an over emphasis upon curriculum-based teacher education preparation to the exclusion of higher order research skills in many programmes. Vaughan, Beers and Burnaford (2015) noted that critical, participative inquiry approaches of traditional higher education action research are not pervasive in teacher education programmes, and suggest this may be due to the political and social pressure exerted on colleges of education to adhere to standards-based teacher preparation that is aligned with kindergarten–12 school goals.

Whilst it is widely agreed that capstone research courses can provide links between theory and professional practice in teaching, the need for greater emphasis upon authentic inquiry and reflection of inquiry to lead to transformed practice is also required. Fulmer and Bodner (2017) have identified the core tensions of capstones in pre-service teacher education as the unsustainability of the academic requirements of the capstone research course beyond graduation and into practice and the disconnect between the research inquiry and actual teaching practice in which graduates will be engaged. They note: "these tensions are likely to dissuade beginning teacher-researchers from further cultivating an inquiry stance once their program requirements have been met" (Fulmer & Bodner, 2017, p.11).

If this linkage is to be achieved, then the need for transformed teacher research capstones that are rooted in practitioner inquiry must be characterised by authentic assessment and strengthened by reflective pedagogy (Loughran, 2007). Several researchers have called for the establishment of sustainable research inquiry practices and authentic assessment approaches so that both the pre-service teachers and practising teachers can easily draw upon the outcomes and improve pedagogy (Beck, 2017; Massey et al., 2009). As Darling-Hammond and Synder (2000) noted, the use of authentic assessment practices in teacher education, including capstone research course research projects, appears to hold potential for influencing the learning of pre-service teachers and thereby the learning opportunities of their future students.

Whilst the challenge for pre-service teachers is the capacity to devise and conduct research that is inquiry-based, links with current teaching pedagogy, can be translated to their own professional development and practice, and provides evidence for the profession, the challenge for teacher educators is the authentic assessment to accompany these capstone research courses. Grahe (2018) has proposed that teacher educators should consider including their students in meta-projects so that students' data has a bigger impact, a greater understanding of the contemporary issues in the profession and provide opportunities for impact through publication, thus avenues for authentic assessment by peers. Fulmer and Bodner (2017) have further suggested inviting practicing K-12 teachers to be research guides; and transforming expectations from an academia-oriented paper to participation in a network of teacher researchers.

This chapter explores some of these challenges and opportunities through examining the development of authentic assessments within the Master of Teaching Practice capstone research course projects for three pedagogical areas explored by students over a five-year period:
– Global education and remote learning and teaching
– Cross disciplinary collaborative learning
– STEM and 21st century skills

4 Theoretical Framework

Narrative is a theory of research and methodological approach that enables researchers to look into professional experiences and in turn trace out possible constructions and changes in their identities as professionals and their own trajectories (Ntinda & Bidwell, 2018; Dickie, 2000). Narrative research is increasingly used in fields of education to identify and communicate (Rhodes & Brown, 2005; Atkinson & Delamont, 2006; Spector-Mersel, 2010). Bruner and Austin (1986) revealed that narrative is a fundamental aspect of humans' sense making, thus the narration of story can work to bridge individual understanding to understanding of larger society. Kim and Latta (2009) noted that finding connections between and among examples is an educative process.

Ponte and Santos (2005) support this position of narrative research by noting that teachers as professionals are assumed to be able to construct their own knowledge about the causes and consequences of their actions to give answers to specific practical problems and questions, and to provide evidence of what works in practice and why. Expanding upon this position, this chapter uses a narrative framework as both an opportunity to illustrate and to present the Master of Teaching Practice capstone research course projects at RMIT University as a resource and an enabler that allows other readers to examine their own practice and thus develop new practice. Through this process, this chapter contributes to an expanding knowledge of possibilities for teacher educators engaged with pre-service teachers in capstone research and authentic assessment.

5   The Master of Teaching Practice Capstone Research Course at RMIT University

The capstone research course in the Master of Teaching Practice at RMIT University is a 12-credit point course conducted over one semester in the final stages of the 24 month postgraduate teaching degree. The course is preceded by a compulsory semester-long course in research methods and inquiry approaches.

The capstone research course allows pre-service teachers to engage in learning through experiential activities and research skills in a comprehensive, intensive project set around a teacher education theme. The capstone research course also allows pre-service teachers to showcase their knowledge, skills, and abilities in a unique and individualised manner. Pre-service teachers are free to plan and construct their own teacher education investigation or connect with one of the three themes currently offered by teacher educators at RMIT University: global education and remote teaching; STEM and 21st century skills; and cross-disciplinary collaborative education. Each pre-service teacher has opportunities for group learning and one to one mentoring and research supervision during the course.

The assessment of the capstone research course is based upon authentic learning principles and aligns with professional teaching capabilities and skills. The next section discusses three of the main projects that have been explored by significant numbers of pre-service teachers over the last three years and examines the authentic assessment involved in each area. The following projects areas were explored:
i.   Global education and remote learning
ii. Cross-disciplinary collaborative learning
iii. STEM and 21st century skills

5.1 Global Education and Remote Learning and Teaching

Australian universities in recent years have seen increased student interest in skills that evidence graduate capacity in global contexts. Schech et al. (2017) have found that higher education institutions often attempt to anticipate the future skills needed beyond a university degree by providing global learning opportunities within study programmes, and that many promote global experiences that will directly assist in developing a diverse range of employability skills such as communication, teamwork, cultural empathy and 21st century skills.

Given the diversity of the national landscape and the remoteness of many indigenous and small mining and farming communities, Australian pre-service teachers need opportunities to experience educational provision in remote and rural regions. As many graduates often commence their teaching careers in these settings within Australia and surrounding island nations, providing experiences in teaching within these remote communities, especially indigenous and isolated communities is an important element of pre-service teacher education and skills development. Pre-service teachers also increasingly understand that as well as 'looking good on the resume' such experiences also provide evidence of teaching in and understanding remote communities, personal growth and satisfaction, cultural empathy and cultural capital along with unique global perspectives (Miller & Gonzalez, 2016; Schech et al., 2017). Graduates who acquire international educational knowledge and global teaching experience are highly competitive in the current and future job market (Knutson Miller & Gonzalez, 2016).

In 2015, RMIT University commenced the Yasawa Islands (Fiji) Water Sanitation Project, which provided opportunities for pre-service teachers to work on the remote islands of Yasawa Islands in Fiji. Whilst COVID-19 has limited opportunities to participate in physical exchanges in remote and indigenous communities in the recent past, the Yasawa Islands (Fiji) Water Sanitation Project has been conducted over the previous five years with the active involvement of 24 Master of Teaching Practice pre-service teachers who have selected a research capstone project within this area. The Yasawa Project draws heavily upon principles of authentic assessment and learner reflection. This has included professional development projects with teachers on Yasawa islands, teaching and remote education, and health ecosystem research projects alongside other RMIT University's multidisciplinary teams.

Pre-service teachers spend five weeks pre-visit undertaking cultural awareness programmes and readiness activities for remote teaching and professional practice skills as well as research inquiry skills. They are then assigned a teacher/school and contact on the Yasawa islands. Over this time the pre-service teacher undertakes the co-design of a capstone project that addresses local challenges and incorporates evidence collected locally from village schools and staff. The capstone research project is co-created with the professional teacher contact and thus the local communities. The pre-visit work provides professional development for local teachers, gives pre-service teachers insights into the use of evidence-based teaching and allows for the development of sustainable peer relationships. Pre-service teachers then visit the Yasawa communities where they are based until the completion of their projects – normally between two and four weeks.

Over the past three years, more than 24 pre-service teachers have completed capstone projects in a range of authentic areas through the Yasawa island project. These include projects that: research and build innovative pedagogy suited to remote learning in complex conditions; measure and analyse educational resources; analyse student data and research suitable pedagogy; record and track student and school performance across disciplines and key indicators; develop, research, co-design and teach in community (village) schools; and build educational links to new professional development projects. The pre-service teachers form new collaborations with an ever-expanding group of village communities and local teachers, supported by a strong steering group of RMIT University academics and industry partners. In all cases, the pre-service teachers live in the village communities for the duration of their time on the islands.

There are two key pieces of authentic assessment. The first piece is the feedback from Yasawa island teachers, principals and schools on the capstone project itself and its capacity to meet the needs of remote, complex village education and improve teaching and learning in the islands. The feedback from local teachers is based upon the outcomes set for each of the individual capstone projects at the beginning of the capstone through the co-design process and may or may not include classroom teaching by the pre-service teachers. The second piece of assessment is the pre-service teacher's reflection on their work and their professional development, their acquired and transferrable skills and their personal reflections on their experiences of the capstone. This can be presented in any format, but is normally a written piece of work built during the capstone, but finalised upon return to Australia.

The first piece of assessment provides links and a connection between the practice of the profession and the research capstone. Through the co-design with village teachers and principals, it reflects a connection between the research inquiry and actual teaching practice in which many graduates will be engaged post-graduation (Fulmer & Bodner, 2017). The assessment links pre-service teachers into a meta-project from which wider impacts upon both

Yasawa students and schools can be measured and illustrated (Grahe, 2018), thus enabling their understanding of research inquiry and its impact upon society. By using current teachers and principals as communities of professional practice in which to design and conduct their research, the pre-service teachers also engage in sustainable research that benefits the wider sector (Beck, 2017; Massey et al., 2009). As the capstone projects are evaluated by their peers in the profession, the opportunities to monitor and test their knowledge in the context of the discipline, which Wiggins (2006) notes as fundamental to the foundation of authentic assessment, is clear. Pre-service teachers constantly adjust and manage their research projects in light of this feedback, so that the assessments are both dynamic and ongoing. This in turn fosters an interest in teaching research, which Yancovic-Allen (2017) has suggested provides an avenue of combining teaching and research with authentic approaches and creates improved teaching and an interest in teaching in remote contexts.

An important part of authentic assessment used in these capstone projects is the second piece of assessment – the reflective reports prepared by the pre-service teachers. In these reports pre-service teachers evaluate their own work seeking to understand their motives and rationales as well as their practice, and taking from the assessment, the capacity to improve upon their work as it relates to remote teaching and learning. Bailey (2012) called this "a stance toward educational professionalism" and it underlines the importance of the authenticity of the assessments.

5.2 *Cross-Disciplinary Collaborative Learning*

The cross-disciplinary collaborative project undertaken by the Master of Teaching Practice pre-service teachers from the School of Education, together with the Master of Clinical Psychology pre-service teachers students from the School of Health Sciences at RMIT University also exemplifies this approach of authentic assessment. The project occurred as a response to the COVID lockdown in Melbourne, in 2020. Pre-service teachers were tasked with creating content targeted at the undergraduate student population, to be incorporated in a series of short wellbeing webinars related to mental health and wellbeing. The aim of the webinars was to provide useful tools that undergraduate pre-service teachers could relate to in an appropriate and accessible mode during lockdown.

This project was initiated by the RMIT University's Mental Health and Wellbeing Team with an invitation for the education and psychology pre-service teachers students to participate, as each group was viewed as being able to bring certain strengths to the work. This collaborative, authentic assessment brought together the mental health expertise of the clinical psychology pre-service students with the educational expertise of the teaching pre-service teachers. It provided a cross-curricular vehicle for expert knowledge to be shared and for the pre-service teachers to achieve the important understandings, attitudes and skills identified through the course learning outcomes of both the Master of Teaching Practice and the Master of Clinical Psychology programs.

The decision to use an authentic assessment process was driven partly by the COVID-19 situation. The lockdown led to a rethinking of the traditional assessments previously used that relied on pre-service teachers being in face-to-face learning environments. It was decided by the staff involved, that the assessment would be as authentic as possible and for the pre-service teachers to create real tools that were to be used within the university. Rutherford and Slade (2018) noted that pre-service teachers value authentic assessment highly and it is believed to "encourage them to engage in deeper and more productive learning" (p. 4). The assessment was planned using a backward design process (Wiggins & McTighe, 2005), by firstly considering what the desired outcome should be (the health promotion webinar), secondly determining the assessment evidence (the development of the skills and knowledge to plan, research, present and evaluate a health webinar) and finally the planning of the learning experiences and instruction (supporting the pre-service teachers to achieve the desired results).

Each pre-service teacher was provided with the opportunity to select from set topics in the area that most interested them, as personal motivation and interest was viewed as an important factor in this assessment process. Staff then allocated students via their preferences, into groups that consisted of approximately half education and half psychology students. The topic areas were:
- Enhancing Positive Wellbeing
- Staying Connected: Managing Isolation and Loneliness
- Being Kind to Yourself
- Social Media and You

Online information sessions were conducted by academic staff from both behavioural sciences and education to set the parameters for the projects, and to familiarise pre-service teachers with the World Health Organisation principles of health promotion. Additionally, pre-service teachers were shown a range of health promotion webinars that provided quality work exemplars by which they would be able to make formative judgements about their own work. Pre-service teachers were encouraged to develop the topics in a way that captured their respective expertise and their own real experiences of being students during lockdown.

Pre-service teachers were not able to meet and work face-to-face, so online mechanisms such as Zoom meetings were employed to facilitate the groups to meet. Pre-service teachers worked together to plan, deliver, and evaluate their webinars and were encouraged to research their selected areas to make use of existing wellbeing resources, as well as create new material where needed. The webinar development made use of free online tools. Pre-service teachers had different levels of expertise in using these tools but worked collaboratively to develop the skills required to produce interactive webinars that contained well-researched and pertinent content that was accessible and engaging for the target audience.

Pre-service teachers had eight weeks in which to develop their webinars. During this time, they met periodically with teachers to present work updates related to project milestones, and to talk through any successes or difficulties they were having. This process provided valuable formative feedback to pre-service teachers and enabled them to be aware of the "student progress towards the learning outcomes" (Rutherford & Slade, 2018, p. 5) as well to support learning by adjusting instruction if required. This enabled the learning environment to be flexible and responsive to individual and group needs and resulted in enhanced learning about developing an authentic and useful webinar product and about working as a member of a cross-curricular diverse team.

The groups formally presented their work to their teachers and class peers in the last two weeks of the course. Verbal and written feedback was provided by teachers at the end of each presentation against set criteria related to course learning outcomes. An advantage of authentic assessment is that "both the process and the final product are important for measuring student performance" (Rutherford & Slade, 2018, p.4). Accordingly, pre-service teachers also undertook self-assessments related to working as part of a group and were required to produce an individual, teacher assessed project report which identified the following:

- The process by which they went about the task
- Planning and evaluation of the webinar
- Group collaboration
- Reflections on the task

When compared to more traditional forms of assessment such as individual essays, multiple choice or standardised tests, the authentic assessment undertaken in this collaborative cross curricular project approach, demonstrated an increased level of student responsibility with less extensive summative feedback required by the teachers (Villarroel et al., 2018). Pre-service teachers were able to make judgements about their work against the exemplars they had been shown early in the process, which provided them with the ability to self-generate formative feedback. As a result, the pre-service teachers were able to recognise the elements of a quality webinar and were able to make the appropriate reflective judgments to improve the quality of their webinars in an ongoing manner (Loughran, 2007; Bailey, 2012). These skills are not only important attributes of lifelong learners but are highly sought-after employability skills.

5.3 STEM and 21st Century Skills

The term 21st century skills refers to a set of knowledge, skills, work habits and character traits that are critically important to success in today and tomorrow's world and workplaces (Siekmann & Korble, 2016; Binkley et al., 2012). Deloitte (2015) and West (2012) noted the intrinsic overlap between 21st century skills and STEM (science, technology, engineering and maths) skills, and provide evidence that employment success across a wide range of current and future industries is related to 21st century STEM ways of thinking such as analytical skills; logical and critical thinking; systematic, structured understandings; evaluative approaches; independent reasoning with sceptical and evidence-based rational approaches to problem solving and innovative, creative and lateral solutions. West (2012) described 21st century skills as knowledge, skills and ways of thinking so that graduates can function in a "STEM-core" world.

As nations strive to reform the delivery and relevance of STEM and 21st century skill education, an ongoing challenge is addressing the under-representation of particular groups, particularly females and low socio-economic students. There is evidence to indicate the engagement, participation and performance of females in STEM is in decline both at tertiary and senior secondary levels of education (Kennedy, Lyons, & Quinn, 2014; Timms et al., 2018). As noted by several researchers in this field, without a diverse female-targeted STEM pipeline attempts to change this situation will be marginal (Marginson et al., 2013; Watt, 2016). A pipeline implies a flow of engaged students in primary schools leading to participation of students in secondary STEM subjects.

In response to this "pipeline" effect, in 2016 RMIT University commenced the STEM in-situ project. The project was a nationally funded Australian Government outreach initiative which introduced 221 female students aged between 11 and 16 years (grades/years 5–9) from regional schools, to STEM workshops in technology-rich facilities at RMIT University. The female students came from twelve schools in the northern and western suburbs of Melbourne, a major city in Australia, up to 25 kilometres distance from the university. Emphasising STEM skills in creativity, design, entrepreneurship, problem solving, adaptive thinking, digital literacy and technology-confidence, the project attempted to build the students' STEM self-identity, interest and capacity. Over four workshop days per school term (totalling sixteen days) the schoolgirls explored STEM skills and knowledge across many industries as diverse as: fashion, virtual reality, additive manufacturing, nanotechnology and robotics; in emerging growth industries; and in entrepreneurial opportunities. This involved interactive talks and maker workshops. The schoolgirls were led in these workshops by pre-service teachers who had spent time in the regional schools planning the workshops and mapping the workshops to the needs of the cohort under the mentoring of the local teachers. Within the workshops, the female students were in groups of mixed ages, abilities and under the tutoring of the pre-service teachers. Post workshops, the pre-service teachers returned to the regional schools to co-produce workshop-related outcomes such as displays, parent evenings, projects or ongoing exhibitions.

There were two pieces of authentic assessment within this project: the workshop response sheets completed by the schoolgirls at the end of each workshop day and the pre-service teachers reflective diary. The first workshop response sheet was distributed to each schoolgirl upon completion of the workshop day and asked the individual schoolgirl to rate their understandings of STEM skills, the workshop, the guidance provided by the pre-service teachers and other general questions about the workshop and STEM knowledge. The aim of the response sheet was to indicate to the schoolgirls and the workshop organisers areas of concern, requirements for change or greater emphasis, skill development by the schoolgirls and leadership and professional skill development by the pre-service teachers. As the response sheets were completed by the end-users, the pre-service teachers had a chance to read timely feedback (Wiggins, 2006), reflect upon their pedagogy and pedagogical approaches especially in STEM (Loughran, 2007; Beck, 2017) and improve their professional capacity (Darling-Hammond & Snyder, 2000). A distinct feature of the response sheet feedback was that the pre-service teachers also had opportunities to discuss the outcomes and responses in a professional peer community, which is added to their own identity as professionals in the discipline of teaching, but also built their self-identity as teachers (Fulmer & Bodner, 2017).

The second piece of assessment was the pre-service teachers reflective diary, in which their interactions with the workshop design, development and relationship to STEM curricular was detailed, along with their reflections on their teaching performance pre and post workshop. If, as Maxwell (2012) has indicated, the learning of the discourse of action research-based outcomes that impact upon their understanding of the complexity of their profession and potential ways to improve it is required, then the pre-service teachers reflective diary provided such an opportunity. In addition, it served to remind the student of their own pedagogical practice and the challenges and successes of their place in that professional growth. At the conclusion of the workshops and the school visits, the pre-service teachers were able to present their work in a visual or written format highlighting their own growth in linking 21st century skills and STEM to their future practice. The assessment also links pre-service teachers into a meta-project from which wider impacts upon the schoolgirls and schools can be measured and illustrated (Grahe, 2018), thus enabling their understanding of research inquiry and its impact upon society. By using current teachers and current schoolgirls as communities of professional practice in which to design and conduct their research, the pre-service teachers also engage in sustainable research that benefits the wider sector (Beck, 2017; Massey et al., 2009). This approach of monitoring and "testing one's knowledge in the context of the discipline" (Wiggins, 2006 p. 41) is fundamental to the foundation of authentic assessment.

6 Conclusion

Whilst each of these projects have been fundamentally different in context and learner cohort, the narrative methodological approach enables the detailed examination of these professional experiences and allows possible constructions by the reader (Ntinda & Bidwell, 2018). This examination reveals there are a number of key features that are common to all of the project areas. It is these features, supported by contemporary literature and theory on authentic assessment that have contributed to the authenticity of the student assessments within these projects. These key features included:
- Input into the design and research practice by local practising teachers and other stakeholders across disciplines
- Support by teacher educators and professional peers who were involved in the wider research project
- Opportunities for collaboration and testing of research pedagogy in "real world" teaching environments/contexts
- Development of professional knowledge based upon both action research and reflective practice

These projects illustrate how assessment work can be a strong measure of a student's skills and knowledge as it relates to specific contexts and relates to future work skills (Aitken & Pungur, 2005), thus illustrating the authenticity of the tasks. In addition to relating to the future profession and real-world contexts, the authentic assessments in these contexts allowed the pre-service teachers students to extrapolate the lessons learnt through such assessment to their own understanding of the world (Lloyd & Davidson, 2005).

The learning in each of the contexts required input, advice, discussion and feedback from others in the teaching communities, which is a key feature of authentic assessment (Sheehy, 2002; Yancovic-Allen, 2018). The assessments were situated within a socially constructed model requiring participation in a community of peers (Gee, 2001); allowed for reflective pedagogy (Loughran, 2007); and allowed for feedback and evaluation from other practising professionals such as teachers, teacher educators or psychologists (Fulmer & Bodner, 2017).

This chapter also illustrated the authentic assessments in three areas explored by students within the Master of Teaching Practice capstone research course at RMIT University: global education and remote learning and teaching; STEM and 21st century skills and cross-disciplinary collaborative learning. The authors have provided insights into the assessment tasks developed around these capstone research course projects and the authenticity of such assessment tasks. In this chapter it has also been illustrated how authentic assessment models were built with stakeholders in these areas and differentiated to allow students to develop and display their skills in a unique format.

Finally, in this chapter insights around authentic assessment in capstone research course projects in teacher education have been provided, which illustrate how the use of authentic assessment practices in teacher education capstone research courses has the potential to improve the learning and professional identity of pre-service teachers students and thereby the learning opportunities of their future students.

References

Aitken, N., & Pungur, L. (2005). *Literature synopsis: Authentic assessment.* http://education.alberta.ca/apps/aisi/literature/pdfs/Authentic_Assessment_UofAb_UofL.PDF

Atkinson, P., & Delamont, S. (2006). Rescuing narrative from qualitative research. *Narrative Inquiry, 16*(1), 164–172. https://doi.org/10.1075/ni.16.1.21atk

Bailey, M. T. (2012). *The relationship between secondary school teacher perceptions of grading practices and secondary school teacher perceptions of student motivation.* https://irl.umsl.edu/cgi/viewcontent.cgi?article=1375&context=dissertation

Beck, C. (2017). Informal action research: The nature and contribution of everyday classroom inquiry. In L. L. Rowell, C. D. Bruce, J. M. Shosh, & M. M. Riel (Eds.), *The Palgrave international handbook of action research* (pp. 37–48). Palgrave Macmillan. https://onlinelibrary.wiley.com/doi/book/10.1002/9781119399490

Berheide, C. W. (2007). Doing less work, collecting better data: Using capstone courses to assess learning. *Peer Review, 9*(2), 27–30. https://tomprof.stanford.edu/posting/821

Binkley, M., Erstad, O., Herman, J., Raizen, S., Ripley, M., Miller-Ricci, M., & Rumble, M. (2012). Defining twenty-first century skills. In P. Griffin, B. McGaw, & E. Care (Eds.), *Assessment and teaching of 21st century skills* (pp. 17–66). Springer. http://dx.doi.org/10.1007/978-94-007-2324-5_2

Boud, D., & Falchikov, N. (2005). Redesigning assessment for learning beyond higher education. *Research and Development in Higher Education, 28* (Special issue), 34–41.

Brown, A. H., & Benson, B. (2005). Making sense of the capstone process: Reflections from the front line. *Education, 125*(4).

Bruner, J. S., & Austin, G. A. (1986). *A study of thinking*. Transaction Publishers. https://researchers.mq.edu.au/en/publications/a-study-of-thinking

Cochran-Smith, M., & Lytle, S. L. (1999). Chapter 8: Relationships of knowledge and practice: Teacher learning in communities. *Review of Research in Education, 24*(1), 249–305. doi:10.3102/0091732X024001249

Darling-Hammond, L., & Snyder, J. (2000). Authentic assessment of teaching in context. *Teaching and Teacher Education, 16*(5–6), 523–545. http://www.brjonesphd.com/uploads/1/6/9/4/16946150/authentic_assessment.pdf

Deloitte. (2015). *Mind the gaps: The 2015 Deloitte Millennial Survey*. Retrieved January 30, 2021, from https://www2.deloitte.com/content/dam/Deloitte/global/Documents/About-Deloitte/gx-wef-2015-millennial-survey-executivesummary.pdf

Dickie, V. (2000). Narratives in education and practice. *American Journal of Occupational Therapy, 54*(2), 227–229. doi:10.5014/ajot.54.2.227

Fulmer, E. F., & Bodner, J. (2017). Detached and unsustainable: Central tensions in teacher research capstones and the possibilities for reimagined inquiry. *i.e.: Inquiry in Education, 9*(2), 5. https://digitalcommons.nl.edu/ie/vol9/iss2/5

Gee, J. P. (2001). Reading as situated language: A sociocognitive perspective. *Journal of Adolescent & Adult Literacy, 44*(8), 714–725. https://www.jstor.org/stable/40018744

Grahe, J. (2018). Another step towards scientific transparency: Requiring research materials for publication. *The Journal of Social Psychology, 158*(1), 1–6. https://doi.org/10.1080/00224545.2018.1416272

Hine, G. S. (2013). The importance of action research in teacher education programs. *Issues in Educational Research, 23*(2), 151–163. http://www.iier.org.au/iier23/hine.html

Jordan, K., Littlewood, K., Kennedy, B., & McLaughlin, P. (2019). Tracking graduate teacher preparedness through a national capstone assessment. In B. Tynan, T. McLaughlin, A. Chester, C. Hall-van den Elsen, & B. Kennedy (Eds.), *Transformations in tertiary education*. Springer. https://doi-org.ezproxy.lib.rmit.edu.au/10.1007/978-981-13-9957-2_14

Kerrigan, S., & Jhaj, S. (2007). Assessing general education capstone courses: An in-depth look at a nationally recognized capstone assessment model. *Peer Review, 9*(2), 13. https://phobos.ramapo.edu/~vasishth/Assessing%20Learning%20Outcomes/Kerrigan+GE_Capstones+Assessment.pdf

Kim, J. H., & Latta, M. M. (2009). Narrative inquiry: Seeking relations as modes of interactions. *The Journal of Educational Research, 103*(2), 69–71. https://doi.org/10.1080/00220670903323164

Knutson Miller, K., & Gonzalez, A. M. (2016). Short-term international internship experiences for future teachers and other child development professionals. *Issues in Educational Research, 26*(2), 241. http://www.iier.org.au/iier26/knutson-miller.pdf

Lattimer, H. (2012). Action research in pre-service teacher education: Is there value added? *i.e.: Inquiry in Education, 3*(1), Article 5. http://digitalcommons.nl.edu/ie/vol3/iss1/5

Lloyd, D., & Davidson, P. (2005). *Task-based integrated-skills assessment. The fundamentals of language assessment: A practical guide for teachers in the Gulf* (pp. 157–166). TESOL Arabia.

Loughran, J. (2007). Researching teacher education practices: Responding to the challenges, demands, and expectations of self-study. *Journal of Teacher Education, 58*(1), 12–20. https://doi.org/10.1177%2F0022487106296217

Kennedy, J., Lyons, T., & Quinn, F. (2014). The continuing decline of science and mathematics enrolments in Australian high schools. *Teaching Science, 60*(2), 34. https://eprints.qut.edu.au/73153/1/Continuing_decline_of_science_proof.pdf

Marginson, S., Tytler, R., Freeman, B., & Roberts, K. (2013). *STEM: Country comparisons: International comparisons of Science, Technology, Engineering and Mathematics (STEM) education.* Final report. Melbourne, Australia: Australia Academy of Learned Academies (ACOLA). https://acola.org.au/wp/PDF/SAF02Consultants/SAF02_STEM_%20FINAL.pdf

Massey, D. D., Allred, M., Baber, P., Lowe, J., Ormond, A., & Weatherly, J. (2009). Teacher research: Who is it for and what is the point? *Journal of Curriculum and Instruction, 3*(1), 47–61.

Maxwell, J. A. (2012). *Qualitative research design: An interactive approach.* Sage Publications.

Miller, K., & Gonzalez, A. (2016). Short-term international internship experiences for future teachers and other child development professionals. *Issues in Educational Research, 26*, 241–259.

Ntinda, M. N., & Bidwell, N. J. (2018, December). Solo or peers: Technology mediated learning of programming. In Winschiers-Theophilus, H., van Zyl, I., Goagoses, N., Singh Jat, D., Belay, E. G., Orji, R., & Peters, A. (Eds.), *Proceedings of the second African conference for human computer interaction: Thriving communities* (pp. 1–4). Association for Computing Machinery New York, NY, United States. https://doi.org/10.1145/3283458.3283473

Osterman, K. F., & Kottkamp, R. B. (2004). *Reflective practice for educators: Professional development to improve student learning.* Corwin Press.

Ponte, J. P. D., & Santos, L. (2005). A distance in-service teacher education setting focused on mathematics investigations: The role of reflection and collaboration. *Interactive Educational Multimedia*, 104–126. https://core.ac.uk/download/pdf/39131057.pdf

Rhodes, C., & Brown, A. D. (2005). Narrative, organizations and research. *International Journal of Management Reviews, 7*(3), 167–188. https://doi.org/10.1111/j.1468-2370.2005.00112.x

Rutherford, P., & Slade, C. (2018, November 23). *Authentic assessment at the University of Queensland: A scoping paper*. Institute for Teaching and Learning Innovation. https://itali.uq.edu.au/files/4529/AuthenticAssessment%40UQscoping_paper_v1_0.pdf

Sanford, K., & Hopper, T. (2010). ePortfolio for development of teaching identity: Identifying learning stages. In S. Ravet (Ed.), *Learning Forum London 2010 proceedings* (pp. 90–97). ElfEL (Extensible library for finite element programming). https://epic.openrecognition.org/wp-content/uploads/sites/6/2018/02/LFL-2010-2.pdf#page=90

Schech, S., Kelton, M., Carati, C., & Kingsmill, V. (2017). Simulating the global workplace for graduate employability. *Higher Education Research & Development, 36*(7), 1476–1489. https://doi.org/10.1080/07294360.2017.1325856

Schlichting, K., & Fox, K. R. (2015). An authentic assessment at the graduate level: A reflective capstone experience. *Teaching Education, 26*(3), 310–324. https://doi.org/10.1080/10476210.2014.996748

Sheehy, M. (2002). Illuminating constructivism: Structure, discourse, and subjectivity in a middle school classroom. *Reading Research Quarterly, 37*(3), 278–308. https://doi.org/10.1598/RRQ.37.3.2

Siekmann, G., & Korbel, P. (2016). *Defining 'STEM' skills: Review and synthesis of the literature – support document 1*. NCVER. http://www.ncvre.edu.au

Spector-Mersel, G. (2010). Narrative research: Time for a paradigm. *Narrative inquiry, 20*(1), 204–224. https://www.jbe-platform.com/content/journals/15699935

Szecsi, T., Gunnels, C., Greene, J., Johnston, V., & Vazquez-Montilla, E. (2019). Teaching and evaluating skills for undergraduate research in the teacher education program. *Scholarship and Practice of Undergraduate Research, 3*(1), 20–29. doi:10.18833/spur/3/1/5

Timms, M. J., Moyle, K., Weldon, P. R., & Mitchell, P. (2018). *Challenges in STEM learning in Australian schools: Literature and policy review*. Australian Council for Educational Research (ACER). https://research.acer.edu.au/policy_analysis_misc/28

Vaughan, M., Beers, C., & Burnaford, G. (2015). The impact of iPads on teacher educator practice: A collaborative professional development initiative. *International Journal of Technology in Teaching and Learning, 11*(1), 21–34. https://files.eric.ed.gov/fulltext/EJ1213362.pdf

Villarroel, V., Bloxham, S., Bruna, D., Bruna, C., & Herrera-Seda, C. (2018). Authentic assessment: Creating a blueprint for course design. *Assessment & Evaluation in Higher Education, 43*(5), 840–854. https://doi.org/10.1080/02602938.2017.1412396

Watt, H. (2016, August 8). *Promoting girls' and boys' engagement and participation in senior secondary STEM fields and occupational aspirations* [Paper presentation]. Research Conference 2016 - Improving STEM Learning : What will it take? https://research.acer.edu.au/research_conference/RC2016/8august/9

West, M. (2012). *Mobile learning for teachers: Global themes.* UNESCO Working Paper Series on Mobile Learning. http://www.unesco.org/new/en/unesco/themes/icts/m4ed .

White, S., & Forgasz, R. (2016). The practicum: The place of experience? In J. Loughran & M. Hamilton (Eds.), *International handbook of teacher education.* Springer. https://link.springer.com/chapter/10.1007/978-981-10-0366-0_6

Wiggins, G. (2006). Healthier testing made easy: The idea of authentic assessment. *Edutopia Magazine.* https://www.edutopia.org/authentic-assessment-grant-wiggins

Wiggins, G., & McTighe, J. (2005). *Understanding by design* (2e). Association for Supervision and Curriculum Development (ASCD).

Yancovic-Allen, M. (2018). Pre-service elementary teachers' perceptions of conducting and consuming research in their future professional practice. *Teachers and Teaching, 24*(5), 487–499. https://doi.org/10.1080/13540602.2018.1438389

Zeichner, K. M., & Noffke, S. (2001). Practitioner research. In V. Richardson (Ed.), *Handbook of research on teaching* (4th ed., pp. 298–330). American Educational Research Association.

CHAPTER 8

Making It Happen

A Case Study of Authentic Assessment for Learning in a Final Year Capstone Course

Gráinne Ryan and Dallas Wingrove

Abstract

Capstones are well recognised as a culminating and integrating experience in higher education creating important opportunities for students to engage in authentic and transformative learning. Authentic learning and assessment is undeniably critical to effective capstone course design and teaching, and to education more broadly. This chapter presents a unique case study of authentic assessment in a capstone course which encompasses innovative, industry relevant assessment and learning approaches and practices. We draw upon our professional learning partnership to reflect upon and analyse our experiences in designing and, in the case of the first author, teaching a final year capstone course in Construction Management. The first author works as an industry fellow and early career educator within a Built Environment Faculty where the second author worked as Academic Developer. We situate our study in the literature to identify the particular characteristics of course design and assessment, which created authentic learning experiences for students. We analyse the student experience via quantitative and qualitative course experience data captured from 2016 to 2020 and apply Rule's (2006) authentic assessment principles to determine the degree and nature of authenticity that the course provided. By triangulating our reflections, good practice principles and course experience data we provide valuable findings and practical strategies to support educators to foster authentic assessment *for and of learning* (Boud, 2000).

Keywords

lifelong learning – authentic assessment – capstone – assessment for learning – construction management capstone

1   Introduction

As the literature attests (Barrie & Prosser, 2004; Kaider, 2017; Stephenson & Yorke 1998), over recent decades universities have increasingly been challenged to ensure they produce graduates who are ready for life and work. The attention given to preparing students for their future professional practice reflects the widely accepted view that to do so represents a core purpose of higher education (Boud & Falchikov, 2006; Smith, 2012). The value of higher education, both here and internationally, is now commonly measured through the prism of work readiness and employability (Klopper & Drew, 2015).

The employer driven expectation for graduates to seamlessly transition from university to the workplace as work ready has impacted upon the sector in significant ways, including infusing learning and teaching practice with situational and experiential guided pedagogies. The expectation that universities prepare graduates for their future professional practice creates an institutional imprimatur which extends to expectations regarding the types of learning experiences students engage in and how their learning is assessed (Ashford-Rowe et al., 2014; Kaider, 2017; Hains-Wesson & Young, 2017).

This chapter focuses on a capstone course which was purposefully designed and taught to engage students in meaningful, active, industry aligned learning that immerses them in authentic industry contexts. As we explore, from both educator and student perspective, capstone pedagogies offer rich and wide-ranging possibilities to foster an authentic and quality learning experience.

To contribute to knowledge of ways to foster authentic assessment *for and of learning* (Boud, 2000), we triangulate our reflections with Rule's (2006) authentic learning principles and five years of student course evaluation quantitative and qualitative data. We reflect on the effectiveness of the authentic design and delivery of the capstone course through the lens of the student's perceptions. We look back to look forward, building knowledge of how to foster authentic assessments on the ground. Drawing upon Rule (2006), we make explicit the characteristics that promote this course's authenticity through analysis of the student and educator perspective.

Lee and Loton (2019) importantly found in their study in which they determined the efficacy of capstone design principles across multiple disciplines that a key factor which contributes to differences in student learning experiences and outcomes is educator's perceptions of the purpose of a capstone course and what makes for an authentic capstone experience.

We demonstrate here that the educator perspective is all powerful. We view academic's identities as multi-dimensional and recognise that identity formation and reformation can be characterised by tensions when different values and beliefs about teaching converge (Curwood, 2014; Watson, 2006). In line with McCune's (2019) theorising, we understand the concept of 'identities' to mean "the dynamic interplay over time of personal narratives, values and processes of identification with diverse groups and communities" (McCune, 2019, p. 3).

We further note, as Entwistle (1991) amongst others theorised, that how a student perceives their learning environment directly influences how a student learns. As the literature attests, when students experience their assessment as authentic, they are more likely to engage in deeper learning and are more motivated to learn (Gulikers et al., 2004).

2   Capstones for Authentic Learning

To examine the principles and practices which promoted authentic learning and assessment in our capstone course it is important to give some attention to the capstone pedagogy. Capstones are well recognised as a culminating and transformative experience in higher education (Lee & Loton, 2019). Capstones commonly draw upon problem based, experiential and situational learning pedagogies such as those espoused by Kolb (1984) and Lave and Wegner (1991).

As the literature identifies (Healy et al., 2013; Lee & Loton, 2019), the culminating learning experience provided by capstones is intended to provide rich opportunities for students to hone their previously acquired knowledge and skills by addressing real world industry problems. It is through the capstone pedagogy that students can engage in learning that is industry aligned, and which fosters higher order metacognitive skills such as critical reflection, analysis and synthesis.

The design, scope, intent and delivery of capstone courses varies across disciplines, qualification types, learning levels and so on. Capstone courseware is commonly predicated on a constructivist approach to course design (Bowden & Marton, 1998; Stephenson & Yorke, 1998), whereby learning is viewed as a meaning-making process, as graduate generic attributes emphasise "what students have to do, rather than how they represent knowledge" (Biggs, 1996, p. 13). In the race for work readiness, the notion of employability presupposes that universities will produce graduates who are attractive in the marketplace and sought after by their respective industries.

In Australia, generic graduate attributes, the hallmarks of employability and work readiness, are conceptualised as comprising skills, qualities and attributes which are integrated to produce work readiness and capable performance

(Bowden & Marton, 1998; Stephenson & Yorke, 1998). As Boyer (1998, p. 28) explains, the capstone course brings "to a symbolic conclusion the acquisition of knowledge and skills that has preceded this final effort".

As the 2015 OLT Capstone Report outlines, there is broad agreement that capstones are underpinned by the following elements:
- integration and extension of prior learning;
- authentic and contextualised experiences;
- challenging and complex problems;
- student independence and agency;
- a concern with critical inquiry and creativity, and;
- active dissemination and celebration.

There is further consensus that capstones should involve students in a process of addressing authentic and complex problems (Healey et al., 2013). Authenticity in this context is commonly understood as assuring alignment between capstone activities and the contexts, methods and issues of professional settings (Herrington et al., 2014).

Conceptually, the notion of authentic learning and assessment draws upon a number of seminal learning theories. These theoretical frameworks ascribe to experiential, immersive and transformative learning pedagogies (Andresen et al., 1995; Kolb, 1984; Lave & Wegner, 1991; Mezirow, 1997).

Whilst a range of definitions of authentic assessment abound in the literature, we adopt Guliker et al. (2004) conception. Guiliker et al. (2004) classify authentic assessment as any assessment which requires students to integrate and apply attributes, capabilities, or combinations of knowledge, skills and dispositions that they need in real life settings. Congruent with this definition we embrace Rule's (2006) authentic assessment principles and apply these overarching principles to critically reflect on our practice and analyse our data. Rule's (2006) principles conceptualise authenticity in relation to four interrelated themes. Rule's four themes stem from the author's analysis of forty-five peer reviewed articles which analyse authentic learning across multiple and diverse disciplines.
- The activity involves real-world problems that mimic the work of professionals in the discipline with presentation of findings to audiences beyond the classroom.
- Open-ended inquiry, thinking skills, and metacognition are addressed.
- Students engage in discourse and social learning in a community of learners.
- Students are empowered through choice to direct their own learning in relevant project work.

3   The Purpose of Study

The purpose of this research is to contribute to knowledge of how to foster authentic learning and assessment in a capstone by making explicit:
- how a final year capstone's course aligns with Rule's authentic principles,
- how students perceive and experience authenticity through their learning and assessment,
- what strategies promote authentic learning and assessment in a capstone course.

4   Methodology

The methodological framework for this study draws upon case study research (Stake, 2000) and insider research inquiry (Humphrey, 2012; Mercer, 2007).

To critically reflect on our practice and explore the challenges and principles which promote authentic assessment, we draw upon the notion of reflective practice (Brookfield, 1998; Mezirow, 1997). We adapt Brookfield's (1998) four reflective lenses as a way to promote reflection. This involved sharing our autobiographies as learner, our perspectives on teaching and situating our reflections in the literature. As insider researchers, we acknowledge the complex ethical, methodological and political dilemmas of the insider method and our hybrid and fluid positioning as researchers (Humphrey, 2012; Mercer, 2007).

Students' perceptions and experiences were captured over five years via student survey quantitative and qualitative course experience data reported from 2016 to 2020. Utilising data from these university run anonymised Course Experience Surveys (CES) does not require ethics approval.

As case study research, our study applied a mixed methods approach involving quantitative and qualitative data since "the use of both approaches in tandem" enhances the overall credibility and validity of the study (Creswell 2009). We further adopted a mixed methods approach to facilitate as Merriam and Tisdell (2016, p. 48) describe "a richer understanding of the subject under study".

Quantitative data was drawn from eight Likert scale questions chosen by the first author and asked of students each semester from 2017 through to 2020. Statements were chosen from a bank of 200 standardised Likert scale statements supplied by the university which can be included in the CES. Questions were chosen for various reasons over the years (not solely to assess authentic learning). Questions have changed from year to year. A sample of the quantitative student survey structure can be seen in Table 8.1 and all questions asked from 2017 through to 2020 have been detailed in Table 8.3.

TABLE 8.1   Sample quantitative student survey

This section asks you about your experience in your course

Thinking about the course please respond to each statement	Strongly disagree	Disagree	Neither agree nor disagree	Agree	Strongly agree
1 I found the assessment in this course challenging.	o	o	o	o	o
2 I learnt a lot through the process of drafting and resubmitting my assignments.	o	o	o	o	o

We captured qualitative data via the open-ended question "what are the best aspects of this course". This question is a mandatory open-ended question asked by the university at the end of each course semester under the CES.

The rationale for using this open-ended question in our study was to elicit the student perspective on what was the most useful and meaningful learning in the course. It is through capturing student's open-ended responses that the authors were able to determine the degree to which authenticity was experienced and valued by the learner in relation to the broader context of their course experience and learning. The use of the open-ended question provides "a means for exploring and understanding the meaning individuals or groups ascribe to a social or human problem" (Creswell, 2009, p. 4). Over seven semesters, 116 free text comments were provided by students in their Course Experience Surveys.

4.1   *Data Analysis*

Our analysis of student data was to determine whether authenticity was valued by the students in the course. To analyse and map the student quantitative and qualitative data we firstly met to discuss Rule's authentic learning principles which involved unpacking these principles to establish a shared understanding of their meaning in practice. We then reviewed both sets of data independently to individually code the themes found in accordance with Rule's authentic learning principles. Where a Likert statement or a student free-text response was deemed to align with more than one of Rule's interrelated principles, multiple codes were assigned.

This process of thematic data analysis (Braun & Clarke, 2006) was inductive and comparative (Merriam & Tisdell, 2016) and involved seeking descriptive and theoretical links between students' perceptions of their experiences of the course and Rule's four intersecting assessment principles. We then subsequently undertook consistency checking by cross referencing our results.

Sharing our respective analysis of the data required us to make explicit our reasoning in assigning codes. Our critical conversations supported us to stand back from the data, to make explicit our unconscious selective impressions, opening our choices up to further scrutiny (Linneberg & Korsgaard, 2019).

This method of triangulating analysts was purposefully adopted to assure validity in the study (Patton, 2015). Our critical conversations supported the process of triangulation from different perspectives (Robson, 2016).

To conclude the process of data analysis we critically reflected on our findings to make explicit the pedagogic principles and practices which promoted authenticity through the lens of the student perspective.

5 A Reflection on the Course in Practice

5.1 *Our Learning Partnership*

We acknowledge the role our identities played in guiding the assessment and learning design and consider how our professional relationship informed what authenticity looked like in the course.

In line with Senge's (2011) theorising, which posits that a learningful community fosters reflective practice, the authors' critical professional conversations and a semi-structured process of reflection has informed both the course design and teaching practice. Throughout the course design, our learningful partnership has enabled us to draw upon our tacit knowledge to deepen our conceptual understandings of authenticity and to practically apply these understandings to foster meaningful and authentic learning experiences for our students.

Our critical conversations informed the design, development and implementation of the capstone course from the initial planning phase in 2016. These conversations created developmental opportunities for us to share and reflect on the course design and examine the efficacy of its implementation by triangulating our individual reflections with student feedback, both formal and informal. Our conversations supported us to make explicit and examine our conceptions of authentic assessment. Our epistemological starting points were integral to guiding the course design and teaching method, and these were made explicit and re-examined and reformed throughout our learning journey. Our professional learning partnership was formative in shaping the course design and delivery, and supported reflection on practice to inform ongoing improvements in teaching. Our partnership created rich and unique opportunities for critical reflection and promoted our reciprocal developmental learning. The process of writing this chapter provides a catalyst for further knowledge building and it speaks to the value in assuring agency in course design and teaching practice.

Much of our earlier conversations focused on how, in their final year of Construction Management (CM), it is critical that students are encouraged to hone their professional practice techniques. The construction industry requires high levels of autonomy while solving genuine industry problems. Furthermore, a student's understanding of what industry best practice looks like, how to practice the required skills and knowledge and the implications of their decision-making on a wide range of deliverables was noted as important.

5.2   Course Design

The capstone is a core final year course delivered each semester to all final year students undertaking a four-year Bachelor Construction Management program. Students numbers average between 80 and 180 per semester. Prior to Covid, the course was taught solely face-to-face via a mix of lectures and tutorials. The course is currently offered as both face-to-face and fully online.

Prior to the course redesign in 2016, there were mixed levels of student engagement reported. OSI (Overall satisfaction indicator) recorded 50% and 23.8% for 2013 and 2014 respectively.

To enhance the quality of the course, the authors came together to share and reflect on this data. Work was required to ensure the course curriculum and teaching was aligned with sound capstone pedagogies. At the time, we shared our beliefs about good teaching, our goals, and how to ultimately promote authentic learning through the course's learning and assessment design.

The first author brought to our learning partnership her identity as an industry fellow with vast and specialised industry knowledge and practice experience. Her identity as industry specialist fueled her passion to engage students in learning that replicates complex and nuanced CM practices. Key to her conception of good teaching practice was how best to authentically contextualise and design the curriculum and its assessment. Furthermore, the first author's focus was on supporting students to become autonomous learners who engaged in authentic real-world practice and to foster their capabilities as work ready, critical and independent thinkers.

As Academic Developer the second author's focus was far more on the process of learning and teaching, on pedagogical practices and principles that would promote engaged and authentic learning for students through a constructivist course design. Through our critical conversations we discovered that our respective conceptions of teaching and our values and beliefs were bridged by a shared vision of authentic learning primarily through a commitment to experiential learning pedagogies (Kolb, 1984; Lave & Wegner, 1991). Our philosophical and pedagogical intent was to assure the integration and application of knowledge.

Assuring that capstones are a culminating and integrating experience requires, as Lee and Loton (2019) attest, that various strands of the CM program needed to be drawn together to consolidate learning and prepare students for their industry profession. The unique characteristics of a capstone needed to act as a foundation where higher order metacognitive skills and authentic assessment for learning could flourish. During the course design, experiential learning pedagogies (Kolb, 1984) were applied to ensure students were engaged in real-life construction projects and authentic assessments each semester.

Through our critical conversations we shared our values and professional expertise and experiences and our perspectives on the course design were continually reframed (Schon, 1983). Through each iteration of the course our developing experiential knowledge informed the next phase of the teaching and learning cycle.

The process of writing this chapter has promoted our further reflections on the course, particularly in relation to the design and degree of authenticity relative to Rule's principles. As we look back to look forward, we found that the following elements were critical to fostering authenticity in tertiary teaching:
– Replicate and measure the knowledge, skills, and attitudes expected in real-world practice
– Create opportunities for authentic conversations
– Foster autonomous learning to empower students
– Challenge students, fostering higher order learning and evidencing metacognition
– Immerse students in the discourses of their field
– Create opportunities for collaboration between peers and with industry
– Integrate self-assessment and critical reflection and teacher feedback as part of the assessment process
– Enable learning and development which signals transference of knowledge and skills

The course assessments mapped to Rule's principles are outlined in Table 8.2.

5.3   *Promoting Authenticity through the Course Delivery and Resources*
The scope of the course design and teaching practices that particularly align with Rule's principles (2006) has been outlined below in greater detail.

6 The Activity Involves Real-World Problems That Mimic the Work of Professionals in the Discipline with Presentation of Findings to Audiences beyond the Classroom

Commencing in 2016, the first author has cultivated a unique educational partnership with the Capital Works department of her university. Industry-partnered learning experiences are facilitated by the first author to engage students directly with site teams on live construction projects. Students explore real-time industry problems and critically appraise emerging trends and approaches to industry practices.

The assessment design further enables students to work collaboratively to create authentic industry tools. The CM industry commonly requires communication to be brief and to the point while also acting as an aid in the effective delivery of construction projects. Students are encouraged throughout the course to produce realistic documentation as concisely as possible. To maintain the integrity of the documents produced, complex management theory and depth of knowledge is communicated with fully referenced footnotes.

The capstone course resources act as a "contextual anchor" (McLellan, 1994) which reflect industry practices. The first author brought to her teaching her unique perspective as both early career educator and industry fellow and harnessed her disciplinary, professional and educational expertise to continually adapt these resources to complement each live construction project studied. Examples of authentic resources include: sample solutions to industry problems; knowledge-building interviews with industry; sample procurement strategies, use of project drawings and contract conditions; site photographs, construction time lapse records, 3D VR scans of construction site progress; reflective group charters which act as collaborative tools; and viva voce panel presentations.

6.1 *Open-Ended Inquiry, Thinking Skills, and Metacognition Are Addressed*

Students are immersed in CM industry best practices as they contextualised and explored various pathways to possible industry solutions. The first author spends time at key points in each semester in critical conversations with students. Wearing her two hats as educator and industry fellow, she partners with students to explore (using industry conventions and language) why open ended, autonomous critical inquiry matters. Using the technique of role-play, students measure the cause and effect of possible solutions gaining further depth of understanding while decision-making capabilities are enhanced.

Assessments are designed to promote and engaged autonomous learning. These authentic conversations put front and centre connections to industry experience, real world case studies inquiry, and do so in ways which assures that the student's practice are in turn subject to critique, review and reflection.

6.2 Students Engage in Discourse and Social Learning in a Community of Learners

While critical conversations immerse students in the discourse of CM, a community of learners is further nurtured using additional strategies. Students deliver the majority of their course assessments as a group. Through the formulation of a detailed group charter group members must adopt individual group process roles to strengthen equal contribution. Additionally, different industry roles are adopted by students during assessment submissions which encourages students, from different perspectives, to explore and unravel problems together.

Given the course is underpinned by the principle of *assessment for learning* (Boud, 2000), there is time and space in workshops each week to work on solutions to problems together. Further formative feedback sessions are available each week for students to present their work for feedback prior to submission. Meaningful and personalised authentic conversations and interactions take place here.

Progressive site visits throughout the semester and visiting lectures undertaken by construction and client teams add further to this community of learners setting.

6.3 Students Are Empowered through Choice to Direct Their Own Learning in Relevant Project Work

Mindful of effective capstone pedagogy which fosters formative learning and authentic assessment (Villarroel et al., 2018), a structured iterative feedback learning cycle is embedded into the curriculum and assessment design. This involves allowing for the resubmission of previously assessed work whereby students can choose to resubmit one task. The purpose of this feedback strategy is to support students to critically reflect on their learning and feedback. In order to gain any additional marks students are required to demonstrate improvement. This type of closing the feedback loop also replicates industry practices.

7 Results

Table 8.3 includes quantitative student feedback mapped to Rule's principles.

Tables 8.4 and 8.5 present the thematic analysis of the qualitative data – student responses to the open-ended question "What were the best aspects of the course?" To note, there were 236 occurrences of Rule's themes which emerged across the 116 student comments.

TABLE 8.2   Capstone course assessment outline

Rule's principles		Assessment	Assessment description and assessment criteria
1, 2, 3, 4	1	*Group charter, tender submission* Weighting: 20% Assessment type: Groupwork	Students are presented with an industry based problem relating to the case study. As a group, the students work through the planning, preparation and submission of a tender proposal and preliminary cost estimate for an industry-based construction project. A group charter is also submitted. The group is assessed on their ability to interpret and integrate knowledge and understanding of construction tender and estimating fundamentals with an industry specific problem based scenario.
1, 2, 3, 4	2	*Design management/site management* Weighting: 20% Assessment type: Groupwork	Students are presented with an industry based problem relating to the case study. As a group, the students work through the planning, preparation and submission of a Site Management Plan and a Request for Information with an appended design sketch for the specific industry-based construction project. The group is assessed on their ability to interpret and integrate knowledge and understanding of site management best practice and design management processes with an industry specific problem based scenario.
1, 2, 3, 4	3	*Contract administration/ project scheduling* Weighting: 20% Assessment type: Groupwork	Students are presented with an industry based problem relating to the case study. As a group, the students work through the planning, preparation and submission of a Procurement Schedule, Scope of Works, Contract Program and Memorandum for the specific industry-based construction project. The group is assessed on their ability to interpret and integrate knowledge and understanding of contract administration best practice and project scheduling processes with an industry specific problem based scenario.
1, 2, 4	4a	*Resubmission of key documents* Words: 750 Weighting: 10% Assessment type: Individual	Individually, students are required to resubmit a key document that was submitted and assessed previously under the course. The student must critically reflect on the formative and summative feedback previously received while integrating and applying their developing knowledge to further improve their work. The student is assessed on their ability to interpret previously received feedback to further improve their work.

(cont.)

TABLE 8.2   Capstone course assessment outline (*cont.*)

Rule's principles	Assessment	Assessment description and assessment criteria
1, 2, 3, 4	4b *Panel presentations* Duration: 20 mins per group Weighting: 25% Assessment type: Individual	The end of semester assessment comprises an industry-attended viva voce panel presentation designed to challenge students through role-playing real-life industry interactions. Students must verbally defend the work that they have undertaken on their case study throughout the semester while playing the role of a chosen industry professional. The student is assessed on their ability to apply autonomous, logical, critical and creative thinking to analyse, synthesise and apply theoretical knowledge, and technical skills, to formulate evidenced based solutions to industry problems or issues.
3	4c *Reflection* Words: Google Form Weighting: 5% Assessment type: Individual mark – peer assessed	Students complete a peer review of each individual group member's performance over the semester. Students reflect on each performance in line with the commitments the group made to each other in their group charters submitted under assessment 1. Marks associated with this reflection come from an average of the mark received from peers in their group.

Legend:
1   The activity involves real-world problems that mimic the work of professionals in the discipline with presentation of findings to audiences beyond the classroom.
2   Open-ended inquiry, thinking skills, and metacognition are addressed.
3   Students engage in discourse and social learning in a community of learners.
4   Students are empowered through choice to direct their own learning in relevant project work.

8   Data Analysis

The results of the data validate the teaching approach and assessment design in accordance with Rule's four principles.

8.1   *The Activity Involves Real-World Problems That Mimic the Work of Professionals in the Discipline with Presentation of Findings to Audiences beyond the Classroom*

As indicated in Table 8.3 a minimum of 94% of respondents agreed that "the course has made effective connections between theory and practice". In

MAKING IT HAPPEN   175

TABLE 8.3   CES additional Likert scale statement responses from 145 students which have been mapped to Rule's four authentic principles

Semester		2017 S2	2018 S2	2019 S1	2019 S2	2020 S1	2020 S2
Number of student responses against cohort size		41/140	47/172	7/36	12/144	21/60	17/152

Rule's principle	Statement	Percentage of students who agreed with the statement[a]					
2	I found the assessment in this course challenging.	96	88	–	–	–	–
1, 4	I learnt a lot through the process of drafting and resubmitting my assignments.	–	91	86	75	95	76
4	I consider what I learned valuable for my future.	96	88	–	–	–	–
2, 4	As a result of my course, I feel confident about tackling unfamiliar problems.	91	79	–	–	–	–
1, 3	The course has made effective connections between theory and practice.	96	94	–	–	–	–
na	I would prefer tutorials in place of some of the lectures.	70	–	–	–	–	–
3	In-class activities for this course were useful in completing the assignments.	100	76	–	–	–	–
3	The role plays used in class were effective learning tools.	–	–	86	58	–	82
4	I worked hard in this class.	–	–	100	92	–	94
1, 2, 3, 4	The examples, applications or analogies that were used prompted me to make new connections or interpretations.	–	–	100	67	100	82
na	The lectures I attended contributed greatly to my learning in this course.	–	–	–	50	95	76
na	The lecture and laboratory notes provided were of high quality.	–	–	100	–	–	–
na	The amount of work required in this course is about right.	100	85	–	–	–	–
1	I can see how this course will help me in the workplace.	–	–	100	83	100	88
4	The industry based project was useful in developing knowledge and skills.	–					

(cont.)

TABLE 8.3 CES additional Likert scale statement responses from 145 students which have been mapped to Rule's four authentic principles (*cont.*)

Semester	2017 S2	2018 S2	2019 S1	2019 S2	2020 S1	2020 S2
Number of student responses against cohort size	41/140	47/172	7/36	12/144	21/60	17/152

Rule's principle	Statement	Percentage of students who agreed with the statement[a]
1, 2, 3	I found that the course team was approachable and passionate about the subject.	100
1, 3	The teaching staff appear engaged with current industry practice.	–

a % agree is the number of students who "agree" or "strongly agree" as a percentage of the number who responded to that question

Legend:
1   The activity involves real-world problems that mimic the work of professionals in the discipline with presentation of findings to audiences beyond the classroom
2   Open-ended inquiry, thinking skills, and metacognition are addressed
3   Students engage in discourse and social learning in a community of learners
4   Students are empowered through choice to direct their own learning in relevant project work

TABLE 8.4 CES responses from 116 students that map to Rule's four authentic principles

Authentic assessment principle	Frequency (116)
1) The activity involves real-world problems that mimic the work of professionals in the discipline with presentation of findings to audiences beyond the classroom	79 (68%)
2) Open-ended inquiry, thinking skills, and metacognition are addressed	50 (43%)
3) Students engage in discourse and social learning in a community of learners	65 (56%)
4) Students are empowered through choice to direct their own learning in relevant project work	42 (36%)

TABLE 8.5   CES responses from 116 students produced 236 individual comments that map to Rule's four authentic principles

Authentic assessment principle	Frequency (236)
1) The activity involves real-world problems that mimic the work of professionals in the discipline with presentation of findings to audiences beyond the classroom	79 (33%)
2) Open-ended inquiry, thinking skills, and metacognition are addressed	50 (21%)
3) Students engage in discourse and social learning in a community of learners	65 (28%)
4) Students are empowered through choice to direct their own learning in relevant project work	42 (18%)

addition to this, respondents between a range of 83% and 100% agreed they could "see how this course will help me in the workplace" and that "the industry based project was useful in developing knowledge and skills". Furthermore, at least 75% of respondents agreed on any specific semester that they "learnt a lot through the process of drafting and resubmitting my assignments" and "the teaching staff appear engaged with current industry practice". Lastly, respondents found "the examples, applications or analogies that were used prompted me to make new connections or interpretations" were valuable (2019, S1 – 100%; 2019, S2 – 67%; 2020, S1 – 100%; 2020, S2 – 82%).

Student responses presented in Tables 8.4 and 8.5 support these findings. As seen in Table 8.4, 68% of respondents made a positive comment relating to engaging in real world problems. The real-world connections we purposefully created were widely valued. Table 8.5 shows that this principle was the most valued of Rules four authentic principles quoted with 33% of 236 individual comments related to this theme.

8.2   Open-Ended Inquiry, Thinking Skills, and Metacognition Are Addressed

As indicated in Table 8.3, a minimum of 79% of respondents agreed on any specific semester that "as a result of my course, I feel confident about tackling unfamiliar problems". In addition to this, respondents between a range of 83% and 100% agreed that "the industry based project was useful in developing knowledge and skills". Furthermore, at least 88% of respondents, when asked, agreed that they "found the assessment in this course challenging".

Lastly, respondents found "the examples, applications or analogies that were used prompted me to make new connections or interpretations" were valuable (2019, S1 – 100%; 2019, S2 – 67%; 2020, S1 – 100%; 2020, S2 – 82%).

Student responses in Tables 8.4 and 8.5 support these findings. As seen in Table 8.4, 43% of respondents made a positive comment relating to this principle. Table 8.5 shows that this principle was the third most valued of Rule's four authentic principles quoted with 21% of 236 individual comments related to this theme.

8.3 Students Engage in Discourse and Social Learning in a Community of Learner

As indicated in Table 8.3 at least 75% of respondents agreed on any specific semester that "the teaching staff appear engaged with current industry practice" and 76% agreed that "in-class activities for this course were useful in completing the assignments". In addition to this, respondents between a range of 83% and 100% agreed that "the industry based project was useful in developing knowledge and skills". Furthermore, a minimum of 94% of respondents agreed that "the course has made effective connections between theory and practice". Lastly, respondents found "the examples, applications or analogies that were used prompted me to make new connections or interpretations" were valuable (2019, S1 – 100%; 2019, S2 – 67%; 2020, S1 – 100%; 2020, S2 – 82%) and "the role plays used in class were effective learning tools" (2019, S1 – 86%; 2019, S2 – 58%; 2020, S2 – 82%).

Student responses in Tables 8.4 and 8.5 support these findings. As seen in Table 8.4, 56% of respondents made a positive comment relating to this principle. Table 8.5 shows that this principle was the second most valued of Rule's four authentic principles quoted with 28% of 236 individual comments related to this theme.

8.4 Students Are Empowered through Choice to Direct Their Own Learning in Relevant Project Work

As indicated in Table 8.3, a minimum of 79% of respondents agreed on any specific semester that "as a result of my course, I feel confident about tackling unfamiliar problems". Respondents between a range of 83% and 100% each semester agreed they could "see how this course will help me in the workplace". In addition to this, a range of 88% and 96% "consider what I learned valuable for my future" and a range of 92% and 100% of students across 3 semesters reported they "worked hard in this class". Furthermore, at least 75% of respondents agreed on any specific semester that they "learnt a lot through the process of drafting and resubmitting my assignments". Lastly, respondents

TABLE 8.6   Course Experience Survey (CES)

Semester	2016 S2	2017 S2	2018 S2	2019 S1	2019 S2	2020 S1	2020 S2
GTS – Good teaching score (%)	61.9	91.7	84	95.2	79.2	98.4	87.3
OSI – Overall satisfaction index (%)	63.2	95.7	87.9	71.4	75	100	93.8

found "the examples, applications or analogies that were used prompted me to make new connections or interpretations" were valuable (2019, S1 – 100%; 2019, S2 – 67%; 2020, S1 – 100%; 2020, S2 – 82%).

Student responses in Tables 8.4 and 8.5 support these findings. As seen in Table 8.4, 36% of respondents made a positive comment relating to this principle. Table 8.5 shows that this principle was the least valued of Rules four authentic principles quoted with 18% of 236 individual comments related to this theme.

9   Our Chapter Reflections

We purposefully embedded structured authentic learning experiences in the course design. From the student perspective, the efficacy of this approach was demonstrated. The course created learning for students that authentically deepened and broadened their critical understandings of their future profession and role as professional practitioners.

Whilst student satisfaction rates improved significantly from 2016 onwards (refer Table 8.6), the course was not without its challenges. It was highly challenging for example to encourage students to harness their own thinking and ideas, to trust their own judgements and decision making, and to initially see the value of the *process* of learning, not just the final product and outcomes.

We acknowledge that a number of authentic learning frameworks exist in the literature, such as Ashford-Rowe et al.'s (2014) eight Critical Elements to Determine Authenticity. As demonstrated, Rule's (2006) four principles can be usefully applied to examine the integrity of assessments designed to foster and evidence authentic learning. By applying Rule's principles, our data demonstrates that the assessment design and teaching practice successfully immersed students in industry ready and contextualised experiences which they valued as authentic.

10 Conclusions

Based on our data analysis and reflections, we suggest the following practical strategies as useful to foster authentic assessment:

- Design real world assessments which require the application of industry focused knowledge, skills and attributes.
- Establish complex and industry relevant problems which can be explored and responded to.
- Design assessments to foster and evidence metacognition and higher order learning, enhancing learner autonomy and decision-making.
- Enrich the assessment design and learning experience with industry aligned authentic resources.
- Disseminate beyond the classroom by critically engaging students with real world projects. Problems can be contextualised, authentic conversations facilitated, and real-life industry practices observed.
- Enable learning and development which signals transference of knowledge and skills.
- Engage students in authentic conversations using industry conventions and language, making explicit the social practice of the discipline and field. Articulation of ideas are promoted, and student's tacit knowledge is made explicit.
- Embed iterative opportunities for formative feedback. Students are challenged to measure the cause and effect of possible solutions, analyse alternative perspectives and critically appraise emerging trends and approaches to industry practices in a community of learners.
- Optimise student's opportunities for success, supporting students to do their best work by scaffolding learning underpinned by criterion referenced assessment.
- Embed both opportunities for shared contributions and learner autonomy in the process of groupwork.
- Create opportunities for student choice through a flexible feedback loop which allows for iterative feedback through a process of self-assessment, critical reflection, redrafting and resubmission where improvement must be demonstrated (metacognition).
- Harness the expertise of an industry fellow, and/or industry more broadly, to simulate the work of professionals: to create authentic problems, design authentic resources, engage in authentic conversations and deliver authentic real-world feedback.
- Create a learning community for the educator which assures supported opportunities for critical reflection on practice to foster good teaching. The professional relationship created between the authors has contributed to the authentic course design in a positive and sustained way.

Our case study is testament to the intrinsic value of investing in authentic learning. Of giving life to graduate capability-based curriculum to harness the intrinsic value of integrating theory with practice "within a purposefully designed curriculum" (Patrick et al., 2008, p. iv).

The study is also testament to the importance of engaging in authentic reflective conversations with each other as educators. Writing this chapter has supported us to make explicit the role of our identities in guiding the assessment and learning design and consider how our professional relationship informed what authenticity looked like in the course. In looking back, we look forward to our future critical conversations, as we continue to reflect on educational practice to improve teaching for all.

References

Andresen, L., Boud D., & Cohen R. (1995). Experience-based learning. In G. Foley (Ed.), *Understanding adult education and training* (2nd ed., pp. 225–239). Allen & Unwin.

Ashford-Rowe, K., Herrington, J., & Brown, C. (2014). Establishing the critical elements that determine authentic assessment. *Assessment & Evaluation in Higher Education, 39*(2), 205–222.

Barrie, S. C., & Prosser, M. (2004). Generic graduate attributes: Citizens for an unknown future. *Higher Education Research and Development, 23*(3), 243–246.

Biggs, J. (1996). Enhancing teaching through constructive alignment. *Higher Education, 32,* 347–364.

Boud, D. (2000). Sustainable assessment: Rethinking assessment for the learning society. *Studies in Continuing Education, 22*(2), 151–167.

Boud, D., & Falchikov, N. (2006). Aligning assessment with long-term learning. *Assessment & Evaluation in Higher Education, 31*(4), 399–413.

Bowden, J., & Marton, F. (1998). *The university of learning: Beyond quality and competence in higher education.* Kogan Page.

Boyer Commission on Educating Undergraduates in the Research University. (1998). *Reinventing undergraduate education: A blueprint for America's research universities.* Carnegie Foundation for the Advancement of Teaching.

Braun, V., & Clarke, V. (2006). Using thematic analysis in psychology. *Qualitative Research in Psychology, 3,* 77–101.

Brookfield, S. (1998). Critically reflective practice. *Journal of Continuing Education in the Health Professions, 18*(4), 197–205.

Creswell, J. W. (2009). *Research design qualitative, quantitative and mixed methods approaches.* Sage Publications.

Curwood, J. (2014). Between continuity and change: Identities and narratives within teacher professional development. *Teaching Education, 25*(2), 156–183.

Entwistle, N. J. (1991). Approaches to learning and perceptions of the learning environment: Introduction to the special issue. *Higher Education, 22*(3), 201–204.

Gulikers, J., Bastiaens, T., & Kirschner, P. (2004). A five-dimensional framework for authentic assessment. *Educational Technology Research and Development, 52*(3), 67–85.

Hains-Wesson, R., & Young, K. (2017). A collaborative autoethnography study to inform the teaching of reflective practice in STEM. *Higher Education Research and Development, 36*(2), 297–310.

Healey, M., & Lannin, L., & Stibbe, A., & Derounian, J. (2013). *Developing and enhancing undergraduate final-year projects and dissertations*. The Higher Education Academy.

Herrington, J., Reeves, T. C., & Oliver, R. (2014). Authentic learning environments. In J. M. Spector, M. D. Merrill, J. Elen, & M. J. Bishop (Eds.), *Handbook of research on educational communications and technology* (4th ed., pp. 401–412). Springer.

Humphrey, C. (2012). Dilemmas in doing insider research in professional education. *Qualitative Social Work, 12*(5), 572–586.

Kaider, F., Hains-Wesson, R., & Young, K. (2017). Practical typology of authentic work-integrated learning activities and assessments. *Asia-Pacific Journal of Cooperative Education, 18*(2) (Special issue), 153–165.

Klopper, C., & Drew, S. (2015). Teaching for learning and learning for teaching. In C. Klopper & S. Drew (Eds.), *Teaching for learning and learning for teaching: Peer review of teaching in higher education* (pp. 1–11). Sense Publishers.

Kolb, D. (1984). *Experiential learning: Experience as the source of learning and development*. Prentice-Hall.

Lave, J., & Wenger, E. (1991). *Situated learning: Legitimate peripheral participation*. Cambridge University Press.

Lee, N., & Loton, D. (2019). Capstone purposes across disciplines. *Studies in Higher Education, 44*(1), 134–150.

Linneberg, M. S., & Korsgaard, S. (2019). Coding qualitative data: A synthesis guiding the novice. *Qualitative Research Journal, 19*(3), 259–370.

McCune, V. (2019). Academic identities in contemporary higher education: Sustaining identities that value teaching. *Teaching in Higher Education, 26*(1), 20–35.

McLellan, H. (1994). Situated learning: Continuing the conversation. *Educational Technology, 34*(10), 7–8.

Mercer, J. (2007). The challenges of insider research in educational institutions: Wielding a double-edged sword and resolving delicate dilemmas. *Oxford Review of Education, 33*(1), 1–17.

Merriam, S. B., & Tisdell, E. J. (2016). *Qualitative research: A guide to design and implementation* (4th ed.). Jossey-Bass.

Mezirow, J. (1997). Transformative learning: Theory to practice. *New Directions for Adult and Continuing Education, 74*, 5–12.

Patrick, C., Peach, D., Pocknee, C., Webb, F., Fletcher, M., & Pretto, G. (2008). *The WIL (work integrated learning) report: National scoping study.* Queensland University of Technology.

Patton, M. Q. (2015). *Qualitative research and evaluation methods* (4th ed.). Sage.

Robson, C., & McCartan, K. (2016). *Real world research: A resource for users of social research methods in applied settings* (4th ed.). Wiley.

Rule, A. C. (2006). Editorial: The components of authentic learning. *Journal of Authentic Learning*, 1–10.

Schön, D. (1983). *The reflective practitioner: How professionals think in action.* Basic Books.

Senge, P. (2011). *The fifth discipline fieldbook: Strategies and tools for building a learning organisation.* Nicholas Brealey Publishing.

Smith, C. (2012). Evaluating the quality of work-integrated learning curricula: A comprehensive framework. *Higher Education Research & Development*, 31(2), 247–262.

Stake, R. E. (2000). Case studies. In N. K. Denzin & Y. S. Lincoln (Eds.), *Handbook of qualitative research* (2nd ed., pp. 435–454). Sage.

Stephenson, J., & Yorke, M. (1998). *Capability and quality in higher education.* Kogan Page.

The Office for Learning and Teaching (OLT) National Senior Teaching Fellowship. (2015). *Capstone curriculum across disciplines: Synthesising theory, practice and policy to provide practical tools for curriculum design.*

Villarroel, V., Bloxham, S., Bruna, D., Bruna, C., & Herrera-Seda, C. (2018). Authentic assessment: Creating a blueprint for course design. *Assessment & Evaluation in Higher Education*, 43(5), 840–854.

Watson, C. (2006). Narratives of practice and the construction of identity in teaching. *Teachers and Teaching: Theory and Practice*, 12(5), 509–526.

PART 2

Authentic Assessment Approaches and Practices in Primary and Secondary Education

CHAPTER 9

Using Learning Trajectory-Based Ratio Curriculum and Diagnostic Assessments for Promoting Learner-Centred Instruction

Jere Confrey, Meetal Shah and Michael Belcher

Abstract

Learning trajectory (LT)-based diagnostic formative assessments answer Wiggins's call for authentic assessments that do not "lose sight" of the learner (Wiggins, 1989, p. 712). Based on empirical patterns in learning, LTs are structured in terms of increasingly sophisticated levels of thinking towards a target mathematical concept, and thus provide teachers a roadmap to proficiency on those concepts. This chapter reports on a design study, with sixth-grade classes at a diverse middle school, that investigated five mathematics teachers' implementation of an LT-based diagnostic formative assessment tool and an associated curriculum on ratio reasoning. Results show that students achieved moderate post-test scores with significant positive learning gains, equitably distributed across sub-groups. Students expressed enthusiasm for revising and resubmitting answers. Although the teachers in this study did not fully leverage the structures of the LTs in the learner-centred way anticipated by the tool's designers during data reviews, the chapter gives insights into potential additional components. Additional components needed to scaffold learner-centred assessment practices include a more explicit model of learner-centred instruction, a framework for LT-based data-driven decision-making, and a design for short- and long-feedback cycles for data use, including one involving collective data reviews and instructional planning by groups of teachers.

Keywords

learning trajectories – learner-centred instruction – classroom assessment – ratio reasoning – diagnostic formative assessment

1 Introduction

It makes sense to reject high stakes testing as a means to improve ongoing instruction: the return of results is delayed, and those results lack detail about specific students' strengths and weaknesses in relation to content topics (Supovitz, 2009). This only highlights the urgency for an alternative means of meaningful, systematic, and timely feedback to teachers and to students as students' progress in learning, to facilitate teachers in making effective, data-driven, instructional modifications. Without systematic feedback, students and teachers "fly blind", lacking information they need for guidance. This has become obvious during the recent pandemic, with teachers and administrators avoiding assessments to "lessen pressure on students", sending the message that assessment is not essential for learning. On the contrary, gathering actionable and valid data on specific content-based needs of students has never been so urgent. As stated, three decades ago, and not yet realised, "We need a new philosophy of assessment in this country that never loses sight of the student" (Wiggins, 1989, p. 712). To this end, a definition of "authentic assessment" whose goal is to strengthen "learner-centred instruction" is discussed (Confrey & Shah, 2021). The chapter also defines learner-centred instruction as instruction that elicits and builds on students' ideas, strategies, discourse, and representations as they solve challenging tasks.

Authentic assessment can be defined in diverse ways, utilising criteria such as performance-based, real-world, formative, cognitively complex, collaborative, justified, self-regulated, and mastery-oriented (Frey, Schmitt, & Allen, 2012; Gulikers, Bastiaens, & Kirschner, 2004). This chapter locates our work in a subset of these terms, focusing on ideas of being formative, addressing progressively more cognitively complex thinking, building on student strengths, promoting their self-regulation, and being mastery-oriented.

In this chapter, the focus on "diagnostic formative assessment based on the foundation of learning trajectories" (Confrey, Gianopulos, McGowan, Shah, & Belcher, 2017) is described in our work at scale across all of the middle grades mathematical content. The goal of the approach is to provide students and teachers with a variety of assessment tools for monitoring students' progress along learning trajectories (LTs) during instruction, to document strengths and needs and to allow for personalised instructional modifications to be rendered to address those documented needs. The reports are designed to help teachers know where to concentrate their instructional time and resources, and to inform students of their areas of proficiency and what remains to be learned, all in real time. The chapter commences with a review of the underlying theoretical base in our key constructs. The chapter then describes the software application used and reports on an initial design study on ratio reasoning that revealed the promise and challenges of using a LT-based curriculum with an accompanying set of diagnostic assessments. Despite significant improvement from pre- to post-tests, overall performance remained low, and observations of teachers using the system to return data revealed few learner-centred strategies. The chapter further discusses the need for greater elaboration on how to leverage the hierarchical structure and content of the LT to adapt instruction in K-12 mathematics to students' needs. Finally, the chapter identifies a set of supports needed for teachers to effectively use these data to help students achieve proficiency in key ideas.

2   Theoretical Background

This study theorises that if teachers have access both to data reports on students' progress along LTs and to an LT-based curriculum, they will be more successful in fostering learner-centred instruction; and this in turn will produce stronger student learning outcomes. The study proposes the use of LT-based, diagnostic, formative classroom assessment as the means to achieve these connections. The study commences by explaining our theoretical approaches to three constructs – *learning trajectories, learner-centred instruction,* and *classroom assessment.*

LTs delineate how students are likely to move from naive and intuitive starting points to more sophisticated thinking, by describing intermediate behaviours, utterances, beliefs, and strategies that are likely to arise during learning (Confrey et al., 2009). LTs are synthesised from empirical studies (clinical interviews, teaching experiments, and design studies) of children engaging with challenging, developmentally-appropriate, instructional tasks (Battista, 2011; Barrett et al., 2012; Confrey, 2019; Confrey et al., 2014; Maloney et al., 2014; Sarama & Clements, 2009; Siemon, Barkatsas, & Seah, 2019; van den Heuvel-Panhuizen & Buys, 2008). The developmental process towards understanding a target mathematical idea or concept is viewed as genetic-epistemological (Piaget, 1970) or guided reinvention (Freudenthal, 1987). LT levels comprise a variety of epistemological objects: representations, strategies, cases, forms of reasoning, inventions, and partial conceptions arranged in levels of sophistication. LTs do not constitute a stage theory; instead, they offer descriptions of thinking that are likely to emerge in classrooms when rich learning opportunities are made available (Lehrer & Schauble, 2015).

By articulating likely levels of student reasoning, LTs also afford teachers a tool to strengthen their own mathematical knowledge for teaching (Ball, Thames, & Phelps, 2008). Teachers can examine the development of important concepts, deepen their understanding of underlying cases, connections,

FIGURE 9.1   Observable characteristics of learner-centred instruction (Confrey & Shah, 2021)

and justifications, and see new possibilities for mathematical modeling or applications.

Thus, LTs can be viewed as a means to strengthen learner-centred instruction and help teachers to focus on students – their ideas, approaches, and reasoning. The study conceptualises learner-centred instruction as encouraging and supporting students to engage in the set of behaviours shown in Figure 9.1 (Confrey & Shah, 2021; O'Shea & Leavy, 2013). Instead of treating an absence of knowledge as a deficit, LTs support insight into specific ideas that lead to more sophisticated conceptual understanding.

LTs can be used to improve learner-centred instruction by providing teachers data on student progress along LTs during instruction and informing instructional modifications that address specific student needs. This approach implies a formative use of assessment. New forms of formative assessment – more systematic, comprehensive, and based on specific theories of learning (Shepard et al., 2018) – are emerging under the descriptor "classroom assessment" (NRC, 2001). Thus, classroom assessment can enhance learning by helping teachers and students to focus on what is to be learned, how that learning is progressing among different learners in relation to the curriculum or assessment tasks, and to increase students' participation in assessment, and hence their self-regulation (Heritage, 2016).

2.1   A Diagnostic Learning Trajectory-Based Formative Assessment System

Math Mapper 6-8 (MM6-8) is the diagnostic LT-based formative assessment system used in the study. It was designed as a digital tool for classroom assessment and feedback to support rich classroom discourse around diverse patterns in student thinking evidenced in their responses to diagnostic items/

tasks. It provides systematic feedback on students' progress along 60 mathematical constructs that span the entire middle school curriculum. The LTs that underpin each construct are developed from a synthesis of empirical research on learning. In MM6-8, LTs are positioned within a hierarchical learning map of nine big ideas (sudds.co). Each big idea contains a set of clusters of related constructs which can be assessed as a group or individually.

MM6-8's diagnostic assessments comprise 8–12 conceptually rich items associated with specific LT-levels. Items were all newly developed by the research team. Item types include numeric entry, multiple choice, multiple select, or matching with options and are designed to diagnose student understanding, misconceptions, or errors. Teachers typically assign assessments about ⅔ of the way through the instructional schedule for a unit. Students take about 20–30 minutes to complete the assessments. Upon completion, students and teachers immediately receive reports that allow students to review their overall percent correct, their item-by-item and level-by-level performance, and to revise or reveal answers to missed questions (Figure 9.2).[1] The assessments are conceptual, rather than focused on skills and procedures. They are calibrated to be diagnostic, so when students first encounter them, their scores tend to be in the middle range of percentiles, allowing space for improvement. These scores initially shock students, especially those accustomed to high scores; the

FIGURE 9.2   Math-Mapper 6–8's student report display

assessments' purpose – to support growth – has to be explained and situated in a formative, growth-oriented context (Dweck, 2006). Prior studies indicate that once their expectations are adjusted, students feel empowered by gaining immediate access to their data, feeling a renewed sense of what they need to do to learn the material (Matlen et al., 2017).

Teacher reports display detailed results for all students in a class in the form of heatmaps (Figure 9.3). The LT levels are displayed along the vertical axes; clicking a level label displays the actual items administered. Students are listed along the horizontal axes, ordered from lowest performing to highest performing on each construct, from left to right. The stack of colour-coded boxes above their initials represents their results by level. The colour coding varies from shades of blue for varying levels of correctness (darker blue indicates a greater percent correct) to orange for incorrect responses.[2] Because the difficulty of items increases at higher levels, one typically finds mostly blue on the lower levels gradually shifting to mostly orange near the top. As illustrated in Figure 9.3, construct A, the general shift from blue to orange forms a diagonal curved boundary (black curve; known as a Guttman curve (Guttman, 1950)), that distinguishes stronger from weaker performance across the class. The heat map also allows teachers to know where to focus their modifications to instruction by level (horizontal purple box) or by student group (vertical purple box).

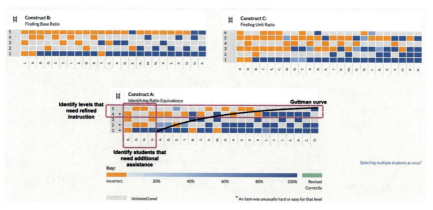

FIGURE 9.3   Math-Mapper 6–8's teacher report, heatmap display

3 The Study

3.1 *Purpose*

Curious about the degree to which MM6-8 could be used effectively by teachers to modify their instruction to be more learner-centred and achieve improved student outcomes, the authors conducted a study focusing on how teachers use and respond to MM6-8 diagnostic assessment data. In order to minimise variation due to differences in curricular materials, the authors designed an LT-based curriculum for participating teachers and conducted related professional development (PD). The authors were interested to see if the focus on LTs and use of level-by-level data from MM6-8 would support teachers to engage students in discussions that drew out their reasoning. The authors expected to see variation in student outcomes across classes, so the study investigated whether different groups of students benefited equally.

3.2 Research Questions
This study investigated three related research questions:
- Can the use of a common sixth-grade LT-based curriculum and accompanying formative diagnostic assessment tool lead to gains in students' learning outcomes in ratio, and, if so, who benefits? Do the gains vary across teachers?
- Are teachers able to interpret and review their class's formative diagnostic assessment data with students, so as to focus attention on appropriate levels of the LT to address student needs, foster student participation, and promote learner-centred discussions?
- Did any of the patterns of assessment results appear to be connected to curricular treatment of topics?

3.3 Participants
The study was conducted at a high-needs middle school (n = 939 students, 56% eligible for free and reduced lunch). The demographic breakdown by ethnic subgroup was: 24% African-American, 19% Hispanic, 10% who identify as multi-racial, and 46% White. All five sixth grade teachers, each teaching two sections, participated. A half-day PD session was conducted before the study on the curriculum use.

3.4 Materials and Methods
3.4.1 Ratio Reasoning in the Learning Map
In the learning map, ratio reasoning resides in two clusters: Cluster 4, "Finding Key Ratio Relationships" and cluster 5, "Comparing Ratios and Solving for Missing Values in Proportions". The cluster "Finding Key Ratio Relationships" consists of three constructs: "Ratio Equivalence", "Base Ratios", and "Unit Ratios" (Table 9.1). The second cluster, "Comparing Ratios and Solving for Missing Values in Proportions", consists of "Comparing Ratios" and "Solving for Missing Values" (Table 9.2). These clusters were constructed through a synthesis of research on ratio reasoning by multiple authors, including members of the Rational Number Project (Behr et al., 1992; Cramer et al., 1993; Post et al., 1998; Vergnaud, 1994; Streefland, 1984, 1985; Confrey & Scarano, 1995).

TABLE 9.1 LT-levels for constructs in the *Finding Key Ratio Relationships* cluster[a]

L	Ratio equivalence	Base ratio	Unit ratio
1	Creates equivalent ratios to make "more" by multiplying both quantities by the same whole number factor (Gr. 6)	Understands base ratio as smallest whole number equivalent ratio (Gr. 6)	Finds unit ratios with whole number quantities [(1: n) or (m: 1) where n, or m, is a whole number] and multiplies by integer values to find equivalent ratios (Gr. 6)
2	Creates equivalent ratios to make "less" by dividing both quantities by 2 one or more times (Gr. 6)	Finds base ratio when common factors are powers of 2 (Gr. 6)	Given one unit ratio with whole number quantities [(1: n) or (m: 1) where n, or m, is a whole number], finds the other ($\frac{1}{n}$:1) or 1:$\frac{1}{m}$ (Gr. 6)
3	Creates equivalent ratios to make "less" by dividing both quantities by an odd factor (Gr. 6)	Finds base ratio for an even and odd or odd and odd quantity that are not relatively prime (Gr. 6)	Identifies both unit ratios on a graph and uses in context (Gr. 6)
4	Uses a table of values to show ratio equivalence always preserved when both quantities are multiplied or divided by the same factor (Gr. 6)	Finds base ratio through prime factorisation (Gr. 6)	For non-unit base ratios, finds unit ratio using equipartitioning or fair sharing (Gr. 6)
5	Recognises equivalent ratios as points on the plane that lie on a line through the origin (Gr. 6)	Understands base ratio as "so much of this for so much of that" (Gr. 6)	Given any non-unit ratio (a:b), finds both unit ratios using division (ab:1 and 1:ba) and uses in context (Gr. 6)

[a] These are the five ratio constructs and associated levels used in the study. Since that time, a new construct, "Building Up/Down with Ratios", and revisions to existing constructs, have been completed. These can be viewed at sudds.co

3.4.2 The Curriculum

The 6-lesson curriculum[3] (Table 9.3) was designed to address two relevant clusters with a shared set of materials that would support learner-centred

TABLE 9.2 LT-levels for constructs in *Comparing Ratios and Solving for Missing Values in Proportions* cluster

L	Comparing ratios	Solving for missing values in proportions
1	Compares and orders ratios $(a:b)$ and $(c:d)$ which have an equivalent corresponding value ($a = c$ or $b = d$) (Gr. 6)	Builds up to a specific value of one quantity by incrementally adding base ratios or unit ratios (Gr. 6)
2	Identifies an equivalent corresponding value in ratio table or graph to compare ratios (Gr. 6)	Builds equivalent ratios from base ratios or unit ratios by multiplying by n (Gr. 6)
3	Creates an equivalent corresponding value in ratio table or graph to compare ratios (Gr. 6)	Builds to equivalent ratios by multiplying quantities by n and adjusts by adding or subtracting base and unit ratios (Gr. 6)
4	Compares ratios using unit ratio (Gr. 6)	Finds missing value in a ratio box (2×2 ratio table) using whole number multiplication or division of both values horizontally and vertically (Gr. 6)
5	Compares ratios by examining relative steepness (later slope) of graph (Gr. 7)	Finds missing value in a ratio box with whole number entries by combination of multiplication and division of both values horizontally and vertically (Gr. 6)
6	–	Uses ratio boxes that include fractional entries to solve for missing value (Gr. 7)
7	–	Distinguishes proportional from non-proportional relationships (Gr. 7)
8	–	Given a set of values in a proportional relationship in tables and graphs, identifies the constant of proportionality and relates it to the unit ratio/rate $(1, k)$ and to the equation, $y = kx$ (Gr. 7)

instruction. The lessons combined problem-based (lessons 1 through 4) and project-based instruction (lessons 5 and 6). They were written to elicit and support the discussion of diverse student strategies. Each lesson included open-ended tasks built around engaging and familiar contexts, such as making more/less lemonade and comparing donut eating speeds, as well as independent practice opportunities and homework assignments. In the first four days of

TABLE 9.3   Overview of curriculum aligned to MM6-8's ratio clusters

Day	Cluster (Construct)	L's	Content	Context
1	4(9)	1–4	Building and identifying equivalent ratios	Making more/less lemonade that tastes the same as a given recipe
2	4(10)	1–5	Finding the base ratio and graphing equivalent ratios	Making smaller batches of trail mix that taste the same as a given recipe
3	4(11), 5(12)	1–3, 1–4	Finding and comparing unit ratios, in tables and graphs	Given a donut-eating race and a ratio of donuts: seconds, determine the number of seconds it takes to eat 1 donut and the number of donuts that can be eaten in 1 second
4	4(11), 5(12)	4–5, 1–4	Finding and comparing unit ratios	Unit prices (e.g., number of dollars for 1 apple and number of apples for 1 dollar)
5	Cluster 4 Diagnostic Assessment			
6	5(13)	1–3	Finding missing values using build-up	Making distracted driving data understandable
7	5(13)	4–5	Finding missing values using ratio boxes	Making distracted driving data understandable
8	Cluster 5 Diagnostic Assessment			

the curriculum, students explored cluster 4, "Finding Key Ratio Relationships", engaging with equivalent ratios, base ratios, and unit ratios. Days 5 and 6 used a project-based approach to address cluster 5, "Comparing Ratios and Solving for Missing Values in Proportions". Students investigated distracted-driving statistics, using ratio boxes to compare ratios and solve for missing values in proportions.

3.4.3   The Professional Development

All the middle grades teachers at the school participated in a two-day PD workshop on the use of the tool during the summer and a half-day targeted PD workshop that reviewed the ratio LTs and the curriculum. Teachers also participated in researcher-led PLC workshops.

All PD activities focused on how to connect the LTs with student thinking to promote learner-centred instruction. The LTs were related to constructivist learning theory, specifically to Piagetian theory of the growth of knowledge. Emphasis was placed on coordinating the representations of ratio in tables and graphs. Teachers were provided opportunities to work the problems and discuss their solutions. Examples of student thinking and work and typical students' misconceptions were shared along with strategies to address them.

3.5   Data Sources and Analysis

3.5.1   Outcome Measures/Assessments

The following assessments, measuring only the 6th grade levels of the LTs, were administered during the study[4] (Figure 9.4):

- A pre-test administered before beginning the ratio curriculum; included items from both MM6-8 ratio clusters
- A diagnostic assessment for cluster 4, administered after completion of its curriculum
- A diagnostic assessment for cluster 5, administered after completion of its curriculum
- MM6-8 survey of students' perceptions of the assessments and reports, administered after each assessment event
- A post-test containing items from both MM6-8 ratio clusters, administered after completion and review of content from both clusters

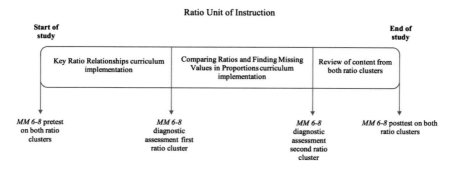

FIGURE 9.4   Schedule of instruction and corresponding diagnostic assessments

The research team conducted 25 observations over the course of the study. Most observations focused on teachers' use of MM6-8 during data review sessions, specifically on whether and how they presented and discussed class heat maps, identified items for whole-group or small-group review, and elicited and built upon student thinking. Some additional class observations were conducted to record the degree and substance of student participation on non-testing days, observe any instructional modifications, and identify necessary changes to the curriculum. Table 9.4 outlines the components of the research questions, the data sources used to investigate them, and the method of analysis.

3.6 Results

In this section, the results from the pre- and post-test on ratio reasoning are discussed. To determine the magnitude of growth in student performance, the

TABLE 9.4 Data sources used to investigate components of the research questions

Connection to research question	Data sources	Method of analysis
Did students show gains in learning outcomes? Which students showed increases? Did the results vary by teacher?	A pre- and post-test administered before beginning work on the ratio curriculum that included items from both MM 6-8 ratio clusters	Descriptive statistics for pre- and post-test Average gain scores from pre- to post-test, by group and by teacher Standard error to determine significance of observed differences between groups
What was the distribution of correct answers by LT level?	Data from cluster tests	Review of compound bar diagram of results by cluster
How do teachers review the data? How did students relate to the assessment reports?	Observations of classroom data reviews for both ratio cluster tests MM6-8 student survey	Summaries from daily debriefs
Do the curricular observations shed light on the student results? Were learner-centred practices witnessed during instruction?	Observations of curriculum implementation	Summaries from daily debriefs

authors calculated the difference between the mean percentage correct scores on the pre- and post-test for students who completed *both* tests (n = 165 for cluster 4 and n = 146 for cluster 5). Figure 9.5 compares the pre- and post-test distributions of overall student scores on cluster 4 and cluster 5 items.

Overall, performance improved on both cluster 4 and cluster 5 tests. Cluster 4's pre-test mean was 35.6% (s.d. 20.7%) and post-test mean was 50.2% (s.d. 22.8%). Cluster 5's pre-test mean was 31.6% (s.d. 21.5%) and post-test mean was 47.1% (s.d. 26.3%). The observed score differences from pre- to post-test were +14.6 (cluster 4, n = 165) and +15.5 (cluster 5, n = 146) percentage points. The effect sizes (Cohen's d) were 0.67 (cluster 4) and 0.65 (cluster 5). Figure 9.6 shows the average gain scores (post-test score − pre-test score) for all students combined with standard error bars, separated by subgroup. For the "All group", the height of the gain score is more than five times greater than the standard

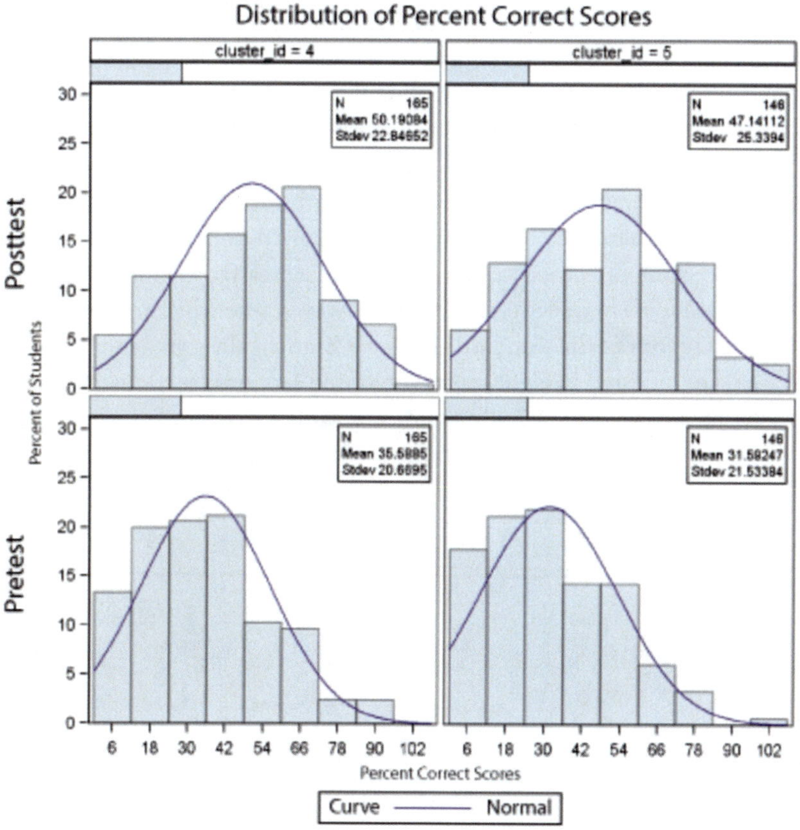

FIGURE 9.5   Pre-test and post-test score distributions of percentage correct on items for cluster 4, "Finding Key Ratio Relationships", and cluster 5, "Comparing Ratios and Solving for Missing Values in Proportions" (for students who took pre-test and post-test)

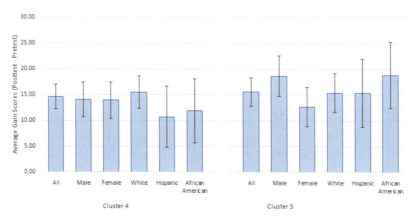

FIGURE 9.6 Average gain scores (post-test – pre-test score) by cluster and group. Error bars represent standard errors

error of the gain score for both clusters, indicating a statistically significant difference. The sample sizes in cluster 4 for each reported subgroup (male, female, white, Hispanic, and African-American students) were 82, 83, 86, 32, and 30, respectively. The sample sizes in cluster 5 for each reported subgroup (male, female, white, Hispanic, and African-American students) were 70, 76, 77, 26, and 26, respectively. Because all standard error bars are overlapping, the conclusion is there are no statistically significant differences across groups.

Figure 9.7 compares the pre- and post-test scores by section. The mean number of students in a section taking a test was 15. The whiskers on the bars in Figure 9.7 represent the standard error bars. Statistically significant gains for cluster 4 were reported in eight out of ten of the sections (sections 86, 88, 89, 90, 91, 92, 94, and 95). Statistically significant gains for cluster 5 were reported in seven out of the ten sections (sections 86, 87, 88, 89, 90, 91, and 92).

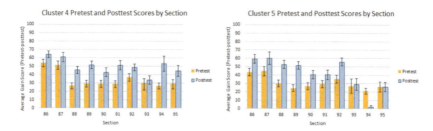

FIGURE 9.7 Pre- and post-test comparisons, by sections, for Cluster 4 and Cluster 5

Pairs of consecutively numbered sections (e.g., 86–87) were taught by the same teacher; sections 86 and 87 were the only two sections identified as "advanced". Pre-test to post-test gains were more variable for cluster 5 than for cluster 4. The non-overlapping error bars on certain sections suggest that some sections attained greater gains than others. For instance, in cluster 5, it appears that sections 90 and 91 did not attain as much growth as sections 88, 89, and 92. For cluster 5, it appears that sections 93 and 95 did not attain as much growth as 90 and 91. (Section 94 shows a negative change, has a very low n due to a teacher error in test assignment, and should be disregarded.) These data by section show that some teachers have more success with a particular cluster than others, while other teachers appear to support significant gains in learning with students who begin the unit with low pre-test results.

Lastly, the authors compared students' performance in this study with students' performance from the same school during the previous year. During the previous school year, the authors had gathered field test data at that school for the same clusters. On items that were administered during both field testing and the current study, the authors observed an average gain of +16 percentage points in favour of the current study. No major efflux or influx of students suggested any major change in the schools' demographics. From current data, it is not possible to differentiate the percentage of variance that can be explained by the curriculum, use of software tool, staffing changes, teacher PD, or item sampling, but some combination of these factors seems to account for the increase in students' average score in ratio reasoning.

3.6.1   Level-by-Level Results for Constructs in Clusters 4 and 5

The authors investigated student results by level and by construct, and compiled the data from the two cluster assessments into compound bar diagrams with confidence intervals (Figures 9.8a–9.8e). These diagrams resemble individual teacher's heat maps in that they display performance (proportion correct/incorrect) by levels; however, they differ in that they display accumulated data for all the sixth-grade sections. The authors looked for the expected pattern of increasing difficulty with higher LT levels. If there were discrepant performance reported on levels (i.e., levels that performed unexpectedly hard or easy), the authors examined the assessment items at that level, as well as the surrounding levels, to seek an explanation for the discrepancy.

Below are general observations from the compound bar diagrams by cluster, accompanied by a more in-depth exploration of the students' responses in the "Finding Unit Ratio" construct. The authors conducted a closer analysis of unit ratio, because it had particularly weak results and classroom observations had revealed the topic was particularly challenging to teach and required supplemental curricular materials (see Section 3.6.3).

The percentage of correct responses at levels ranged from 20–70%. As expected, the proportion of incorrect responses generally tended to increase as one proceeded up the levels. An exception was observed at L1 of ratio equivalence, which was unexpectedly difficult for the students. The item at that level

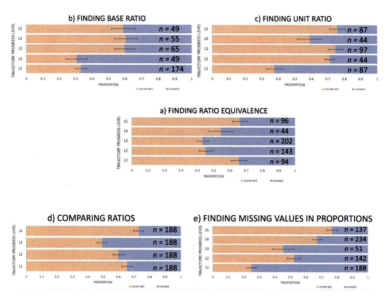

FIGURES 9.8 (a, b, and c) Compound bar diagrams for constructs in Cluster 4. (d) and (e) Compound bar diagrams for constructs in Cluster 5. Orange and blue represent proportion incorrect and correct, respectively

required students to multiply a decimal by a factor, which without a calculator may have been difficult for these students. In base ratio, students exhibited struggles at level 3 (L3), when required them to factor out values other than 2, and at L4, which involved prime factoring. These results suggested students' weaknesses in multiplication and division may have negatively affected their performance.

On unit ratio, the data showed that while students were able to work with whole numbered-valued unit ratios (L1), they struggled at levels involving fractional values. One minor exception was evidenced at L4, where questions involved using fair-sharing strategies to find unit ratios. The fair sharing item (Figure 9.9) required students to notice that dividing a half into fourths results in a share that is an eighth of the original quantity (not a fourth). While 41% of the responses to this item were entirely correct ($n = 44$), the 21% who selected the response that both students were correct may have understood how to share fairly, but failed to recognise the mistake in naming the result. This may indicate a problem understanding referent units in fractions.

In the L5 item (Figure 9.9), students were required to find both unit ratios (number of feet of snow per 1 day and the number of days it takes for 1 foot of snow to fall). The item responses show that finding the answer ($\frac{5}{4} = 1.25$) (37% of responses) was slightly easier than $\frac{4}{5} = .8$ (30% of responses), supporting

PROMOTING LEARNER-CENTRED INSTRUCTION 203

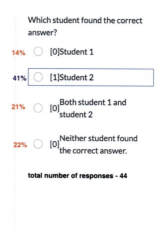

Every fall, a town in Wisconsin hosts an apple pie eating contest. This year, the winner ate 5 apple pies in 8 minutes. Two students want to report how many pies the winner ate each minute, if the winner ate steadily.

The students described the methods they used to determine how much pie the winner ate each minute.

Student 1:
- Divide each of the five pies into halves, making 10 halves.
- Distribute 1 half to each of the eight minutes, leaving 2 halves.
- Divide each half into 4 parts, which makes 8 parts.
- Give one of those parts to each of the eight minutes.
- Solution: The winner ate $\frac{1}{2} + \frac{1}{4}$ pies per minute.

Student 2:
- Divide each of the five pies into eighths.
- Distribute one eighth from each pie to each minute.
- Solution: The winner ate $\frac{5}{8}$ pies per minute.

Which student found the correct answer?

14% ○ [0]Student 1
41% ○ [1]Student 2
21% ○ [0] Both student 1 and student 2
22% ○ [0] Neither student found the correct answer.

total number of responses - 44

FIGURE 9.9   L4 item (for non-unit base ratios, finds unit ratio using equipartitioning or fair sharing). Correct responses are shown in blue and incorrect responses are shown in red

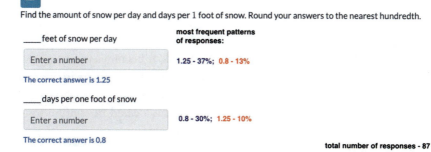

FIGURE 9.10   Item for L5 ("Given any non-unit ratio $(a:b)$, finds both unit ratios using division ($\frac{a}{b}:1$ and $1:\frac{b}{a}$) and uses in context")

prior research demonstrating that equipartitioning a objects among b sharers tends to prove easier for learners when $a > b$ (Confrey et al., 2014). Only 25% ($n = 87$) of the responses were correct for both unit ratios and about 8% of responses reversed the answers. If students had internalised algorithmically dividing through by 4 to get the first answer and by 5 to get the second, the percentage correct on the two parts of the item would have likely been equivalent. The fact that the difficulty pattern corresponds more closely to the pattern predicted from research on partitioning suggests that many students may not have successfully transitioned from L4 to L5.

Students' overall performance on Cluster 5 was weaker than on Cluster 4, suggesting that they lacked key insights from Cluster 4, which was likely to have impeded their progress on Cluster 5. This suggests that instructional modifications following the return of data from Cluster 4 may not have remediated the weakness. However, without retesting, this cannot be directly inferred. Students' overall performance in "Comparing Ratios" conformed to the expectation of increased difficulty at higher levels in the LT, with the exception of L3. Analysis of the L3 item revealed that the item did not conform properly to the level. It was subsequently revised. Students' difficulties with unit ratios, especially those with decimal values, may explain the weaker performance at L4 ("Compares ratios using unit ratio").

L1 of Finding Missing Values in Proportions indicated that students were able to build up to specific quantities in equivalent ratios and hence solve for a missing value by using unit ratios of the form 1: n at L1. However, they seemed to struggle with the remainder of levels that had items with ratios of the form where, $a, b \neq 0$ or 1. L3 was the only exception; review of the values used in the item suggested number choice may account for the slightly stronger performance. Overall, the authors suspect that students' performance on both cluster 4 and 5 may indicate weakness with the big idea on number ("Position, compare and operate on quantities involving one-dimensional number") involving fluency in multiplication and division facts and understanding of fractions and decimals.

Using analysis of the compound bar diagrams, it becomes more apparent how student performance data can be analysed within LTs to create far more specific observations about student understanding. Not only can weakness in topics be identified, but those weaknesses can be located in relation to the overall hierarchical structure of the LTs and the relationships among the constructs and clusters.

3.6.2 Observations Regarding Review of Diagnostic Assessment Data

After teachers administered diagnostic assessments, researchers observed how they discussed results with students. Several teachers began their reviews by leading a whole-class discussion of their class heat maps, which they displayed (student initials hidden) at the front of the classroom. They then asked students to reflect on the class performance, drawing their attention to relevant features of the heat map. For example, one teacher, after explaining the meanings of the different colours, asked her students, "What colour pops out at you" and then, "Why is [orange] popping out?" She then expressed a growth mindset

(Dweck, 2006), explaining to students, "That means we got more wrong ... than we [got] right ... the great thing is, it is a way for us to learn, so we have some work to do".

Typically, teachers walked through the items step-by-step, by simply putting the responses up on the board, identifying the correct answers, and explaining why they were correct. Sometimes these exchanges were animated with the teachers reminding students with advice such as "Many of you did not make the chart. Make a chart. It is not optional". Or "Keep the balance by dividing both columns by the same number". With this type of review, teachers simply reinforced a correct procedure. Student participation was limited to giving the correct response; only occasionally were they asked for an explanation. At no point during the data review were teachers observed facilitating a conceptual discussion around incorrect answers.

For the most part, the teachers focused on demonstrating why techniques recommended in class would have helped students do better. The review provided an opportunity to demonstrate and reinforce those approaches. Notably less evident was the implementation of the tenets expressed in the classroom or formative assessment framework, such as encouraging students to reflect on and establish learning goals or engaging in self- and peer-assessment. While some teachers did try to help students recognise the gap between their current performance and the desired outcomes, they did not use many techniques to strengthen student agency, nor did they leverage the LTs in those conversations.

Overall, watching teachers discuss class results revealed that rapid and automated return of data to students and teachers resulted in significant excitement and interest, but did not necessarily accomplish the goal of supporting learner-centred instruction within a classroom assessment framework. Students were animated by seeing their results and excited by the possibility of revising and resubmitting their responses. However, teachers demonstrated little evidence of working with students to diagnose the reasons behind their incorrect responses. The authors also saw no use of peer-to-peer interactions as an opportunity for students to share insights and approaches with each other.

Although teachers did focus on levels most in need of attention at the classroom level, there was virtually no evidence that they viewed the items as representative of a level or as a level as situated in the sequence of the LT levels. An item's connection to the description of its level, or to another item from the same level, was not discussed. Nor was any mention made of how an item's level built on the earlier level and set up the subsequent level.

Having observed data reviews where students typically did not play a significant role, the authors were interested in understanding how students related to their own data reports based on their survey responses ($n = 269$). Students found the reports mostly useful (somewhat useful – 46%; definitely useful – 25%; not useful – 29%). The authors also asked students what one action they would take now that they've seen their report. A total of 42 responses to this question were recorded (16% response rate), 80% of which indicated that students want to improve and work harder e.g. "I want to study harder", "More ratios on my own time", "Keep practicing!", "Study and practice finding missing values in proportions", etc. These responses highlight that students began to take more responsibility for their own learning and partner in the assessment process.

3.6.3   Classroom Observations on Curricular Use

To explore the extent to which patterns observed in the compound bar diagrams (Figures 9.8a–9.8c) could be connected to the treatment of the content in the curricular materials and their use, the authors compared the results from the compound bar diagrams with those from the classroom observations. The report focuses upon one example on unit ratios, where the authors saw possible connections between the classroom observations and students' performance on the diagnostic assessments.

The compound bar diagram for unit ratios (Figure 9.8c) showed a drop in student performance from L1 (finds and builds up with unit ratios of the form $1: n$ where n is a whole-number) to L2 (given the ratio $1: n$, where n is a whole-number, finds the other unit ratio). During L3, given ratios of the form $(a: an)$ and asked to find the unit ratio $(1: n)$, teachers directed students to divide both columns in the ratio table by the same number to get a column equal to 1, reminding them that equivalence in a ratio table is maintained by multiplying or dividing the quantities by the same number (Figure 9.11).

Number of donuts	Number of seconds
6	30
1	5
0.2	1

FIGURE 9.11
Strategy one teacher used to show students how to find unit ratios

In this example, one teacher was observed showing students how they could divide both the number of donuts (6) and the number of seconds (30) by 6 to find the unit ratio 1:5 (row 3 in the table). Students' active role was then restricted to calculating the unit ratio using calculators or long division to find the second unit ratio, 0.2: 1. No discussion of the contextual meaning of that unit ratio was observed.

Emphasising the process of division instead of fair sharing to find unit ratios probably affected students' performance on the assessment for two reasons. First, it was not clear whether students viewed the decimal answers to their division calculations as ratios, which may have affected their performance on L2 assessment items. For example, they were able to find the correct value for the bottom row of the tables (0.2), but the meaning of the unit ratio (i.e., 1/5 donut for every 1 second) was not discussed in class, so it was unlikely to make sense to students.

Second, this procedure used by the teacher, while likely to produce a correct answer, is difficult to apply consecutively when both unit ratios include fractions, as shown in the L5 example in Figure 9.12. The procedure could lead students to correctly divide both 5 and 4 by 5 to find the unit ratio 1 foot of snow: 4/5 days, but then struggle with how to divide both 1 and 4/5 by 4/5 to find the second unit ratio. In this instance, the strategy requires a sophisticated understanding of how to divide 1 by ⅘, a challenge to many students. While they could go back to the 5:4 represented in the first row and divide both quantities by 4, the authors doubt this would help students interpret the result of 1 ¼ feet of snow in 1 day.

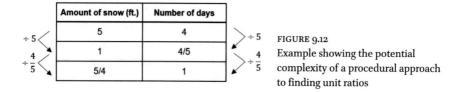

FIGURE 9.12
Example showing the potential complexity of a procedural approach to finding unit ratios

Despite the teachers' reliance on a procedural calculation of unit ratios, students were observed in two instances exploring how to find the unit ratio via a fair sharing approach (L4), in one case drawing representations of sharing a number of donuts among a set of single seconds (lesson 3), and of sharing apples among a set of dollars (lesson 4) in the other. In neither case was the teacher observed following the student approach to completion and discussing it. This procedural approach to L2 and insufficient treatment of L4 (fair sharing) of the LT (despite some students' attempts at such an approach) may have led to students' weaknesses at L5, which involves recognising that the two unit ratios for the ratio $a:b$ are $\frac{a}{b}:1$ and $1:\frac{b}{a}$.

Based on these observations and the data provided by the compound bar diagrams, the authors later edited the curriculum to: (1) simplify the numbers used in the tasks to decrease the procedural demand and to encourage focusing on understanding the meaning of unit ratio in context, and (2) strengthen the connection between the unit ratio and fair sharing.

4 Discussion

Regarding research question 1, based on the pre- and post-test results, students achieved significant learning outcome gains. The gains were achieved by all subgroups (boys, girls, and all race and ethnicities), suggesting that the benefits were equitably distributed. Sections taught by different teachers showed different amounts of gain, with the advanced classes achieving the largest gains and with some evidence of weakness in both classes' performance taught by different teachers. The scores were substantially greater than those achieved during the prior year (by a different but likely comparable group), suggesting a positive effect of the curriculum/diagnostic assessment tool combination. However, the absence of a comparison group makes it difficult to gauge the meaningfulness of the gains. And finally, the post-test score means, were low (50–60%), this suggests that despite improvements, students' understanding of ratio was still well-below grade-level expectations based on assignment of levels to grades.

The answer to the second research question, concerning the use of data to promote learner-involvement and -centredness, was more complex. Most of the teachers (4 out of 5) projected the heat maps on the board to review with their students, and used the language of the LTs to communicate about student progress. Those teachers selected appropriate levels for attention, and opened and reexamined the items with their classes. However, for the most part, they did not solicit student input as they reviewed the items. None of the teachers asked students who answered an item incorrectly to explain their reasoning. Typically, teachers instead simply re-told the students how to solve the problem, often admonishing them that, had they only followed the teachers' instruction, they would have got the answer correct.

Secondly, the teachers neither treated the items as examples of the reasoning germane to their levels, nor the levels as positioned within a sequence of levels. The way the authors interpreted and reported on the compound bar diagrams illustrates what is meant by conducting a hierarchical analysis of results by analysing the patterns across levels and looking for explanations across items at a level. It is not surprising that teachers struggle to conduct a hierarchical analysis, given that their experience of test review has been grounded in domain-sampling tests (Briggs & Peck, 2015), where items only represent examples of a broadly-defined topic. Teachers did not express to students that the learning goal was to reach proficiency in a target idea positioned at the top of the LT –they did not share with students where they were headed so the students could more readily recognise their progress toward the target understanding. Nonetheless, students demonstrated an increased sense of agency and satisfaction when they received and reviewed their own results and articulated what their next steps needed to be.

How then can diagnostic assessment data support teachers to reflect on and improve the learner-centredness of their own instruction? In answer to the third research question, observations of teachers implementing the curriculum did provide some curricular insights that could explain students' performance on the unit ratio assessment. In particular, compound bar diagrams revealed weak performance on L2 and L5. The authors observed in some cases that teachers overemphasised division as a procedure lacking conceptual depth with which to calculate unit ratios, which may have negatively impacted students' success finding and interpreting both unit ratios (1: n and $1/n$: 1). This treatment also appeared to have obscured the meaning of a unit ratio and its connection to fair sharing, which could explain students' performance on L5. Based on these observations, the authors modified the curriculum to strengthen the connection between fair sharing and unit ratios.

It appeared that the LT-based assessments and associated curriculum were being assimilated into everyday teacher-driven instructional practices but were not yet being leveraged by the teachers to explicitly strengthen learner-centred aspects of their practice. That the combination of the curriculum and the assessment tools resulted in improvements in learning, improvements that were well-distributed across student groups, suggests significant value in the approach. Students' enthusiasm for receiving the data and revising and submitting answers suggests the potential to amplify their agency. However, when they received low scores, they were not simultaneously supported by robust formative practices to invite their active participation and convince them of their potential for success; this dampened further excitement. More effort needs to be devoted to encouraging persistence and student agency. These overall results suggest that a 'bare bones' integrating diagnostic feedback does not by itself stimulate a robust culture of learner-centred instruction. It denotes a step toward that end only, at least over the short term. So, the results raise the question of what more or else is needed to support teachers in developing assessment practices that keep students at the center.

The study catalysed for us three subsequent actions that will scaffold stronger advances towards learner-centred instruction and assessment (Confrey et al., 2018; Confrey & Shah, 2021):
- Strengthen teachers' understanding of the nature of the LTs, and their trust of the LTs as a robust, research-based source of understanding student learning. Teachers often view them as just another instructional support, instead of recognising the coherence of their structure for informing teachers about student cognitive behaviours. The authors believe that this

points to the need for more emphasis on two principles: (a) understanding that the LTs are a guide to the "genetic epistemology" of mathematical concepts", connecting students' naive ideas and everyday experiences to how those ideas and experiences can be refined gradually to develop deep and sound understanding of those concepts, and (b) recognising that if a gradual process of knowledge development is disrupted by early introduction of a procedural shortcut (e.g., a procedure to calculate the unit ratio), students will needlessly stumble on non-routinised problems and be more likely to internalise misconceptions. To provide them more reasons to trust the LTs, the authors are writing a set of rationale documents that explain, for each LT the underlying ideas, related research, and examples of student work. Further, the authors have articulated a model of learner-centred instruction (Figure 9.13) in MM6-8's professional learning materials that emphasises the centrality of student actions within an overall inquiry approach.

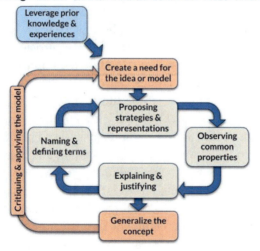

FIGURE 9.13
Model for learner-centred instruction

– Provide teachers with a framework for data interpretation. To this end, the authors have developed a learning-trajectory data-driven decision-making framework (Confrey and Shah, 2021). The framework (Figure 9.14) is organised around an inquiry cycle – scanning, interpreting, modifying instruction, reassessing, and review – that results in instructional interventions that accurately target and efficiently address the students' needs and reassessments to document that those needs have been met. Specifically, the framework scaffolds teachers on how to read heat maps and situate the results at the item-level within the hierarchy of the LT, that is, an item represents a level, which resides within a sequence of levels, all building to understanding of a target concept. Teachers learn to create conjectures that are carefully supported through contextualising the data in relation to curricular treatments and student needs, and, further, to actively test those conjectures through instructional modifications and reassessment to gauge their success.

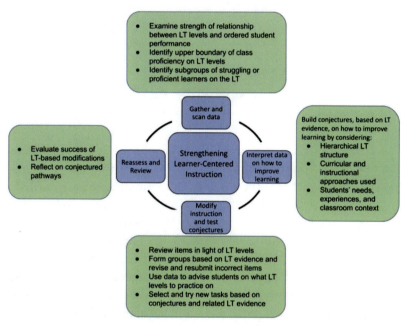

FIGURE 9.14   Framework for LT-based data-driven decision making (LT-DDDM) (from Confrey & Shah, 2021)

– Organise professional learning communities (PLCs) to support grade-level data reviews and discussions of alternative approaches. Our data revealed that: (a) different teachers were more or less successful in promoting learning gains, and (b) success varied by cluster. This suggests that schools have internal capacity for improvement, via colleagues' sharing of data and insights. Our data also suggest that curriculum can be strengthened by data examination, which can in turn lead to both immediate instructional modifications based on data and longer-term revisions (Figure 9.15). The authors have described the use of a two-cycle feedback loop called the Agile Curriculum Framework with successive school partnerships (Confrey et al., 2018).

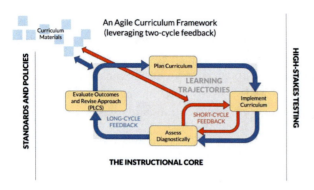

FIGURE 9.15   The agile curriculum framework, leveraging two-cycle feedback (from Confrey et al., 2018, p. 161)

5   Conclusion

To achieve Wiggins's call for authentic assessment that never loses sight of the student, one has to elaborate the meaning of, and directly scaffold, learner-centredness. Too often, the advocates of formative assessment suggest that it simply requires teachers to solicit student work or explanations, independent of an underlying model of longer-term student learning into which to sequence these contributions. In contrast, while the authors of this work certainly share the belief that student contributions are essential, they have to be understood in the context of a goal of instruction, an explicit target concept to be understood, and a pathway to reach the target. This requires more than a formal disciplinary interpretation; it requires – an understanding of how that idea evolves in learners' thinking, closely aligned to Confrey's "interactional path" (1990) and Simon's (1995) "hypothetical learning trajectory". It is also imperative that teachers have a deep commitment to the value of student thinking, to be curious about understanding it, and to recognise the importance of providing students with opportunities to build those understandings gradually and express them during the course of instruction and/or data review. Students must feel welcomed and validated in expressing their ideas and see their contributions as critical to gaining sophisticated understanding of a concept, i.e., learning.

This chapter described an LT-based diagnostic assessment tool and showed that when it is accompanied by an LT-based curriculum, teachers can successfully implement it to some degree, resulting in significant achievement gains and evenly distributed positive results. Some teachers' implementation of the curriculum appeared to be somewhat limited by overly procedural approaches to the content, which can cut-off students' contributions to learner-centred instruction as described by our model (Figure 9.13). The study thus identifies the need to direct more attention to the mathematical content and to the pedagogical content knowledge. This enables teachers to anticipate how the content unfolds and how to support students' movement up the LT both during initial instruction and during the review of diagnostic formative assessment data. The study also shows PD must be ongoing and systematic and include PLCs that require teachers to jointly plan for the future by communicating specifically about the mathematical content. Based on the variability of teacher effects on instructional gain, schools might profit by leveraging capacity within their own teaching ranks.

Notes

1 Since this study was completed, a practice component to support personalisation has been added, allowing students to choose and work at any level on any construct.
2 For any cluster, there are more levels overall than are practical to test for each student, so teachers can assign multiple forms of the test to cover all the levels across a class. If a particular student did not receive an item assessing a level, the cell is grey.
3 The curriculum was subsequently revised based on the findings of this study and is available on Math-Mapper 6-8's Resourcer at sudds.co
4 Students were provided opportunities to opt out of the research. Teachers' consent for participation was also collected.

References

Barrett, J., Clements, D., Sarama, J., Cullen, C., McCool, J., Witkowski-Rumsey, C., & Klanderman, D. (2012). Evaluating and improving a learning trajectory for linear measurement in elementary grades 2 and 3: A longitudinal study. *Mathematical Thinking and Learning, 14*(1), 28–54.

Battista, M. T. (2011). Conceptualizations and issues related to learning progressions, learning trajectories, and levels of sophistication. *The Mathematics Enthusiast, 8*(3), 507–570.

Behr, M., Harel, G., Post, T., & Lesh, R. (1992). Rational number, ratio and proportion. In D. Grouws (Ed.), *Handbook of research on mathematics teaching and learning* (pp. 296–333). Macmillan Publishing.

Black, P., & Wiliam, D. (1998). Inside the black box: Raising standards through classroom assessment. *Phi Delta Kappan, 80*(2), 139–144.

Briggs, D. C., & Peck, F. A. (2015). Using learning progressions to design vertical scales that support coherent inferences about student growth. *Measurement: Interdisciplinary Research and Perspectives, 13*(2), 75–99.

Cobb, P., Confrey, J., Lehrer, R., & Schauble, L. (2003). Design experiments in educational research. *Educational Researcher, 32*(1), 9–13.

Confrey, J. (1990). What constructivism implies for teaching. In R. B. Davis, C. A. Maher, & N. Noddings (Eds.), *Constructivist views on the teaching and learning of mathematics, Journal for Research in Mathematics Education Monograph, 4* (pp. 107–122). NCTM.

Confrey, J. (2015). *SUDDS digital learning system and learning map.* https://sudds.ced.ncsu.edu/wp-content/uploads/2017/02/gates-report-07-2015-smaller_2.pdf

Confrey, J., Gianopulos, G., McGowan, W., Shah, M., & Belcher, M. (2017). Scaffolding learner-centered curricular coherence using learning maps and diagnostic assessments designed around mathematics learning trajectories. *ZDM Mathematics Education, 49*(5), 717–734.

Confrey, J., & Maloney, A. (2012). A next generation digital classroom assessment based on learning trajectories. In C. Dede & J. Richards (Eds.), *Steps toward a digital teaching platform* (pp. 134–152). Teachers College Press.

Confrey, J., Maloney, A., Belcher, M. P., McGowan, W. P., Hennessey, M. P., & Shah, M. (2018). The concept of an agile curriculum as applied to a middle school mathematics Digital Learning System (DLS). *International Journal of Educational Research, 92*, 158–172.

Confrey, J., Maloney, A., Nguyen, K., Mojica, G., & Myers, M. (2009). Equipartitioning/splitting as a foundation of rational number reasoning using learning trajectories. In M. Tzekaki, M. Kaldrimidou, & H. Sakonidis (Eds.), *Proceedings of the 33rd conference of the International Group for the Psychology of Mathematics Education* (Vol. 2, pp. 345–352). International Group for the Psychology of Mathematics Education.

Confrey, J., Maloney, A. P., Nguyen, K. H. & Rupp, A. A. (2014). Equipartitioning, a foundation for rational number reasoning: Elucidation of a learning trajectory. In A. P. Maloney, J. Confrey, & K. H. Nguyen (Eds.), *Learning over time: Learning trajectories in mathematics education* (pp. 61–96). Information Age Publishing.

Confrey, J., & Scarano, G. (1995). Splitting reexamined: Results from a three-year longitudinal study of children in grades three to five. In D. Owens, M. Reed, & M. Millsaps (Eds.), *Proceedings of the seventeenth annual meeting of the North American Chapter of the International Group for the Psychology of Mathematics Education* (Vol. 1, pp. 421–426). Ohio State University.

Confrey, J., & Shah, M. (2021). Examining instructional change at scale using data from diagnostic assessments built on learning trajectories. *ZDM.* Manuscript in press.

Cramer, K., Post, T., & Currier, S. (1993). Learning and teaching ratio and proportion: Research implications. In D. Owens (Ed.), *Research ideas for the classroom* (pp. 159–178). Macmillan Publishing Company.

Dweck, C. S. (2006). *Mindset: The new psychology of success*. Random House Incorporated.

Frey, B. B., Schmitt, V. L., & Allen, J. P. (2012). Defining authentic classroom assessment. *Practical Assessment, Research & Evaluation, 17*(2), 1–18.

Gulikers, J., Bastiaens, T., & Kirschner, P. (2004). A five-dimensional framework for authentic assessment. *Educational Technology Research and Development, 52*(3), 67–85.

Guttman, L. (1950). The principal components of scale analysis. In S. A. Stouffer (Ed.), *Measurement and prediction* (pp. 312–361). University Press.

Heritage, M. (2016). Assessment for learning: Co-regulation in and as student–teacher interaction. In D. Laveault & L. Allal (Eds.), *Assessment for learning: Meeting the challenge of implementation* (Vol. 4, pp. 327–343). Springer International Publishing.

Lehrer, R., & Schauble, L. (2015). Learning progressions: The whole world is NOT a stage. *Science Education, 99*(3), 432–437.

Maloney, A. P., Confrey, J., & Nguyen, K. H. (Eds.). (2014). *Learning over time: Learning trajectories in mathematics education*. IAP.

Matlen, B., Tiu, M., Luu, R., & Green, J. (2017). *The learning sciences group instrument development and classroom implementation study memo*. West-Ed.

National Research Council. (2001). *Knowing what students know: The science and design of educational assessment*. National Academies Press.

O'Shea, J., & Leavy, A. M. (2013). Teaching mathematical problem-solving from an emergent constructivist perspective: The experiences of Irish primary teachers. *Journal of Mathematics Teacher Education, 16*(4), 293–318.

Post, T. R., Cramer, K., Harel, G., Kiernen, T., & Lesh, R. (1998). Research on rational number, ratio and proportionality. In S. Berenson (Ed.), *Proceedings of the twentieth annual meeting of the North American chapter of the International Group for the Psychology of Mathematics Education, PME-NA 98* (Vol. 1, pp. 89–93). North Carolina State University.

Sarama, J., & Clements, D. H. (2009). *Early childhood mathematics education research: Learning trajectories for young children*. Routledge.

Siemon, D., Barkatsas, T., & Seah, R. (Eds.). (2019). *Researching and using learning progressions (trajectories) in mathematics education*. Brill.

Simon, M. (1995). Reconstructing mathematics pedagogy from a constructivist perspective. *Journal for Research in Mathematics Education, 26*(2), 114–145.

Streefland, L. (1984). Search for the roots of ratio: Some thoughts on the long-term learning process (Towards ... a theory): Part I: Reflections on a teaching experiment. *Educational Studies in Mathematics, 15*(4), 327–348.

Streefland, L. (1985). Search for the roots of ratio: Some thoughts on the long-term learning process (Towards ... a theory): Part II: The outline of the long-term learning process. *Educational Studies in Mathematics, 16*(1), 75–94.

Supovitz, J. (2009). Can high stakes testing leverage educational improvement? Prospects from the last decade of testing and accountability reform. *Journal of Educational Change, 10*(2–3), 211–227.

Van den Heuvel-Panhuizen, M., & Buys, K. (Eds.). (2008). *Young children learn measurement and geometry*. Sense Publishers.

Vergnaud, G. (1994). Multiplicative conceptual field: What and why? In G. Harel & J. Confrey (Eds.), *The development of multiplicative reasoning in the learning of mathematics*. SUNY Press.

Wiggins, G. (1989). A true test: Towards more equitable and authentic assessment. *Phi Delta Kappan, 70*(9), 703–713.

CHAPTER 10

Removing the Teacher 'Blind Spot'
Developing a Comprehensive Online Place Value Assessment Tool for Year 3–6 Teachers

Angela Rogers

Abstract

As we move into the 21st century, educationalists are continuing to explore the myriad of possibilities offered by Computer Based Assessment (CBA). CBA is particularly relevant in the field of Mathematics Education, where dichotomous items are commonplace. This chapter compares the validity, reliability and practicality of a paper and online place value assessment for Upper Primary students.

The Place Value Assessment Tool (PVAT) and its online equivalent (the PVAT-O) were administered, using a counterbalanced research design, to 253 Year 3–6 students across 9 classes at a primary school in metropolitan Melbourne. Rasch analysis was used to quantitatively determine if the tests were comparable. Students and teachers (n = 7) were surveyed to provide qualitative insight into the advantages and disadvantages of CBA from each perspective. The findings presented in this chapter suggest there is little or no difference between the paper and pen and online version of the PVAT in terms of difficulty or student preference, however the online mode was preferred by teachers. Threats to validity including speediness, practical considerations including a schools' technological infrastructure and the importance of developing a teacher's assessment literacy skills are highlighted. The chapter suggests providing comparable online and paper version of assessments, and allowing teachers to select the mode which best suits their needs, affords numerous advantages for schools.

Keywords

maths education – online assessment – place value

1   Introduction

Over the past 5–10 years there has been a rapid uptake of Mathematics Computer Based Assessments (CBA) in Australian primary schools. This push has been led by commercial testing firms who have identified the obvious advantages presented by this mode of assessment. Computer Based Assessments provide time-poor teachers with immediate access to student achievement data. Yet, as this is a relatively new platform, one questions whether teachers have developed the skills and knowledge required to effectively appreciate the affordances and constraints of this assessment mode.

Many commercially developed CBAs use adaptive testing technology. Computer-adaptive testing means items are selected from a central bank and presented in accordance with individual student's responses throughout a test (Davey, 2011). While this flexibility is promoted as a positive feature of test design, and is reported to lead to increased measurement accuracy (Martin & Lazendic, 2018), it also poses potential issues for teachers. Adaptive testing means every student completing an assessment is presented with a different set of assessment items. This variety makes it difficult for teachers to determine the content each student has encountered, and evaluate the quality and relevance of the items presented. At the completion of the adaptive testing session, teachers are provided with a score report on each student. Popham (2018) describes these score reports as often being too narrow or too broad to effectively guide instruction. Without being able to readily access the items presented to their students, and being provided with score reports which are often unhelpful, teachers face a potential 'blind spot' in the online assessment process.

At first glance the CBA mode of assessment seems to provide many exciting opportunities in the mathematics domain. The most obvious advantages of CBA are the speed and accuracy of accessing results and the opportunities for innovative item development. However, one must question the purpose of each CBA tool and whether our school systems, students and teachers are equipped to harness this form of assessment.

In Australia there are very few comprehensive place value assessment tools for Year 3–6 students, and almost none are presented as Computer Based Assessments (CBA). Place value knowledge has been described to be as important as the framework of a house, such that if a student's knowledge in this area is shaky, his/her understanding of mathematics as a whole is affected (Major, 2011). An understanding of place value has been shown to be closely related to students' sense of number (McIntosh et al., 1992), understanding of decimals (Moloney & Stacey, 1997) and comprehension of multi-digit operations

(Fuson, 1990). Furthermore, it is seen to underpin almost every aspect of the mathematics curriculum, from counting, estimating, money, addition, subtraction, multiplication, division and measurement through to percentages. Place value is fundamental to a student's ability to experience success in mathematics and, as such, is an integral part of the Primary school syllabus.

Generalist mathematics assessments can provide a snapshot of a student's place value understanding, by asking 3 or 4 questions related to this construct. However, very few assessments are comprehensive enough to allow teachers to identify student misconceptions and assist them to teach place value effectively.

This chapter outlines the process to design an online place value assessment tool for Year 3–6 students and teachers. The assessment tool was required to be valid, reliable and comparable to the PVAT (the paper version of the test developed in earlier research). The purpose of creating the online version (PVAT-O) was to address the concern of teachers in the original research project (Rogers, 2014), that the PVAT took too long to mark manually (approximately 5–7 minutes per student). The PVAT-O was intended to be used alongside the PVAT – allowing teachers to have access to both forms and providing them with complete transparency on the items their students encounter. The chapter highlights the process to trial the PVAT-O and the related psychometric and practical considerations involved, including the use of Rasch analysis and the opinions of students and teachers.

2   Literature Review

An assessment is essentially a small sample of selected tasks that are intended to allow inferences to be made about a student's level of achievement. However, the strength of these inferences relies heavily on the quality of the tasks used (Izard, 2002b). An assessment tool that includes a selection of items that are too easy or too difficult will not provide teachers with a complete picture of each student's knowledge. Similarly, an assessment that does not comprehensively cover content may cause the omitted content to be devalued by teachers (Webb, 2007). In both cases the inaccurate inferences gathered from such assessments can influence the quality of instruction.

There are several types of assessment, including summative and formative, both of which have distinct implications for teaching and learning. Summative assessments measure students' achievement at a particular point in time. As Wiliam et al. (2004) and Izard (2004) suggest, summative assessments are commonly an assessment *of* learning, while formative assessments are an assessment *for* learning. Formative assessment is a process (Popham, 2018) that allows students' progress to be monitored and provides teachers with information that can be used to support future learning.

One of the most important considerations when developing assessments is practicality (Masters & Forster, 1996). If an assessment instrument does not justify the time or money required for its administration and scoring, it will not be used. Ketterlin-Geller (2009) noted that some educators avoided using interview-based assessments simply because of their administration time. Doig (2011) noted similar problems with interviews, stating that by the time a whole class is assessed, some student data may be obsolete. Further, as teacher bias and variation in administration can lead interview-based assessments to be less reliable (Callingham, 2003), it appears paper-and-pen tests are a practical and reliable assessment option. Yet, proponents of interview-based assessments disagree, stating paper-and-pen assessments place a considerable reading-load on students.

Research has shown that students' inability to read items on a paper-and-pen assessment can interfere with their engagement and achievement, suggesting the text is a source of construct-irrelevant variance (Bielinski et al., 2001). While this variance appears to be most relevant with younger children and students with reading difficulties, it has led to the inclusion of 'read aloud' accommodations in some assessments (Bielinski et al., 2001). These accommodations permit teachers to read the questions to students during paper and pen assessments. Such accommodations are particularly relevant in mathematics, where reading is not the central construct being assessed. This is a feature that can readily be included on a CBA platform.

Further supporting interview-based assessment, several studies have found that interviews provided higher quality assessment information and enhanced teacher knowledge of mathematics compared to paper-and-pen assessments (Caygill & Eley, 2001; Clements & Ellerton, 1995; Kamii & Lewis, 1991). The place value research conducted by Kamii and Lewis (1991) assessed the knowledge of 87 Year 2 students. They observed dramatic differences between when the students were interviewed and when they completed a paper-and-pen place value test. Many of the students who performed well on traditional paper-and-pen place value items struggled to answer higher order thinking interview items. As different items were used in the two formats, one would question whether the differences observed were related to the content of the questions rather than the format of the assessment. Nonetheless, the research suggests that interviews may provide teachers, particularly those teaching in Junior Primary school, the opportunity to probe students' knowledge more comprehensively than paper-and-pen assessments (Caygill & Eley, 2001).

The literature presented above suggests there are advantages and disadvantages for both paper-and-pen and interview-based assessment. There will always be disagreements over the most effective mode of assessment. Therefore, as asserted by Callingham (2003), a pragmatic decision based upon the test purpose, test construct and test population is necessary. This is particularly important in the context of computer-based assessments (CBA).

While Mathematics assessments have traditionally been delivered via paper-and-pen or interview (Griffin et al., 2012), as we move further into the 21st century, CBA provides exciting opportunities for the advancement of the mathematics evaluative process. This, coupled with the recognition that "doing mathematics with the assistance of a computer is now part of mathematical literacy'" (Stacey, 2012, p. 11), has led many, including those responsible for large scale tests like PISA and NAPLAN, to investigate the potential of CBA (Tout & Spithill, 2012; ACARA, 2020).

CBA can facilitate the design of assessments that better address existing constructs (Csapo et al., 2012), address totally new constructs (Stacey & Wiliam, 2013) and deliver traditional assessment in a more efficient and effective manner (Bridgeman, 2009). One of the biggest advantages claimed for CBA is the instant and precise feedback it may provide to teachers. CBA has the potential to save teachers marking test papers, and also means that the results provided are current and can be used immediately to guide instruction (Csapo et al., 2012). Yet as Popham (2008) points out, gathering this data is only the beginning of the process. Teachers need to possess the assessment literacy skills to *interpret* this data successfully. Popham (2018) defines assessment literacy as an "individual's understanding of the fundamental assessment concepts and procedures deemed likely to influence educational decisions" (p. 13). As CBA is a relatively new form of assessment, teachers need to be supported to develop their assessment literacy in this mode.

For schools, CBA has the prospect of becoming the most convenient mode of assessment. However, as Thompson and Weiss (2009) explain, many school's technological capabilities are not at the standard required to successfully implement CBA, often leading to test administration problems (McGowan, 2019). These issues can result in teachers feeling anxious and fearful of this mode (Jones & Truran, 2011). Thus, while CBA has great potential in schools, further developmental work is required to ensure its success.

Much of the research associated with CBA has addressed the comparison of a traditional pen-and-paper based test with its CBA equivalent (e.g., Bennett et al., 2008; Poggio et al., 2004; Thompson & Weiss, 2009; Wang et al., 2007). Wang et al. (2007) conducted a meta-analysis of 44 mathematics-based assessments which compared paper-and-pen and CBA versions of the same test.

Only research that provided mean and standard deviation data were included in the study to ensure Effect Size measures could be calculated and compared. Overall, they reported that the mode of administration did not have a substantive effect on the students' performance (ES = −0.059). These results supported the work of Poggio et al. (2004) who reported that "there existed no meaningful statistical differences" (p. 30) between the two modes in their research (ES = 0.015). This study also considered the effect of gender, socioeconomic status and academic placement (gifted, general or special education) and detected no substantive Effect Size differences between test modes within each category.

While observing no overall mode differences, several studies have noted differences at an item level. Poggio et al. (2005) noted that some pen-and-paper items were more difficult or easier than their equivalent item in the CBA mode. Item level functioning differences were also explored by Bennett et al. (2008), whose study used two randomly parallel groups of students and found that the difficulty of the computer items were generally greater by an average of 0.22 logits. Although unable to determine the exact reasons for this, Bennett et al. (2008) noted that many of the items that were more difficult on the computer were 'constructed response' as opposed to 'multiple choice' items. Bennett et al. (2008) suggested that students' responses to these items may be influenced by their computer skills. This is supported by Csapo et al. (2012) who noted that the level of proficiency and the general familiarity students have with computers can affect their level of interest and approach to CBA. Csapo et al. (2012) suggest the use of item formats such as 'drop and drag', 'radio buttons' and the possibility of using "dynamic stimuli" (Csapo et al., 2012, p. 149) like audio, video or animation may influence student performance on CBA items. Huff and Sireci (2001) suggest these features have the potential to cause construct-irrelevant variance by changing the construct that is intended to be assessed (assuming coping with this stimulus is not the intended outcome of the assessment). This phenomenon was noted in the Program for International Student Assessment (PISA) 2006 computer-based assessment of science (CBAS) trial, where differences in item scores were not a result of the mode of delivery but of a feature that was associated with the delivery mode (Csapo et al., 2012). As such, construct-irrelevant variance poses significant challenges for CBA test developers.

Item response modelling (IRM) is a proven approach which measures the relationship between student achievement and item difficulty on the same scale (Wright & Stone, 1979). The IRM approach to test design has well-established methods for analysis (Wright & Masters, 1982; Wright & Stone, 1979). IRM has been successfully applied to a variety of test modes and is used in both large scale and classroom-based assessments throughout the world (Izard,

1992). The Program for International School Assessment (PISA) and the Trends in International Mathematics and Science Study (TIMMS) have both used IRM, and the Australian national educational tests, NAPLAN, are also based on this technique. Similarly, several classroom-based assessment tools have used this approach (e.g., Australian Council for Educational Research, 2012; Doig, 2000; Siemon et al., 2006; Watson et al., 2008; Wu & Adams, 2006). Many of these assessments have used a popular IRM model devised by Rasch (1960).

The Rasch (1960) model is based around the interplay of candidates and items in an assessment. While analysis of assessments traditionally generates a score that summarises the number of items correctly answered by students, Rasch considers the students who correctly answered each item (Izard, 2004). Rasch examines the extent to which the item distinguishes between those who are more and less knowledgeable (Izard et al., 2003). That is, the model assumes that less knowledgeable students have lower probability of answering a difficult item compared with those who are more knowledgeable (Rasch, 1960). Items that are considered not to follow this pattern do not fit the Rasch model and are generally removed from the test. This process verifies that the test content is meaningful and appropriate so that useful inferences can be made about the knowledge of candidates (Izard et al., 2003). Rasch analysis also provides test designers with further important information that is critical for the design of formative assessments. Rasch allows different tests to be located on the same scale (Wright & Masters, 1982) and thus test designers can determine if two tests are of comparable difficulty.

The next section discusses the creation of the online PVAT-O assessment. It describes the quantitative Rasch based methods used to compare the PVAT and PVAT-O, and the qualitative methods used to gather the insights from teachers and students related to the online platform.

3   Methodology

Prior to this research, a Rasch analysis-based methodology was used to construct a valid and reliable place value paper and pen assessment for Year 3–6 students. This was called the Place Value Assessment Tool (PVAT) (see Rogers, 2014). While this tool was found by teachers to provide a comprehensive picture of their students' knowledge in this construct, the time taken to mark the test was mentioned as a potential issue for teachers.

In order to address this, the researcher decided to investigate if an online version of the test could be created whilst retaining the test's reliability and validity. The methodology below documents the process to create the PVAT-O as an alternate assessment. It explores the use of quantitative Rasch methods and the inclusion of computer-based features, such as 'Audio Assist' and 'Drag and Drop' to enhance the design of the PVAT-O.

3.1   PVAT-O Creation

Multiple technologies including HyperText Markup Language (HTML5), Javascript and PHP: Hypertext Preprocessor (PHP) were used to create the PVAT-O assessment. The mathematical content and format of each PVAT-O item was as close as possible to the equivalent PVAT items. However, some items required the inclusion of computer-based features. For example, Figure 10.1 shows how the 'drag and drop' feature was used in an item requiring students to place numbers in order from smallest to largest. Several other computer-based features were also used in the PVAT-O items including: 'radio buttons' in multiple choice items, 'fill in the gap' boxes in counting pattern items, and colour images rather than the black and white paper images. Each item also included an 'Audio Assist' button which allowed students to listen to the question being read aloud so as to overcome any potential issues associated with reading the item text (Bielinski et al., 2001).

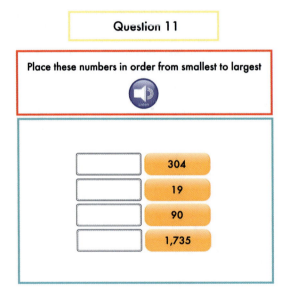

FIGURE 10.1
PVAT-O item using the drag and drop feature

3.2   The Counterbalanced Trial

The online and paper and pen PVAT trial was conducted at School C, a Catholic Primary school in metropolitan Melbourne where approximately 11% of students were from NESB families (ACARA, 2012).

All Year 3 to 6 students (N = 253) from nine classes took part in the trial (Male = 47%, Female = 53%). The trial took place over a two-week period during Term Three in the school Library. The library was closed to all other students during the trial period to ensure the students were not interrupted. In each trial the students were supervised by both the researcher and their classroom teacher. The trial was taken using a counterbalanced measures design (Shuttleworth, 2009). Half of the students in each class (randomly selected) completed the PVAT-O, while the other half of the class completed the paper-and-pen PVAT. Exactly one week later – that is, on the same day and in the same time block – the students completed the alternate version of the test. This research design was used to minimise factors such as learning effects and order of treatment, adversely influencing the results of the trials (Perlini et al., 1998).

Although 253 students were involved in the trial, 227 students (Male = 45%, Female = 55%) completed both forms of the test. The remaining 26 students were either absent for one trial, experienced technological issues uploading their data, or their PVAT and PVAT-O data could not be matched.

3.3   *Audio Assist*

During the trial each student was provided with headphones and could choose to use the 'audio assist' button to hear the item text being read aloud. It was originally envisaged that the website would be able to record the frequency of audio assist usage automatically for each student on individual items, however, unfortunately, this feature was not available in time for the PVAT-O trial. As a consequence, students were asked to manually record the number of times they used the audio assist feature.

3.4   *Test Duration*

The time each student took to complete each form was also measured and recorded by the researcher for overall comparison.

3.5   *Student and Teacher Surveys*

When considering child-computer interaction it is common for researchers to use a survey method to elicit students' opinions on the appeal or usefulness of a product (Read & Fine, 2005). Thus, a short survey was used to collect data on the students' preferred mode of delivery for the PVAT. Students completed the survey after they had completed both forms of the test. The survey asked students to indicate the mode they preferred when completing the test and which they found 'easier'. The survey used simple language, took less than five minutes to complete (Read & Fine, 2005) and did not include 'yes/no' questions, which have been observed to produce inaccuracies (Bruck et al., 1997).

The survey data was aggregated and analysed by gender and year level in order to determine any patterns in student mode preference.

A short survey was also given to the Year 3 to 6 classroom teachers (n = 7) who observed their students completing the PVAT-O trials. The purpose of this survey was to gain an indication of the preferred testing mode of the teachers. The survey only gathered information from seven teachers therefore this data was not aggregated but was interpreted by the researcher and reported as individual responses (Neuman, 2006).

3.6 Rasch Analysis

The paper PVAT test papers were scored and coded by the researcher and the online PVAT-O was scored by the website database and then rechecked by the researcher to ensure consistency and accuracy in the test scoring. A Rasch analysis was conducted to determine if the PVAT and PVAT-O could be considered comparable in their mean item difficulty and mean student achievement (Kolen & Brennan, 2004). Three Rasch analyses (Run A, B and C) were completed to determine this comparability.

3.6.1   Run A

The purpose of Run A was to re-confirm that the paper-and-pen PVAT is an internally consistent test (although this has already been completed in 2 previous schools (see Rogers, 2014)). The items which fit the model were used to create an anchor file for Run C. This allowed the PVAT and PVAT-O items to be placed on the same scale.

3.6.2   Run B

The purpose of Run B was to look at the PVAT-O test items in isolation. The Rasch analysis was used to determine which PVAT-O items fit the model and determine if the PVAT-O was an internally consistent test.

3.6.3   Run C

The purpose of Run C was to investigate if the PVAT and PVAT-O could be placed on the same uni-dimensional scale and thus determine if they were comparable in item difficulty and student achievement. The anchor file from Run A was used to fix the difficulty estimates of the PVAT items that fit the model. This allowed the PVAT-O items to be calibrated against the PVAT items (Izard, 2005). The mean item difficulty and mean student achievement for the PVAT and PVAT-O was then calculated from this run. Effect Size measures were used to quantify the standardised mean difference between the two tests

(Izard, 2004). Cohen's (1969) descriptors for the magnitude of Effect Sizes, alongside the assigned ranges for each descriptor as suggested by Izard (2004) were then be used to describe the Effect Sizes in plain language.

The following section presents the results gathered from the PVAT-O trial and highlights that the PVAT and PVAT-O were found to be comparable.

4 Results

4.1 Test Comparison

The mean and standard deviation of the PVAT (n = 65) and PVAT-O (n = 59) items which fit the model in Run C were calculated in order to determine if the PVAT and PVAT-O could be considered comparable tests.

The Effect Size measure calculated for the comparison of the PVAT and the PVAT-O was calculated to be 0.14, while the difference in student achievement between the tests was 0.01. This is described to be a "very small (0.00 to 0.14)" (Izard, 2004, p. 8) magnitude of Effect Size. This suggests that there was not a substantive difference between the mean of item difficulties in the two modes of administration, nor the students' achievement (which is to be expected if the tests are of similar difficulty). While beyond the scope of this chapter, at an item level some items appeared to display a mode difference. That is, they were substantively more or less difficult in one mode compared to the other. This supports the findings of Bennett et al. (2008) and Csapo et al. (2012).

The PVAT-O took slightly longer, 36.80 minutes (SD 7.42) than the PVAT to complete 32.43 minutes (SD 9.67).

4.2 Student Opinions

After completing both the PVAT and PVAT-O each student was asked to complete a brief student survey related to their preferred mode of PVAT testing. The survey data from N = 201 student surveys were analysed. The data show that 55% (n = 111) of students indicated that they preferred the PVAT-O. These data suggest that overall students did not display a substantive preference towards either the PVAT or the PVAT-O.

From the 55% (n = 111) of students who indicated they preferred the online version of the test, the following reasons the most common:
– 'It's easier to see the graphics'
– 'I like using computers more'
– 'You can listen to the question if you get stuck'
– 'It's more fun on the computer'

From the 45% (n = 90) of students who preferred the PVAT, the following reasons were the most common:
- 'It takes longer on the computer'
- 'You can do more working out when you have it on paper in front of you'
- 'The computer is frustrating'
- 'You can lose all your answers on the computer'

These responses provide important insights into the opinions of students in relation to each mode. They provide examples of considerations test developers must address to ensure students feel comfortable using computer-based assessments.

To determine whether there was any particular year-level group or gender with a strong preference for one mode of PVAT testing over another, the responses of several different cohorts of students to the student survey were analysed. Males in Year 3 and 4 show a substantive preference for the PVAT-O compared to the PVAT (80% and 70% respectively). Females, apart from Year 3 where 61% preferred the PVAT, showed no preference for either mode. The relatively small size of each cohort suggests these results need to be confirmed through further research, however it was found that younger males showed a clear preference for online assessment.

4.3 Audio Assist

The PVAT-O platform provided students with an inbuilt 'audio assist' button on each item so they could listen to a recording of the item being read aloud to them. The results collected indicate that 104 (46%) of the 227 students used the audio assist at some point throughout the test. The average number of items students used audio assist on was 3.79 items (SD = 3.5) and the range was 1 to 23 items. This suggests that although the feature was used by around half of the students it was commonly only used on a small sample of items. Nonetheless the range of usage suggests that some students did access the feature on a substantive number of items, confirming the usefulness of its inclusion in the test.

4.4 Teachers

The class teachers (N = 7) at School C completed a brief survey asking them to indicate their preferred mode of administration for the PVAT. Five teachers preferred the PVAT-O, while two preferred the PVAT. The teachers were asked to indicate the reasons for their preference. The five teachers who indicated they preferred the PVAT-O mode provided the following reasons:
- 'It will save me correcting it all'
- 'The results are immediate and I can use them the next day in my teaching'

- 'If the computers all work, online is much better'
- 'I don't have to correct it'
- 'The corrections would save me a lot of time and effort … I can use the results tomorrow'

The two teachers who indicated they preferred the PVAT mode provided the following reasons:
- 'Correcting them myself gives me a sense of each child's understanding'
- 'I am always concerned the computers will break down and students will lose their responses'

Again, the small sample size of teachers completing this survey limits the inferences that can be made from the data, but within this group of teachers there is a clear preference for the PVAT-O mode of test administration.

The following section discusses the issues this study has raised, including the possible advantages of providing *both* an online and paper version of the PVAT, and the importance of teachers developing their assessment literacy skills in relation to CBA.

5 Discussion

The 21st century presents many possibilities for computer-based assessment (CBA) to be expanded and implemented within schools. This new direction is currently being embraced by schools, teachers, educationalists and test developers, but CBA and paper-and-pen assessment should not be seen as mutually exclusive entities. These testing modes can be designed to work in harmony to develop the quality and flexibility of assessment practices in schools.

Providing teachers with access to a comprehensive place value assessment that could be administered in two modes is considered to increase the usability and practicality of the assessment tool. The PVAT-O was designed to support teachers by providing instant feedback on their students' achievement. Yet because the online and paper tests were found to be comparable, teachers can choose the mode which works best for them and their students.

The relatively small sample size gathered from only one school limits the scope of conclusions that can be made from the PVAT and PVAT-O trial. However, very little difference was detected between the mean difficulties and student achievement of the PVAT and PVAT-O test items at School C.

Similarly, the student achievement on the PVAT and PVAT-O was found to be comparable. This supports the results of the meta-analysis conducted by Wang et al. (2007), which noted that the mode of administration did not have a substantive effect on student achievement in computer-based and paper-based mathematics assessments. Wang et al. (2007) noted a mean Effect Size difference of −0.059 between tests, which was similar to the Effect Size difference of 0.14 noted in this research. Research by Poggio et al. (2004) also supports the PVAT findings, with Effect Size difference of 0.015 noted between paper and CBA tests of the same content. It is important to note that research by Poggio et al. (2004) did note a difference in the performance of individual items in each mode. Differences at an item level were also observed in the PVAT and PVAT-O trial. For this reason, further investigation is required to determine the possible causes and implications of these item-level differences.

A concern when looking at the PVAT-O and PVAT was the effect of the construct-irrelevant factor: speededness. Speededness is defined as the ability to work quickly when taking a test (Huff & Sireci, 2001). It was hypothesised that the PVAT-O would take longer than the PVAT to complete and this was confirmed in the trial. Two possible explanations for this were found in the research literature. Muter (1996) noted that reading speed was slower on a computer compared to printed text, while Pommerich (2004) observed that students took time to navigate using the mouse, particularly when the interface was new or unfamiliar. The design of the PVAT-O interface and the navigation of the site were purposely kept as simple as possible to not confuse the students. However, students did take time to become accustomed to locating the navigation buttons and placing the cursor in the appropriate location to answer items. This finding supports the need to allow students longer to complete online assessments compared to paper and pen tests and the importance of providing tutorials or practice sessions on CBA platforms to ensure the students are familiar with the interface (Martin & Lazendic, 2018).

Another significant influence on the speed of the PVAT-O was the technological infrastructure available at School C. The technological requirements to facilitate an online assessment program rely heavily on the capacity of the school's connection to the Internet and their computer resources. As Csapo et al. (2012) noted, at a minimum a school must have the capacity to allow all the children completing the assessment concurrent access to the Internet while still supporting the Internet requirements of the other students and teachers at the school. In the PVAT-O trial it was noted that some computers took a great deal longer than others to move through the PVAT-O. This probably frustrated and disadvantaged the students working on the 'slow' computers. Likewise, at different times the Internet took more time to load the website, again frustrating the students who were eager to begin the PVAT-O.

Another issue encountered at School C was that there were only 15 co-located computers. While the counter-balanced nature of this trial meant that only 15 computers were required at any one time, in reality classroom teachers at this school would need two sittings of the test before all their students were assessed. As Huff and Sireci (2001) correctly note such issues may influence the validity of the test and thus are important considerations before a school undertakes a CBA program.

The reading requirements of mathematics assessments can increase the construct-irrelevant difficulties students experience (Messick, 1995). As a result, students can be disadvantaged from answering mathematics assessment items simply because they struggle to read the stimulus. With this in mind, wherever possible the reading complexity of PVAT items was kept to a minimum. However, in a paper-and-pen assessment, reading is almost unavoidable. By contrast, the CBA platform allowed the inclusion of the 'audio assist' feature to reduce the reading demands of the assessment.

Parshall and Balizet (2001) state that speech audio can be used to supplement or enhance communication with students in a computer-based assessment. The audio assist feature allowed students to click on a button and hear the item read aloud to them through headphones. Audio assist is particularly relevant in mathematics assessments, where reading is often a supplementary skill that is not being assessed. While few CBA assessments have included audio assist, the work of Williams et al. (1999) suggested that this feature could result in improved measurement of the mathematics skills of those students with reading deficiencies. In the case of the PVAT-O, all students, irrespective of their level of reading ability, were provided with access to the audio assist. This type of test design is described as a universal design for assessment (Johnstone, 2003; Thompson et al., 2002). Such design principles have the potential to 'even the playing field' for students by providing them with the choice of whether or not to use the audio assist.

The audio assist feature also provides possibilities for the assessment of Language Background Other Than English (LBOTE) students. Item stimuli may be written in English but supported by audio translations in a second language. Including these translations may diminish construct-irrelevant variance due to second language proficiency noted by Sireci and Wells (2010). In the USA, the No Child Left Behind Act (2002) requires assessments to be provided "in the language and form most likely to yield accurate data on what such students know and can do in academic content areas, until such students have achieved English language proficiency" (Sec. 1111(b)(3)(C)(ix)(III)). Yet this rarely occurs in Australia, particularly in remote Australian Indigenous schools.

Students in remote Indigenous communities have been found to be disadvantaged by the linguistic and cultural demands of having to complete traditional assessments in English (Meaney et al., 2012). Siemon et al. (2009) found that when Indigenous students completed assessments which had been translated into their native language their results on the same assessments improved. Warren and de Viers (2009) noted the importance of teachers providing a 'bridge' for young Indigenous students as they come to understand new language, concepts and vocabulary associated with numeracy. A dual-language version of the PVAT-O could be a means of providing this 'bridge' between Indigenous languages and Standard Australian English. Clearly this is no easy task in Australia where there are over 50 Indigenous languages reported to be in use (Klenowski, 2009). Nonetheless, the use of recorded translation presents the possibility to improve the test administration integrity and importantly the equity of assessments within these communities. With considerable work required by mathematics educators, teachers and native language speakers to ensure the integrity of these translations, and notwithstanding the need for schools to have appropriate technological infrastructure, the audio assist feature appears to warrant further investigation.

It is also worthwhile to consider affective aspects of the CBA mode from the perspective students. Huff and Sireci (2001) note that students may experience test anxiety simply because they feel a lack of familiarity with the CBA mode. This was evident in the PVAT-O trial. Student comments such as 'you can lose all your work on the computer' and 'the computer is frustrating' show the concerns students felt whilst completing the PVAT-O. Furthermore, observations of the students as they completed the tests showed that, as noted in the research by Pommerich and Burden (2000), many students were anxious to ensure their work was 'saved'.

Csapo et al. (2012) noted that the level of proficiency and familiarity students have with computers can affect their level of interest and approach to CBA. While the results of the survey conducted in the PVAT-O trial by no means provide a definitive indication of students' proficiency or familiarity with computers, it was interesting to note that Year 3 and 4 males did show a clear preference towards the computer-based assessment (80% and 73%). This supports the findings of Colley and Comber (2003) who noted that age and gender can influence the attitude of students to computers. This suggests the need to assist children to develop familiarity and confidence in the online mode of testing in order to ensure their performance is not influenced negatively.

Yet, as Jones and Truran (2011) note, it is not only students who need to feel comfortable and familiar with CBA, so too must teachers.

Teachers are a critical stakeholder in the computer-based assessment process. They are required to administer the CBA and their interpretation of the results influences the fidelity of the assessment process.

Although the sample of teachers surveyed in the PVAT-O trial was limited (N = 7), their insights highlight some of the important issues in the CBA debate. These include the advantages associated with the speed and accuracy of CBA results and the disadvantages associated with the technological fragility of the mode.

Research into computer education has shown that some teachers lack confidence with computers and feel scared and anxious about using them (Russell & Bradley, 1997). Considering that this research took place in 1997, one questions the extent to which this still holds true. Yet the results from the PVAT-O teacher survey suggest that the pressure associated with administering a test on an unfamiliar website or testing platform makes teachers feel anxious about CBA. These findings highlight the importance of explaining CBA tools thoroughly to teachers and providing them with assistance from a technician, or someone who is confident with the testing interface to ensure the teachers feel confident in administering the test. Providing teachers with a 'back up' paper version of the test is also another way to alleviate these fears.

It is not just when administering the tests that teachers require support. Teachers also need to be supported to develop their assessment literacy (Popham, 2008) around CBA. This includes helping them to determine if the CBA provides a valid and reliable summary of student knowledge. As mentioned in the introduction to this chapter, the added challenge CBA presents is teachers may not be able to access the questions their students complete. This is particularly true in computer-adaptive testing (Martin & Lazendic, 2018). When each student is presented with different items, teachers are unable to judge if the items are relevant, cover appropriate content and provide a true indication of the student's ability. Without complete transparency, teachers are essentially outsourcing the judgement of student knowledge to test designers. This concern was echoed by one of the teachers at School C who was worried she would not have access to important diagnostic information when the test was marked by the computer database. Doig (2011) supports this concern by noting that 'off site marking' does little to assist teachers to develop their knowledge of common student errors and misconceptions, because teachers are provided with an overall score rather than information on individual items.

The Specific Mathematics Assessments that Reveal Thinking (SMART) tests (University of Melbourne, 2012), provide an example of a CBA platform which sees the importance of assisting teachers to recognise common student errors. The SMART assessment platform presents teachers with a summary of common misconceptions identified from a pool of student responses. As Stacey and Wiliam (2013) note, this provides teachers with useful diagnostic information rather than just a raw score, ensuing the fidelity of the CBA process.

6   Conclusion

Classroom teachers are busy. The demands on their time have never been greater (Collinson & Cook, 2001; Gallant & Riley, 2017). So an online assessment which saves teachers individually interviewing or marking each student's work, is understandably a favored option. Yet educationalists must carefully consider the affordances and constraints of these tools. It is critical that CBAs provide an accurate summary of student knowledge and that teachers remain invested in the process to develop their own understanding of the data each tool provides. Teachers must be supported to develop their assessment literacy skills, particularly in reading and interpreting CBA data.

Without doubt it is useful for a teacher to be provided with instant information about their students. Yet data that is not valid or reliable is unusable. It is important for teachers and schools to be part of the assessment process. Teachers need to be able to see the items presented to their students and be allowed to analyse common student misconceptions. This is particularly important for early career teachers who are developing their craft.

This chapter highlights the value in providing teachers statistically comparable paper and online versions of the same assessment. Through having both modes available, teachers can decide which best suits their needs. Access to both modes allows complete transparency in the assessment process and overcomes the potential 'blind spot' CBA presents for teachers.

References

Australian Council for Educational Research. (2012). *Progressive Achievement Tests in Mathematics Plus (PATMaths Plus)*. http://www.acer.edu.au/tests/patmaths-plus

Australian Curriculum Assessment and Reporting Authority. (2012). *My school: "School C"*. http://www.myschool.edu.au/

Australian Curriculum Assessment and Reporting Authority. (2021). *NAPLAN online: Research and development*. https://www.nap.edu.au/online-assessment/research-and-development

Bennett, R. E., Braswell, J., Oranhe, A., Sandene, B., Kaplan, B., & Yan, F. (2008). Does it matter if I take my mathematics test on computer? A second empirical study of mode effects in NEAP. *Journal of Technology, Learning and Assessment, 6*(9).

Bielinski, J., Thurlow, M., Ysseldyke, J., Freidebach, J., & Freidebach, M. (2001). *Read-aloud accommodations: Effects on multiple-choice reading and math Items.* Technical report 31. University of Minnesota, National Centre on Educational Outcomes. http://education.umn.edu/NCEO/OnlinePubs/Technical31.htm

Black, P., & Wiliam, D. (2004). The formative purpose: Assessment must first promote learning. *Yearbook of the National Society for the Study of Education, 103*(2), 20–50.

Bridgeman, B. (2009). Experiences from large-scale computer-based testing in the USA. In F. Scheuermann & J. Bjornsson (Eds.), *The transition to computer-based assessment. New approaches to skills assessment and implications for large scale testing* (pp. 39–44). Office for Official Publications of the European Communities.

Bruck, M., Ceci, S. J., & Melnyk, L. (1997). External and internal sources of variation in the creation of false reports in children. *Learning and Individual Differences, 9*(4), 269–316.

Callingham, R. (2003). *A comparison among three different approaches to mathematics assessment. Mathematics education research: Innovation, networking, opportunity.* Paper presented at the 26th Annual Conference of the Mathematics Education Research Group of Australasia. http://www.merga.net.au/publications/counter.php?pub=pub_conf&id=1353

Caygill, R., & Eley, L. (2001). *Evidence about the effects of assessment task format on student achievement.* Paper presented at the Annual Conference of the British Educational Research Association. http://www.leeds.ac.uk/educol/documents/00001841.htm

Clements, M., & Ellerton, N. (1995). Assessing the effectiveness of pencil-and-paper tests for school mathematics. In B. Atweh & S. Flavel (Eds.), *MERGA18: Galtha. Proceedings of 18th annual conference of Mathematics Education Research Group of Australasia* (pp. 184–188). Mathematics Education Research Group of Australasia.

Cohen, J. (1969). *Statistical power analysis for the behavioural sciences.* Academic Press.

Colley, A., & Comber, C. (2003). Age and gender differences in computer use and attitudes among secondary school students: What has changed? *Educational Research, 45*(2), 155–165.

Collinson, V., & Cook, T. (2001). "I don't have enough time" – Teachers' interpretations of time as a key to learning and school change. *Journal of Educational Administration, 39*(3), 266–281.

Csapo, B., Ainley, J., Bennett, R., Latour, T., & Law, N. (2012). Technological issues for computer-based assessment. In P. Griffin, B. McGaw, & E. Care (Eds.), *Assessment and teaching of 21st century skills* (pp. 143–231). Springer.

Davey, T. (2011). *A guide to computer adaptive testing systems.* Council of Chief State School Officers

Doig, B. (2000). *I can do maths.* Australian Council for Educational Research.

Doig, B. (2011). *Reporting large-scale assessment on a single formative-summative scale* [Unpublished doctoral dissertation]. Deakin University, Melbourne, Victoria, Australia.

Fuson, K. (1990). Conceptual structures for multiunit numbers: Implications for learning and teaching multidigit addition, subtraction, and place value. *Cognition and Instruction, 7*(4), 343–403.

Gallant, A., & Riley, P. (2017). Early career teacher attrition in Australia: inconvenient truths about new public management. *Teachers and Teaching, 23*(8), 896–913. doi:10.1080/13540602.2017.1358707

Griffin, P., McGaw, B., & Care, E. (Eds.). (2012). *Assessment and teaching of 21st century skills*. Springer.

Huff, K., & Sireci, S. (2001). Validity issues in computer-based testing. *Educational Measurement: Issues and Practice, 20*(3), 16–25.

Izard, J. (2002b). *Using assessment strategies to inform student learning*. Paper presented at the Annual Conference of the Australian Association for Research in Education. http://www.aare.edu.au/data/publications/2002/iza02378.pdf

Izard, J. (2004). *Best practice in assessment for learning*. Paper presented at the Third Conference of the Association of Commonwealth Examinations and Accreditation Bodies on Redefining the Roles of Educational Assessment.

Izard, J. (2005). *Trial testing and item analysis in test construction: Module 7*. International Institute for Educational Planning (UNESCO).

Izard, J., Haines, C., Crouch, R., Houston, S., & Neill, N. (2003). Assessing the impact of the teaching of modelling: Some implications. In S. Lamon, W. Parker, & K. Houston (Eds.), *Mathematical modelling: A way of life: ICTMA 11* (pp. 165–177). Horwood Publishing.

Johnstone, C. (2003). *Improving validity of large-scale tests: Universal design and student performance*. Technical Report 37. National Center on Educational Outcomes.

Jones, A., & Truran, L. (2011). *Paper and online testing: Establishing and crossing boundaries*. http://www.aare.edu.au/data/publications/2011/aarefinal00704.pdf

Kamii, C., & Lewis, B. (1991). Achievement tests in lower primary mathematics: Perpetuating lower-order thinking. *Arithmetic Teacher, 38*(9), 4–9.

Ketterlin-Geller, L. (2009). Diagnostic assessments in mathematics to support instructional decision making. *Practical Assessment, Research and Evaluation, 14*(16), 1–11.

Klenowski, V. (2009). Australian Indigenous students: Addressing equity issues in assessment. *Teaching Education, 20*(1), 77–93.

Kolen, M. J., & Brennan, R. L. (2004). *Test equating, scaling and linking: Methods and practices* (2nd ed.). Springer.

Major, K. (2011). *Place value: Get it. Got it. Good enough?* [Unpublished master's thesis]. University of Auckland, Auckland, New Zealand.

Martin, A. J., & Lazendic, G. (2018). Computer-adaptive testing: Implications for students' achievement, motivation, engagement, and subjective test experience. *Journal of Educational Psychology, 110*(1), 27–45. https://doi.org/10.1037/edu0000205

Masters, G., & Forster, M. (1996). *Developmental assessment*. Australian Council for Educational Research.

Meaney, T., McMurchy-Pilkington, C., & Trinick, T. (2012). Indigenous students and the learning of mathematics. In B. Perry, T. Lowrie, T. Logan, A. MacDonald, & J. Greenless (Eds.), *Research in mathematics education in Australasia 2008–2011* (pp. 67–87). Sense Publishers.

Messick, S. (1995). Validity of psychological assessment: Validation of inferences from person's responses and performances as scientific inquiry into score meaning. *American Psychologist, 50*, 741–749.

McGowan, M. (2019, May 27). Naplan's online testing to be reviewed after botched rollout. *The Guardian*. https://www.theguardian.com/australia-news/2019/may/27/naplans-online-testing-to-be-reviewed-after-botched-rollout

McIntosh, A., Reys, B., & Reys, R. (1992). A proposed framework for examining basic number sense. *For the Learning of Mathematics, 12*(3), 2–8.

Moloney, K., & Stacey, K. (1997). Changes with age in students' conception of decimal notation. *Mathematics Education Research Journal, 9*(1), 25–38.

Muter, P. (1996). Interface design and optimization of reading of continuous text. In H. van Oostendorp & S. de Mul (Eds.), *Cognitive aspects of electronic text processing* (pp. 161–180). Ablex.

Neuman, L. W. (2006). *Social research methods* (6th ed.). Pearson Education Inc.

No Child Left Behind Act of 2002 (US), Pub. L. No. 107-110,115 Stat.1425. (2002).

Parshall, C., & Balizet, S. (2001). Audio Computer-Based Tests (CBTs): An initial framework for the use of sound in computerized tests. *Educational Measurement: Issues and Practice, 20*(2), 5–15.

Perlini, A., Lind, D., & Zumbo, B. (1998). Context effects on examinations: The effects of time, item order and item difficulty. *Canadian Psychology/Psychologie Canadienne, 39*(4), 299–307.

Poggio, J., Glasnapp, D., Yang, X., & Poggio, A. (2004). A comparative evaluation of score results from computerized and paper and pencil mathematics testing in a large scale state assessment program. *Journal of Technology, Learning and Assessment, 3*(6), 30–38.

Pommerich, M. (2004). Developing computerized versions of paper-and-pencil tests: Mode effects for passage-based tests. *The Journal of Technology, Learning and Assessment, 2*(6).

Pommerich, M., & Burden, T. (2000). *From simulation to application: Examinees react to computerized testing*. Paper presented at the annual meeting of the National Council on Measurement in Education.

Popham, W. J. (2008). *Transformative assessment.* ASCD.

Popham, W. J. (2018). Assessment literacy for educators in a hurry. ASCD.

Rasch, G. (1960). *Probabilistic models for some intelligence and attainment tests.* Denmark's Paedagogiske Institut.

Read, J., & Fine, K. (2005). *Using survey methods for design and evaluation in child computer interaction.* Paper presented Interact 2005. http://www.chici.org/references/using_survey_methods.pdf

Rogers, A. (2014). *Investigating whole number place value assessment in Years 3–6: Creating an evidence-based Developmental Progression* [Unpublished PhD thesis]. RMIT University.

Russell, G., & Bradley, G. (1997). Teachers' computer anxiety: Implications for professional development. *Education and Information Technologies, 2,* 1–14.

Shuttleworth, M. (2009). *Counterbalanced measures design.* http://explorable.com/counterbalanced-measures-design.html

Siemon, D., Bradbury, J., Christie, M., Johnstone, C., McMahon, K., Virgona, J., & Walta, C. (2009). *Building community capital to support sustainable numeracy education in remote locations – Project findings, materials and resources* [CD ROM]. RMIT University.

Siemon, D., Breed, M., Dole, S., Izard, J., & Virgona, J. (2006). *Scaffolding numeracy in the middle years – Project findings, material and resources.* Final report. RMIT University. www.eduweb.vic.gov.au/edulibrary/public/teachlearn/student/snmy.ppt

Sireci, S., & Wells, C. (2010). Evaluating the comparability of English and Spanish video accommodations for English language learners. In P. Winter (Ed.), *Evaluating the comparability of scores from achievement test variations* (pp. 33–68). Council of Chief State School Officers.

Stacey, K., & Wiliam, D. (2013). Technology and assessment in mathematics. In M. Clements, A. Bishop, C. Keitel, J. Kilpatrick, & F. Leung (Eds.), *Third international handbook of mathematics education* (pp. 721–752). Springer.

Thompson, S., Johnstone, C., & Thurlow, M. (2002). *Universal design applied to large scale assessments.* Synthesis Report 44. National Center on Educational Outcomes.

Thompson, N., & Weiss, D. (2009). Computer and adaptive testing in educational assessment. In F. Scheuermann & J. Björnsson (Eds.), *The transition to computer-based assessment. New approaches to skills assessment and implications for large scale testing* (pp. 127–133). Office for Official Publications of the European Communities.

Tout, D., & Spithill, J. (2012). *From paper to screen: Computer-based assessment of mathematics-lessons from PISA.* Paper presented at the Mathematical Association of Victoria Conference.

University of Melbourne. (2012). *Specific Mathematics Assessments that Reveal Thinking (SMART).* http://www.smartvic.com/smart/samples/select_preset.html

Wang, S., Jiao, H., Young, M., Brooks, T., & Olson, J. (2007). A meta-analysis of testing mode effects in grade K-12 mathematics tests. *Educational and Psychological Measurement, 67*(2), 219–238.

Warren, E., & de Viers, E. (2009). Young Australian Indigenous students' engagement with numeracy: Actions that assist to bridge the gap. *Australian Journal of Education, 53*(2), 159–175.

Watson, J., Kelly, B., & Izard, J. (2008). *Improving the quality of assessments and evaluations: Student understanding of chance and data: A longitudinal study.* Paper presented at the Fifth Conference of the Association of Commonwealth Examinations and Accreditation Bodies. Improving the quality of public education in the Commonwealth: Assessment, accreditation and evaluation.

Webb, N. (2007). Mathematics content specification in the age of assessment. In F. Lester (Ed.), *Second handbook of research on mathematics teaching and learning* (Vol. 2, pp. 1281–1292). National Council of Teachers of Mathematics.

William, D., Lee, C., Harrison, C., & Black, P. (2004). Teachers developing assessment for learning: Impact on student achievement. *Assessment in Education: Principles, Policy & Practice, 11*(1) 49–64.

Williams, V., Sweeny, S., & Bethke, A. (1999). *The development and cognitive laboratory evaluation of an audio-assisted computer-adaptive test for eighth-grade mathematics.* Paper presented at the Annual Meeting of the National Council on Measurement in Education.

Wright, B., & Masters, G. (1982). *Rating scale analysis*. MESA Press.

Wright, B., & Stone, M. (1979). *Best test design*. MESA Press.

Wu, M., & Adams, R. (2006). Modelling mathematics problem solving item responses using a multidimensional IRT model. *Mathematics Education Research Journal, 18*(2), 93–113.

CHAPTER 11

How Much Do They Know about 3D Objects

Using Authentic Assessment to Inform Teaching Practice

Rebecca Seah and Marj Horne

Abstract

Although geometric reasoning is recognised as a key component for promoting STEM disciplines, very little research has been done on its promotion in middle years in Australia. There have been few studies on how to teach students to reason about three-dimensional (3D) objects. Fanned by a need to ensure authentic achievement, assessment for learning has been the centre of much research effort. It is characterised by using evidence-based data to inform teaching and learning. This chapter presents a geometric thinking model, consisting of visualisation, representation, and language and discourse as key to supporting geometric reasoning. A total of 775 Year 4 to 10 students completed a task based on reasoning about 3D objects. Analysis of results show that the thinking model can assist in identifying student knowledge and help shape learning goals that support reasoning.

Keywords

authentic assessment for learning – 3D objects – geometric reasoning

1 Introduction

Promoting STEM education is a key agenda of the 21st century global education. STEM, the combination of Science, Technology, Engineering and Mathematics is a recognition of the critical roles these disciplines play in our current world, the world of the near future and of the interactions between these disciplines. Since 1990, employment in STEM occupations has grown 79% (Graf, Fry, & Funk, 2018, January 9), while 75% of the fastest growing occupations require STEM (PricewaterhouseCoopers, 2015). There are clear and obvious connections between STEM and many aspects of geometry such as measurement, transformations and spatial visualisation, yet there has been a reduction in the amount of geometry being taught at school in many countries (Mammana & Villani, 1998; Sinclair & Bruce, 2015). Research has shown, for example, that spatial visualisation is important for STEM generally (Wai, Lubinski, & Benbow, 2009) and also for the development of number understanding (Gunderson, Ramirez, Beilock, & Levine, 2012; Uttal et al., 2013; Verdine, Golinkoff, Hirsh-Pasek, & Newcombe, 2017). However, there has been a reduction in geometry being taught in schools in favour of arithmetic and new topics such as probability and computer science. When geometry is taught the approach tends to focus on procedure rather than developing understanding and reasoning. In consequence, Australian students are particularly weak in geometry in the *Trends in International Mathematics and Science Study* (TIMSS) (Thomson, Wernert, O'Grady, & Rodrigues, 2017).

The improvement of the teaching and learning of geometry requires not only attention to the curriculum but also enabling teachers to implement the curriculum more effectively. The use of authentic assessment *for* learning can help bring about such change.

The aim of this chapter is to discuss the characteristics of authentic assessment that can facilitate the design and use of assessment of tasks that promote reasoning in three-dimensional (3D) space. Firstly, issues surrounding the elements of authentic assessment will be addressed. We will then show how evidence-based assessment data, based on the use of authentic assessment task, can be used to inform the teaching of three-dimensional concepts.

2 Authentic Assessment *for* Learning and the Case for Its Use in Geometry

Assessment is a key part of the teaching and learning process as it underscores what is important in learning. Current understanding of assessment practices involves three types: assessment *as* learning (self-assessment), assessment *of* learning (summative assessment) and assessment *for* learning (formative assessment). The distinction relates to the purposes of assessment and the focus in this chapter is on assessment for learning (Wiliam, 2014). Cumming and Maxwell (1999) expound that the relationships between learning goals, teaching activities, learning processes and assessment procedures are in dynamic tension or balance. The underlying theoretical assumptions relating to the learning goals and the assessment procedures need to match not only each other but also those relating to the teaching processes and the nature of learning and achievement. It is in relation to the issue of school achievement that the term 'authentic' first appeared.

At the time, there was concern that 'what counts for success in school is often considered trivial, meaningless, and contrived by students and adults alike' (Newmann & Archbald, 1992, p. 71). Newmann and Archbald argued that authentic achievement should be about: (1) the production of knowledge rather than reproducing what was taught, (2) embracing disciplined enquiry that draws on prior knowledge, develops in-depth understanding, and produces knowledge, and (3) acknowledging aesthetic, utilitarian, and personal value beyond assessment. Wiggins (1989) defined authentic assessments as tasks that replicate the challenges and standards of performance faced by professional in the fields. He asserts that students must use knowledge to fashion performances effectively and creatively (Wiggins, 1993, p. 229). Replicating or analogising the work of professionals is problematic since a 'genuine' math task for a mathematician is vastly different from that of an accountant or an artist. Moreover, given the rapid advancement of technology, this approach is insufficient to equip students to face their work future which is as yet unknown.

Assessment *for* learning has been the centre of many research efforts (Black & Wiliam, 1998; Siemon, Tasos, & Seah, 2019). It is based on the premise that assessment is central to instruction and effective use of quality assessment data is vital for improving teaching and learning outcomes (Goss, Hunter, Romanes, & Parsonage, 2015; Siemon et al., 2018; Wiliam, 2014). It is a formative assessment, and centred on identifying where the learners are in their learning, where they need to go and how best to get there (Assessment Reform Group, 2002). For Swaffield (2011), this form of assessment is authentic (in the sense of genuine), centred on the 'interaction' between the students and their teacher in the immediate and near future. This view closely relates to the original meaning of the word assessment, which has its roots in the Latin verb *assidere* to mean 'to sit beside'. It also posits that learning (that resulted in authentic achievement) is connected to, constrained by, and afforded by the social situations within the classrooms between the teacher and the students. In short, what the teacher does in class matters.

Until recently, geometry in schools was viewed as a topic about shapes and objects with few practical purposes used in relation to teaching. As such, its teaching was reduced to memorising vocabularies and applying formulae in routine arithmetic calculations (Barrantes & Blanco, 2006). Decades of neglect have resulted in many teachers having insufficient geometry knowledge and sharing similar misconceptions with their students (Marchis, 2012; Owens & Outhred, 2006; Seah, 2015), thus perpetuating the issue.

Geometry is a diverse subject with over 50 methodologies and theories and is needed in robotics, medical imaging, and all forms of computer aided design and modelling technology (Whiteley, 1999). Geometric principles help create stents to clear blocked arteries, and send the Eyeglass Telescope, a 100 m diameter lens to space (Lang, 2008, February). In these situations, geometry is combined with other disciplines in STEM to advance technology. In a world that is increasingly governed by technology, there is a need to realign school geometry, focusing on what is important.

The use of authentic assessment *for* learning can help with this process. Such assessment connects the geometric concepts with applications, going beyond rote memorisation to focus on conceptual understanding, problem solving and reasoning. Such assessment provides teachers (and learners) with data that enables more targeted teaching and learning.

3 Characteristics of Authentic Assessment *for* Learning

Swaffield (2011) identifies three characteristics that undergird authentic assessment *for* learning. First, it must have at its core practices that support learning. This means seeing learning as a process, a continually developing capacity rather than the acquisition of commodities. The focus on learning is crucial in mathematics education. Those who love mathematics sees it as a way of thinking, reasoning and problem solving. But for the majority, it is learning procedural skills and applying steps to solve routine problems without understanding. The emphasis on developing capacity and knowledge production situates 'knowledge' as a dynamic, negotiable practice within the taken-as-shared mathematics communities. Swaffield points out that 'teachers need to be aware of and think about what underlies the practices, and to check constantly for the actual (as opposed to the intended) effects of practices' (2011, p. 438). Moreover, while teachers can provide opportunities for learning, only the students have the autonomy to regulate learning. Indeed, individuals' emotions, self-regulated learning and mindsets are dynamic, multifaceted phenomenon and are recognised to play an essential role in academic success (Dweck, 2012; Mega, Ronconi, & De Beni, 2014). For authentic learning to take place, students must be interested in and recognise the importance of what they are asked to do. They need to be taught how to learn and feel safe to try new ideas, make mistakes, and learn from them.

The second characteristics of assessment *for* learning is about conceptualising the learning objectives. The question is 'what has been learned and where to go next'. Swaffield warns against seeing learning as checking students' attainment of a pre-determined and tightly sequenced set of learning objects. Rather, the learning objectives should include not just curriculum objectives but also open-ended or problem solving objectives and evaluative objectives that assess the outcomes the students have produced, which are built on in future lessons through evaluation. This is where the analysis of what constitute geometric knowledge comes into play. At its core, geometry is about understanding and reasoning about spatial relations in terms of size, position, orientation, and hierarchy. Studying geometry helps develop the skills of visualisation, critical thinking, intuition, perspective, problem-solving, conjecturing, deductive reasoning, logical argument and proof (Jones, 2002). These are skills vital for STEM related disciplines and handling the everchanging cyberworld.

The third characteristics considers the active involvement of students. Swaffield explains that for assessment to authentically reflect what is learned, the students need to develop an appreciation of 'quality' in various field and forms, be able to critique their work and respond to feedback from others. In short, students should learn to take responsibility for regulating their learning. To achieve this, the role of the teacher is no longer the dispenser of information but rather the engineer that designs and shapes the conditions that enable, encourage, and facilitate student learning. Swaffield asserts that applying these three characteristics can help transform the culture of the classroom and school communities where everyone becoming more self-evaluative, seeing feedback as a valuable tool to learning and improvement. In the following, we will discuss how the three characteristics can be enacted in our work on promoting geometric reasoning.

4   Conceptualising the Geometry Learning Objectives

Our work began with a quest to improve students' geometric reasoning abilities. Given the lack of emphasis on geometry, there has been limited information on 'where the students are in their learning'. We therefore needed to audit Australian students' knowledge, which meant we first needed to identify the building blocks for geometric reasoning abilities. The learning of geometric ideas does not necessarily follow a linear path. Children do not learn all about a particular shape first before learning others. Instead, all types of geometric concepts develop over time, becoming increasingly integrated and synthesised (Jones, 2002). How well a concept is learned and reasoned about is largely dependent on the degree of connectedness among the representations used to express the concepts, and individuals' ability to visualise and communicate the relationships (Figure 11.1).

While these three key ideas can be discussed separately the interplay between them assists in geometric thinking. This is further elaborated here.

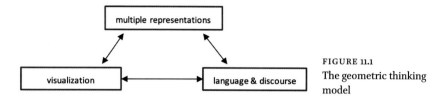

FIGURE 11.1
The geometric thinking model

The use of representations to learn and explain abstract concepts is central to mathematics learning. Representations are configurations of signs, characters, icons, or objects that are used to stand for something else. These may include numerals, diagrams, or geometric symbols to highlight certain properties of a 3D solid. While referring to the use of multiple representations in general in their review, Acevedo et al. (2009) note factors which impact on students use of representations such as students' prior conceptual and procedural knowledge about the different representations, their knowledge about the conventions related to the specific representations and domain specific knowledge. This has implications for teaching geometry in general and 3D objects in particular.

To comprehend the meaning of these representations, most of which are images, one needs visualisation skills to interpret, use, transform and/or construct images in our minds, on paper or with technological tools. The ability to visualise and interpret these representations in connection with earlier learned concepts is part of the sense making process. Visusalisation is a difficult construct to define partly due to the many terminologies associated with it including spatial imagery, visual imagery, spatial reasoning, and visuospatial reasoning (see Owens, 2015; Ramful, Lowrie, & Logan, 2016). For our purpose, visualisation is defined as a cognitive process in which objects are interpreted within the person's existing network of beliefs, experiences, and understanding (Phillips, Norris, & Macnab, 2010). It takes place when an image is viewed and interpreted for the purpose of understanding something other than the object itself. For example, looking at a net consisting of four equilateral triangles and identifying it as a tetrahedron.

To visualise the object requires individuals to introspect possible images similar to a visualisation object and interpret it within the person's existing network of beliefs, experiences and understanding. Since our visual sensory input is constantly bombarded with different imageries, our visual cognition makes a distinction between spatial images (relating to information about the location, size, and orientation of an image) and visual images (such as shapes, colour and depth) (Sima, Schultheis, & Barkowsky, 2013). These two distinct types of visualising style reflect different ways of the brain generate mental images and process visual-spatial information. Those who focus on visual images, the object visualisers, tend to encode images globally as a single perceptual unit based on actual appearances (Kozhevnikov, Kosslyn, & Shephard, 2005). They generate detailed pictorial images of objects and process the information holistically. They are faster and more accurate when performing recognition and memory tasks. When asked to interpret and reconstruct 3D objects using 2D format, object visualisers often reproduce images that resemble the actual object. Conversely, those who focus heavily on spatial images, the spatial visualisers, tend to encode and process images analytically, using spatial relations to generate schematic and abstract images from what they see. These individuals are better able to interpret and analyse abstract representations. Research shows that poor visualisation of 3D objects affects students' ability to reason in measurement situations (Seah & Horne, 2020b; Tan-Sisman & Aksu, 2016).

Language also plays an important role in influencing our visual spatial perception. How one sees an object is influenced by ones' definitions of that object. For example, if a student defines a hexagon as a shape with many corners, or 'roundish', s/he is likely to call an octagon a hexagon. Similarly, if one's sole experience with 3D objects is prism, s/he is likely to call a triangular pyramid a triangular prism. The way a student perceives and talks about geometric visual representations reveals their thought processes and shapes their thinking (Sfard, 2008). A lack of teaching for conceptual understanding can also lead to overgeneralisation, such as calling any shape or object associated with six a hexagon. As such, changing how students visualise 3D objects necessitates changing their discourse – the use of keywords and representations in their narratives and classroom routines. A full discussion of this model is reported in Seah and Horne (2019). Having identified the three building blocks for geometric thinking, we set out to measure Australia students' geometric reasoning skills.

5 Methodology

5.1 *Context*

Reframing Mathematical Futures II project (RMFII) is a large-scale research project funded by the Australian Government Department of Education and Training under the auspices of the Australian Mathematics and Science Partnership Programme (AMSPP). The project worked with industry partners and practitioners in each State and Territory and the Australian Association of Mathematics Teachers (AAMT) to support the development of mathematical reasoning in Years 7 to 10 by developing:

- evidence-based learning progressions that can be used to inform teaching decisions and the choice of mathematics learning activities and resources by teachers and students;
- a range of validated, rich assessment tasks and scoring rubrics that can be used to identify what students know and understand in terms of the learning progressions, inform starting points for teaching and show learning over time;
- detailed teaching advice that (1) establish and consolidate learning at the level identified, and (2) introduce and develop the ideas and strategies needed to progress learning to the next level, and
- indicative resources to support the implementation of a targeted teaching approach in mixed ability classrooms.

Research has shown that inadequate teacher knowledge, ineffective teaching instructions that focus on routine application of rules, deficits in the curriculum and insufficient time allocation to the teaching of geometry and measurement are some of the cause of poor performance in geometry (Owens, 2015; Smith, Males, & Gonulates, 2016). As such, a learning progression research framework was chosen as it could support the design of learning goals, instructions, classroom assessments and teacher professional development (Cobb, Jackson, Smith, & Henrick, 2017). We did this by first drafting a hypothetical geometric learning progression based on the work of van Hiele, Clements and Battista (Battista, 2007; Clements & Battista, 1992). Next, we wrote multiple context based open response assessment tasks that sought to determine students' reasoning abilities. These were compiled into four forms each with about 5 to 7 questions. Our focus in the design of the questions was to determine to what extent a student could visualise and use representations and language to reason in their thinking process.

The assessment forms were trialled with 436 year 4–10 students from 10 trial schools in four states. The resulting data were analysed using the Rasch partial credit model (Masters, 1982) using Winsteps 3.92.0 (Linacre, 2017). This tool allowed both students' performances and item difficulties to be measured using the same log-odds unit (the logit), and placed on an interval scale (Bond & Fox, 2015). Items that did not fit the model were examined and refined.

A total of 32 secondary schools, approximately 80 teachers, and 3500 students in Years 7 to 10 were involved in the project. A refined set of overlapping forms was constructed and used with 3366 students from these participating research schools. This allowed the further refinement of the Draft Learning Progressions. A discussion on how items were validated is in Seah and Horne (2020a). The final version of the assessment forms can be accessed via the AAMT website (Australian Association of Mathematics Teachers, 2020).

The assessment thus designed was authentic in that it focused on students producing knowledge, drawing on prior knowledge and developing in-depth understanding. The question contexts provided connections to real world situations. The nature of the questions allowed students to provide extended responses thus using representations, visualisation and language in their explanations as required by the learning objectives. Most importantly, the purpose was to provide data to teachers which would inform their teaching.

5.2 Method

In this chapter, we report students' performance on a novel task that involves presenting students with a picture showing a dog facing three geometric objects (Figure 11.2). The students were asked first to name the objects, then draw what the dog sees and explain their reasoning. We ask: Can students comprehend the concept of left, and right? Can they name the 3D objects in the

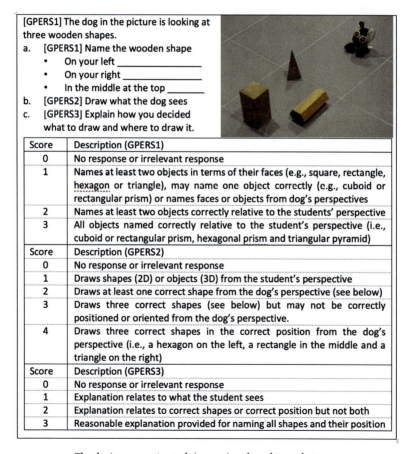

FIGURE 11.2   The dog's perspective task (GPERS) and marking rubric

picture? But more importantly, what spatial skills did they employ to produce an image of what the dog sees? And what was their rationale? The scoring rubric is a conjecture on how a response depends on level of ability or skill. It is a critical aspect of the research feature as it contributes to the refinement of the learning progression. The descriptive data from the task show students' use of *keywords* to name the object and its components and the *narratives*, written utterances, students made to justify their reasoning. The diagrams allow researchers to determine what information best captured individual students' attention when visualising the objects, whether they focus on the spatial or visual images. By comparing their drawing with the reasoning, we seek to determine their use of spatial skills in a novel situation.

Two groups of data were analysed for this item. The first set of data – the trial data, was taken from 436 Year 4–10 students from three primary and seven high schools across social strata and States to allow for a wider spread of data being collected. The teachers were asked to administer the assessment tasks and return the student work. These teachers had not participated in any specific professional learning related to the project. The trial results were marked by two markers and validated by a team of researchers to ascertain the usefulness of the scoring rubric and the accuracy of the data entry. The second set of data – the project data, was taken from 339 Year 7–10 students from six high schools situated in lower socioeconomic regions with diverse populations. The project school teachers were asked to mark and return the raw score instead of individual forms to the researchers. These teachers received two 3 day face-to-face professional learning sessions, each containing about a half day on spatial and geometric reasoning prior to the implementation of the assessment tasks. They also had access to a bank of teaching resources and four on-site visits to support their teaching effort. There was no requirement for them to teach any specific material, or indeed to even teach Geometry in the time frame. However, some expressed a desire to do so at the professional learning days and during subsequent school visits. How they used the available materials was left entirely for each school to decide. In the project schools, some of the teachers may have taught Geometry prior to the assessment while others had not.

While each assessment form had 5–6 contacts based extended response problems, teachers were encouraged to administer and the assessment over a few days with students completing a few tasks only at each sitting then continuing with the a normal lessons. After the assessment was completed and scored in the project schools, teachers could use the resultant information to better target their teaching using the advice provided to them. This sometimes led to discussions in the classroom about similar items to the assessment items.

In this way, the assessments were was formative as an impacted on teachers classroom practise.

6   Findings

Table 11.1 shows the overall percentage breakdown of student responses for GPERS and Table 11.2 shows the breakdown according to each year level. The project schools clearly outperformed trial school students in several areas. This is very encouraging as it shows that the professional learning the teachers in project schools received may have contributed to better awareness and attention given to the teaching of geometry in school. While gender difference was not the aim of our investigation, we nonetheless found no significant differences at the $p < 0.05$ level.

TABLE 11.1   Overall results expressed as percentages for the perspective task GPERS.

Score	Trial schools (n = 436)			Project schools (n = 339)		
	GPERS1	GPERS2	GPERS3	GPERS1	GPERS2	GPERS3
0	12.6	15.4	37.6	8.6	2.1	33.6
1	42.9	18.6	46.3	26.5	17.7	36.9
2	17.7	17.7	14.2	16.2	10.6	14.7
3	26.8	30.5	1.8	48.7	14.2	14.7
4		17.9			55.5	

Overall, students' knowledge of 3D objects was poor as 55.5% and 35% of trial schools project school students respectively were unable to correctly name the 3D objects in the photo (GPERS1). This difficulty was due to a lack of experience rather than based just on year level (e.g., see Table 11.2 Year 7 and Year 10 results in project schools).

More than 50% of the trial school and Yr 9 project school students were unable to name the three objects correctly (GPERS1). Students who score 1 may have named the objects based on the dog's perspective rather than their perspective though the question asked them what they could see. Analysis of the trial school data showed that 46.6% of the students name the squared/rectangular based prism correctly; a further 12% wrote rectangle. 45% named hexagonal prism correctly and 8.7% wrote hexagon. The triangular based

TABLE 11.2 Percentage breakdown for GPERS1, 2, and 3 according to year level

Score	Trial schools						Project schools			
	Yr 4 $n=31$	Yr 5 $n=59$	Yr 7 $n=111$	Yr 8 $n=74$	Yr 9 $n=79$	Yr 10 $n=82$	Yr 7 $n=66$	Yr 8 $n=87$	Yr 9 $n=93$	Yr 10 $n=93$
GPERS1										
0	0	8.5	7.2	12.2	15.2	25.6	3	4.6	11.8	12.9
1	58.1	61	43.2	25.7	342	47.6	16.6	23	44.1	19.4
2	19.4	17	22.5	16.2	15.2	14.6	21.2	26.4	6.5	12.9
3	22.6	13.6	27	46	35.4	12.2	59.1	46	37.6	54.8
GPERS2										
0	12.9	6.8	10.8	13.5	12.7	32.9	6.1	2.3	0	1.1
1	29	33.9	23.4	10.8	2.5	19.5	31.8	24.1	18.3	1.1
2	32.3	22	18	10.8	20.3	12.2	22.7	5.8	15.1	2.2
3	25.8	28.8	28.8	31.1	40.5	25.6	22.7	18.4	12.9	5.4
4	0	8.5	18.9	33.8	24.1	9.8	16.7	49.4	56.8	90.3
GPERS3										
0	38.7	25.4	29.7	40.5	34.2	57.3	24.2	43.7	36.6	28
1	61.3	62.7	47.8	39.2	48.1	31.7	63.6	33.3	25.8	32.3
2	0	11.9	18	18.9	15.2	11	6.1	9.2	8.6	32.3
3	0	0	4.5	1.4	2.6	0	6.1	13.8	29	7.5

pyramid presented the most challenge with 24% named it correctly, a further 14% used the term pyramid and 2% wrote square based pyramid. This may have been a difficulty in their knowledge of left and right, however, only 3% gave a complete reversal, mixing the right and the left and they were spread across year levels, which suggests that their knowledge of left and right was not a real issue. This analysis of student scripts includes all that row schools data but only some of the project school data as project schools were not required to return their scripts.

Analysis of *keywords* used in the trial schools showed that 13% of the cohort did not respond to the question. Around 47% named the rectangular prism, 45% named the hexagonal prism, and 24% name the triangular based pyramid correctly. Misspelling words such as 'prisim' 'prizem', 'prymand', 'pryrimid', 'peyment', were not counted as errors. Some students used 2D shape names for the 3D objects (17% rectangle/square; 15% hexagon and triangle) and 10%

named triangular pyramid as triangular prism. Others named the objects by joining known terms, such as 'hexagonal cilender', 'rectangular hexagon', 'rectangular square', 'pentagon cilender', and 'rectangular cylinder'.

For GPERS2, the project schools showed a clear progression from Year 7 through to Year 10 with 90% of them able to successfully complete the task. The greatest error was that the students drew the objects from their perspective but claimed that that was what the dog saw or reversed the order saying the dog was seeing the objects from the other side. This accounted for between 25% and 40% of the trial school cohort and 5 – 22.7% of the project data.

Students have varying degrees of experience with drawing 3D objects. Many trial schools' students tried to incorporate all the components in their drawing. Eight students (2 Yr 4, 4 Yr 5 and 1 each from Yr 8 and 10) drew a bird eye view of the scene including the dog, like the drawing on the left in Figure 11.3.

 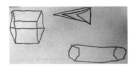

FIGURE 11.3
Students' bird eye views of objects showing all components

The drawing on the right shows that the student may have seen drawings of a square or rectangular prism before but had little experience with the other objects. Even with the prism, this student has included all faces although the dog would be unable to see them all. The hexagonal prism shows both ends for the same reason. With the triangular pyramid he knows that there are three triangular faces on the side but was unable to depict it in 3D.

When comparing the drawings by year levels, Year 4 students tended to produce a wider range of drawings, from 2D shapes or 3D objects drawn on one plane, that show depth, to drawing an octagon as a hexagon and mixing the positions of the objects. From Year 5 onwards, depth and dimensionality became important features. While the rubric did not specify 'depth' as a criterion (placing the rectangular prism to the rear), many trial schools students demonstrated this in their drawing. Three students (1 Yr 4 and 2 Yr 7) included the tile lines although only the Year 7 students provided an explanation that the lines were used for either get the proportions or position correct (see row 3 in Figure 11.4).

Indeed, analysing trial schools' students' drawings, and their explanations led to six strategies: mental rotation, physical rotation of page, mental reflection, perspective drawing, position and depth, and 2D perspective of 3D object. Figure 11.4 shows examples of student drawing and their explanations on how they drew what the dog saw. Some samples used more than one strategy.

HOW MUCH DO THEY KNOW ABOUT 3D OBJECTS 253

Student's drawing	Strategy used and student's justification
	Mental rotation (with position and depth) I did it as if the dog was me. I put myself in the dog position and figured it out as if the shapes were right in front of me.
	I put myself in the *dogs position* and he can only see straight so they look 2D (sic) *(with 2D perspective of 3D object)*.
	Physically rotate page I turned the paper around and figured what shapes it would look like from the *dogs* persoectuve (sic).
	Mental reflection I just flipped it around to *make* a reverse picture. (incorrectly reflected)
	Perspective drawing (mental or physical rotation) I decided to draw some of the shapes 3D because the dog would be able to see he top of the rectangular prism a little bit and the dog would be able to see top and right side of the hexagonal prism, but the triangle he would only be able to see the face.

FIGURE 11.4   Students' representation of the dog's perspective

There is a difference in the sophistication of the drawing and explanations as students attempt to indicate depth and dimensionality, as seen in row 1 and 4 of Figure 11.4. The student's explanation of the perspective drawing (row 4) is correct as the dog would be able to see the top and right side of the hexagonal prism, and at least two sides of the rectangular prism but only one face of the pyramid. Equally, sophistication of drawing may not necessarily reflect the thinking that showed in the explanation (Figure 11.5).

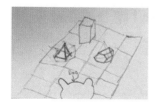

Correct justification, incorrect drawing
If the hexagonal prisim is on my right, the dog is facing the other way so it is on its left, this means that the pyramid that is on my left would be on its right and tha rectangular prisim stays in the same position (sic).

FIGURE 11.5   A correct justification with incorrect drawing of the dog's perspective

Students did not seem to be used to justifying their actions (GPERS3) even when they were able to successfully complete the drawing. Many did not respond but for those who did, the explanation tended to be superficial such as 'I imagined I was the dog', 'I decided to draw it like that because'. Less than 5% of the trial school cohort and between 6–29% of project school students were able to give an adequate explanation.

These results have implications for curriculum and teaching approaches. Skills associated with making representations such as drawings and diagrams, transformation of objects through reflection and rotation and the visualisation of objects from different perspectives need to be specifically in the curriculum. In the classroom there needs to be an emphasis on language and the discourse associated with explanation and argument. The language should include not only the specific geometric language but perhaps more importantly the language of argument and justification. Finally, there needs to be opportunity provided for students to present argument and explanation where they connect their discourse to the representations they use.

The assessment forms used included more items than just the dog perspective task. The variable map for geometric reasoning produced through Rasch analysis of the whole collection of assessment items (Figure 11.6) reflected the

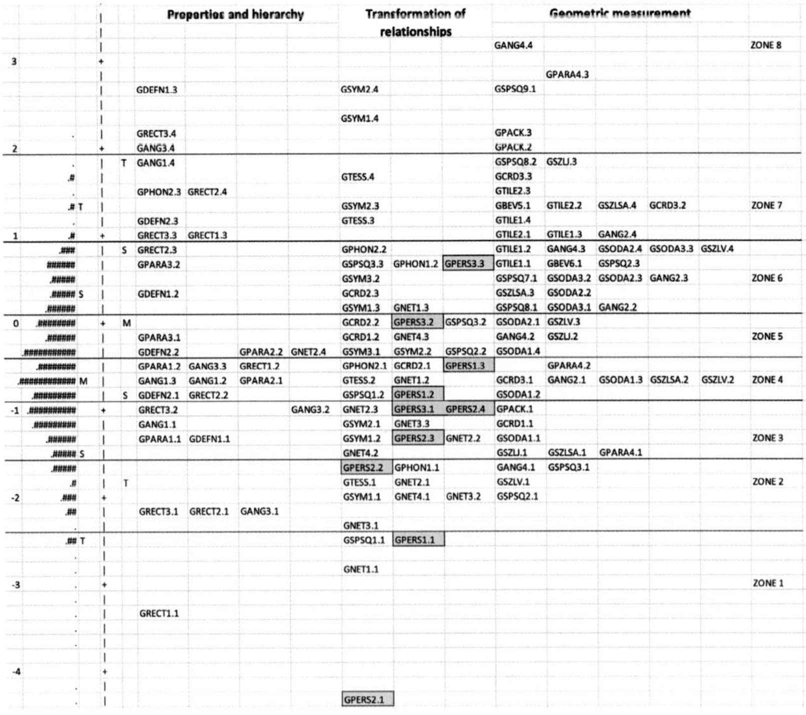

FIGURE 11.6 Excerpt from the variable map for geometric reasoning for GPERS

degrees of reasoning needed for GPERS when compared with other items (see Seah & Horne, 2020a for examples of other items). The map is grouped into three content areas, although some tasks certainly required a combination of knowledge. and we ranked the item responses from easiest (bottom of the map) to most difficult (top of the map). Items at the same or very similar levels of difficulty were interrogated to identify similarities or differences in the reasoning required. The items in the map are referred to by the code letters such as PERS, with a number following for the specific question such as PERS2. Following that is the rubric score so PERS2.3 refers to a student gaining a score of 3 on item PERS2.

Responses exhibiting similar levels of reasoning were grouped together, which resulted in eight relatively discrete, hierarchical zones. For example, GPERS3.3 indicates a correct response (coded as 3) to GPERS3 while GSZLV.4, represents a correct response scoring 4 to item GSZLV, which requires students to explain whether doubling the length of the edges of a shoe box will result in doubling the volume. Both items are in zone 6. Since GPERS spread across multiple zones, there is no construct-irrelevant variance, in that the task allows students at all levels to demonstrate their reasoning ability. It is this multi-stages process that helped to produce an invariant measurement scale that can be used to identify longitudinal changes in students' performance (Siemon & Callingham, 2019).

The Rasch analysis has been included here to show how the task PERS provided data demonstrating a wide range of thinking processes and how the task integrated into the whole of the assessment used. For further explanation of the Rasch analysis and the zones of geometric reasoning in the evidence based learning progression that was produced see Seah and Horne (2019).

7 Discussions and Conclusion

Given the scarcity of research conducted in this area among Australian students, the data collected here provided valuable information on how to shape instructional design and future research direction. In this section, we will discuss two issues:
– How does this task reflect the principles of authentic achievement?
– How does this result assist in the design of activities '*for* learning' and how might it be incorporated into teacher practice?

7.1 *Ascertaining Authenticity*
Authenticity in achievement centred on the production of knowledge, embracing disciplined enquiry and valuing learning experiences beyond assessment

(Newmann & Archbald, 1992). In designing this task, we took into consideration the need to evaluate the depth of students' spatial reasoning skills. That is, can students see things from other's perspective and explain their reasoning to others? The novelty of this task is likely to attract students' interest in attempting the task. This is supported by the completion rate for this task, which was above 97%, higher than that for the other tasks (for example, see Seah & Horne, 2020b). To answer this question, the students needed to rely on their visualisation and prior experience to present their solution in naming, drawing, and explaining. This method of assessment allows us to assess a wider range of student knowledge, including understanding 3D objects, visualisation, interpreting images and using correct terms. Indeed, we documented a range of six strategies students used to answer an essentially mental rotation question, some not recorded in research that used a multiple choice format. The task also alerts students to other's viewpoints, which may influence their own spatial thinking experience beyond the assessment task.

Swaffield (2011) maintains that assessment that claims to be 'for learning' must have learning goals that include curricular, problem solving and evaluative learning objectives. Given the lack of details on how to develop spatial and geometric reasoning in the Australian Curriculum: Mathematics, we hypothesise that the three building blocks in the geometric thinking model–multiple representations, visualisation, and discourse, are key to promoting reasoning. The data showed that Australian students' 3D knowledge and spatial abilities are poor, both in naming the objects, seeing things from other's perspective, and explaining their reasoning. They also showed that project school students are slightly more successful in answering the question than the trial school students. This suggests that teacher professional learning can influence student knowledge. The thinking model can help to identify students' reasoning processes but may also assist in helping students to regulate their own learning. A case in point is a Year 4 student who afterwards was shown his response to this task and asked to double check his work. Upon consideration, he noticed that he had drawn what he saw rather than what the dog saw. It must be said that not all students who were asked to double check their work recant their position.

7.2 *Constructing Authentic Learning Experiences*

Authentic assessment *for* learning is about active involvement of students in the learning process and seeking ways to support learning (Swaffield, 2011). Item analysis of students' geometric knowledge such as those reported here address the question of 'where the learners are in their learning'. Rasch analysis of all items we designed, tested, refined, and retested contributed to the construction of an evidence-based geometric learning progression. The progression serves as a road map to show 'where they need to go' and contributed to the construction of teaching advice and learning activities that show 'how best to get there'. The progression is not a replacement of the curriculum but rather used to inform teaching decisions. Our data has shown that it is possible for some students to reason at a higher zone in one task and a lower zone in another. Since all types of geometric concepts are developed over time, becoming increasingly integrated and synthesised (Jones, 2002), rich use of learning activities that support all students' learning is vital. This means that the focus is not on the product, but rather the thinking processes each student used to complete a task; how students integrated visualisation, representations, and language and discourse when completing the task.

Visualisation involves imagining the shapes and objects and manipulating them in one's mind, picturing what might be seen as the shape/object is rotated, or reflected, stretched or shrunk, or moved to a different position in relation to other shapes/objects, and orientation and location. It is about looking for patterns and relationships and interpreting and reconstruction what is found in the light of existing knowledge. Representations is about different diagrammatic ways of representing objects and mathematical ideas, seeing multiple representations, and making connections between them. Language and discourse encompassing both the common vocabulary used to describe specific mathematical properties, the formal definitions of terms and all other forms of communication such as diagrams and symbols. Participation in discussion using description, explanation and justification is a vital in the development of all mathematical concepts and in being able to reason. These three building blocks of geometric thinking need to be incorporated into teaching approaches and curriculum.

The learning progression which arose from the Rasch analysis referred to in this chapter but described more completely elsewhere has proved to be stable over a number of subsequent data collections. Teachers have access to a small chart which enables them to see roughly in which zones their students are working and thus the progression provides a framework for teachers to enable them to target their teaching appropriately. The use of the rubrics for scoring also assists the teachers to learn about their students reasoning. Accompanying this is advice to teachers with recommendations about strategies for moving the students forward in their learning journey. The resources, learning progression and teaching advice are available free online from the Australian Association of Mathematics Teachers website (2020).

Above all, the three key components of the Geometric Thinking model in Figure 11.1 give teachers a focus enabling the assessments to be authentic for learning. However, there is much still to be learned about how the geometric thinking model can support learning. Clearly, more research is needed in this area of spatial skills and reasoning with specific focus on the impact of classroom experiences on learning, teacher knowledge, and the contribution made by the classroom discourse and the culture of the classroom and how these contribute to the development of visualisation and spatial reasoning.

Acknowledgement

This research was funded by the Australian Government Department of Education and Training under the auspices of the Australian Mathematics and Science Partnership Programme (AMSPP), in partnerships with industry partners and practitioners in each State and Territory and the Australian Association of Mathematics Teachers (AAMT).

References

Acevedo Nistal, A., Dooren, W., Clarebout, G., Elen, J., & Verschaffel, L. (2009). Conceptualising, investigating and stimulating representational flexibility in mathematical problem solving and learning: A critical review. *ZDM, 41*(5), 627–636. doi:10.1007/s11858-009-0189-1

Assessment Reform Group. (2002). *Assessment for learning.* http://arrts.gtcni.org.uk/gtcni/handle/2428/4617

Australian Association of Mathematics Teachers. (2020). *Reframing mathematical futures II: Supporting the development of geometric reasoning.* http://www.mathseducation.org.au/online-resources/geometrical-reasoning/

Barrantes, M., & Blanco, L. J. (2006). A study of prospective primary teachers' conceptions of teaching and learning school geometry. *Journal of Mathematics Teacher Education, 9*, 411–436.

Battista, M. T. (2007). The development of geometric and spatial thinking. In F. K. Lester (Ed.), *Second handbook of research on mathematics teaching and learning.* Information Age Publishing.

Black, P., & Wiliam, D. (1998). Assessment and classroom learning. *Assessment in Education: Principles, Policy & Practice, 5*(1), 7–74. doi:10.1080/0969595980050102

Bond, T. G., & Fox, C. M. (2015). *Applying the Rasch model: Fundamental measurement in the human sciences.* Routledge, Taylor and Francis Group.

Clements, D. H., & Battista, M. T. (1992). Geometry and spatial reasoning. In D. A. Grouws (Ed.), *Handbook of research on mathematics teaching and learning* (pp. 420–464). National Council of Teachers of Mathematics.

Cobb, P., Jackson, K., Smith, H., & Henrick, E. (2017). Supporting improvements in the quality of mathematics teaching on a large scale. In S. Doff & R. Komoss (Eds.), *Making change happen?* (pp. 203–221). Springer.

Cumming, J. J., & Maxwell, G. S. (1999). Contextualising authentic assessment. *Assessment in Education: Principles, Policy & Practice, 6*(2), 177–194. doi:10.1080/09695949992865

Dweck, C. (2012). *Mindset: how you can fulfil your potential.* Constable & Robinson.

Goss, P., Hunter, J., Romanes, D., & Parsonage, H. (2015). *Targeted teaching: how better use of data can improve student learning.* Grattan Institute.

Graf, N., Fry, R., & Funk, C. (2018, January 9). 7 facts about the STEM workforce. *Factank: News in the Numbers.* http://pewrsr.ch/2EpARn

Gunderson, E. A., Ramirez, G., Beilock, S. L., & Levine, S. C. (2012). The relation between spatial skill and early number knowledge: The role of the linear number line. *Developmental Psychology, 48*(5), 1229–1241. doi:10.1037/a0027433

Jones, K. (2002). Issues in the teaching and learning of geometry. In L. Haggarty (Ed.), *Aspects of teaching secondary mathematics: Perspectives on practice* (pp. 121–139). RoutledgeFalmer.

Kozhevnikov, M., Kosslyn, S., & Shephard, J. (2005). Spatial versus object visualizers: A new characterization of visual cognitive style. *Memory & Cognition, 33*(4), 710–726. doi:10.3758/BF03195337

Lang, R. (Producer). (2008, February). *The math and magic of origami* [TED talk]. http://www.ted.com/talks/robert_lang_folds_way_new_origami

Linacre, J. M. (2017). *Winsteps Rasch measurement V4.0.0* [Computer program]. Winsteps.org

Mammana, C., & Villani, V. (1998). *Perspectives on the teaching of geometry for the 21st century.* Kluwer Academic Publishers.

Marchis, I. (2012). Preservice primary school teachers' elementary geometry knowledge. *Acta Didactica Napocensia, 5*(2), 33–40.

Masters, G. N. (1982). A Rasch model for partial credit scoring. *Psychometrika, 47*(2), 149–174. doi:10.1007/BF02296272

Mega, C., Ronconi, L., & De Beni, R. (2014). What makes a good student? How emotions, self-regulated learning, and motivation contribute to academic achievement. *Journal of Educational Psychology, 106*(1), 121–131. doi:10.1037/a0033546

Newmann, F. M., & Archbald, D. A. (1992). The nature of authentic academic achievement. In H. Berlak, F. M. Newmann, E. Adams, D. A. Archbald, T. Burgess, J. Raven, & T. A. Romberg (Eds.), *Toward a new science of educational testing and assessment* (pp. 71–84). State University of New York Press.

Owens, K. (2015). *Visuospatial reasoning: An ecocultural perspective for space, geometry and measurement education* (Vol. 111). Springer International Publishing.

Owens, K., & Outhred, L. (2006). The complexity of learning geometry and measurement. In A. Gutiérrez & P. Boero (Eds.), *Handbook of research on the psychology of mathematics education. PME (1976–2006). Past, Present and future* (pp. 83–115). Sense Publishers.

Phillips, L. M., Norris, S. P., & Macnab, J. S. (2010). *Visualization in mathematics, reading and science education*. Springer.

PricewaterhouseCoopers. (2015). *A smart move: Future proofing Australia's workforce by growing skills in science, mathematics, engineering and maths (STEM)*. https://www.pwc.com.au/pdf/a-smart-move-pwc-stem-report-april-2015.pdf

Ramful, A., Lowrie, T., & Logan, T. (2016). Measurement of spatial ability: Construction and validation of the spatial reasoning instrument for middle school students. *Journal of Psychoeducational Assessment, 35*(7), 709–727. doi:10.1177/0734282916659207

Seah, R. (2015). Understanding geometric ideas: Pre-service primary teachers' knowledge as a basis for teaching. In M. Marshman, V. Geiger, & A. Bennison (Eds.), *Proceedings of the 38th annual conference of the Mathematics Education Research Group of Australasia (MERGA)* (pp. 571–578). MERGA.

Seah, R., & Horne, M. (2019). A learning progression for geometric reasoning. In D. Siemon, T. Barkatsas, & R. Seah (Eds.), *Researching and using progressions (Trajectories) in mathematics education* (pp. 157–180). Brill Sense.

Seah, R., & Horne, M. (2020a). The construction and validation of a geometric reasoning test item to support the development of learning progression. *Mathematics Education Research Journal, 32*, 607–628. doi:10.1007/s13394-019-00273-2

Seah, R., & Horne, M. (2020b). The influence of spatial reasoning on analysing about measurement situations. *Mathematics Education Research Journal, 32*(2), 365–386. doi:10.1007/s13394-020-00327-w

Sfard, A. (2008). *Thinking as communicating: Human development, the growth of discourses and mathematizing*. Cambridge University Press.

Siemon, D., & Callingham, R. (2019). Researching mathematical reasoning: Building evidence-based resources to support targeted teaching in the middle years. In D. Siemon, T. Barkatsas, & R. Seah (Eds.), *Researching and using learning progressions (trajectories) in mathematics education* (pp. 101–125). Brill Sense.

Siemon, D., Callingham, R., Day, L., Horne, M., Seah, R., Stephens, M., & Watson, J. (2018). From research to practice: The case of mathematical reasoning. In J. Hunter, P. Perger, & L. Darragh (Eds.), *Making waves, opening spaces. Proceedings of the 41st annual conference of the Mathematics Education Research Group of Australasia* (pp. 40–49). MERGA.

Siemon, D., Tasos, B., & Seah, R. (Eds.). (2019). *Researching and using progressions (trajectories) in mathematics education*. Brill Sense.

Sima, J. F., Schultheis, H., & Barkowsky, T. (2013). Differences between spatial and visual mental representations. *Frontiers in Psychology, 4*. doi:10.3389/fpsyg.2013.00240

Sinclair, N., & Bruce, C. (2015). New opportunities in geometry education at the primary school. *ZDM, 47*(3), 319–329. doi:10.1007/s11858-015-0693-4

Smith, J. P., Males, L. M., & Gonulates, F. (2016). Conceptual limitations in curricular presentations of area measurement: One nation's challenges. *Mathematical Thinking and Learning, 18*(4), 239–270. doi:10.1080/10986065.2016.1219930

Swaffield, S. (2011). Getting to the heart of authentic assessment for learning. *Assessment in Education: Principles, Policy & Practice, 18*(4), 433–449. doi:10.1080/0969594X.2011.582838

Tan-Sisman, G., & Aksu, M. (2016). A study on sixth grade students' misconceptions and errors in spatial measurement: Length, area, and volume. *International Journal of Science and Mathematics Education, 14*(7), 1293–1319. doi:10.1007/s10763-015-9642-5

Thomson, S., Wernert, N., O'Grady, E., & Rodrigues, S. (2017). *TIMSS 2015: Reporting Australia's results.* Australian Council for Educational Research.

Uttal, D. H., Meadow, N. G., Tipton, E., Hand, L. L., Alden, A. R., Warren, C., & Newcombe, N. S. (2013). The malleability of spatial skills: A meta-analysis of training studies. *Psychological Bulletin, 139*(2), 352–402. doi:10.1037/a0028446

Verdine, B. N., Golinkoff, R. M., Hirsh-Pasek, K., & Newcombe, N. S. (2017). Spatial skills, their development, and their links to mathematics *Monographs of the Society for Research in Child Development, 82*(1), 7–30. doi:10.1111/mono.12280

Wai, J., Lubinski, D., & Benbow, C. P. (2009). Spatial ability for STEM domains: Aligning over 50 years of cumulative psychological knowledge solidifies its importance. *Journal of Educational Psychology, 101*(4), 817–835. doi:10.1037/a0016127

Whiteley, W. (1999). *The decline and rise of geometry in 20th century North America.* Paper presented at the Proceedings of the Canadian Mathematics Education Study Group. https://www.academia.edu/32278314/The_Decline_and_Rise_of_Geometry_in_20th_Century_North_America

Wiggins, G. P. (1989). A true test: Toward more authentic and equitable assessment. *Phi Delta Kappan, 70*(9), 703–713. doi:10.1177/003172171109200721

Wiggins, G. P. (1993). *Assessing student performance.* Jossey-Bass.

Wiliam, D. (2014). *Formative assessment and contingency in the regulation of learning processes.* Paper presented at the Toward a Theory of Classroom Assessment as the Regulation of Learning at the annual meeting of the American Educational Research Association. https://famemichigan.org/wp-content/uploads/2018/06/Wiliam-Formative-assessment-and-contingency-in-the-regulation-of-learning-processes.pdf

CHAPTER 12

Humanising Mathematics Education through Authentic Assessment
The Story of Sarah

Huk-Yuen Law

Abstract

Assessment has a critical role to play in developing the learners' perception of not just how well they learn but also how they can identify themselves as an authentic learner. The purpose of this chapter is to explore the way of how we can address the issue of humanising mathematics education in terms of authentic assessment. The empirical material is drawn from the case study of Sarah – a story about a five-year old girl through which the inquiry into the development of authenticity for self and her own learning would be undertaken. The phenomenological inquiry draws on what began as a humanistic action research project, comprising a university educator, a parent, discourse, observation and documentation, into which the re-conceptualisation of authenticity was unfolded through the girl's questioning into how she could make sense of learning itself. The purposeful choosing of Sarah as the targeted research subject came from the author's conversation with her mother touching on the issue of what a parent could do for fostering a child's well-being through assessing authentically learning in general and learning mathematics in particular. The findings of the study unfolded the child's innate predisposition towards choosing to choose what mattered to her own learning as an authentic learner. And the study reinstates the advocacy of humanising mathematics through the designing of authentic assessment for learning mathematics itself in view of the learners' struggling over the dominant accountability assessment discourse.

Keywords

authentic assessment – humanising mathematics education – authenticity – phenomenological inquiry – learner questioning

1   Introduction

Modern education has long been institutionalised by confining learning to the place called school for some particular learners called students as situated in some particular space called classroom during the particular time period called lesson. Yet, as human beings, we are born a learner with an innate curiosity to explore, to inquire and to learn. Assessing what and how we learn to know is a natural way of making dialogue with our own self in making meaning of learning itself. Very often than not, it would be the teachers and parents rather than the schoolchildren themselves to take up the roles of doing the evaluation of the progress as well as the outcomes of learning. The time has come for us to think seriously of what we can do and should do to help our children to develop themselves into authentic learners in order to make meaning of their learning. Learning itself is closely interrelated with assessment through which a learner knows not just how well she performs in a task but also how that very performance under scrutiny shapes who and what she is as a learner.

In 2020, we witnessed the occurrence of an enormous disruption to formal education at large and schooling in particular. The rapid spread of COVID-19 pandemic has forced schools around the globe to adopt online learning as a substitute to face-to-face learning. This global event urges us to ponder over a question as related to education – What is happening to the learners and how they would prepare themselves in a complex and uncertain world for their future lives through their own learning? In other words, the global impacts of the COVID-19 pandemic challenge us to ponder not just over the physical health but our human responsiveness towards the feel of uncertainty (see Jung, Horta, & Postiglione, 2021).

To answer the above question authentically, it has to be the learners themselves who need to undertake authentic assessment on how learning is experiencing. In other words, the learners need to have feel of "authenticity" (Cummings & Maxwell, 1999). Approaching the era of 21st century, the notion of "authentic" has already been a buzzword as applied to educational intervention (Shaffer & Resnick, 1999). And yet, the inconsistent and inexplicit interpretations of the word render poorly its access to the standpoint that puts its ideas into actual practice (Yarden & Carvalho, 2011). The notion of authentic assessment as inherent in the concept of authenticity should not be a mere buzzword but a serious venture for us to think deeply of how it could be adopted to engage learners in becoming more fully human for living and working in the changing world (Vu & Dall'Alba, 2014).

As a mathematics educator, I see that the orientation of authentic assessment is towards making meaning of learning mathematics as a human activity of its own. Adopting Freire's (1994) metaphor, humanising mathematics is to make learners *matter* in reading (understanding) and writing (acting on and changing) the world (experiencing mathematics). Borrowing the notion adopted by Gutstein (2012), authentic assessment can be seen as "a weapon in the struggle" for humanising mathematics in coping with the struggling of high-stakes accountability-driven school assessment system. As argued by Greer and Skovsmose (2012, pp. 4–5), teaching/learning mathematics is "not a purely intellectual activity" but a human activity entailing "ethical responsibilities" of both the teacher and the students in making meaning of the task activity itself, and the meaning-making process in turn constitutes the kind of "critical agency" that empowers the learners to "speak for themselves". According to White (1993) and Brown (1996), the concept of humanistic mathematics education comprises the didactical approach of caring for the learners' dispositions in personalising their own learning experiences with joy and dignity. In the process of humanising mathematics, the learners should be entitled to have the freedom to choose as they engage themselves into authentic mathematical inquiry (Cibulskaite, 2013).

Four years ago, I proposed an action research project designated as "SARAH" to my former student Amitola (a pseudonym) who had attended the action research course that I taught before she gave birth to her first daughter – Sarah. In the course, Amitola was absorbed in writing up her SARAH story in doing the assignment of "Self-narration: Self As Responsible Agent for Humanities" through which she depicted how she would understand the notion of moral responsibility by highlighting some life experiences that she had undergone. When Sarah was about a few months old, Amitola and I had a lunch gathering in which we had an interesting conversation about what it would be meant to humanise mathematics. The project of SARAH as I proposed to Amitola, which is about Sarah's growth experiences entailing the documentation of how Amitola observed and interacted with her daughter, aims at making sense of three humanistic questions as related to the learning in general and the learning of mathematics in particular, (1) Who is Sarah as a person? (2) Who does she aim to become? (3) What improves her learning as an authentic learner? In telling the story of the told, I would let it be read by Amitola and Sarah as well (through her mother's telling) and would also ask them for their approval in picking the photos as images that I would use for explicating the told.

Before I tell the story of Sarah, I will delineate the conceptualisation of authenticity as inherent in our understanding of what authentic assessment is meant to be. The outline begins with an examination of Heidegger's concept of authenticity in terms of double choosing to choose. I shall elaborate the methodological orientation to authenticity as grounded on the concept and through such idea of how I read and interpret the story of Sarah in supporting for and echoing with my thinking for humanising mathematics education.

2   Methodological Orientation to Authenticity

The notion of "assessment" is generally understood as "the action or an instance of making a judgement about something" (Merriam-Webster, 2021). In the field of education, it has long been adopted for *judging* how well the students learn in terms of tests and examinations. We know from our schooling experiences that it is common for significant others, such as parents and teachers, who have great influence on an individual's well-being, to take up the primary role of judging the learners' performances and defining the meaning of "success". Below, I would describe how and why authentic assessment may alleviate the negative outcomes from such judgement.

Wiggins (1993, cited in Mueller, 2005, p. 2) defines authentic assessment as measures, which entail "engaging and worthy problems or questions of importance, in which students must use knowledge to fashion performances effectively and creatively". According to Mueller (2005), authentic assessment is to assess students' capability of using what they have learnt for performing real-world tasks in a meaningful way. He further argues that authentic assessments provide us the most direct evidence for knowing what makes students' learning meaningful as these kinds of assessment not only "capture the constructive nature of learning" but also "provide multiple paths to demonstration of learning" (ibid., p. 3). According to Wiggins' (1989) widely read article, *A True Test: Toward More Authentic and Equitable Assessment*, the authentic test design constitutes three essential elements for providing evidence of (meaningful) knowing. The first one is *thoughtful understanding* for solving slightly ambiguous problems in a complex situation in an "effective, transformative, or novel" (ibid., p. 705) way. The second is *habits of mind* for learning a new concept through "effortlessly handling information that had previously been confusing" (ibid., p. 706). And the third one is the use of *practical judgement* "to recognize and pose complex problems as a prelude to using one's discrete knowledge to solve them … inherently ambiguous and open-ended" (ibid., p. 706). All these constituents of authentic assessment, as I understand it, unfold the critical role of the *learners' voices* for insuring that both the complex problem itself and the answers or solutions to it would have been understood or explored as fully as possible. It would be an ethical responsibility of the professional teachers to enable the authentic voices from their students to be heard in order to "sit with" (the root of the word *assessment* as Wiggins reminded us) each of the learners for ensuring what is heard really means what it is meant to be. In other words, it requires a "self-as-assessment" (ibid., p. 708) for eliciting the student's response to the assessment through the choice that he or she makes. Authentic assessment enables us to know more and differently of what a learner can learn.

If the choice that we make is meant to be authentic, it would need to undergo a serious test of authenticity by asking ourselves the three humanistic questions, (1) Who are we as a person? (2) Who do we ought to become? (3) What improves our learning in general and our learning in mathematics in particular as an authentic learner?

Such an approach to authenticity, as I argue, would need to put trust on how the teacher and the students have the feel that "authenticity is the way to go" (Cummings & Maxwell, 1999, p. 178; cited in Gulikers, Bastiaens, & Kirschner, 2004) through the *choices* that they make for creating the possibilities of worlds beyond the confine of the everyday world of learning environment. To assess authentically is to open the space of learning possibilities for the learners to make their choices.

In order to enhance student learning in preparation for a changing world, Vu and Dall'Alba (2014) argue by drawing from Heidegger's concepts of inauthenticity and authenticity that authentic assessment is an integration of epistemology with ontology so as to provide "an opportunity for students to learn and reflect on their learning for their personal and career development, in a way that nurtures the spirit of striving for authenticity" (p. 14). By entailing the ontology in our understanding of authentic assessment, it challenges us to think more deeply of the question: Who should bear the ethical responsibility of *making choice* for the learners with regards to the aspects of authentic learning? In attempting to answer the question, we may need to go further in understanding Heidegger's concept of authenticity in order to help us make a better sense of what one become their authentic self.

3 Heidegger's Choice to Choose Oneself: Choosing to Choose Authenticity

The unique lived experience that we have is about the *being* of being a human. *Dasein* is the very word that Heidegger used to depict human being to entail "the subject-object duality of the individual and the world" (Sherman, 2009, p. 1). We are born or "thrown" into the world as a unique authentic being. Once we embark on our life journey, we are getting "lost" and "fallen" in-the-world (called "they") as part of daily-life routine (Heidegger, 1927/1962). There is a price to pay of becoming authentic as it would be associated with "anxiety, guilt, ambiguity and entanglement" (Vu & Dall'Alba, 2014, p. 7). In other words, if we desire to stand against the instrumental conformity of becoming inauthentic, it demands us a kind of ethical courage of making choice "to make a stand on our life projects and seek our own ways of being" (p. 9). Becoming authentic is a puzzle to us as we ask how free we are to make the choice as such. What further puzzling us is the double structure of the "choice to choose oneself" as Heidegger hinted for two tiers of making choice (Han-Pile, 2009, p. 293). The doubling of the choice is to distinguish the passive inauthenticity of "falling" into the world and getting lost from the active inauthenticity of "fleeing" in the face of anxiety as experienced (ibid., p. 297). The possible reason of choosing to live as an inauthentic self, according to Han-Pile, can be too difficult of such a choice or too high the cost of choosing not to.

The choice of choosing authenticity challenges us as educators to think seriously of what kind of calling that education can offer to our students enabling them to undergo ever-lasting return to their own selves as an authentic learner. Choosing to choose one-self entails deep understanding of self as situated in the ever-happening of the world one is living in. Who is responsible for what the learner is to understand of what being learnt? How can the teachers help preparing their students for equipping themselves with the kind of understanding who they are whilst living in the ever complex and uncertain world? Would the conventional assessment in the forms of high-stakes test and examination be a possible root or route of restraining the learners from choosing to live as an authentic self? Could assessment to be done in an authentic way empower a learner to strive at choosing to become a unique being of her own? Perhaps, we might not have the answers but the questions that invite us to keep learning and unlearning from the telling and the told of life stories of being a human. Through the story of Sarah that she is telling, can we pick something up from the told in order to make more sense of doing something for humanising education through which those who teach would offer help to those who learn to assess what is learnt in an authentic way?

4 Humanising Mathematics: Making Learners Matter

As a mathematics educator, I cannot agree more of the claim that "mathematics is a human activity" (White, 1947; Freudenthal, 1973; Hersh, 1994; Peck, 2018). As a human activity, Peck (2018, p. 6) argues mathematics itself is a human achievement incorporating various forms of activity as embedded socially, culturally, contingent-historically across time and space. It could be a "self-constructed cage" in mathematics classroom to adopt an attitude of over-emphasising the need "in a search for procedures, rules, algorithms" rather than to develop the learners' awareness of taking up "the responsibility of making judgments in complex social situations" (Greer & Skovsmose, 2012, p. 6). To humanise mathematics is to provide the students guided reinvention so as to empower them with critical agency to learn beyond the cage and to enable them read (understand) and write (acting on and changing) the world (in a mathematics class) (Freire's metaphor, see Gutstein, 2012, p. 23). In so doing, we need to allow the learners to speak for themselves. As an advocator of humanistic mathematics, Alvin White (1987; cited in Karaali, 2014, p. 41) urged teachers "to place the student more centrally in the position of inquirer ... acknowledging the emotional climate of the activity of learning mathematics" so as to enable the learners "to better understand mathematics as a meaningful rather than arbitrary discipline".

Stephen Brown, in his recent article *Humanistic Mathematics: Personal Evaluation and Excavations* (2004), highlighted three themes in reflecting upon his advocacy for humanising mathematics. These included (1) world and self; (2) "why?"; and (3) problems. Drawn on the myth of how Gauss solved the problem of finding the sum of the natural numbers from 1 to 100, Brown (ibid., p. 3) pointed out that it "left with the mystery of figuring out how it is (why?) anyone ever came up with the idea of writing the sum first in ascending and then in descending order as a starting point" even after we would have been told how the insightful formula for the sum was derived. It would be the "self", with unique way of seeing the particular problem whilst being situated in the world with the asking ("why?") habits of mind, to choose a unique way of solving it.

I could hardly believe that the self being deprived of the authentic learning experience would have genuine interest and value in searching of elegant solutions to a problem. In assessing authentically of what a student has learnt, we have to create space for the learner's hidden voice to be heard and allow her to enjoy the freedom of choosing the way in answering "how it is (why?)" she ever comes up with the idea of performing the task she chooses. Authentic learning in education has the potential for humanising mathematics in the face of dominant assessment discourses that have taken teaching and learning accountability for granted. Authenticity as a kind of phenomenon has "something to say". Groenewald (2004, p. 44) argues that we all are born phenomenologists, like poets and painters, as we understand what we have been practicing through the "task of sharing, by means of word and image, the(their) insights with others". Through the story as told by Sarah, I would argue that we as human being are born authentic learners – to make meaning from the task we choose to perform for answering "how it is (why?)" of the problems as encountered in order to understand something more about the self, about the world, as well as about the relation of self and world.

5 Researching Authentic Learning Experience: A Phenomenological Inquiry

Practicing phenomenology is a project "driven by fascination: being swept up in a spell of wonder, a fascination with meaning" (van Manen, 2007, p. 13). Researching Sarah's learning experiences that she has lived through during the first five years after her birth offers me "the moments of seeing-meaning" – meaning as inherent within lived experience. Through the reflective method of writing, van Manen argues that "a phenomenology of practice aims to open up possibilities for creating *formative relations* [emphasis added] between being and acting, between who we are and how we act, between thoughtfulness and tact" (ibid., p. 13). I regard such kind of formative relation as a way of doing authentic assessment by presenting and re-presenting what and how the self chooses to choose the authenticity with which we read (understand) and write (acting on and changing) the world (of learning through lived experience). Lived experience is "experience-as-live-through-it in our *actions, relations* and *situations* [emphasis added]" (ibid., p. 16). Thus, to research authentic learning experience is to make phenomenological inquiry into how the self makes meaning out of what she would have done, how that relates her with others, as well to make sense of her presence in the situations she is experiencing. To write up the story of Sarah is to measure the depth of authenticity that she has experienced, as well to come to a sense of assessing her depth as an authentic learner.

Research method (see Giles, 2012, p. 216) in the form of phenomenological inquiry is characterised by (1) open response to the question at hand through self-created "signposts" for guiding the inquiry (van Manen, 1990); (2) being contingent upon the phenomenon under study (Ironside, 2005); and (3) open inquiry without preoccupation with research techniques (Gadamer, 1994). The participants in this inquiry were Sarah (the five-year old girl) and her mother, Amitola. The data as gathered in this research inquiry came from the extracts of Amitola's personal log (as fitful documentation of Sarah's growth experiences from the age of three to the age of five) in response to my question, "Would you tell me something about Sarah's lived experience as you have been experiencing the caring practice for her?" The question serves the purpose of creating "a space and a freedom" for Amitola to let me make sense of how Sarah makes meaning for her own lived experience not just from the text itself but also in Sarah's own words (as far as those could be recollected), "unobstructed by rubrics, or interview schedule" in order to let the research ideas emerged and structured into meaningful whole (see Farrell, 2020, p. 6). The data in the form of experience-as-text would also be triangulated with other sources of data as collected, including face-to-face conversations, WhatsApp messaging, and emails. The kind of phenomenological dialogue that I have with Amitola serves as a form of casual interviews through which I made conscious attempt to find out more information about the setting of the research question that I want to address – *What is the lived experience of Sarah during her kindergarten education through which she would make meaning from the performing of the tasks she chooses to accomplish?*

The data, as presented and re-presented here (see Table 12.1), were not following entirely the chronological order but would be arranged instead

TABLE 12.1 A retrospective time-scaled map of the research process

Date/Sarah's age	Phenomenological events: Sarah's lived experiences	The research ideas: The learner's lived experience
February 2020 Aged 4½ October 2019 Aged 4	Sarah enjoyed free time and space for reading and thinking She did not like to do repetitive homework	Creating thinking space for thoughtful understanding
February 2021 Aged 5½ February 2020 Aged 4½ May 2019 Aged 4 October 2020 Aged 5 November 2020 Aged 5	She puzzled why mutes could not be taught to speak She restrained speaking at school with a face mask on She adored private thinking and free chat with her mum at home She overcooked the pancake She asked what zeroth could have meaning of its own	Asking and imagining as habits of mind
January 2019 Aged 3 ½ June 2018 Aged 3–4 October 2020 Aged 5 September 2020 Aged 5	She invented a straight-line cutting method to create perfect circle She made meaning with geometrical objects through life experiencing She used straight lines to make sketch for perfect circle She counted the passage of time	The use of judgement in solving open-ended real-life problems

according to the *meaningful whole* of my interpretations about Sarah's actions, relations and situations as she lived through it. "Data analysis" in the form of "explicitation process" (Hycner, 1999) would be done by transforming the data into the story through interpretation (see Groenewald, 2004, p. 49).

6 The Story of Sarah: Who is Sarah?

6.1 *Sarah Enjoyed Free Time and Space for Reading and Thinking*
Like other schoolchildren during the pandemic, Sarah could hardly know for sure whether she would go to school tomorrow by the end of today's class. Yet, she enjoyed much more freedom within her space of learning – free to choose any books (including National Geography) from her own private collections at home, make her own models, and even lay herself down on the floor to do her untroubled thinking of anything she could possibly imagine. Having gone through a long period of school lockdown, Sarah seemed not to have a vivid memory of the school life in the last year of her kindergarten but envisioned instead a rosy picture of becoming a primary pupil at the end of Summer.

6.2 *She Did Not Like to Do Repetitive Homework*
On the eve of going back to school after a long summer holiday, Amitola felt embarrassed about forgetting to remind Sarah to finish all the teacher-assigned works. Sarah was too sleepy to do anything but said to her mother, "Let me go to sleep and I know how to deal with it tomorrow!" The next morning, Sarah got herself dressed in proper uniform. "I know what to do, mum. I need not do the works as assigned for K2 as now I am in K3!" She was happy to have figured out a reasonable excuse for not doing the tedious and time-consuming exercise of repetitive work such as in writing over pages and pages of her own name and the odd numbers from 1 to 50.

6.3 *She Puzzled Why Mutes Could Not Be Taught to Speak*
As a former kindergarten teacher herself, Amitola did observe that Sarah was inclined to thinking in her own way and would judge without agreeing entirely the responses of others to the questions she asked. This time, Amitola did not expect Sarah to ask her a question that she could hardly satisfy her doubt.

> "Can a mute think if he cannot talk?", Sarah asked with a dubious gesture.
> "What exactly are you thinking of?"
> "I can tell you of what I think. But I won't say it out aloud of everything that I think. Inside, I can speak with my heart. But for the mute not able to speak with heart, how can they think?"

"I think they can". Amitola said.
"That means the mute know how to think!", Sarah kept asking her mum,
"Would we know how to think after born without being taught?"
"It could be".
"We can teach the mute speak again, can't we?" Sarah frowned.
"Not possible!" Her mum remarked.
"Why not?" Sarah felt not satisfied.
"I know not of how to go on the talk with you ..."
"You are not dumb, aren't you?"

Sarah was puzzling about the intriguing relationship between thinking and speaking as well as between teaching and learning – If we are thinking without speaking, no one knows that we are thinking. If we are speaking, we must be thinking though we may not know how to say it clearly enough for others to understand what exactly we are thinking. It seemed that Sarah was questioning whether we could teach everyone everything by asking "Can we teach the mute to speak?" and she was deeply doubtful whether thinking and speaking are innate or whether they have to be taught.

6.4   She Restrained Speaking at School with a Face Mask On
The school closure continued. Online learning had turned itself into a routine for Sarah without chance of going back to meet her classmates. Sarah like all other schoolchildren, was trained to wear a surgical mask when in-person learning was briefly resumed. At home, there was not just no need for Sarah to wear a mask but also no need for her to mask the teeth with her lips and in turn to mask the tongue with her teeth. But at school, not just speaking but smiling behind the mask would be a restraint to Sarah of expressing herself and "such lessons gave the children the capacity to mask their tongues ..., the pair of closed lips turned itself into a mask, the *invisible mask*" (Law, 2009, p. 192).

6.5   She Adored Private Thinking and Free Chat with Her Mum at Home
Whilst at home, Sarah would have much more time to do her private thinking as she lied on the floor with nothing to do and also would have much more chance to have free talk with her mum.

6.6   She Overcooked the Pancake
Amitola shared with me her log about how Sarah overcooked pancakes.

> Sarah made a mess as she prepared for herself some pancakes for her breakfast. She overcooked the pancake as she told me that she was

thinking while doing cooking. I asked her what she was thinking. She said, "I was looking at the seasonings while holding the pan and I wondered what the flavouring was thinking about how I did the cooking". I was greatly surprised by the imagination that she had. (Personal communication, 17 October 2020)

6.7   She Asked What Zeroth Could Have Meaning of Its Own

Sarah's imagination caught my attention especially the way she approached the world of mathematics in her life experiences through visualisation and reasoning as well.

> "Mum, is there something called the zeroth thing?", Sarah asked abruptly after her day-dreaming thinking on the floor of the sitting room.
> "What exactly do you want to ask?"
> "I think there should have such a thing called zeroth", Sarah answered and went further of how she made sense of it.
> "In a queue to the toilet, the zeroth classmate is in front of the first one. If the toilet is empty, the zeroth can go straight in to it. If it is already occupied, it would be the first go into it. So, in other word, the zeroth means there is no one in the queue or no need to queue. And the first in queue means needs waiting as the toilet is already occupied and will be the first to go in after it got empty".

Amitola herself had never thought of such a question in her own schooling nor did her teachers have ever asked the question in class whether there would have such a thing called "zeroth".

6.8   She Invented a Straight-line Cutting Method to Create Perfect Circle

As noted down in her logbook, Amitola recalled that Sarah, at the age of three, appeared to have particular fancy over things of different shapes and especially circle. As I read what was recorded in the log, I noticed that Sarah had gone through different stages of developing her understanding of circle.

> "I like circles!", Sarah told her mum while making various sketching of circles on the paper.
> "Why you like circles so much?", Amitola puzzled.
> "Because the circle looks like face, eyes, nose that like all of us have in the family".

One day, Sarah did her artwork and had to cut out a paper circle. It was not an easy task for a small child to hold the scissor with small hand for tailoring a curvy figure. Having made several unsatisfactory attempts, she decided to adopt a different way of doing it. Instead of cutting the whole circle, she kept cutting along a straight line tangentially with the circle. And finally, she felt excited that she made it and told mum her new discovery, "I can cut a lot of straight lines and make a circle!"

FIGURE 12.1   The left picture shows Sarah's world of circle and the right sees how Sarah used her own way of tailoring circle

6.9   *She Made Meaning with Geometrical Objects through Life Experiencing*

By the age of four, Sarah started exploring different shapes such as square, triangle, and rectangle by comparing their differences with each other. She tried to understand the differences through block-building game as she told her mum, "Square, triangle and rectangle are friends. I can use them to make up the building with the blocks of these shapes. I cannot make it higher up with more of other blocks when I put an extra semi-circular block onto it. I can build a circle with two semi-circular blocks. Circles are naughty. I like it!" As Sarah was making sense of the shapes through the block building, she came to learn the art of doing tessellation. She could not restrain herself from making a big laugh as she explained to her mum why she particularly adored circle among other shapes. "Oh circle! Oh circle! Do you know why I like you so much? You always make gaps that I cannot fill up whenever I try piecing up the blocks altogether. You are the most naughty one. You always disobey and are not following rule. I like you and you are just like me, haha …".

6.10   *She Used Straight Lines to Make Sketch for Perfect Circle*

It was just quite some days after celebrating Sarah's fifth birthday. She was working on her own "perfect circle" project by asking herself, "How can I draw a perfect circle with a ruler?" She had a belief that she could use ruler to make any perfect shape through drawing perfect lines. Amitola WhatsApped the problem that Sarah had to her friends, Jack, Jill and Julia (all are pseudonyms), who were teaching mathematics in schools. Jack (a secondary teacher) told Amitola that there would not be any perfect circle in the world that could be drawn and Jill (a primary teacher) gave the advice of using a compass for Sarah rather than a ruler to draw it. And Julia (a kindergarten teacher) responded to the WhatsApp, "Sarah could not use ruler to draw a circle as there is no straight line in it. Just ask her make sketch of the circle! You know, practice makes perfect!" Nonetheless, Amitola did not tell any of these advices to Sarah. In the morning of a day, Sarah showed with excitement her work on drawing her "perfect circle" with ruler – a picture of circle clock with the word "morning" (in Chinese) written on it and inside the circle clock with the sketches of breakfast and teeth brush. With close examination of it, she could see that Sarah had used the ruler to draw out cluster of straight lines for the making of the circle. A few months later, a causal talk between Sarah and her mum revealed a further understanding of how the notion of "perfect circle" helped her make sense of elliptical shape.

> "I like perfect circle among all of the other shapes I know. Do you know why?", Sarah used to raise questions for her mum to answer.
> "Yes, but why? I have no ideas of how you think of it". Amitola pleaded her to say more.
> "Perfect circle is an all-round curve and its curve is the most beautiful".
> "Can you tell me of what you mean by perfect circle?"
> "It is a perfect circle if I do a good draw. If not, it is an oval but not a circle!"

FIGURE 12.2
Sarah's "perfect circle"

The kind of spatial awareness of geometrical figures that Sarah had developed ever after three years of age reinforced her learning of identifying the shapes that she encountered in her everyday life. More the names of the shape she knew, more questions she would have asked her mum for making sense of those new mathematical lingo. While walking along the street, Sarah spotted a billboard design that constituted an intersecting knot of two inclined squares. She could not stop asking her mum, "Is it a square or rhombus?"

6.11   *She Counted the Passage of Time*

After reading all of Amitola's documented account in the log, I cannot stop telling one more thing before I end the story – Sarah's interpretation of time.

> "How many times do I need to count for 15 minutes?", Sarah asked her mum after she knew that it takes about one second for counting a number. "You need to repeat 15 times of what you have done in your counting after each time you have counted from one up to sixty", said Amitola.
> "I would then need to count many … many times, and I'll get lost! Is it the reason why we need to use clock to help us read the time?" Sarah suddenly realised why her mum taught her how to read the time from the clock, "Ah! Now I know that clock is a really useful thing and why we have to learn to read it".

It comes to my understanding that by the time her mum taught her how to read the clock time Sarah puzzled why on earth she had to learn it as long as she could use counting to make sense of the passing of time. The clock time is what we used to call it as the "physical time", the "objective time", or the "scientific time". Counting of time to her is a way of feeling a real sense of her now-and-here. As she grasps the measure of physical time, she would begin to lose the touching of self which itself is becoming a fiction to her. In other words, the more 'real' Sarah knows of the world through the clock reading, the less 'real' she might have a feel of her own self through the counting of time as elapsed.

> Who is Sarah?
> By any other names, she knows
> What she wants to know.

7   Learning from the Telling of Sarah Story: What Makes Human a Person?

7.1   *Humanising Mathematics through Raising One's Self-Awareness*

Hersh (1997, p. 19) proposed a reawakening interpretation of what mathematics really is by arguing that mathematics as a branch of knowledge is "a world of ideas, created by human beings, existing in their shared consciousness". In line with such an understanding, the goal of doing mathematics education is "to humanize mathematics, to teach tolerance and understanding of the ideas and opinions of others, and thus to learn something of our heritage of ideas, how we came to think the way we do" (Toumasis, 1993, p. 255). If we would take what we want to do with humanising mathematics education seriously, we need to care for student needs as we see each student as a unique human being. Human needs entail human choices. And yet, students in their learning process would hardly defy the shaping mechanism of the cultural force as practicing in school through testing and examination as well as at home through parental judgement on how a child ought to learn. It would not be a simple if not an impossible task for an individual student to make an authentic choice of her own as she struggles to survive through the schooling system. Through the telling of Sarah's story, I attempt to explore from the humanist perspective what constitutes the authenticity of learning as grounded on the documentation of her first five years of growth experience ever after being "thrown" into the world as a unique human being. The telling of Sarah's story is hoped to raise our own self-awareness of the importance of becoming authentic learners. Without such kind of awareness, it would be hard to imagine what could be done to make mathematics meaningful on its own accord.

7.2   Creating Thinking Space for Thoughtful Understanding

From the story of Sarah, we can see that she is the kind of person who adores thinking. The extended closure of school during the pandemic had created the think-alone space at home for Sarah to do the private dialogue with her own self. She tried to make meaning out of the tasks that she needed to do. In so doing, she *chose* to favour more the out-of-school tasks, which appeared to her more real and more meaningful. She was reluctant to do the repetitive work especially when she already had a good knowing of what to do with it.

7.3   Asking and Imagining as Habits of Mind

In choosing to be herself, Sarah realised that language is an utterly important tool for communicating her thoughts with others. The doubt over how to relate thinking and speaking made her ask her mum the hard-to-answer question, "Can a mute think if he cannot talk?" It further intrigued her whether everything could be taught or learnt as she asked, "Can we teach the mute to speak?" Amitola might have a feel of what Wittgenstein (1961) said, "Whereof one cannot speak, thereof one must be silent", as she made the attempt of answering the question that Sarah had. To Sarah, the need of wearing mask when back to school in between the closure periods made her remained silent in class without the chance of voicing out what she was thinking like wearing an extra mask though invisible behind the physical one. That kind of silence might perhaps be a moment of welcome for Sarah to explore the world of her own imagination for anything that she could possibly perceive.

Imagination is of great value for the experiencing of creativity. The discourse of authenticity entails the narratives of insight, imagination, discovery and talent (Wilson & Brown, 2015). The price to pay for Sarah's imagination was making a mess of overcooking the pancake as she helped preparing for her own breakfast. Her mum's understanding and tolerance of the muddle that she had done offered her the affordance as required for fostering the very kind of authentic creativity that constitutes the production of originality not just in the making of artwork but also in the doing of visualisation and reasoning involving abstract mathematical objects. It was remarkable for Sarah to use everyday experience of toilet queue for interpreting the abstract mathematical notion of "zeroth" through her creative imagination. Such kind of creative authenticity could be the driving force behind Sarah's reinvention of using straight lines for the making of circle. Interpreting time is never a simple task for children to grasp. Nonetheless, Sarah has been semiotically active from her early age to make sense of the past, present, and future of what is happening to her in the real-life world through researching her senses of self.

7.4   *The Use of Judgement in Solving Open-ended Real-life Problems*

As Sarah situated herself in the everyday world of learning, she enjoyed the ownership of knowing how the daily-life problems could be solved through her own reasoning as she told her mum that "I know what to do". Through her own questioning, she develops the capacity of answerability to the real-life world where she dwells. Such kind of answerability, as hinted by Bakhtin (1990), is essential for an authentic learner who has the self's responsibility for making the *choice* in what ways to respond to the other in order to retain the uniqueness of integrity of the self as a person (see Markova, 2016, pp. 158–159). Learning, to Sarah, is a kind of "picking something up" (Peters, 1967, p. 8) as she chooses to pick up something with passion for savouring what she has chosen for making meaning of her own life experiences.

"Knowing what one wants to know" is no simple task as it entails sorts of hermeneutical activities constituting differing layers of meanings. To Sarah, the most effective way for her *"to know" is to question* anything which she would have *wonder* of. She would then *judge* what thing or matter is what she really wants to know for making sense of what she has been experiencing – a kind of epistemic choice. "Knowing what" to Sarah would go beyond her knowing from the epistemological point of view but instead would unfold knowing of what to know not just from aspect of epistemology but from that of ontology, judging for herself of what she ought to do, like what she told her mum, "I know what to do, mum". Sarah knew well what she valued were the real-to-life aspects of the tasks that she did and what she favoured would be the design of the tasks that she had the freedom of creating them for herself, engaging "the whole person: what they [she] knows, how they [she] acts and who they are [she is]" (Dall'Alba & Barnacle, 2007, p. 691).

During the closure of school, Sarah would have much more free time and space for choosing the kinds of authentic tasks that she had developed from her real-life experiencing. It was indeed remarkable for Sarah to demonstrate for herself the kind of authenticity of learning by her endeavour to make the construction of the "perfect circle" with straight lines without any mathematical knowledge of what it means to her by the notions of "tangents to circle" or how to get close to a circle through drawing by increasing the number of sides of a polygon. What caught my attention in particular was the sketch of the "perfect circle" embedded with the real-life scenario showing the time frame (in the morning) and the daily routine (having breakfast) in it. It can be to Sarah, semiotically speaking, a signifier of what a "perfect day" is meant to be.

7.5 *The Importance of Human Agency in Choosing to Choose Oneself*

Anowai and Chukwujekwu (2019) outline some fundamental principles of *authentic* humanism that entails free thinking, making choices as grounded on reasoning, make experience meaningful, testing ideas against reality, truth is not absolute – fallibility of human senses and human reason, making sense of value in the context of human life, ethics grounded on human needs, ethics is contextual, and tentative conclusion about the world. In the telling of Sarah's story, we come hopefully at least to have a feel of authenticity which is a way to go with our life journey and come to unfold the importance of human agency in choosing to choose oneself as we are practicing ethics of everyday life. Through education, we seek chance to make a better change of our life project in maintaining our unique relationship with others through dialogues whilst feeling free to make a choice to create a unique life story of our own in preserving the integrity of the self in an intelligent way. Would it be our faith to have authentic humanism in education in general and in mathematics education in particular to afford the growth of schoolchildren in becoming an authentic self of uniqueness and integrity of their own?

8   Reprise

Human as a being once "thrown" into the world would undergo a developmental process of getting "lost" of authenticity through time. Increasing authenticity as self-intentional act in learning would undergo the struggle of two kinds of anxiety that comes from Heidegger's double choosing to choose oneself – the primary anxiety arises as one is aware of getting lost from the active inauthenticity of "fleeing" and the secondary anxiety would surface as one is dwelled in the passive inauthenticity of "falling" into the world. The telling of Sarah's story is to highlight the role of education with a particular aim at supporting the learners as a person to make meaning of real-life experience by making ethical choice of creating the ownership of knowing who they are.

Actions and thoughts "are embodied and have meaning within the context of a particular person's life experience and social world" (Schiff, 2017, pp. 12–13). The story of Sarah as told might raise more questions than answers to know how assessment can be really made authentic for our schoolchildren as we as educators face the ever-challenge of situating ourselves in the world of inauthenticity. Life itself is a learning process but in turn learning is a life process of itself. Does it make sense of doing assessment without highlighting the process and the context of learning mathematics? Would it be an ethical action for teachers not to undertake the task of helping their students make meaning of life? Would authentic assessment be a kind of practicing of listening to our inner voice as calling to choosing to choose each of our own selves?

Every choice Sarah makes, as I see it, is to see the differences of the world as it appears to be. Seeing the mathematics world differently enables her to look into the self and the world within and beyond which she can reach. The telling of the story of Sarah has reinforced my belief that authentic learning entails meaning-making through being self-aware of one's learning experiences (the meaning of learning), being reflexive of one's own transformation as conducive to growth of learning experiences, being conscious of gaining agency for change by reflecting on one's experiences. "Education is an encounter with a person in the horizon of the fundamental exigencies [that is required in a particular situation as an urgent need] of being a human being. As the reawakening of the humanity of the human being, education is a meeting of persons in need. As such, it is a gift, …, not a something, but another human being [the teacher], who opens up in front of us [the learners] a horizon of meaning" (Wiercinski, 2015, p. 504). In other words, education is a private personal encountering through which we come to understand the growth and transformation of our own self as a human in general and as a person in particular. Authentic assessment, as a meeting place for the soul of authenticity and humanism, would be the growth experience of a person who learns how to strive at choosing to become a unique being of her own. We as educators need to learn to transform the assessment itself and develop its spirit as the agency for doing something that means something to our students. Such an understanding of assessment, as I believe, would be particularly important in humanising mathematics education. The meaning of undertaking the moral action for making mathematics meaningful direct us the way of practicing what kind of understanding we have about what humanity is meant to be.

Thanks to Sarah and Amitola for letting me tell the story as told. Before I end my writing here, I would like to share some extracts of the poem of Fernando Pessoa (translated by Chris Daniels, 2009, pp. 14, 16) as a human gift for glorifying the soul of authenticity as we listen to the voice of Sarah through the story she is telling us.

> How do I know what I'll be, when I don't even know what I am?
> Should I be what I think? But I think about being so many things!
> And there are so many thinking they're the same thing – they can't all be?
> Genius? At this moment
> A hundred thousand minds like mine dream themselves geniuses like me, ...
> I see the shops, I see the sidewalks, I see the cars pass by,
> I see the clothed living entities who cross,
> I see the dogs which also exist,
> And all of it weighs upon me like a curse of banishment,
> And all of it is foreign, as is everything.

References

Anowai, E., & Chukwujekwu, S. (2019). Philosophy of authentic humanism: The only way of curbing conflict and violence. *International Journal of History and Philosophical Research, 7*(1), 1–11.

Bakhtin, M. (1990). Art and answerability (V. Liapunov, Trans.). In M. Holquist & V. Liapunov (Eds.), *Art and answerability*. University of Texas Press.

Brown, S. I. (1993). Mathematics and humanistic themes: Sum considerations. In S. I. Brown & M. Walter (Eds.), *Problem posing: Reflections and applications* (pp. 249–278). Lawrence Erlbaum Associates.

Brown, S. I. (1996). Towards humanistic mathematics education. In A. Bishop et al. (Eds.), *First international handbook in mathematics education* (pp. 1289–1331). Kluwer Academic Publishers.

Brown, S. I. (2004). Humanistic mathematics: Personal evaluation and excavations. *Humanistic Mathematics Network Journal, 27*(13).

Cibulskaite, N. (2013). The humanization of mathematics education. *Procedia – Social and Behavioral Sciences, 83*, 134–139.

Cummings, J. J., & Maxwell, G. S. (1999). Contextualising authentic assessment. *Assessment in Education: Principles, Policy and Practice, 1*(2), 143–166.

Dall'Alba, G., & Barnacle, R. (2007). An ontological turn for higher education. *Studies in Higher Education, 32*, 679–691.

Farrell, E. (2020). Researching lived experience in education: Misunderstood or missed opportunity? *International Journal of Qualitative Methods, 19*, 1–8.

Fought, S. S., Misfeldt, M., & Shaffer, D. W. (2019). Realistic authenticity. *Journal of Interactive Learning Research, 30*(4), 477–504.

Freire, P. (1994). *Pedagogy of hope: Reliving "Pedagogy of the oppressed"* (R. R. Barr, Trans.). Continuum.

Freudenthal, H. (1973). *Mathematics as an educational task*. D. Reidel.

Gadamer, H. G. (1994). *Truth and method* (2nd rev. ed., J. Weinsheimer & D. G. Marshall, Trans.). Continuum.

Giles, D., Smythe, E., & Spence, D. (2012). Exploring relationships in education: A phenomenological inquiry. *Australian Journal of Adult Learning, 52*(2), 214–236.

Greer, B., & Skovsmose, O. (2012). Introduction: Seeing the cage? The emergence of critical mathematics education. In O. Skovsmose & B. Greer (Eds.), *Opening the cage: Critique and politics of mathematics education*, 1–20. Sense Publishers.

Groenewald, T. (2004). A phenomenological research design illustrated. *International Journal of Qualitative Methods, 3*(1), 42–55.

Gulikers, J., Bastiaens, Th., & Kirschner, P. (2004). A five-dimensional framework for authentic assessment. *Educational Technology Research & Development, 52*(3), 67–85.

Gutstein, E. (2012). Mathematics as a weapon in the struggle. In O. Skovsmose & B. Greer (Eds.), *Opening the cage: Critique and politics of mathematics education* (pp. 23–48). Sense Publishers.

Han-Pile, B. (2009). Freedom and the "choice to choose oneself" in being and time. In M. Wrathall (Ed.), *The Cambridge companions to Heidegger's being and time (Cambridge companion to philosophy)* (pp. 291–309). Cambridge University.

Heidegger, M. (1962). *Being and time* (J. Macquarrie & E. Robinson, Trans.). Harper & Row. (Original work published 1927)

Hersh, R. (1994). Fresh breezes in the philosophy of mathematics. In P. Ernest (Ed.), *Mathematics, education, and philosophy: An international perspective* (pp. 11–20). The Falmer Press.

Hersh, R. (1997). *What is mathematics, really?* Oxford University Press.

Hycner, R. H. (1999). Some guidelines for the phenomenological analysis of interview data. In A. Bryman & R. G. Burgess (Eds.), *Qualitative Research,* (Vol. 3, pp. 143-164). Sage.

Ironside, P. M. (2005). Introduction: Thinking beyond method. In P. M. Ironside (Ed.), *Beyond method: Philosophical conversations in healthcare research and scholarship* (pp. ix–xx). University of Wisconsin Press.

Jung, J., Horta, H., & Postiglione, G. A. (2021). Living in uncertainty: The COVID-19 pandemic and higher education in Hong Kong. *Studies in Higher Education*, January, 1–14.

Karaali, G. (2014). Can zombies write mathematical poetry? Mathematical poetry as a model for humanistic mathematics. *Journal of Mathematics and the Arts, 8*(1–2), 38–45.

Law, H. Y. (2009). *Learning to ask: The role of communication in the teaching and learning of mathematics* [Unpublished doctoral dissertation]. University of East Anglia, Norwich.

Marková, I. (2016). *The dialogical mind: Common sense and ethics*. Cambridge University Press.

Mueller, J. (2005). The authentic assessment toolbox: Enhancing student learning through online faculty development. *Journal of Online Learning and Teaching, 1*(1), 1–7.

Peck, F.A. (2018). Rejecting Platonism: Recovering humanity in mathematics education. *Education Sciences, 8*(43), 1–13.

Pessoa, F. (2009). *The collected poems of Álvaro de Campos, Vol. 2 (1928–1935)* (C. Daniels, Trans.). Shearsman Books.

Peters, R. S. (1967). What is an educational process. In R. S. Peters (Ed.), *The concept of education* (pp. 1–16). Routledge & Kegan Paul.

Schiff, B. (2017). *A new narrative for psychology*. Oxford University Press.

Shaffer, D. W., & Resnick, M. (1999). "Thick" authenticity: New media and authentic learning. *Journal of Interactive Learning Research, 10*(2), 195–215.

Sherman, G. L. (2009). Martin Heidegger's concept of authenticity: A philosophical contribution to student affairs theory. *Journal of College and Character, 10*(7), 1–8.

Toumasis, C. (1993). Ideas and processes in mathematics: A course in history and philosophy of mathematics. *Studies in Philosophy and Education, 12*, 245–256.

Van Manen, M. (1990). *Researching lived experience: Human science for an action sensitive pedagogy*. SUNY Press.

Van Manen, M. (2007). Phenomenology of practice. *Phenomenology & Practice, 1*(1), 11–30.

Vu, T. T., & Dall'Alba, G. (2014). Authentic assessment for student learning: An ontological conceptualisation. *Educational Philosophy and Theory, 46*(7), 778–791.

Wiercinski, A. (2015). Educative encounter as a meeting of people in need. In A. Wiercinski (Ed.), *Hermeneutics-ethics-education* (pp. 491–504). LIT Verlag.

Wilson, C., & Brown, M. (2015). Creativity and authenticity: Perspectives of creative value, utility and quality. *Proceedings of the 5th contemporary arts conference*. DAKAM-Eastern Mediterrean Academic Research Center.

White, A. (1987). Letter from the editor (untitled). *Humanistic Mathematics Network Newsletter, 1*.

White, A. (Ed.). (1993). *Essays in humanistic mathematics*. MAA Notes no. 32. The Mathematical Association of America.

White, L. A. (1947). The locus of mathematical reality: An anthropological footnote. *Philosophy of Science, 14*, 289–303.

Wiggins, G. (1989). A true test: Toward more authentic and equitable assessment. *The Phi Delta Kappan, 70*(9), 703–713.

Wittgenstein, L. (1961). *Tractatus Logico-Philosophicus*. Routledge & Kegan.

Yarden, A., & Carvalho, G. S. (2011). Authenticity in biology education: Benefits and challenges. *Journal of Biological Education, 45*(3), 118–120.

CHAPTER 13

Translanguaging Pedagogies for Multilingual Learner Assessment

Naomi Wilks-Smith

Abstract

There is substantial linguistic diversity amongst students in Melbourne Australia and these students' competencies also span across languages. Despite this, assessments in schools are most often monolingual English practices. The languages that students have in addition to English are, in most cases, left at the school gate and their valuable multilingual skills are generally not utilised or celebrated in any meaningful pedagogic way or considered when assessing students. Reducing assessment to English-only disadvantages multilingual learners by ignoring the full range of language skills that these learners have and also failing to acknowledge their content and conceptual knowledge and understandings in languages other than English. Although there is an increasing awareness of the need to include learners' home languages in classroom practice, it is not common place, and in most cases has not extended to the assessment of learners. Translanguaging pedagogies have much to offer education practice and assessment by connecting the entire repertoire of a student's linguistic skill-set with their overall learning. Doing so brings languages into the classroom by recognising, valuing and building upon the many different language skills of students to enrich their learning. Within this chapter, translanguaging pedagogical approaches are explored through examples of practice designed for a linguistically and culturally diverse primary school context. The examples of practice draw on the varied multilingual abilities of students, and by integrating their linguistic repertoires into classroom learning, students use their multilingual skills as learning resources that can also be acknowledged in assessment. In sharing these, the potential of translanguaging to add an important lens to student assessment is revealed which, in turn, contributes towards a more widespread use of translanguaging pedagogical approaches for teaching, learning and assessment in linguistically and culturally diverse schools.

Keywords

translanguaging – assessment – linguistic diversity – multilingual learners – EAL

1 Introduction

The myriad of languages spoken in Australia is a striking feature of the country's population. 263 different languages and dialects are regularly spoken in Australian homes and communities (Australian Bureau of Statistics, 2016) and 32% of students in the state of Victoria in Australia are from language backgrounds other than English (Department of Education and Training Victoria, 2020a). Despite this incredible linguistic diversity amongst students, Victorian schools are overwhelmingly monolingual English-centred spaces where "… languages are often 'left at the school gate' and are not recognised or celebrated at school" (Wilks-Smith, 2017) and English is the medium for teaching and assessing students. This practice ignores the valuable skills of multilingual students.

In the field of education broadly, academics and teachers often talk about students' 'virtual school bags' (Thomson, 2002), referring to the knowledge, understandings and experiences students bring with them to school, and the importance of these virtual school bags to leverage in-school learning. Often however, on a practical level, "… school only draws on the contents of some children's school bags, those whose resources match those required in the game of education" (Thomson & Hall, 2008, p. 4). It is widely recognised that language is a key element of students' school bags that privileges some and disadvantages others. Monolingual English-speaking students enter Australian classrooms where their English literacy knowledge is readily understood, whilst bilingual and multilingual learners discard much of their school bags that do not seem to 'fit' the classroom environment. Schooling therefore commences from these inequitable starting points. Bilingual and multilingual students have linguistic competencies in their languages, have had experiences, and have developed conceptual understandings and cultural knowledge across their languages. However, often teachers know little of students' prior experiences, knowledge and understandings that are not in English or about their skills in additional languages, so they are not validated or utilised in their learning and even more rarely, considered in assessment. This lack of validation and inclusion of learners' knowledge and capabilities across languages means that only a portion of learners' knowledge is being assessed, that which can be expressed in English. This situation leads to inequalities and unfair assessment. This highlights a need for teachers to find out about students' capabilities across their languages. The Australian Institute for Teaching and School Leadership (AITSL) sets professional standards for teachers (Australian Institute for Teaching and School Leadership, 2017) which includes a requirement that teachers 'Know students and how they learn' (Standard 1) including 'students with diverse linguistic, cultural, religious and socioeconomic backgrounds' (Focus area 1.3). This national requirement expects teachers to consider learners' linguistic diversity when teaching, however, despite a growing awareness amongst teachers of the need to consider students' languages, there is limited practical uptake of this in classrooms.

There is a plethora of research that point to the many cognitive and academic advantages of being bilingual or multilingual (such as Bialystok & Werker, 2017; Cummins, 2003; Fernandez, Language and Society Centre & Bayswater South Primary School 1992; García, 2009; Liddicoat, 2013; Molyneux, 2011) and a growing body of research that identifies the benefits of including learners' full repertoires of languages into their classroom learning (Chau, 2007; Conteh, 2018; Cummins & Persad, 2014; French, 2016; García, 2009; Liu, 2010; Swain & Lapkin, 2013), which will be explored further in the literature review. In order to realise these benefits, learners' languages must be present in their learning. This draws attention to the need to recognise and value students' knowledge and skills in languages that are not English or the 'majority' language. It also presents an untapped potential to utilise students' languages and prior knowledge to leverage their classroom learning which leads to further depth of learning.

Despite this extensive research, in schools, multilingual learners are often referred to as English as additional language (EAL) learners and the focus of teachers is usually on what these students are lacking in English and on supporting their English language development. This viewpoint places emphasis on students' deficit in English, without acknowledgement of the broad range of skills that multilingual learners have across their repertoires of languages. Students' knowledge of languages is connected and should be integrated into their learning to continue the development of each language. Too often, in the quest to improve English, learners' additional languages are ignored in the classroom, and outside the classroom are either used less or cease to be used. This unfortunate practice contributes towards the erasing of these languages, and along with them, aspects of culture, and connections with family and community. In order to embrace all languages in the classroom and more fairly assess students, teaching practice needs to include strategies that provide opportunities for students to showcase their capabilities using their full repertoires of languages.

Translanguaging offers a practical way to bring languages that are often invisible at school into classrooms. It utilises pedagogical ways that promote students' use of their full set of linguistic resources, and importantly, supports further learning. Translanguaging pedagogies connect students' entire repertoire of languages with their learning by embracing and integrating multilinguals' linguistic skills, experiences and cultural knowledge into classroom practice. Through such an approach, multilingual students "integrate their knowledge of multiple languages in a way that enriches their communication and learning in all languages" (VCAA, 2020, p. 1). Learning is enhanced this way because "… knowledge of their multiple languages is interconnected and integrated …" (Department of Education and Training Victoria, 2020b, p. 1). By utilising translanguaging practices in the classroom and embedding translanguaging pedagogies into assessment, a more complete picture of learners' current capabilities can be understood and drawn on for future teaching that builds on learners' capabilities. Whilst an understanding of this concept is growing in schools, there remains limited evidence of its practical uptake in classrooms, and even less evidence of consideration or integration of translanguaging in assessment practices. Often when teachers are not bilingual or multilingual themselves, or do not share languages in common with students, and do not know how to bring languages into the classroom, an English-only context prevails.

This chapter aims to encourage and support all teachers to integrate learners' languages into classroom teaching and assessment practices. It provides an overview of relevant literature and then shares examples of classroom practice that demonstrate translanguaging pedagogical approaches for teaching and assessment that could be used as models for teachers to consider in their own teaching practice.

2 Literature Review

2.1 *Translanguaging*

Bilinguals and multilinguals routinely use a range of language and semiotic resources for a variety of purposes in their daily lives. Their languages are part of an interconnected system (García & Kleyn, 2016). For these speakers, languages are "… tools in their communicative toolkits, which they use flexibly according to need and circumstance" and prohibiting such use would be "… like telling a carpenter to build a house using only half of the tools in his or her toolbox" (Faulstich, 2015, p. 105). Translanguaging reflects these out-of-school language practices of multilinguals and considers their full "linguistic repertoire" whilst bringing their language practices into the classroom (García, 2009).

Translanguaging focuses on the 'language user' (Baynham & Lee, 2019) rather than the language system or aspects of the languages, and "… there are no clear-cut boundaries between the languages …" (García, 2009, p. 115). In practice, this means multilingual students access their full linguistic repertoires in a variety of ways and for a variety of purposes in the classroom without separating languages for certain contexts or tasks. Mixing languages is an accepted practice whilst students make full use of their multilingual resources. The concurrent use of languages makes use of the "interdependence of skills and knowledge across languages" (Creese & Blackledge, 2010). In this way, translanguaging "... gives legitimacy to the practices of multilingual speakers and encourages us as educators to leverage their full language repertoire to support their understanding of content, develop their language performances, and buttress their socioemotional development" (García & Kleyn, 2016, p. 14).

Critical to adopting a translanguaging pedagogy are García, Johnson and Seltzer's (2017) notions of *'stance', 'design'* and *'shift'*. A teacher's *stance* whereby they view students' multilingualism as central to their identities is important. Teachers must believe that multilingualism is a resource for learners to think and learn in, should allow learners to determine how they use their linguistic repertoires, and believe that translanguaging enables learners to use languages in a natural way for them. Teachers need to *design* instruction that integrates students' linguistic repertoires. "Designing instruction based on translanguaging theory requires three elements: (1) constructing collaborative/cooperative structures, (2) collecting varied multilingual and multimodal instructional resources, and (3) using translanguaging pedagogical practices" (García & Kleyn, 2016, p. 21). Translanguaging capitalises on social interaction between students who share common languages, such as through discussion and collaboration. It also gives power to students to use languages for their learning. Multilingual and multimodal resources such as texts, videos, movies and internet resources are important to facilitate these translanguaging practices. The design of teaching with translanguaging also includes family and community in school. Teaching needs to respond to learners' linguistic repertoires which are varied, so *shifts* are required to respond to individual differences in students' language repertoires and *shift* to students' linguistic needs and practices during learning.

French (2019) recognises that students will have varying levels of proficiency in their languages and their skills may be in some or all language modes (listening, speaking, reading, writing) so it is important that there is flexibility and choice in the inclusion of languages in tasks. Therefore, "... multilingual strategies and tasks should build on the existing multilingual practices of students" (French, 2019, p. 36) and "Tasks should be designed with flexibility to allow students to make choices about how and to what extent they apply their multilingual resources to learning" (French, 2019, p. 38). These teaching practices do not require teachers to know the languages of their students in order to embrace translanguaging pedagogy, rather, they facilitate classroom practice that encourages learners to interact using their languages, think in their languages, and integrate their knowledge across languages in their learning of new content.

2.2 Benefits of Translanguaging

There are a wide range of reasons for including translanguaging in classrooms and benefits to learners of doing so. One important reason is that students come to school with 'funds of knowledge' (Moll, Amanti, Neff & Gonzalez, 1992, p. 132) that can be used to inform and support teaching and learning. Languages are part of these 'funds of knowledge' that students bring with them to school in their 'virtual school bags' (Thomson, 2002; Thomson & Hall, 2008). Building on these existing resources by making connections with students' full linguistic repertoires acts as springboards for their learning in classrooms (Somerville, Sawyer & D'warte, 2016).

There are many benefits of translanguaging and making connections with learners' home languages for their further learning. Translanguaging helps learners make links between their languages and between experiences outside and within school (Conteh, 2018). The use of all languages helps "… to build shared knowledge, both everyday and academic, helps EAL/D [English as an additional language or dialect] learners expand and re-situate the meanings they can already make, and the concepts they already have, to engage with the curriculum" (Feez & Harper, 2021, p. 12). Permitting use of home languages in classrooms can help learners activate higher order thinking skills (García, 2009) and can activate and extend their conceptual knowledge (Cummins & Persad, 2014). Use of home languages in classrooms also helps learners process new and complex material in class (Swain and Lapkin, 2013). There are clear benefits to both languages and content learning when learners' linguistic resources are included in the process of learning.

Translanguaging also supports English language development. Home languages can be productively used to support English literacy acquisition at school (Liu, 2010). In an English as an additional language (EAL) learning context, learners can use home languages with other speakers of the same language to help understand informational content and in doing so, supports them to stay involved in their learning and share their language learning experiences (Chau, 2007). Learners use their first language (L1) to check comprehension, to clarify meaning, and to work out second language (L2) meaning and decide on L2 words, as well as to provide additional information (Chau, 2007). Often in an EAL context, learners can understand aspects of the L2 but are unable to generate responses in L2 so using L1 with peers can help them negotiate meaning and form L2 utterances together. This shows a variety of ways in which L1 can be used as a language learning resource for students to support their EAL communication and learning.

In an Australian context where there is great diversity in the range of languages within classrooms, a wide range of advantages have been identified for multilingual students when using their multilingual resources. These include "... access to additional cognitive tools, further language learning ability, expanded spheres of communication, and affective development" and using translanguaging also "... benefitted their thinking" (French, 2016, p. 304). These students "... used their multilingual resources individually to support language, literacy, conceptual learning, and access to information" and "... helped facilitate thought processes through the home language ..." (French, 2016, p. 309). As well as students using their home languages as resources, many also used additional languages to interact with each other for social and academic purposes. Importantly, it was found that the greatest benefit is attained when teachers purposefully integrate learners' multilingual resources into learning tasks rather than merely allowing languages to be used.

2.3 Translanguaging for Social Justice

There are also important social justice reasons for including translanguaging in classroom practice. Greater educational equity is realised when students' 'virtual school bags' (Thomson, 2002) are understood, valued and used at school. When students have their home language practices validated in the classroom and are able to use their full range of linguistic resources for their learning, their overall learning is improved. The use of home languages in classrooms gives visibility to students' languages and places value on them (Pacheco & Miller, 2016) which has socio-emotional benefits for learners.

More accurate judgements of students' capabilities are made when multilingualism is invited into classrooms. There is often a deficit positioning around the limited English skills that bilingual and multilingual students have rather than viewing bi/multilingual students' linguistic skills across languages. "If, as teachers, we make judgements based on what a learner can produce in English only, we make a narrow judgement of their overall literacy knowledge and skills" (Wilks-Smith, 2017), however, by inviting students' full set of linguistic resources into classrooms, teachers have a clearer, more complete picture of students' literacy skills. Translanguaging supports a move away from the "monolingual mindset" (Clyne, 2005) that prevails in schools and offers practice that embraces all languages. In this way, translanguaging brings students' languages into classrooms where English is dominant, overcoming injustices of ignoring minority languages (de los Rios & Seltzer, 2017). A more language-inclusive context for learning is more equitable for 'minority' students and disrupts the inequalities of English-dominant practice (Robinson, Tian, Martinez, & Qarqeen, 2018).

Translanguaging is also important for language maintenance. Far too often students sacrifice home languages in the process of learning English at school. Students languages, other than English, are often used less or stop being used. This contributes towards individuals' loss of languages, languages disappearing in families over generations, and globally endangered languages. Translanguaging offers a practical solution where languages can be strengthened and preserved by using them and continuing the development of all languages together.

2.4 Assessment of Multilingual Learners

A hesitation often mentioned by teachers when considering translanguaging is that assessment is done in English, and teachers unfamiliar with learners' home languages cannot assess these languages. Although some formal summative assessment is required in English, translanguaging can play an important and powerful role in formative ongoing assessment as diagnostic assessment for informing teaching practice, and multilingual practices can be included in classroom summative assessments. Translanguaging can be used to gather evidence to assess where learners are in their learning development and inform further teaching practice and learning. It is not necessary for assessment evidence to be only in English. For example, teachers can learn a lot about a learner's literacy by viewing samples of their writing in each of their languages. Judgements that may be made if we only viewed their English work may be expanded when viewing a learner's capabilities in other languages (Wilks-Smith, 2017). Teachers do not need to know learners' languages to see that they can write words, a sentence or a page of text in their additional language/s. Similarly, when finding out about students' prior knowledge on a new class topic, an often-used strategy is to ask students to 'brainstorm' what they already know. If students are encouraged to include what they know, such as by writing or orally recording in any language, the extent of their prior knowledge may be better understood by teachers. Additionally, the knowledge, skills and concepts learners understand can be demonstrated by drawing, making or doing, also opening up opportunities for non-verbal evidence of learning. In these ways, assessment practices that include translanguaging provide more in-depth information about students' capabilities which then enable teachers to plan for learning to address individual needs. Integrating translanguaging pedagogies into assessment allows learners to demonstrate their capabilities across languages and in doing this helps "… ensure that assessment activities are equitable for, and accessible to, all learners" (Department of Education and Training Victoria, 2019a, p. 1).

Overwhelmingly, assessment is designed for monolingual students and doesn't include considerations for multicultural and multilingual students (van de Vijver, 2016). Assessment often has method bias (including norm samples and test instruments), test item bias (including linguistic items), and issues with equivalence in meanings across cultural groups (van de Vijver, 2016). These problems and inequities with monolingual summative assessment (that are often national assessments that teachers must administer) are important to identify so that judgements made from these assessments are better understood. Considering this, it is important that teachers harness the opportunities to include the full linguistic repertoires of learners in their ongoing formative assessment so that knowledge gleaned from more inclusive practices inform their overall assessments of students' learning. This calls for classroom teaching and assessment practices to reflect multilinguals' language practices, to consider languages as resources and include the full linguistic repertoires of learners (Gorter & Cenoz, 2017). This can be achieved through the use of translanguaging.

Relating specifically to translanguaging, García and Kleyn (2016) stress the importance of students' languages and knowledge across languages being recognised in assessment:

> ... translanguaging in assessment levels the playing field between bilingual and monolingual children. Whereas monolingual children are allowed to use most of the features of their language repertoire (with few exceptions) in expressing what they know, bilingual children are asked to suppress more than half of the features in their repertoire in one or the other language. Thus, a translanguaging theory in assessment also promotes equal educational opportunity and social justice. It offers a more accurate assessment of what bilingual students know and can do with language. (García & Kleyn, 2016, pp. 24–25)

This calls for teachers to include translanguaging theory "... to design formative and summative assessments in which students are given opportunity to show what they know by using their full language repertoire" (García & Kleyn, 2016, p. 25).

Despite the vast multilingual population in Australian schools, "... national and state curricula reflect a monolingual English-based approach to learning and assessment" (French & Armitage, 2020, p. 104). Nevertheless, there is considerable flexibility in how teachers reach broad learning outcomes, and teaching pedagogy can include multilingualism. French and Armitage (2020) provide examples of students using translanguaging pedagogies within secondary school units of work that included a Year 12 analysis of Tagalog and English in text messaging, a Year 10 webpage of a recount based on an interview with a family member, and Year 12 individual research projects which included bilingual references. These examples demonstrate that there are still opportunities for students to use their multilingual resources in their learning and to build on their knowledge and skills across languages. Important to note is that these translanguaging practices were conducted in classroom contexts where teachers did not share the languages of their students, as is most often the case in Australian schools. This shows that "It does not need to be difficult for teachers to create opportunities for multilingual learning, as simple changes to task information can invite home languages to enter the learning space" (French & Armitage, 2020, p. 105).

3 Translanguaging Pedagogies for Multilingual Learners

3.1 *Designing Tasks with Translanguaging Pedagogies*

The literature review identified the need for teaching pedagogy to be inclusive of multilingual learners and pointed to translanguaging as a practical way to include learners' languages in classroom practice. Although there is an increasing understanding of the need to include learners' languages in schools, there is little uptake of it practically, mostly because many teachers don't know how to include learners' languages and because they feel ill-prepared to do so when they don't know their students' languages, and there is even less consideration of the role of learners' languages within assessment practices. This points to the need for 'examples of practice' that demonstrate how translanguaging can be practically enacted in classrooms for teaching and assessment purposes. So, a lecturer-researcher and pre-service teachers from one university course within a Bachelor of Education programme in Melbourne, Australia worked to design a collection of examples of practice.

The concept of translanguaging was introduced to pre-service teachers within a university course that focused on teaching English as an additional language or dialect (EAL/D) learners. At the commencement of the course, the lecturer-researcher and pre-service teachers went to a primary school that was linguistically and culturally diverse for EAL/D teaching-learning experiences. The pre-service teachers were paired with EAL/D learner buddies and familiarised themselves with the school, the classroom context, and the unique learning needs of their buddies. It was within this context that pre-service teachers saw first-hand the extent of the languages and cultures that were represented in the school. The pre-service teachers were then encouraged to consider how translanguaging could be used within this context, with the original aim to regularly teach these EAL/D learners. Unfortunately, the COVID pandemic abruptly stopped the visits to the school and the teaching of these students, but nevertheless, the initial experiences in this school provided stimulus for planning with translanguaging pedagogies. As part of their course work, pre-service teachers designed units of work that incorporated translanguaging pedagogies, and excerpts from ten pre-service teachers' work were selected that clearly demonstrated a practical application of translanguaging for the purpose of creating a collection of examples of practice for this chapter. In some cases, the excerpts were combined to expand on similar themes or ideas in order to provide examples of practice that reflect the theory of translanguaging, have scope to be adapted for different year levels or topics, and to include suggestions for assessment. Each example includes a purposeful integration of learners' languages into the task, provides learners with the opportunity to showcase their abilities across languages, and have these capabilities included in assessment. The result is the following examples of practice.

3.2 Examples of Practice

This collection of examples of practice demonstrate how translanguaging pedagogies can be used in a wide variety of ways for a wide variety of teaching and assessment purposes. They can be easily modified for use with a diversity of topics and with students that range in languages and year levels. Consideration has been given to students who are the only speakers of their L1 in classrooms amongst a diversity of languages, as is often the case in many Australian schools. Additionally, many Australian teachers are monolingual or do not share the languages of their students, so strategies that model inviting students to use their languages without relying on teachers' use of these languages were required. The translanguaging design principles (Rowe, 2018) were also considered and reflected on whilst creating the examples of practice. The principles, compiled by Rowe from the research are "… valuing students' languages and cultures, modelling translanguaging, providing authentic opportunities for multilingual communication, inviting two-way translation, composing dual-language texts, and connecting students with bilingual or multilingual audiences" (Rowe, 2018, p. 31). The relationship between the examples of practice and Rowe's design principles are included in a summary table after the examples of practice are described. Following these considerations and principles, the examples of practice move beyond valuing students' languages in classrooms and demonstrate how to practically include and actively encourage multilingualism in classroom learning and assessment.

3.3 *Categorising*

Students in a Year 1 class learning about 'Animal Habitats' are provided with a collection of images of animals and habitats. They are asked to categorise which animals live in each habitat. The teacher models placing each habitat picture in a different place and in-turn thinking about each animal and moving them between habitats before deciding. Pairs of students are then given a set of pictures to categorise. The task can be done non-verbally, by moving the pictures into their categories, providing the opportunity for students to demonstrate their knowledge regardless of their English language ability. The use of pairs encourages student discussion about their choices. Same-L1 pairs can be selected by the teacher when possible so that discussion about the task and their category choices can be in L1. Pairs can then share their choices with the teacher or the class; this may be done by showing a category of pictures and may include L1 and/or L2 English and may also include L1 or L2 written labels for the pictures. This task could also include word cards provided by the teacher or created by learners (in any language/s) to match with the images.

This task demonstrates students' knowledge of the content; in this example, of which animals live in which habitats. It can be used as formative assessment providing the teacher with knowledge about students' prior knowledge on the topic and can be used to inform planning and teaching. The image-based nature of the task allows for students to demonstrate their knowledge non-verbally which can be a useful way to gauge conceptual knowledge of students who may not yet be able to verbally demonstrate their knowledge in English. Visuals support learners in understanding class content and provide context for the language. The task also provides students with an authentic opportunity to communicate with their peers in L1 where possible, depending on the languages in the classroom. Opportunities can be provided for students to discuss their work in pairs, in L1, L2 or a combination of both. The task may also include writing labels or descriptions in L1 or L2 further demonstrating students' content knowledge as well as linguistic skills. Observations of students during this task is also important as formative assessment, supporting teachers to understand individual learning needs and modify tasks to suit learners.

3.4 KWL *Charts*

KWL charts are graphic organisers that can be used to track what students 'know', 'want to know' and have 'learned' during class. They can be used with any topic by learners in any year level. The KWL is designed to engage students throughout their learning. The 'know' section helps students to activate their schema on the topic and make explicit what they already know. The 'want to know' section helps students generate questions to guide their learning and make sense of new thoughts. Students add to their KWL chart throughout a unit, eventually completing the 'learned' section to demonstrate their progress and as a reflection on their learning of the topic content and their skill development. Individual knowledge over time can be tracked by students using a different coloured pen each time they add to the chart and contributions could be dated. Students can respond in L1, L2, or a combination of both. The use of L1 and L2 has an important cognitive function for students helping them make connections between their prior knowledge in L1 with new in-class learning in L2. Although the teacher may not be able to understand what the student has written in L1, they will know that the student has a certain number of points of information that they may otherwise have not have known if the chart was only in English. When students do these individually, the KWL chart can be used as assessment of students' prior knowledge at the commencement of a topic, for ongoing formative assessment of learning throughout the topic informing teaching practice, and as a summative assessment at the end of a topic. The chart is also important for learners own self-assessment of their learning.

3.5 *Multilingual Brainstorming*

A small group of Year 1 English as additional language (EAL) learners brainstorm what they do in a day within the broad topic of 'All about me'. They write in L1, L2, or both, possibly including mixed language sentences or multilingual text. They also draw or select digital images, searching using L1 or L2. Students share what they do in a day with each other, where possible using L1, L2, or both. L1 can be used to clarify meaning and also to ask for support for L2 English words or to form English sentences. Differentiation can be provided through options to label, write, draw, point to visuals, code-switch between home language and English in their writing or when speaking about their work, and through use of a same-L1 peer when possible to share work and/or help each other. The task can be scaffolded with explicit instruction, with teacher-student collaboration, peer collaboration, and worked examples. The task can be used as diagnostic assessment to find out about students' literacy skills, including their writing skills. Assessment may also include informal and formal observations, peer discussions, and an analysis of student work.

When students use L1 and/or L2 when brainstorming they can focus on the brainstorming of ideas rather than being restrained by their English language skills. Brainstorming may include oral and written modes as well as images. The inclusion of images, drawn by the students and/or digital images, demonstrates content information. These visuals enable the teacher to understand the message the student is communicating and support the teacher to provide targeted EAL support to students at the precise time of need as they are working by providing the words or phrases in English for the information expressed in the images. The task may also include plurilingual strategies such as using home language words and words copied from various sources. When students are encouraged to use their home language, it reassures them that their prior literacy knowledge is considered and valued and subsequently boosts their self-esteem. When students of the same home language collaborate and use their L1 to communicate and clarify meaning, it not only supports their learning but also strengthens social skills. In this way the task facilitates student interaction, important for friendships and social interaction. When EAL students have friends, they have a need and a purpose to communicate and use language/s meaningfully.

3.6 *Multimodal Texts*

Students in Year 2 explore key concepts about living things within the topic 'Lifecycles', a unit of work integrating literacy and science. Three related tasks that incorporate translanguaging using multimodal texts are shared. The first task is the creation of a multimodal, dual-language or multilingual text that illustrates the lifecycle of a plant or butterfly. Choice is provided for students (plant or butterfly) to increase their motivation. Students demonstrate their knowledge using multiple modes such as drawing, including digital images, labelling using supplied or student-created labels (in L1 and/or L2), writing information (L1 and/or L2), and including audio of themselves verbalising information (L1 and/or L2). The inclusion of illustrations softens the boundaries between languages and supports the meaning of the written text. Multilingual students often have different linguistic abilities in different modes of language, so it is important that various modes are included in the task. Focus of the task is on the information and the students' knowledge rather than being reliant on English. The task could be carried out on commencement of a unit as a pre-assessment to find out about what students already know. It could also be a form of formative assessment to monitor student learning during the unit of work, or as summative assessment at the end of the unit to identify the learning that has been achieved throughout the unit. The same task could even be carried out twice, as a pre-assessment and summative assessment to identify individual learning growth between these two time periods.

The second task is an information-gap task using a partially labelled diagram of an insect. Working in pairs, partners A and B have the same insect but with differing information and need to communicate to find out their missing information. The activity is modelled by the teacher before students begin. Pairs can be formed to provide same-L1 use and support or to provide an L2 English peer model for a developing English language learner. Through questioning each other they complete their diagrams, add drawings, labels, writing, and personal notes demonstrating the information they collected in multimodal ways. Information-gap tasks provide an authentic purpose for communication and can provide multilingual learners with opportunities to display their knowledge and understanding of the content across their languages. This also enables teachers to understand students' competencies across their languages and assess their knowledge.

The third task includes the growing of a plant. Each student is given a pot, soil and seeds to plant and watch grow. This is a 'hands-on' learning experience where students are actively involved in their learning. The task does not rely on a strong command of English because it is supported with the physical involvement of learners and physical objects or images. The process of planting is modelled, further utilising visual cues. There are many opportunities for learners to discuss their learning during the process, and afterwards students also talk about their learning experience using any language. This may be to a peer in class in L1 or L2 or to a parent in L1. Students also record their experience by drawing and writing. Depending on students' writing abilities, their writing may include copied text, modelled text such as by completing provided sentence starters, using or writing labels, or writing extended descriptions, using any language or mix of languages. This task reflects the 'language experience' approach (Department of Education and Training Victoria, 2019b) which draws upon all areas of literacy. It integrates speaking, listening, reading and writing through the development of a text based on first-hand experiences. It can also include drawings, digital images, and photographs taken during the learning experience. In this way, it elicits the creation of a multimodal, dual-language or multilingual text. These learner-centred texts are personal and meaningful and become texts that the students read and reflect upon. This task is not only a task which includes translanguaging practices but can also be used for various assessment purposes as the combined information included in a multimodal text provides more information about a learner's literacy capabilities and content knowledge than when only one mode is used.

3.7   *Research Project Reports*

A commonly used open-ended task, particularly suitable for Years 3 to 6 students, is research project reports. These can be about any topic and can be teacher- or student-driven. Once a topic is selected, and perhaps key questions to investigate are decided upon, students search for information and read. Immediately this invites a multitude of opportunities for students to use their full range of linguistic resources across languages. It can include searching for and locating internet sources of information in any language and the reading of them, reading L1, L2 or bilingual texts, using dictionaries in any language including bilingual dictionaries and picture dictionaries, and speaking with and communicating (emails, letters, text messages, phone interviews) with resource people (anywhere in the world). Each of these, build content knowledge on the topic. Allowing research to be done in any language enables a greater depth and detail in the project because students are able to use their linguistic strengths. Graphic organisers (such as Venn diagrams, mindmaps, T-charts, see Teach Starter, 2021) can then be used to support the writing process. Graphic organisers provide a structure for writing, support students to plan their work, and provide a way for students to get down their knowledge, thoughts, ideas and questions. These can be used with any language and are important to support the thinking and planning process for learners' writing. It is not important for teachers to be able to read students work for it to be valuable for them, for it to enhance their learning and increase their confidence in their learning. Observations and student conferencing can be used as formative assessment, leading to teachers providing targeted support. Scaffolding is one form of targeted support during the project writing process including such things as guided writing, joint construction, modelled writing, shared writing and teacher- or peer-editing. Multilingual resources such as bilingual texts, dictionaries and L1-speakers are valuable forms of support at this stage too. The final product is a written research project report. The final stage may also include project presentations. Multilingual learners' languages could be drawn on in oral presentations by using a language of choice with an audience of choice. For example, students may choose to present their project to peers or another class in L2 English or may choose to present in L1 to their family, a community group, or L1-speaking friends.

3.8 *Multilingual Interviews and Surveys*

Multilingual interviews and surveys can be carried out with learners of all year levels for a variety of purposes, within a variety of topics. One task that involves multilingual interviews is interviewing family members from different generations to find out about daily life for them at your age. Learners design a set of questions to ask them, ask the questions orally (L1, L2, mix of L1 & L2, possibly even L3, L4+) and record the responses (in any language/s). Students then summarise what they found out (in any language) and create a way to show what they learned (oral, written, multimodal, using L1, L2, or both). Students then share what they learned with a classmate (L1 or L2) which may involve two-way (or more) translation, then with a group, then with the teacher and whole class (L2 English). This process moves from a small supportive one-to-one sharing, increasingly building the size of the group that is being communicated with. The familiarity and repetition of presenting to new audiences supports students' confidence with larger group presentations. Finally, students write letters of thanks to the family members that were interviewed in the language used with them if possible. This task is a powerful way to use multilingual learners' repertoires to gather information, demonstrates value in gaining knowledge using languages and engages families in class work.

Similarly, multilingual surveys can be conducted which authentically utilise the language repertoires of students. One example of a topic that could be explored beyond the classroom is 'favourite food'. Students can survey their family and friends for their responses. The surveys may be done face-to-face, on paper, over the phone, via text, email, or other social media (with parental consent), and these surveys can be conducted in a range of languages depending on who students survey. Multilingual use can be particularly encouraged by having a class challenge to gather responses from as many countries as possible and using as many languages as possible. The information can then be collated and graphed, individually, and then again with whole class data. Connections can be made with the mathematics skills of presenting data and interpreting data. There are a multitude of possibilities for assessment. In this example, students' understanding of mathematical concepts and their ability to present and interpret data could be a focus for assessment. In this case, these understandings can be visually demonstrated regardless of the languages used in the gathering of the data.

3.9   Community Flyers

Students in a Year 6 class learning about 'Natural Disasters' create information flyers to tell the community about natural disasters. Each student selects one natural disaster relating to a region of choice, for example, the risk of bushfires in a rural region of Australia in Summer. The flyer needs to include information about the natural disaster and practical strategies that can prepare people to respond to it. This creates an authentic scenario for students work and an authentic audience. Students are told that the community needs to know this information to be aware of the natural disaster and to know how to be prepared for it and respond to it. The flyers are needed in as many languages as possible so that everyone in the community gets the information. Visuals and writing in any language can be used to convey information. This culminating task for a unit of work reflects an important stage of students' learning, consolidating their knowledge and leading to action. Students' work during the task can be used as formative assessment, including informal observations of students' on-task behaviour, use of information resources, and demonstration of their conceptual knowledge. Teacher-to-student and student-to-student questioning, both structured & open-ended, also provide formative assessment that provides diagnostic information to teachers to enable them to target support to learners. A focused analysis of student work can be used during the unit as formative assessment and at the end of the unit as summative assessment of their learning.

3.10 *Multilingual Promotional Travel Materials*

A Year 5/6 class comprising a range of languages have been learning about places in Australia. They have been tasked to create a promotional travel brochure or video for international visitors coming to their location of choice in Australia. The promotional materials are needed in as many languages as possible to provide information to the international travellers. The materials will include information about the travel location and what the visitors can see and do there. The research to gather the information can be done in L1, L2, or a combination of both. It may include such things as books, online resources and resource people. Students' use of their languages when doing research enables a greater depth of content understanding than if the task is restricted to only English. It also helps them to make connections between their knowledge in L1 and L2. The task includes various elements of choice. Students can create a promotional travel brochure or video, select their travel location, and have choice in which language it will be presented in. The options to create a brochure or video provide opportunities for students to be creative whilst selecting their preferred mode of communication. The brochure will rely more on writing ability, whilst the video will rely more on oral ability, and both utilise images. The task includes an authentic international audience for the authentic use of students' languages. Formative assessment can be carried out during the task, observing and questioning students about the information they are gathering and what they have found out. The use of images and English text or oral description can support teachers to understand promotional materials that are in languages other than English. This knowledge may support teachers to scaffold the task and guide students' work.

Table 13.1 provides an overview of the eight examples of practice.

It is hoped that these examples of practice contribute towards impetus for change in historically monolingual school contexts and drive motivation for more multilingual-inclusive classroom practices. These examples may kick-start other school programmes to embed a range of translanguaging practices into their pedagogy and drive their own creation of and contributions to multilingual practices. A future follow-up study of the implementation of these examples of practice is recommended because a limitation of the current study is that the examples have been designed but not yet implemented.

TABLE 13.1 Overview of examples of practice

Task name	Learning experience	Language use	Type of assessment	What is being assessed	Rowe's (2018) design principles for translanguaging
Categorising	Sort images of animals and habitats into categories.	Can be non-verbal (moving images). Pair oral discussions in L1 and/or L2. May include reading of teacher-provided labels. May include student-created written labels (or extended descriptions) in L1 and/or L2. Share categories (verbally or non-verbally) with the teacher and/or class. Authentic use of language; L1 if in like-L1 pairings, or L2 depending on languages.	Formative assessment. Diagnostic assessment (to inform teaching). Teacher observations.	Knowledge of content. May assess prior knowledge. Teacher observations of students' oral communication, reading of labels, writing.	Valuing languages and cultures; Modelling translanguaging (pairs); Opportunities for bi-/multilingual communication (pairs); Two-way translation (translation between L1 and L2 in pair discussions); Dual-language texts (L1 and L2 written labels).
KWL charts	Graphic organiser used by learners to write what they 'know,' 'want to know,' and 'have learned'.	Written language; L1, L2 or a combination of both.	Pre-assessment. Formative. Diagnostic assessment. Summative. Student self-assessment of learning.	Assesses students' prior knowledge. Ongoing, formative assessment of learning during a unit of work (to inform teaching). Summative assessment of learning at the end of the topic.	Valuing languages and cultures; Modelling translanguaging; Opportunities for bi-/multilingual communication; Two-way translation; Dual-language texts (KWL chart).

(cont.)

TABLE 13.1 Overview of examples of practice (cont.)

Task name	Learning experience	Language use	Type of assessment	What is being assessed	Rowe's (2018) design principles for translanguaging
Multilingual brainstorming	Brainstorm what you do in a day.	Write in L1, L2, or a combination of both. May include mixed-language sentences. Internet search of images using L1 or L2. L1 to clarify meaning or ask for support. Options to label, write, draw, point to visuals, bi-/multilingual written work may include peer oral interactions.	Formative assessment. Diagnostic assessment. Informal & formal observations.	Student knowledge of topic content. Peer discussions. Analysis of student work.	Valuing languages and cultures; Modelling translanguaging; May include opportunities for bi-/multilingual communication; Dual-language texts.
Multimodal texts	Three tasks: Task 1: Students create a multimodal, dual-language text illustrating the lifecycle of a plant or butterfly.	Reading of supplied labels (and matching with images/ content). Student-created labels or extended writing (L1, L2, both). Oral explanations.	Pre-assessment. Formative. Summative.	Students' knowledge of content (demonstrated through drawings, selection of digital images, labels, writing, verbal ability). Assessment of oral language ability, reading, writing,	Valuing languages and cultures; Modelling translanguaging; May include opportunities for bi-/multilingual communication; Two-way translation; Dual-language texts.

(cont.)

TABLE 13.1 Overview of examples of practice (*cont.*)

Task name	Learning experience	Language use	Type of assessment	What is being assessed	Rowe's (2018) design principles for translanguaging
Task 2: Information gap task. Pairs have differing information on a partially labelled diagram and communicate orally to find out their missing information.		Oral language; L1, L2, both (like-L1 pairs or mixed language pairs).	Formative. Self-assessment. Partner feedback.	Student knowledge and understanding demonstrated in multimodal ways.	Valuing languages and cultures; Modelling translanguaging; Opportunities for bi-/multilingual communication; Two-way translation; Dual-language texts; Connecting with bi-/multilingual audiences.
Task 3: Growing a plant.		Discuss learning and observations (L1, L2) during process and afterwards. Writing (L1, L2); copied text, modelled text, independent text. Reading; own text and class peers' work.	Formative. Self-assessment. Reflection.	Content knowledge. Literacy capabilities (L1, L2).	Valuing languages and cultures; Modelling translanguaging; Opportunities for bi-/multilingual communication; Two-way translation; Dual-language texts; Connecting with bi-/multilingual audiences.

(*cont.*)

TABLE 13.1   Overview of examples of practice (cont.)

Task name	Learning experience	Language use	Type of assessment	What is being assessed	Rowe's (2018) design principles for translanguaging
Research project reports	Research a topic of interest, undertake the project, complete a written report, and orally present the project to an audience.	Read information; L1, L2, bilingual texts. Use dictionaries including bilingual dictionaries & picture dictionaries. Oral communication; phone interviews, discussions. Written communication; emails, text messages, letters. Guided writing, joint construction, modelled writing, shared writing, Teacher- or peer-editing (audience). Oral presentation in L1 or L2 depending on audience; class peers (L2), family (L1), community group (L1 or L2), L1-speaking friends.	Formative. Summative.	Content knowledge. Written skills. Oral communication and presentation skills.	Valuing languages and cultures; Modelling translanguaging; Opportunities for bi-/multilingual communication; Two-way translation; Dual-language texts; Connecting with bi-/multilingual audiences.
Multilingual interviews and surveys	Interview example; interview family members from different generations to find out about daily life for them at your age.	Writing; create questions (L1, L2, both), record interview responses (L1, L2, both), summarise findings. Demonstrate learning (oral, written, multimodal, L1, L2). Oral; share work with a classmate (L1 or L2), then with a group, then with the teacher and whole class (L2). Writing; letters of thanks (L1 or L2).	Formative. Summative.	Gathering of information. Oral and written communication skills.	Valuing languages and cultures; Modelling translanguaging; Opportunities for bi-/multilingual communication; Two-way translation; Dual-language texts; Connecting with bi-/multilingual audiences.

(cont.)

TABLE 13.1 Overview of examples of practice (cont.)

Task name	Learning experience	Language use	Type of assessment	What is being assessed	Rowe's (2018) design principles for translanguaging
	Survey example; survey family and friends about their favourite food. Gather as many responses as you can from as many locations/countries as possible, using as many languages as possible.	Oral language; questioning face-to-face or over the phone (L1, L2, both). Writing; paper survey, email, text message, social media, and written responses (L1, L2, both).	Formative. Summative.	Students' ability to gather information, present information (in a graph), analyse then explain information/findings.	Valuing languages and cultures; Modelling translanguaging; Opportunities for bi-/multilingual communication; Two-way translation; Dual-language texts; Connecting with bi-/multilingual audiences.
Community flyers	Create information flyers about a natural disaster.	Information searching and reading (L1, L2, both). Written flyer (L1, L2).	Formative assessment. Diagnostic assessment. Summative assessment. Informal observations. Teacher-student & student-student questioning.	Conceptual knowledge. Analysis of student work.	Valuing languages and cultures; Modelling translanguaging; Opportunities for bi-/multilingual communication; Two-way translation; Dual-language texts; Connecting with bi-/multilingual audiences.
Multilingual promotional travel materials	Create a travel brochure or video for international visitors coming to a location of choice.	Research (L1, L2). Brochure; writing (L1, L2). Video; oral language (L1, L2).	Formative assessment. Diagnostic assessment for student support and to guide learning. Observations. Questioning.	Content knowledge. Communication skills (oral or written).	Valuing languages and cultures; Modelling translanguaging; Opportunities for bi-/multilingual communication; Two-way translation; Dual-language texts; Connecting with bi-/multilingual audiences.

4 Conclusion

This chapter has drawn attention to the "monolingual mindset" (Clyne, 2005) that prevails in schools and highlights the inequities for multilingual learners when their languages are not included in classroom practice or considered in assessment. Translanguaging is proposed as a practical way to challenge traditional monolingual practices and invite the plethora of multilingual students' languages into classrooms. This practice demonstrates linguistic inclusion, acknowledges the capabilities of learners that are across languages, and can be used to leverage classroom learning. In this way, translanguaging contributes towards more equitable teaching and assessment practices for multilingual learners and fosters social and educational justice.

Although the need to include multilingual learners' languages in classroom practice is becoming more widely understood, actual classroom practice enacting linguistically-inclusive pedagogy is less developed, and even less consideration is given to the role of learners' languages in assessment. In particular, the way in which translanguaging can be undertaken by monolingual teachers or teachers that do not share the same languages as their learners needs to be recognised. Also, the way in which learners can use their languages in classrooms when they are the only speaker of the language needs to be addressed. For these reasons, examples of practice were created that demonstrate a variety of practical applications of translanguaging pedagogy for teaching and assessment purposes and identify a range of ways that multilingual learners' full range of linguistic resources can be leveraged in classrooms. In doing so, the potential of translanguaging to embrace multilingualism in classrooms is revealed. It is hoped that teachers that have not considered translanguaging before or have wanted to embrace languages in their classrooms but have been unsure how to do so, can use the examples presented in this chapter, leading to a wider uptake and transformative action in schools and more equitable learning experiences and assessment for multilingual students.

Acknowledgements

I sincerely thank the wonderful pre-service teachers whom I had the pleasure to work with during 2020 and thank them for their contributions to the examples of practice included in this chapter. Thank-you Jane Dempsey, Laura Hicks, Kate O'Donnell, Emillie Pistone, Zoe Robinson, Georgia Royse, Narelle Smith, Iesha Taha, Anita Tran and Rhianna Wallace.

References

Australian Bureau of Statistics. (2016). https://www.abs.gov.au/statistics

Australian Institute for Teaching and School Leadership. (2017). *Australian professional standards for teachers.* https://www.aitsl.edu.au/teach/standards

Baynham, M., & Lee, T. (2019). *Translation and translanguaging.* https://ebookcentral.proquest.com

Bialystok, E., & Werker, J. (2017). Editorial: The systematic effects of bilingualism on children's development. *Developmental Science, 20.* doi:10.1111/desc.12535

Chau, E. (2007). Learners' use of their first language in ESL classroom interactions. *TESOL in Context, 16*(2), 11–18. https://search-informit-com-au.ezproxy.lib.rmit.edu.au/fullText;dn=162863;res=AEIPT

Clyne, M. (2005). *Australia's language potential.* University of New South Wales Press.

Conteh, J. (2018). Translanguaging. *ELT Journal, 72*(4), 445–447. https://primo-direct-apac.hosted.exlibrisgroup.com/primo-explore/fulldisplay?docid=TN_oxford10.1093%2Felt%2Fccy034&context=PC&vid=RMITU&lang=en_US&search_scope=Books_articles_and_more&adaptor=primo_central_multiple_fe&tab=default_tab&query=any,contains,translanguaging&offset=0

Creese, A., & Blackledge, A. (2010). Translanguaging in the bilingual classroom: A pedagogy for learning and teaching? *The Modern Language Journal, 94*(1), 103–115. www.jstor.org/stable/25612290

Cummins, J. (2003). Bilingual education. In J. Bourne & E. Reid (Eds.), *World yearbook of education: Language education* (pp. 3–20). Kogan Page.

Cummins, J., & Persad, R. (2014). Teaching through a multilingual lens: The evolution of EAL policy and practice in Canada. *Education Matters, 2,* 3–40. http://em.journalhosting.ucalgary.ca/index.php/em/article/view/67/34

De Courcy, M., Dooley, K., Jackson, R., Miller, J., & Rushton, K. (2012). *Teaching EAL/D learners in Australian classrooms.* PETAA.

de los Ríos, C. V., & Seltzer, K. (2017). Translanguaging, coloniality, and English classrooms: An exploration of two bicoastal urban classrooms. *Research in the Teaching of English, 52*(1), 55–76. http://ezproxy.its.rmit.edu.au/login?url=https://search-proquest-com.ezproxy.lib.rmit.edu.au/docview/1927801652?accountid=13552

Department of Education and Training Victoria. (2019a). *Assessment in principle.* https://www.education.vic.gov.au/school/teachers/teachingresources/practice/Pages/insight-principle.aspx

Department of Education and Training Victoria. (2019b). *The language experience approach.* https://www.education.vic.gov.au/school/teachers/teachingresources/discipline/english/literacy/readingviewing/Pages/teachingpraclangexp.aspx Melbourne, Australia.

Department of Education and Training Victoria. (2020a). *EAL annual reports. 2019 English as an additional language report.* https://www.education.vic.gov.au/school/teachers/support/diversity/eal/Pages/ealonlinereports.aspx

Department of Education and Training Victoria. (2020b). *EAL/D learners are plurilingual.* https://www.education.vic.gov.au/school/teachers/support/diversity/eal/Pages/EALD-learners-are-plurilingual.aspx

Faulstich, O. (2015). *Immigrant children in transcultural spaces: Language, learning, and love.* https://ebookcentral.proquest.com

Feez, S., & Harper, H. (2021). Learning and teaching English as an additional language or dialect in mainstream classrooms. In H. Harper & S. Feez (Eds.), *An EAL/D handbook: Teaching and learning across the curriculum when English is an additional language or dialect* (chapter 1). Primary English Teaching Association Australia.

Fernandez, S., Language and Society Centre, & Bayswater South Primary School. (1992). *Room for two: A study of bilingual education at Bayswater South Primary School.* Produced on behalf of the Language and Society Centre of the National Languages and Literacy Institute of Australia.

French, M. (2016). Students' multilingual resources and policy-in-action: An Australian case study, *Language and Education, 30*(4), 298–316. doi:10.1080/09500782.2015.1114628

French, M. (2019). Multilingual pedagogies in practice. *TESOL in Context, 28*(1), 21–44. doi:10.21153/tesol2019vol28no1art869

French, M., & Armitage, J. (2020). Eroding the Monolingual Monolith. *Australian Journal of Applied Linguistics, 3*(1), 91–114. https://doi.org/10.29140/ajal.v3n1.302

García, O. (2009). *Bilingual education in the 21st century: A global perspective.* Wiley-Blackwell. https://ebookcentral.proquest.com

García, O., Johnson, S., & Seltzer, K. (2017). *The translanguaging classroom: Leveraging student bilingualism for learning* (1st ed.). Caslon.

García, O., & Kleyn, T. (Eds.). (2016). *Translanguaging with multilingual students: Learning from classroom moments.* Routledge. https://ebookcentral.proquest.com

Gorter, D., & Cenoz, J. (2017). Language education policy and multilingual assessment. *Language and Education, 31*(3), 231–248. doi:10.1080/09500782.2016.1261892

Liddicoat, A. (2013). *Plurilingual individuals: Languages, literacies and cultures.* Camberwell Primary School.

Liu, C. (2010). Home language: A Stigma or a vehicle to literacy? *Literacy Learning: The Middle Years, 18*(1), 26–40. https://search-informit-com-au.ezproxy.lib.rmit.edu.au/fullText;dn=180164;res=AEIPT

Moll, L., Amanti, C., Neff, D., & Gonzalez, N. (1992). Funds of knowledge for teaching: Using a qualitative approach to connect homes and classrooms. *Theory into Practice, 31*(2), 132–141.

Molyneux, P. (2011). *Collaborating effectively to enhance literacy*. Paper presented at the Workshop Session for Bilingual Schools Network.

Pacheco, M., & Miller, M. (2016). Making meaning through translanguaging in the literacy classroom. *The Reading Teacher, 69*(5), 533–537. www.jstor.org/stable/44002002

Robinson, E., Tian, Z., Martínez, T., & Qarqeen, A. (2018). Teaching for justice: Introducing translanguaging in an undergraduate TESOL course. *Journal of Language and Education, 4*(3), 77–87. https://www.researchgate.net/profile/Zhongfeng_Tian/publication/327988176_Teaching_For_Justice_Introducing_Translanguaging_in_an_Undergraduate_TESOL_Course/links/5bb234ef45851574f7f415c3/Teaching-For-Justice-Introducing-Translanguaging-in-an-Undergraduate-TESOL-Course.pdf

Rowe, L. (2018). Say it in your language: Supporting translanguaging in multilingual classes. *Reading Teacher, 72*(1), 31–38. https://ila-onlinelibrary-wiley-com.ezproxy.lib.rmit.edu.au/doi/full/10.1002/trtr.1673

Somerville, M., Sawyer, W., & D'warte, J. (2016). *Building on children's linguistic repertoires to enrich learning: A project report for the NSW department of education*. https://www.researchgate.net/publication/305181658_Building_on_Children's_Linguistic_Repertoires_to_Enrich_Learning_A_Project_Report_for_the_NSW_Department_of_Education'_Research_Report

Swain, M., & Lapkin, S. (2013). A Vygotskian sociocultural perspective on immersion education: The L1/L2 debate. *Journal of Immersion and Content Based Education, 1*, 101–129. http://dx.doi.org/10.1075/jicb.1.1.05swa

Teach Starter Pty. Ltd. (2021). *Graphic organisers teaching resources*. https://www.teachstarter.com/au/teaching-resource-collection/graphic-organisers-2/

Thomson, P. (2002). *Schooling the rustbelt kids. Making the difference in changing times*. Allen & Unwin.

Thomson, P., & Hall, C. (2008). Opportunities missed and/or thwarted? 'Funds of knowledge' meet the English national curriculum. *The Curriculum Journal, 19*(2), 87–103. doi:10.1080/09585170802079488

van de Vijver, F. (2016). Assessment in education in multicultural populations. In C. Brown & L. Harris (Eds.), *Handbook of human and social conditions in assessment* (chapter 25). Taylor and Francis.

Victorian Curriculum and Assessment Authority (VCAA). (2020). *English as an Additional Language (EAL) curriculum*. https://victoriancurriculum.vcaa.vic.edu.au/english/english-as-an-additional-language-eal/introduction/rationale-and-aims

Wilks-Smith, N. (2017). The place of learners' languages in literacy programs: Bringing learners' home languages in through the school gate. *Babel, 52*(1), 27–34.

PART 3

Educational Evaluation Approaches and Practices

CHAPTER 14

Teacher Performance Evaluation Approach from a Brazilian Perspective

A Literature Review

Fabiano Pereira dos Santos, Ivan Fortunato and Juanjo Mena

Abstract

This study discusses the theme of teacher performance evaluation in Brazil. It aims to carry out an inventory of research published in five Brazilian journals in the field of education (and related fields), which specialise from early childhood education to tertiary education evaluation.

Thus, our interest is to identify major concepts and the possible teaching performance evaluation methods and techniques already developed and in use in Brazil. A mapping of the themes, objectives, methodologies and results from the papers published in four specialised journals was conducted: *Estudos em Avaliação Educacional, Ensaio: Avaliação e Políticas Públicas em Educação, Meta: Avaliação* and *Avaliação: Revista da Avaliação da Educação Superior*. The ultimate purpose is to create a theoretical-methodological inventory that can serve as a basis for reviewing and/or implementing assertive policies for teachers' evaluation, eliminating this important gap between teacher training and work.

Main results indicate that teacher performance evaluation is an incipient topic in Brazilian specialised literature in educational evaluation from which only 18 papers out of 2400 where found. This can be interpreted as an important gap to be filled with new and deeper studies.

Keywords

teacher evaluation – teacher education – literature review

1 Prologue or Why Evaluation Is Important

Evaluation is one of the themes that permeates educational processes and which gains great relevance after the neoliberal turn in education in several countries around the globe. Although it is a very recurrent and important theme for education, much is said about student evaluation, large-scale evaluations, international testing, but very little is said and done about teacher evaluation, at least in Brazil. Still, there are many papers and thesis on "teacher training", however little is studied about how to evaluate our profession.

That being stated, this starts from the following research question: how is teaching evaluation in Brazil understood in the teaching and teacher education literature?

An inventory of published papers in four major Brazilian journals in the area of educational evaluation from kindergarten to graduate school was conducted. These journals are: *Estudos em Avaliação Educacional, Ensaio: Avaliação e Políticas Públicas em Educação, Avaliação: Revista da Avaliação da Educação Superior* and *Meta: Avaliação*.[1] These journals were selected based on the classification criteria of Brazilian journals, as detailed in the following section and the timeframe covered starts with journal's first online edition until the last one available online in 2020.

This is an exploratory research under a qualitative approach (Richardson, 2012), in which we took as an initial methodological strategy the search of keywords on the websites of the aforementioned journals, repeating the previous research procedures of systematic survey (Fortunato & Schwartz, 2019).

Thus, our interest is to identify, through an inventory and analysis of the themes treated in the listed journals, trying to understand author's evaluation perspective. With this, we find the influence of several agents and organisations in the structuring of teacher evaluation systems.

In view of these categories described in the main body of this chapter, it is expected to create an evaluation frame that can serve as a basis for reviewing and/or implementing assertive teacher evaluation policies, eliminating this important gap in teacher training and work. This mapping, although superficial, can serve as an indicator of the paths of the evaluation processes studied, proposed or implemented in the Brazilian educational context.

2 Data Collection from Brazilian Journals

The initial research work was to select the journals to be inventoried. For that, we use the Brazilian database and a classification evaluation system called "Qualis Periódicos".[2] It is a national system, created and maintained by the National Bureau for the Improvement of Higher Education Personnel (its acronym is CAPES, in Portuguese), whose list of journals is classified in 8 strata at the time of this writing, with A1 being the highest. Although the system is under discussion and may possibly be changed in this year 2021, our mapping was carried out based on the currently available classification. The journals were selected according to the following selection criteria were: (a) it is a reference journal of the scientific area of Education listed in the "Qualis Periódicos", specifically containing the term "avaliação" (evaluation/assessment) in its title and journal description; (b) its access is available on the internet and free of charge; (c) it is listed in the highest levels of Brazilian journal quality appraisal as explained next.

When doing this search in the system "Qualis Periódicos", we found only seven journals. Of these, one of them is in the lowest stratum, considered a periodical for dissemination (stratum C) and two in the lowest scientific stratum (B5). On the other hand, four of these journals are in the highest rankings, being *Meta: Avaliação* listed as B1 (or the highest level of a national journal) and *Estudos em Avaliação Educacional* listed as A2 (the second level of international journal). And last but not least *Avaliação: Revista da avaliação da educação superior* and *Ensaio: Avaliação e políticas públicas em educação* as both appear as A1, that is, the highest stratum including international journals.

Although restricted to only four journals, our research sought only publications of excellence and with a specific focus on evaluation, a central theme of our concerns.

So, to construct this mapping, the first step was to access the page of each journal and, through the search field, we insert the terms, in various ways "evaluation", "teacher", "teaching". As we populated each journal search field with these terms combined a short list of papers would return. Then we read these papers titles and/or abstracts in order to check whether they were related to teacher/teaching evaluation rather than teachers evaluating students, or if the paper was about institutional evaluations.

After applying this procedure in all four journals, we created a list of all papers located in the journals database, from which only 22 out of 2463 papers published in 275 editions about the subject of teacher evaluation. Four of these papers were not included in the analyses because they are about other countries rather than Brazil, either specific about Portugal (Tomás & Costa, 2011; Ferreira & Oliveira, 2015; Frederico-Ferreira; Camarneiro; Loureiro, & Ventura, 2017) or other countries from OECD and Latin America (Vaillant, 2010). So the total papers mapped are 18. This represents less than 1% of papers published about teacher evaluation.

After mapping these 18 papers, we read them looking for the central theme of study on teacher evaluation. As there were no specific categories for this type of analysis yet, it was necessary, through discourse analysis (Bardin, 2006) to establish some categories, such as, for example, "self-assessment" or "student assessment" or "internal assessment" and etc., which we explored a little deeper in the following section. It is worth mentioning that, often, due to the methodology or approach used in the research, the themes were not very evident, or clearly delineated. Therefore, in some cases we had to infer the theme addressed by its predominance throughout the manuscript, or its degree of relevance for the construction of the authors' ideas.

In any case, we systematised information in the form of a table. The inventory by journal, indicating only the title, the date of publication and the central theme of the teacher evaluation identified in each of the papers found and read.

The systematisation is shown in Table 14.1.

By looking at Table 14.1 we realised that the theme is quite incipient, as stated by Vailant (2010) regarding teaching evaluation proposals in Latin American countries. The majority of papers found focused on institutional evaluation, either from the students standpoint or performed or not within the classroom by the teacher, or its effects on learning. Whether it was large-scale external evaluation or its impacts on national education management policies.

Although the number of studies on teacher evaluation is limited (in contrast to the number of articles on "teacher training"), the central themes of research, analysis and reflections are very varied, making this paper a first approach in this field of study. After all, it is a fundamental element for teaching, but it is foreshadowed in a dispersed way in the literature.

So, in the next session, we go a little deeper into the analysis of Table 14.1, trying to identify some possible paths to be worked on in future investigations regarding teacher evaluation.

3   Results and Discussion

We begin the analysis with the following note: the periodisation of the papers stands out, of which the first dates from 2004 until 2020, which demonstrates a small, but recurring concern with the theme. In addition, 13 out of 18 (representing 72.22%) of the papers were produced as of 2010, with only 5 papers published in the first decade of the 21st century.

The specifications of the themes addressed in the selected papers are diversified, with a predominance of studies aimed at higher education, whether at undergraduate or graduate level, which can be stated from paper's abstract review. A quantitative analysis of these data reveals that among the 18 selected papers, 66.67%, that is, 12, were dedicated to the analysis of evaluation strategies related to higher education. In contrast, only 6 studies were held to analyse

TABLE 14.1   Paper inventory about teacher evaluation[a]

Journal	Paper title and publication date	Evaluation categories
Avaliação: revista de avaliação da educação superior	Competências docentes como antecedentes da avaliação de desempenho do professor: percepção de mestrandos de administração (2012)	Teacher evaluation from student's perception
	Reflexões sobre o processo de avaliar docente contribuindo com sua formação (2007)	Teacher performance evaluation critical analysis
	Validade e confiabilidade de instrumento de avaliação da docência sob a ótica dos modelos de equação estrutural (2011)	Teacher evaluation from student's perception
Estudos em Avaliação Educacional	Análise da participação discente na avaliação docente no ensino superior (2020)	Teacher evaluation from student's perception
	Autoavaliação: observando e analisando a prática docente. (2020)	Teacher self-assessment
	Indicadores de desenvolvimento profissional da docência: construção, avaliação e usos (2015)	Proposal of a qualitative instrument for basic school teaching evaluation
Ensaio: Avaliação e políticas públicas em educação	A Pesquisa-ação como Instrumento de Análise e Avaliação da Prática Docente (2005)	Proposal of a qualitative method for basic school teaching evaluation
	Avaliação de Docentes do Ensino Superior: Um Estudo de Caso (2004)	Teacher evaluation from student's perception
	Avaliação do docente pelo discente na melhoria do desempenho institucional: UTFPR/SIAVI (2013)	Teacher evaluation from student's perception
	Políticas de Avaliação Docente: tendências e estratégias (2012)	Teacher performance evaluation critical analysis
	Plano de carreira e avaliação dos professores: encontros e desencontros (2009)	Teacher evaluation from student's perception
	Um indicador para a avaliação do desempenho docente em Instituições de Ensino Superior (2010)	Proposal of quantitative instrument for university teaching evaluation

(cont.)

TABLE 14.1 Paper inventory about teacher evaluation[a] (cont.)

Journal	Paper title and publication date	Evaluation categories
Meta: Avaliação	Avaliação da Atuação dos Docentes de Instituições de Ensino Superior: o caso da Faculdade Cearense (FAC) (2012)	Teacher evaluation from student's perception
	Avaliação da qualidade docente (2009)	Teacher performance evaluation critical analysis
	Avaliação do Docente pelo Discente no Âmbito do Ensino Técnico Integrado: evidências de validade da Escala SIR-II (2019)	Teacher evaluation from student's perception
	Avaliação do Docente pelo Discente: análise das percepções de utilização ideal e efetiva (2016)	Teacher evaluation from student's perception
	Como Avaliar Docentes? A Percepção dos Docentes na Implantação da Gestão por Competências em uma Instituição de Ensino Superior Privada (2017)	Miscellaneous (Competency Management)
	Mapas Conceituais na Avaliação de Professores (2018)	Miscellaneous (Concept Maps)

a Journal and paper titles are registered in Portuguese.

the evaluation processes and instruments applied to basic education (in Brazil, basic education refers to school education from kindergarten to high school).

A point to be highlighted in this predominance of studies aimed at studying higher education refers to the higher education assessment policies outlined based on national legislation. Thus, we perceive the preponderance of the influence of institutions such as MEC,[3] CAPES[4] and SINAES[5] in the construction of the assessment instruments of this level of education. These institutions are responsible for financing, evaluating and organising the Brazilian educational system so they are responsible for creating policies and control mechanisms. In addition, managerial practices and strategies with evaluation strategies dimensioned from administrative instruments and techniques have proved to be an important factor in the design of the evaluations that impact on the teacher evaluation processes.

Finally, through content analysis, we identified categories of teacher evaluation as seen in Table 14.1. This is an initial attempt to provide some important elements for teacher evaluation, which needs to be tested in future investigations. These categories can be specific to a level and modality of education, or they can be broader, applied to teaching in general. In the sequence, we present some important highlights of this categorization.

3.1 Miscellaneous

In relation to basic or technical education, we have to highlight the fact that, in the absence of a public policy provided for in the legislation, except in the case of Portugal, and experiences in countries such as Chile, Colombia, Canada, Mexico and the United States (Tomás & Costa, 2011; Vailant, 2010) the evaluation of basic education teachers does not seem to have predisposed examples of effective evaluative application in the education networks.

However, a miscellaneous category can be retrieved from the paper "Mapas Conceituais na Avaliação de Professores" (Kruchelski, Moraes, & Lang, 2010). The authors conducted a systematic review about the use of "Concept Maps in school teacher assessment" and after the analyses of 11 papers they could not present any substantial information about the use of Concept Maps for this purpose. Yet they claim that they are "an efficient learning and assessment tool teaching-learning process" (p. 593), but not could be stated about teacher assessment.

Another miscellaneous category is in the paper "Como Avaliar Docentes? A Percepção dos Docentes na Implantação da Gestão por Competências em uma Instituição de Ensino Superior Privada" (Gallon, Taufer, Just, Batistella, & Ruas, 2017) in which authors mention the "Competency Management" but their paper is not about this kind of management. They conducted interviews with a few lectures from a private university to verify their perception regarding this method of assessment. This paper does not help to understand teacher performance evaluation.

3.2 Proposal of a Quantitative Instrument for University Teaching Evaluation

This category was found from the paper "Um indicador para a avaliação do desempenho docente em Instituições de Ensino Superior" written by Embiruçu, Fontes and Almeida (2010, p. 795). In this paper the authors "proposes the creation of a teacher evaluation indicator, objective and quantitative, to be used as an instrument of evaluation of the performance of teachers in Higher Education Institutions". Thus, based on various attributions of university teaching, such as number of subjects and classes taught, thesis supervised, scholarships granted for students, funded research etc., these authors established a preliminary instrument capable of quantifying all this to assess the effectiveness of teachers.

3.3 Proposal of a Qualitative Instrument for Basic School Teaching Evaluation

This category could be found from the paper "Indicadores de desenvolvimento profissional da docência: construção, avaliação e usos" in which Leal and Reali (2015, p. 83) coined not a quantitative instrument for teacher performance evaluation but a qualitative inventory of "educational indicators related to teacher professional development". Unlike the previous instrument whereas the evaluation could be objectively measured, this indicator demands a complex and subjective analyses in context, yet it is not quite clear of who or how or when or even why a teacher should be submitted to these specific indicators.

3.4 Proposal of a Qualitative Method for Basic School Teaching Evaluation

This category is derived from the previous and it could be found in the paper: "A Pesquisa-ação como instrumento de análise e avaliação da prática docente". Its author, Maria Abdalla (2005) shows interest in a qualitative method for teacher performance evaluation but she does not present any instruments but develops a research-action methodology with a group of teachers using daily logs, case studies and reality check methods to stimulate the perception of everyday life at school by these teachers.

3.5 Teacher Self-Assessment

This category was found in the paper "Autoavaliação: observando e analisando a prática docente" by Pereira, Barro, Trezzi, Spicer-Escalante and Felicetti (2020). Authors present the SATS (Self-assessment of Teaching Statement) which is a relatively new instrument designed by one of the authors and still in a trial version – yet this is not stated. This instrument consists of a five-step process starting with a class plan submitted to an observer, then the class is developed and both videotaped and analysed by the observer who takes specific notes about what he/she liked during class, what he/she would have done differently and why. After the class, the teacher watches it and takes notes about the same things. Then, the observer sends his/her notes to the teacher who makes the comparison between the forms and writes down the final the Self-Assessment Teaching Declaration to be approved by the observer. It does not seem to be a self-assessment tool par excellence, as it involves "approval", a script, in short, everything prepared around this form; but it is an attempt

3.6 Teacher Performance Evaluation Critical Analysis

Two papers are representative of this category which can be understood from the theoretical or philosophical or epistemological point of view. These authors do not present any instruments, methods or categories about teacher evaluation, yet they rise very good questions about this matter that anticipate any practical actions to be taken. Bernadete Gatti (2014, p. 373), in the paper "Avaliação e qualidade do desenvolvimento profissional docente" brings three basic questions: "Which evaluative perspective do we take when carrying out an educational evaluation? What do we mean by quality? and What do we mean by professional development?". Gatti (2014, p. 373) then concludes her argumentation by stating that "evaluative processes places formative and attitudinal demands on evaluators and evaluates".

The other paper "Políticas de Avaliação Docente: tendências e estratégias" was written by Rodrigues (2012, p. 749) and its author presented a deep discussion about "some trends of educational policies aimed at improving the quality of teaching strategies which involve the evaluation of teachers". She brought some ideas about the profile for a good teacher that range from content mastery to communication and relationship skills, including a good understanding about learning processes. Finally, the author refers to a national public policy of entering and remaining in the teaching career that was actually never implemented.

3.7 *Teacher Evaluation from Student's Perception*

The predominant category within the papers was the Teacher Evaluation from Student's Perception, represented by a total number of nine manuscripts. It is a category of teacher evaluation in which students assume the centrality as subjects of the evaluation process, either by filling out surveys, or by answering essay questions in which students expose their perceptions about the teacher's performance.

The oldest paper from the list is "Avaliação de Docentes do Ensino Superior: um estudo de caso", by Roberto Boclin (2004), whose approach, as stated in the title, is based on a case study developed at the Institute of Social and Applied Sciences of the Veiga de Almeida University. In this study, the author considers that teacher evaluation is indispensable in the teaching-learning processes and he understands that the use of standardised tests through survey made available to students is an efficient strategy both to awaken the critical sense of students, as well as for the improvement of educational practices.

The paper "Plano de Carreira e Avaliação dos Professores: encontros e desencontros" written by Janete Palazzo and Candido Alberto Gomes (2009) uses the qualitative approach to relate the teachers' evaluation criteria, such as the degree, experience in higher education, length of service in the institution and the scientific publications to the evaluation made by the students from a Higher Education Institution in the Federal District. Focusing on the teaching career plan, the authors found that in the researched institution, there was no significant relationship between the students' assessment of teachers and the variables valued by the Career Plan.

On the other hand, there is the idea that teacher success depends on four factors presented on the paper "Validade e confiabilidade de instrumento de avaliação da docência sob a ótica dos modelos de equação estrutural", Amilton Barreto de Bem, Edgar Augusto Lanzer, Elmo Tambosi Filho, Otávio Próspero Sanchez and Plínio Bernardi Junior (2011). The authors attempt to demonstrate through an exploratory and confirmatory factor analysis that the evaluation made by the students presents consistent results in face of the evaluation technique developed by them in their case study at the University of the South of Santa Catarina. From this point of view, the authors consider the evaluation by the students to be a model of reliable structural equation to evaluate the work of the teacher.

Márcia Zampieri Grohmann and Márcio Sampedro Ramos (2012), using theoretical models used by Latin American authors, wrote the paper "Competências docentes como antecedentes da avaliação de desempenho do professor: percepção de mestrandos de administração" seeking to map teaching skills (behaviour in class, didactics and knowledge, relationship, evaluation and utility) through a survey applied to a group of students. With that, they come to the conclusion that "a good teacher must have, above all, mastery of the content he teaches and a good teaching to transmit it to students; and conduct fair assessments, showing the practical usefulness of the content that is taught".

Still from the year 2012, the experience report published by Wagner Bandeira Andriola and Cristiany Gomes Andriola, named "Avaliação da Atuação dos Docentes de Instituições de Ensino Superior: o caso da Faculdade Cearense (FAC)", seeks to demonstrate the validation of survey usage to evaluate the teaching work by the students. For the authors, this type of evaluation assumes great importance in the educational management process, since from the results, managers can plan pedagogical actions in order to improve the performance of teachers individually and collectively.

This idea is in line with Miraldo Matuichuk and Maclovia Corrêa da Silva's (2013) paper "Avaliação do docente pelo discente na melhoria do desempenho institucional: UTFPR/SIAVI". The authors describe the stages of the teachers' evaluation process by the students at the institution mentioned, pointing to the relationship between evaluation and training that aims to assess the quality of the academic and administrative actions of the courses. In the institution studies for the paper, the teacher evaluation by the students is made through a survey with only five questions about "didactics", "content", "planning", "evaluation" and "relationship", graded from one to five stars. With this, the institution expects to evaluate its teachers, but this a poor instrument.

Paixão and Almeida (2016), in the paper "Avaliação do Docente pelo Discente: análise das percepções de utilização ideal e efetiva", they analyse the process of teacher evaluation by the student, through a survey, carried out at a federal teaching institution. The authors' belief that the evaluation of the teacher by the student is a positive influence in the pedagogical practice, guaranteeing the valorisation, employment merit, which can contribute with the quality of education.

Roberto Brazileiro Paixão, Anamaria Azevedo Lafeta Rabelo and Adriano Leal Bruni (2019) analysed the Student Instructional Report (SIR-II) of the Educational Testing Service (ETS) in the paper "Avaliação do Docente pelo Discente no Âmbito do Ensino Técnico Integrado: evidências de validade da Escala SIR-II". They realised the need for translation of tests developed in foreign countries before being applied in Brazil, but the SIR-II is a good instrument since it involves the dimensions of planning and organisation of the discipline, teacher communication, teacher-student interaction, assessments given by teachers and teaching methods and materials used by teachers.

Finally, there is the paper "Análise da participação discente na avaliação docente no ensino superior", written by Tomás, D'Albuquerque, Neves and Mesquista (2020). Although the authors bring some comments and a literature review on teacher evaluation from the student's perspective, their interest is to identify the profile of students who voluntarily participate in the evaluation of their teachers, in a specific higher education institution.

4 Final Remarks

The aim of this chapter was to identify educational policies (public, government and/or management), major concepts and the possible teaching performance evaluation methods and techniques in the current educational system in Brazil. A literature review of four major educational journals in the country was conducted.

The main results out of our study revealed quite a few categories of teacher evaluation as from the inventory we collected seven distinguished categories: (1) Miscellaneous, in which papers did not quite explore teacher evaluation through mind maps and competency management, in addition to bringing good experiences from abroad, but not from Brazil; (2) Proposal of a quantitative instrument for university teaching evaluation as a way of control teaching work through objective results; (3) Proposal of a qualitative instrument for basic school teaching evaluation that is not objective and stands no metrics, yet it becomes very loose, backed only by the subjectivity of "I believe";

(4) Proposal of qualitative method for basic school teaching evaluation that also does not have any objective support, it is a reflective process and not an instrument; (5) Teacher self-assessment from a new instrument involving a third party and his/her approval; (6) Teacher performance evaluation critical analysis which brings theoretical analysis of the possible conjunctures of teacher evaluation in Brazil; (7) Teacher evaluation from student's perception using the student point of view as the most important element for evaluating teacher performance – something close to a "customer satisfaction survey", since, increasingly, education has resembled commercial relations.

From the inventory we could identify multiple approaches that variate a lot. Even though the evaluation of the teacher performance, understood as the impact on the students' learning, is of crucial importance, it is still missing in Brazilian education. There is a need of substantial analysis on teachers' practice by observing pedagogical strategies used, teachers' dispositions and beliefs, tests scores, or students' surveys.

In our study we found these criteria scattered across the papers in which some sought to approach them from an institutional point of view, or from a self-evaluation point of view, but mainly through the perception of students. After all, we were interested in identifying *how* teacher evaluation is carried out in Brazil.

This type of literature review is much needed in the context of the Brazilian education and more extensively to the Latin-American framework. This is an initial attempt to provide some important elements for teacher evaluation, which needs to be tested in future investigations. It is evident that only four resources have been put under scrutiny. Other journals in the country should be also checked in order to expand the review and be able to ratify or refute the results and extract other conclusions. Besides, it would be advisable for future research to extract metrics from the main categories in a metanalysis to measure the extent to which the weight of the extracted categories is sufficient as to be considered their relevance in the field of study.

Notes

1 Journals could be translated as following: "Studies in Education Evaluation", "Essay: Evaluation and Education Public Policy", "Evaluation: Higher Education Journal" and "Goal: Evaluation".
2 2 Direct link: https://sucupira.capes.gov.br/sucupira/public/consultas/coleta/veiculoPublicacaoQualis/listaConsultaGeralPeriodicos.jsf
3 MEC is the Brazilian Ministry of Education: http://portal.mec.gov.br/

4 CAPES is the National Bureau for the Improvement of Higher Education Personnel: https://www.gov.br/capes/pt-br
5 SINAES is the Brazilian Higher Education Assessment System: http://portal.inep.gov.br/sinaes

References

Abdalla, M. F. B. (2005). A pesquisa-ação como instrumento de análise e avaliação da prática docente. *Ensaio: Avaliação e Políticas Públicas em Educação, 13*(48), 383–400. https://doi.org/10.1590/S0104-40362005000300008

Andriola, W. B., & Adriola, C. G. (2012). Avaliação da atuação dos docentes de instituições de ensino superior: o caso da Faculdade Cearense (FAC). *Meta: Avaliação, 4*(11), 91–119. https://dx.doi.org/10.22347/2175-2753v9i26.1300

Bardin, L. (2006). *Análise de conteúdo*. Edições 70.

Bem, A. B. de, Lanzer, E. A., Tambosi Filho, E., Sanchez, O. P., & Bernardi Junior, P. (2011). Validade e confiabilidade de instrumento de avaliação da docência sob a ótica dos modelos de equação estrutural. *Avaliação: revista da avaliação da educação superior, 16*(2), 375–401. https://doi.org/10.1590/S1414-40772011000200008.

Boclin, R. (2004). Avaliação de docentes do ensino superior: um estudo de caso. *Ensaio: Avaliação e Políticas Públicas em Educação, 12*(45), 959–980. https://doi.org/10.1590/S0104-40362004000400004

Embiruçu, M., Fontes, C., & Almeida. (2010). Um indicador para a avaliação do desempenho docente em Instituições de Ensinos Superior. *Ensaio: Avaliação e Políticas Públicas em Educação, 18*(69), 795–820. https://dx.doi.org/10.1590/S0104-40362010000400008

Ferreira, C. A., & Oliveira, C. (2015). Auto-avaliação docente e melhoria das práticas pedagógicas: percepções de professores portugueses. *Estudos em Avaliação Educacional, 26*(63), 806–836. https://dx.doi.org/10.18222/eae.v0ix.3592

Fortunato, I., & Schwartz, G. M. (2019). Cinema, Psicologia Positiva e resiliência: uma revisão sistemática. *Interfaces Científicas Humanas e Sociais, 8*(2), 83–98. https://doi.org/10.17564/2316-3801.2019v8n2p83-98

Frederico-Ferreira, M. M., Camarneiro, A. P. F., Loureiro, C. R. E. C., & Ventura, M. C. A. A. (2017). Tradução e adaptação do questionário de validade das avaliações dos estudantes ao ensino e aos professores. Avaliação: *Revista da Avaliação da Educação Superior, 22*(2), 458–468. https://dx.doi.org/10.1590/s1414-40772017000200011

Gallon, S., Taufer, E., Just, M. G., Batistella, C., & Ruas, R. L. (2017). Como avaliar docentes? A percepção dos docentes na implantação da gestão por competências em uma instituição de ensino superior privada. *Meta: Avaliação, 9*(26), 223–254. https://dx.doi.org/10.22347/2175-2753v9i26.1300

Gatti, B. A. (2014). Avaliação e qualidade do desenvolvimento profissional docente. *Avaliação: revista da avaliação da educação superior, 19*(2), 373–384. https://doi.org/10.1590/S1414-40772014000200006

Grohmann, M. Z., & Ramos, M. S. (2012). Competências docentes como antecedentes da avaliação de desempenho do professor: percepção de mestrandos de administração. *Avaliação: revista da avaliação da educação superior, 17*(63), 375–401. https://doi.org/10.1590/S1414-40772012000100004

Kruchelski, S., Moraes, A., & Lang, C. R. (2018). Mapas conceituais na avaliação de professores. *Meta: Avaliação, 10*(30), 579–599. https://dx.doi.org/10.22347/2175-2753v10i30.1593

Leal, P. H., & Reali, A. M. M. R. (2015). Indicadores de desenvolvimento profissional da docência: construção, avaliação e usos. *Estudos em Avaliação Educacional, 26*(61), 82–122. https://dx.doi.org/10.18222/eae266102859

Matuichuk, M., & Silva, M. C. (2013). Avaliação do docente pelo discente na melhoria do desempenho institucional: UTFPR/SIAVI. *Ensaio: Avaliação e Políticas Públicas em Educação, 21*(79), 323–348. https://doi.org/10.1590/S0104-40362013000200008

Paixão, R. B., & Almeida, B. C. (2016). Avaliação docente pelo discente: análise das percepções de utilização ideal e efetiva. *Meta: Avaliação, 8*(1), 48–68. https://dx.doi.org/10.22347/2175-2753v8i22.794

Paixão, R. B., Rabelo, A. A. L., & Bruni, A. L. (2019). Avaliação do Docente pelo Discente no Âmbito do Ensino Técnico Integrado: evidências de validade da Escala SIR-II. *Meta: Avaliação, 11*(1), 154–176. http://dx.doi.org/10.22347/2175-2753v11i31.1738

Palazzo, J., & Gomes, C. A. (2009). Plano de carreira e avaliação dos professores: encontros e desencontros. *Ensaio: Avaliação e Políticas Públicas em Educação, 17*(63), 205–234. https://dx.doi.org/10.1590/S0104-40362009000200003

Pereira, M. A. C., Barro, D., Trezzi, C., Spicer-Escalante, M. L., & Felicetti. (2020). Autoavaliação: observando e analisando a prática docente. *Estudos em Avaliação Educacional, 31*(76), 7–27. https://dx.doi.org/10.18222/eae.v31i76.7010

Richardson, R. J. (2012). *Pesquisa social:* métodos e técnicas (3. ed.). Atlas.

Rodrigues, S. S. (2016). Políticas de avaliação docente: tendencias e estratégias. *Ensaio: Avaliação e Políticas Públicas em Educação, 20*(77), 749–768. https://doi.org/10.1590/S0104-40362012000400007

Tomás, I., & Costa, J. A. (2011). Avaliação de professores nas escolas públicas portuguesas. *Ensaio: Avaliação e Políticas Públicas em Educação, 19*(72), 457–484. https://dx.doi.org/10.1590/S0104-40362011000400002

Tomás, M., D'Albuquerque, R. W., Neves, O. F., & Mesquista, M. C. (2020). Análise da participação discente na avaliação docente no ensino superior. *Estudos em Avaliação Educacional, 31*(76), 28–49. http://dx.doi.org/10.18222/eae.v0ix.6815

Vailant, D. (2010). Avaliação de Professores em vários países da OCDE e da América Latina. *Meta: Avaliação, 2*(6), 459–477. http://dx.doi.org/10.22347/2175-2753v2i6.84

CHAPTER 15

A Systemic Approach to Authentic Evaluation in Education

The Case of Mathematics Teaching Effectiveness in Tertiary Engineering Education

Katerina Kasimatis, Andreas Moutsios-Rentzos and Fragkiskos Kalavasis

Abstract

In this chapter, we introduce a systemic approach to authentic evaluation in tertiary engineering education about mathematics teaching effectiveness. We conceptualise the educational unit as a learning organisation and we obtain multiple viewings of the lived realities as experienced by different educational protagonists, including the evaluator. By communicating the diversely experienced lived realities to the protagonists, the system becomes aware of its existence as such, whilst through a series of reflections the disjointed protagonists become intentional systemic actors. The discussion of our theoretical methodological approach is complemented with a discussion of its ongoing empirical implementation in a tertiary educational unit in Greece.

Keywords

systemic approach – authentic evaluation – mathematics teaching effectiveness – engineering education

1 Setting the Scene

As scientific modelling is transferred to the area of social sciences and humanities, mathematics appears to be the language in which models are communicated, transcending the descriptions, the engineering and the decision making of these areas. Mathematical representations and forms of argumentation appear in many fields of education, in the organisation of education, and in the evaluation of processes and objectives. In these circumstances, the efficient study and comprehension of the mathematics influence includes and supersedes the mathematics courses, didactic situations or pedagogical practices. The phenomenology of learning and teaching mathematics becomes a fundamental component for the interpretation of cognitive difficulties or epistemological obstacles both in the level of intra-school pedagogical practices and in the organisational level of the educational units (including their management and their transformation processes). Mathematical notation and terminology seem to be at the crux of modern sciences and in the contemporary socio-political interactions, thus constituting mathematics as a dominant discourse in the modern socio-scientific contexts. Though the ways that mathematics appears in our everyday lived reality may conceptually differ from mathematics as a discipline, its notation, reasoning, argumentation, tools and practices are present in our everyday communications. This holds especially true for the teaching and learning courses related with the sciences and engineering.

Acknowledging this lived complexity and the contradictions that it may entail; we propose an authentic evaluation of mathematics teaching effectiveness. The proposed approach is authentic in the sense that is relevant and meaningful for the specific educational unit and the ways that mathematics functions, interacts, *is* within the unit. In this chapter, we concentrate on theoretical basis of our approach. Subsequently, we present empirical data of an ongoing implementation about mathematics teaching effectiveness in a Greek tertiary education institution of the School of Pedagogical and Technological Education (ASPETE), which incorporates a particular educational complexity: its graduates hold an engineer degree and a pedagogical degree as engineer educators. It is crucial to support the development of mathematics teaching that is meaningful for the ASPETE students; both about their studies and their future career, through authentic evaluation processes of mathematics teaching effectiveness. Though the present chapter is relevant to educational environments where mathematics is positioned as the supporting character, rather than the protagonist, our approach may be implemented to diverse educational units.

2   Towards a Systemic Approach to Authentic Evaluation about Mathematics Teaching Effectiveness

Following these, we draw upon a systemic approach to mathematics education research (Begg, 2003; Chen & Stroup, 1993; Davis & Simmt, 2003; Davis & Sumara, 2005; English, 2007, 2008; Kalavasis & Kazadi, 2015; Moutsios-Rentzos & Kalavasis, 2016, 2021; Pepin & Roesken-Winter, 2014; Wittmann, 2001) to introduce a conceptualisation of mathematics teaching effectiveness as an emergent systemic phenomenon. A system refers to a whole, clearly defined within its environment, the parts of which are linked and interrelated in complex ways towards specific goals, behaviour and connectivity with other systems that the constructed whole significantly differs from a simple adding of its parts (Bertalanffy, 1968). The properties of the system *emerge non-deterministically* as a result of the complexity of its structure, links and interactions.

We posit that an authentic evaluation of an emergent systemic phenomenon essentially entails the *purposeful engineering* on the system, to overcome its inertia and its current equilibrium. At the crux of the proposed engineering lies the activation of a series of systemic reflections by allowing *the (disjointed) protagonists* of the educational system to be transformed towards their being *intentional (systemic) actors*; by shedding light on the links amongst mathematics, techniques and technologies, as well as by including the perspectives of crucial actors within the educational system (faculty members, students and Heads of the departments) and the researchers whose lenses inevitably affect the system. Through these reflections the system is allowed to become a *learning organisation* "where new and expansive patterns of thinking are nurtured, where collective aspiration is set free, and where people are continually learning how to learn together" (Senge, 1990, p. 3).

This approach attempts to link seemingly disjunct or even incongruent realities within the educational unit, explicitly acknowledging also the role of the observer in the dynamics of the observed phenomenon. In this sense, the proposed evaluation approach is *fundamentally and inherently authentic as it is meaningful and representative* for each protagonist *and* for the system (cf. Herrington & Herrington, 2006), as the sharing of the diverse views and reflections facilitates the emergence of shared, intersubjective meanings that characterise and are relevant to the system.

Following these, we propose an authentic and meaningful evaluation approach for mathematics teaching effectiveness in an educational unit, viewed as a *learning organisation* in constant interaction with its broader educational and sociocultural environment. A learning organisation is characterised by its developing systems thinking, personal mastery, mental models, team development and building a shared vision (Senge, 1990; Senge, Roberts, Ross, Smith, & Kleiner, 2000).

The proposed approach is authentic and meaningful because it voices, rather than silences, the variety of perspectives and roles, allowing for the identified variety to be a tool for reflection and decision-making for all the stakeholders. We posit that such an approach is particularly important in the emerging (and rapidly spreading) dynamic, hybrid (analog-digital) era that the educational protagonists experience (Moutsios-Rentzos, Kalavasis, & Sofos, 2017), especially since the digital means of data collection and representation may facilitate the aforementioned systemic reflections, actions and re-actions.

3   The Proposed Approach

According to this perspective, in order to identify and/or propose authentic evaluation practices about mathematics teaching, we also need to conceptualise mathematics teaching effectiveness and its authentic evaluation as emergent systemic phenomena. We first present the foundational elements of our approach (Moutsios-Rentzos & Kalavasis, 2016, 2021), followed by the proposed model of authentic evaluation about mathematics teaching effectiveness.

We posit that an authentic evaluation approach that draws upon a systemic perspective crucially includes the evaluating system within the evaluated system (Roth & Tobin, 2001); there is a living, dynamic relationship that (at the very least, for the interacting protagonists) should be explicitly included (cf. Kershner, 2021). Hence, according to the first foundational element of our approach, mathematics teaching effectiveness emerges amongst the interactions of the lived realities of the educational protagonists (including, the lecturers, the students, the head of the department) *and* of those who perform the assessment and evaluation processes, allowing for the investigation of the potentially diverse lived realities that co-exist in the under-evaluation system.

Moreover, the educational system produces cultures: of thinking, learning and coping within the affiliated domain of knowledge, within the linked professional domains, as well as within the broader sociocultural environment. The educational system as a learning organisation needs to address the nature of the produced learning, conceptualised as *linking links* (Moutsios-Rentzos & Kalavasis, 2016) amongst roles of the educational protagonists, courses, scientific disciplines, and professions. Hence, in the educational unit, learning emerges through the transformations of the qualities and/or the quantity of these linkings and at the same time, signifies a new state of equilibrium i.e. the state of the system that needs to be transformed for subsequent learning to be realised. Furthermore, mathematics is linked with the other courses that are taught within an educational system; for example, the students experience mathematical notation, formulas and tools in other courses. Hence, fundamental to our approach is the view that, within a specific educational system, learning mathematics has inherent interdisciplinary aspects and the corpus of mathematics knowledge is linked not only with the subject related to the course at hand (mathematics), but with the whole complex corpus of knowledge that a degree entails (including, physics, engineering, etc).

At the same time, the educational protagonists as intending beings (Husserl, 2001; Zahavi, 2003) develop an *intentional relationship with mathematics* within the educational system. This intentional relationship spans across co-existing *lived realities* (Moutsios-Rentzos & Kalavasis, 2016; Moutsios-Rentzos, Kritikos, & Kalavasis, 2017, 2019): actuality (*pragmatic*; what is perceived as actually happening), potentiality (*desired/intentioned*; what is intended to happen, assuming the power of implementation), normativity (*symbolic/normative*; what is perceived to officially happen). Different lived realities may elicit qualitatively different aspects of the intentional relationship among the same and/or the different protagonists.

Consequently, the complex, non-deterministic nature of the aforementioned phenomena implies that a conceptually appropriate approach to evaluation should be implemented. A process of conscious, intentional linking of the diverse views and experiences, of individual and collective reflections, as well as of teaching and administrative practices, may facilitate the system to reach a new equilibrium. Such linkings are realised through a series of engineered individual and collective reflections (Jay & Johnson, 2002; Nissilä, 2005), aiming to allow for interdisciplinary communication to develop (Nikitina & Mansilla, 2003). This intentional, reflective process gradually enables the system's organisational knowledge maturing, referring to "goal-oriented learning on a collective level, emphasising that it is always purposeful" (Kump et al., 2011, p. 31). Thus, learning refers to a transformation of the whole system, affecting and being affected by the lived realities that the protagonist experience (Begg, Davis, & Bramald, 2003). Nevertheless, the different protagonists may experience diverse qualities and aspects of the systemic learning, crucially determined by their intentional relationship with the system; by their point of view of a whole that includes them. Thus, an authentic evaluation system of mathematics teaching effectiveness, conceptualised as a systemic phenomenon, needs to functionally incorporate these dimensions.

Following these foundational elements of our approach, in this study, we conceptualise mathematics teaching effectiveness as an emerging phenomenon that characterises the mathematics class subsystem, including the *students*, the *lecturer*, and, crucially, the *evaluator* (in our case, the *observing researcher*). Moreover, mathematics experience is differentiated between the pragmatic level (what they experienced in actuality) and the desired/intentioned level (what they would prefer to experience). Through a process of systemic reflections, the protagonists observe, reflect and act upon a system

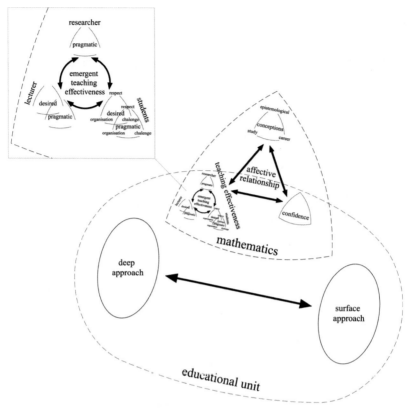

FIGURE 15.1   Mathematics teaching effectiveness as an emergent phenomenon in a learning organisation: multiple, multileveled lived realities

that explicitly includes the protagonists themselves. Consequently, the evaluation of mathematics teaching effectiveness is becoming part of mathematics teaching effectiveness itself, in the form of a continuous interplay of systemic observing-acting-reflecting that is iterated in cycles, thus becoming an integral, transforming process of the system and, consequently, authentic for the given educational system. In this study, amongst the general models of teaching effectiveness (Creemers & Kyriakides, 2008; Muijs & Reynolds, 2017) and models explicitly focussed on mathematics teaching effectiveness (Backes, Goldhaber, Cade, Sullivan, & Dodson, 2018; Cai, Kaiser, Perry, & Wong, 2009), we adopted a general model introduced by Patrick and Smart (1998). This model includes three core dimensions identified in other models: *respect for students*; *ability to challenge students*; *organisation and presentation skills*. In each dimension, we allowed for the identification of two levels of reality (the pragmatic and the desired/intentioned) as experienced by the different protagonists.

Furthermore, mathematics learning within the ASPETE system is theorised to occur in two interacting levels of educational experience: *specific to mathematics courses* and *broader* (related to the broad educational experience with the under-evaluation educational system). The students' narrow affective relationship with mathematics was conceptualised as a *dynamic affect system* (Pepin & Roesken-Winter, 2014), including their *conceptions about mathematics* and their *confidence about coping with mathematics*, whilst their broader educational experience was identified through their *approaches to study*.

Focussing on the narrow affective relationship with mathematics, considering *conceptions about mathematics*, we drew upon Wood, Petocz and Reid (2012) who identify three dimensions of mathematics conceptions: epistemological conceptions; conceptions about the role of mathematics in their future studies; conceptions about the role of mathematics in their future career. The students' epistemological conceptions are categorised as 'numbers/components' (individual and isolated components, techniques and calculations), 'abstract/models' (models of the real-world phenomena), and 'life' (a way of thinking and interpreting the world). Moreover, Wood et al. (2012) identify three roles of mathematics in their future studies and career: 'practical' (calculations, problem solving, and logical thinking), b) 'generic' (a generic mathematical way of thinking that is important in studies and career), and c) (lack of) 'knowledge' (lack of knowing of the exact role of mathematics in studies and career). Moreover, we adopted the conceptualisation of Fennema and Sherman (1976) who identify the degree of *confidence coping with mathematics* that an individual experiences with respect to his/her "ability to learn and to perform well on mathematical tasks" (p. 326).

Regarding the students' broader experience in ASPETE, we employed the notion of *approaches to study* (Biggs, 2001; Marton & Säljö, 1976; Entwistle, McCune, & Walker, 2001), referring to the manner in which the students prefer to study in a specific educational environment, as a "result of the constant negotiation between the students' learning characteristics and the requirements of the specific learning environment, as reflected on the students' academic outcomes" (Kasimatis, Moutsios-Rentzos, Matzakos, Rozou, & Kouloumpis, 2021, p. 52). In particular, we drew upon Biggs (2001) who contrasts *deep approach* (referring to focussing on the meaning and the ideas) with *surface approach* (referring to focussing on the superficial characteristics and requirements of a task).

Overall, we propose a model of authentic evaluation of mathematics teaching effectiveness as an emergent systemic phenomenon, which is focussed on the mathematics class within a learning organisation. We acknowledge that the educational stakeholders are engaged with potentially diverse roles with other subsystems of the broader educational system to which the mathematics class belongs.

4 Implementing our Approach: The Case of ASPETE

4.1 *The School of Pedagogical and Technological Education (ASPETE) in Greece*

The School of Pedagogical and Technological Education (ASPETE) that incorporates a particular educational complexity: its graduates hold an engineer degree (Electrical Engineers, Mechanical Engineers or Civil Engineers) and a pedagogical degree as engineer educators (who may potentially teach in secondary vocational schools). Considering also the fact that the students entering ASPETE have diverse mathematics teaching and learning experiences, deriving from vocational and general education secondary school, we argue that it is crucial to support the development of mathematics teaching that is meaningful for the ASPETE students; both about their studies and their future career, through authentic evaluation processes of the mathematics teaching effectiveness.

In the following sections, we discuss empirical data deriving from a two-year research project implementing this approach (partially discussed elsewhere; Kasimatis et al., 2020, 2021), conducted in ASPETE. We concentrate on the mathematics class in the ASPETE system (the lecturer and the students) and on the observing researcher (in the broader project, we include the lecturers teaching the "core" courses for each department and the heads of the departments).

4.2 *Methods and Procedures*

Our systemic identification of the lived realities focussed on the mathematics class subsystem as experienced by the immediately interacting protagonists (the lecturer and students), as well as by the observing researcher. At the same time, we investigated two levels of experience: the mathematics class in the Department system (including the students, the lecturer, and the observer) and the mathematics class in the ASPETE system (including the students of different departments). Hence, we primarily focussed on the students who were following an Electrical Engineer degree (N_{Electr} = 48; 13 females) in the end of the first semester of the academic year 2018–2019. In line with our systemic approach, we included in the study students who were also in the end of the first semester of the academic year 2018–2019, but following a Mechanical

Engineer degree (N_{Mech} = 43; 4 females). Overall, 91 first-year students of ASPETE (N = 91; 17 females) participated in the study. The participation in the study was optional and no incentives were provided.

In the first semester of their studies, the students of both departments attended the obligatory course Mathematics I. Different lecturers taught in each department with the same syllabus, including Linear Algebra (vectors, eigenvalues, matrices, determinants etc.), Complex Numbers (operations, trigonometric forms, nth roots etc.) and Differential and Integral Calculus (single variable, limits, differentiation, definite/indefinite integrals, etc).

A five-section questionnaire was employed, to identify the students' affective relationship with mathematics and mathematics teaching, and their broader approach to studying in ASPETE. The statistical analyses of the questionnaire data were conducted with SPSS 25, including: One-sample Wilcoxon signed rank tests, Mann-Whitney *U* tests, and Kendall's tau correlations.

- Section A. Socio-demographic details
- Section B. Approaches to study were identified by Revised Two-Factor Study Process Questionnaire (R-SPQ-2F; Biggs, Kember, & Leung, 2001). R-SPQ-2F consists of twenty (10 for each approach) 5-point Likert-type items. A translated to Greek version has been employed with ASPETE students (Kasimati, Moutsios-Rentzos, & Matzakos, 2016), showing good cross-cultural validity and reliability.
- Section C. The students' conceptions about mathematics were identified through the questionnaire of Wood et al. (2012). The questionnaire consists of forty-six 5-point Likert type items organised in three parts, identifying epistemological conceptions (16 items), as well as conceptions about the students' studies (14 items) and their career (16 items). A translated to Greek version has been employed with ASPETE students by Moutsios-Rentzos and Kasimati (2014), showing its good cross-cultural psychometrics.
- Section D. The students' confidence about mathematics was identified through a translated to Greek version of the Confidence in Learning Mathematics Scale (Fennema & Sherman, 1976), which consists of twelve 5-point Likert type items. The factorial analysis (Principal Axis Factoring with Varimax rotation; 55.15% of variance explained) was in line with the unifactorial structure of the original instrument, whilst the Cronbach's alpha was found to be 0.934.
- Section E. The students' views about mathematics teaching effectiveness were identified through a *modified* and translated to Greek version of Patrick and Smart's (1998) instrument. Each of the twenty-four, 5-point Likert type items of the original questionnaire include two parts: a part asking the students' views about the teaching they actually experienced (*pragmatic*)

and a part about their teaching they desire to experience (*desired*). The factorial structure (Principal Axis Factoring with Varimax rotation; 61.58% of variance explained) was in line the tri-factorial structure of the original instrument, whilst the reliability analyses for each factor were good (Cronbach's alphas 0.867, 0.906, and 0.897 for, respectively, respect, organisation and challenge).

The lecturer's conceptions were identified through a two-hour audio-recorded semi-structured interview, in line with the content of the students' questionnaire. For example, it included questions about her views about the role of mathematics in the students' career and studies, about mathematics teaching effectiveness as it happened and as she planned to implement it in subsequent years etc. The interview was transcribed, and thematic analysis (Boyatzis, 1998; Fereday & Muir-Cochrane, 2006) was conducted with the transcriptions, drawing upon Nowell et al. (2017).

The observer's views were obtained through 10 direct structured (three-hour long each) classroom observations of Mathematics I in Electrical Engineers during the whole semester. The number of students attending ranged from 40 to 60, as attendance for this course is not obligatory (though the course is obligatory). The observer was focussed on the lecturer's practices (who voluntarily participated), noting the ongoing activities according to an observation scheme, which included, teaching methods and techniques, communicational techniques. Care was given so that it would be clear to the students that the observer focussed on the teacher's practices. The observer's notes were subjected to thematic analysis, following Nowell et al. (2017).

4.3 Multiple, Co-Existing Lived Realities in the Mathematics Class

Firstly, we present the students' experiences, starting by the whole sample, narrowing down to the Electrical Engineering students. Recall that we investigated the *narrower* affective relationship with mathematics; a dynamic affect system including: the students' conceptions (epistemological, studies, career), their confidence about coping with mathematics, their views about mathematics teaching effectiveness (pragmatic, desired/intentioned) and their links. Subsequently, we explored the *broader* relationship with studying in ASPETE through the students' approaches to study.

Considering the students' epistemological conceptions, mathematics is conceptualised to be about abstract models, techniques and calculations (see Table 15.1, column "*P*"). On the other hand, regarding their conceptions about the role of mathematics in their future studies and their future career, they noted their knowledge about its role, including both its practical and generic role. Moreover, the students appeared to be statistically significant on the positive with respect to their confidence about learning mathematics. When focussing on the students' conceptions about the effectiveness of their mathematics lecturer, on the pragmatic level, the students seemed to be statistically significant satisfied by the teacher's effectiveness on all the dimensions of the measured effectiveness (respect, organisation, challenge). Nevertheless, on the Desired/intentioned level, the students expressed a statistically significant desire for improvement in all the measured dimensions.

Furthermore, we investigated the links *amongst* the components of the dynamic affect system about mathematics. Confidence in learning mathematics appeared to be interrelated with most of the components of the system (see Table 15.1, "*Conf*"): statistically significant positively correlated with the pragmatic representation of respect and of challenge, as well as with seven of the nine conceptions about mathematics (except for with mathematics being numbers/components and with the generic role of mathematics in their studies). Moreover, considering teaching effectiveness and the students' conceptions, the students' conceptions about the generic aspect of mathematics in their future studies were statistically significant negatively correlated with their desire for more respect ($\tau = -0.193$, $P = 0.047$).

Subsequently, we situated the aforementioned viewings in terms of the students' broader experience of studying in ASPETE and of the respective affective experience of the students of another Department of ASPETE. Statistically significant links were found between the broader experience of studying in ASPETE and the narrow experience of learning mathematics, which suggest that learning mathematics is affected by the way that the students experience and relate themselves with ASPETE. The results are summarised as follows (see Table 15.1, columns "Deep", "Surf"):
- Deep approach was statistically significant positively correlated: with confidence; with challenge and respect in teaching (pragmatic); with conceiving mathematics as being abstract and about models; with the knowledge about the role of mathematics in their future studies and career; with the generic aspect of mathematics in their future career
- Surface approach statistically significant negatively correlated: with confidence; with a preference for challenge in teaching (pragmatic), conceiving mathematics as being abstract and about models

After the identification of the lived reality of all the students, we focussed on the Electrical Engineering students. First, the students of the two departments did not statistically significant differ (see Table 15.1, column "P") in their conceptions about mathematics or in their approaches to study, suggesting these may transcend departmental affiliation, thus being characteristics of the ASPETE system, rather than specific to a department.

Considering the dynamic affect system about mathematics, in comparison with the students following the Mechanical Engineering degree, the Electrical Engineering students were statistically significant (see Table 15.1, column "P"): more confident in learning mathematics; more satisfied by the organisation aspect of the mathematics teaching; less desiring more organisation in the mathematics teaching.

The aforementioned statistically significant interconnections of confidence within the affect system were also identified for the Mechanical engineers (see Table 15.1, column "$Conf_{Me}$"), but appeared to disappear when focussing on the Electrical Engineers (see Table 15.1, column "$Conf_{El}$"). We posit that the fact those students appeared to have more positive pragmatic representations of the mathematics teaching they experienced (different lecturers were teaching in the two Departments), as well as that they were on the positive side of the confidence spectrum ($M = 3.5, p = 0.002$) contrasting the Mechanical Engineers who were neutral ($M = 3.1, p = 0.216$) may be linked with these departmentally linked differences. For example, it may be hypothesised that the positive teaching experience combined with confidence may provide the students with a sense of autonomy in their broader affective relationship with mathematics. Moreover, though mathematics as a course taught in both departments may have a similar content, the students' complex affiliation (Bingolbali, Monaghan, & Roper, 2007) and professional identity (practicing engineers and teachers; Garner & Kaplan, 2019) may crucially affect the way that mathematics teaching effectiveness is conceptualised and experienced. Overall, it is argued that the degree of confidence and its links with teaching effectiveness appeared to be crucial in the characteristics of the affective system, which renders important for further investigations to be conducted.

Having obtained a comparative viewing about the students' experiences of mathematics teaching effectiveness, we focussed on the lecturer. The lecturer's interview revealed the complex lived reality she experienced, as she critically reflected upon her teaching experiences of the particular semester, referring at the same time on her past lecturing experiences and at her intentions and thoughts of future teaching practices. The results of the thematic analysis of the lecturer's interview identified three main themes (see also Kasimatis et al., 2020): *mathematics and her role as a mathematics teacher; teaching* (pragmatic; as it happened); *teaching* (intentioned/desired; as she would like it to happen in the future).

Regarding mathematics and her role as a teacher she suggested: "Mathematics are actually the base for all other subjects" and "Mathematics help students

TABLE 15.1   Learning mathematics and studying in ASPETE: the students' lived complexity (based on Kasimatis et al., 2020, 2021)

		M_{Whole}	P		$Deep^i$	$Surf^i$	$Conf^i$	M_{EI}	M_{Me}	P^h	$Conf_{EI}$	$Conf_{Me}$
Deep		3.0^a	0.815^d					3.0^a	3.0	0.891		
Surface		2.6^a	<0.001^d					2.5^a	2.6	0.582		
Confidence		3.3^b	<0.001^e	τ^g	0.207	−0.197		3.5^b	3.1	0.018		
				p	0.013	0.018						
Respect	Pragm^i	4.2^b	<0.001^e	τ	0.222	−0.128	0.184	4.1^b	4.2	0.711	0.133	0.284
				p	0.005	0.102	0.034				0.295	0.022
	Des/Unt^i	3.3^c	<0.001^f	τ	0.057	−0.087	−0.099	3.3^c	3.3^c	0.679	−0.036	−0.118
				p	0.503	0.308	0.297				0.791	0.406
Organisation	Pragm	3.9^b	<0.001^e	τ	0.101	0.021	0.144	4.2^b	3.4	<0.001	0.167	−0.155
				p	0.226	0.803	0.126				0.193	0.300
	Des/Unt	3.7^c	<0.001^f	τ	0.026	−0.097	−0.057	3.3^c	4.4	<0.001	−0.028	0.278
				p	0.748	0.235	0.530				0.838	0.035
Challenge	Pragm	3.9^b	<0.001^e	τ	0.264	−0.159	.0251	3.9^b	3.9	0.994	0.163	0.379
				p	0.001	0.043	0.004				0.204	0.002
	Des/Unt	3.3^c	<0.001^f	τ	0.133	−0.056	−0.015	3.3^c	3.4	0.342	0.117	−0.128
				p	0.115	0.504	0.874				0.383	0.357
Conceptions	Num/Cj	3.7^b	<0.001^e	τ	0.100	0.098	0.124	3.8^b	3.6	0.154	0.138	−0.004
				p	0.226	0.237	0.142				0.281	0.971
	Mo/Abj	4.0^b	<0.001^e	τ	0.207	−0.163	0.289	3.9^b	4.0	0.893	0.210	0.338
				p	0.014	0.054	0.001				0.110	0.004
	Life^j	3.3^b	<0.001^e	τ	0.151	−0.196	0.173	3.3^b	3.3	0.696	0.041	0.289
				p	0.067	0.018	0.041				0.752	0.013

(cont.)

TABLE 15.1 Learning mathematics and studying in ASPETE: the students' lived complexity (based on Kasimatis et al., 2020, 2021) (cont.)

		M_{Whole}	P		$Deep^i$	$Surf^i$	$Conf^i$	M_{El}	M_{Me}	P^h	$Conf_{El}$	$Conf_{Me}$
Studies	Pract[j]	3.9[b]	<0.001[a]	τ	0.092	−0.034	0.212	3.9[b]	3.8	0.423	0.085	0.299
				P	0.267	0.688	0.013				0.510	0.011
	Gen[j]	3.5[b]	<0.001[a]	τ	0.061	−0.074	0.204	3.6[b]	3.4	0.300	0.069	0.259
				P	0.462	0.372	0.015				0.593	0.025
	Know[j]	3.8[b]	<0.001[a]	τ	0.241	−0.008	0.302	4.0[b]	3.6	0.074	0.198	0.277
				P	0.004	0.928	<0.001				0.134	0.019
Career	Pract	3.7[b]	<0.001[a]	τ	0.155	−0.069	0.290	3.8[b]	3.7	0.273	0.175	0.309
				P	0.063	0.414	0.001				0.184	0.009
	Gen	3.2[b]	0.001[a]	τ	0.187	−0.073	0.229	3.3[b]	3.2	0.416	0.078	0.331
				P	0.023	0.379	0.007				0.542	0.004
	Know	3.4[b]	<0.001[a]	τ	0.221	−0.084	0.249	3.6[b]	3.3	0.113	0.195	0.207
				P	0.007	0.311	0.003				0.128	0.077

Notes: 'Whole': Whole sample, 'Me': Mechanical Engineers, 'El': Electrical Engineers.

a '1': never or rarely true of me, '2': sometimes true of me, '3': this item is true of me about half the time, '4': frequently true of me. '5': almost always true of me.
b '1': strongly disagree, '2': disagree, '3': neither agree, nor disagree, '4': agree. '5': strongly agree.
c '1': considerably less frequently, '2': less frequently, '3': as frequently as it did. '4': more frequently. '5': much more frequently.
d One-sample Wilcoxon signed rank test to the hypothesised median "3": "this item is true of me about half the time".
e One-sample Wilcoxon signed rank test to the hypothesised median "3": "neither agree, nor disagree".
f One-sample Wilcoxon signed rank test to the hypothesised median "3": "as frequently as it did".
g Kendall's tau τ non-parametric correlation.
h Mann-Whitney's U test.
i 'Deep': Deep approach, 'Surf': Surface approach, 'Confidence': Confidence in learning mathematics.
j 'Pragm': Pragmatic, 'Des/Unt': Desired/Unintentional, 'Num/C': Number/Components, 'Mo/Ab': Modelling/Abstract, 'Pract': Practical, 'Gen': Generic, 'Know': (lack of) Knowledge

to develop a specific way of thinking. They learn to think outside-the-box – a valuable ability in today's world and their profession". Her view of her role as a teacher is evident in: "I think my role was to build an enabling environment, to motivate my students, to guide and support them".

About her pragmatic views of her teaching, she mentioned that: "I tried to reflect on the mission, values and specialisation of the institution and connect Mathematics through specific examples with the specialisation of my students". She also stressed that she "tried to design and teach this course in a way that fosters all students, but especially the less developed students". Moreover, she highlighted that "I tried to keep my instruction practical and useful, not theoretical, and used a lot of examples", as well as that "I used scaffolding as a teaching strategy and asked open questions, so that each student becomes part of the conversation, and member of the learning community".

Considering her desired/intentioned teaching, she noted that: "if I had to teach this class again, I would re-consider my students' needs and make changes accordingly" ... "some changes in my classroom practice and more attention to students' difficulties, maybe connect more the given examples to their specialisation" ... "I could make more use of e-class".

Subsequently, we concentrated on the observer. The thematic analysis (see also Kasimatis et al., 2020) of the observer's notes revealed that the lecturer conducted well designed and coherent lessons, providing the students opportunities to recall, use and link prior knowledge. She used different instructional techniques and methods (for example, whole-class discussion and working in pairs), as well as different representations (for example, tables and diagrams). Nevertheless, it was noted that almost half of the students were reluctant to participate in the whole-class discussion, but they were engaged in other activities. The lecturer employed a communicative approach to her teaching by often incorporating key questions and examples. Her teaching was student-centred, promoting the students' engagement and motivation. Importantly, she tried to link mathematics with other disciplines.

4.4 Communicating the Multiple Viewings of the System to the System: The Reflective Lecturer as an Intentional (Systemic) Actor

The last part of the cycle of this iterative process is the communication of the obtained viewings of the system to the system. We reveal to all the educational protagonists the obtained multiple viewings, providing them at the same time with suggestions of ways of acting. In this chapter, we discuss aspects of this ongoing process with one educational protagonist, i.e., the lecturer.

First, the viewings were presented and discussed with a member of the research team with the purpose to communicate both the nature of the multiple lenses through which the system was viewed and the results of this process. During this process, care was taken so that the lecturer would have the time and space to reflect and to position herself with the diverse lived realities.

At the same time, though suggestions were offered by the researcher about the ways her teaching may be transformed in future implementations our interest was primarily on allowing them to reflect on her practices, on previous practices and potential future decisions. In other words, the purpose of this communication is to support the lecturers in their intentionally transforming their teaching to be in line with the novel level of awareness presented to them: our multiple viewings enriched their lived reality to be systemic and, consequently, to facilitate their being systemic, intentional actors.

Our current investigations with one of the lecturers includes his documenting in a log his teaching plans and decisions, as a result of the aforementioned process. At the same time, the research team obtains the multiple viewings of another iteration, which we plan to compare with the lecturer's log and to discuss them with the lecturer. In this way, our proposed evaluating process is *dynamic and meaningful for the present system.*

5 Concluding Remarks and Ways Forward

In this chapter, we discussed a systemic approach to authentic evaluation in education and, in particular, in mathematics teaching effectiveness. At the crux of our approach lie the multiple viewings of the system as potentially diversely experienced by the educational protagonists and as observed by the researcher. Hence, we incorporate the perspective of the evaluator in the under-evaluation system.

The presented results reveal the divergences and the convergences of the obtained multiple viewings. The convergences may be interpreted as a characteristic of the system with respect to mathematics teaching effectiveness. For example, the teachers' respect about the students appeared in the obtained viewings of the lived realities of the students, the lecturer and the observer. Nevertheless, it should be stressed that it is the communication of the obtained multiple viewings to the system that explicitly allows for the system *to start experiencing itself as complex whole.* We started our communications from the lecturers. The lecturers were chosen as the significant authority figures who constantly make important decisions about mathematics teaching and, crucially, these decisions and the respective practices are immediately experienced by the students. The purpose of these communications is, through a series of reflections, to allow for the lecturers to be transformed from an isolated, disjointed actor to a systemic, intentional organic part of the system. We argue that through a series of iterations of such authentic evaluation cycles the educational unit becomes a learning organisation, as it becomes *aware of its existence as a complex system*.

In this chapter, we only discussed the communication of the viewings to the lecturers, because, due to the ongoing pandemic, it was not feasible to include the students nor the Heads of the Departments (cf. Teodorović, Stanković, Bodroža, Milin, & Đerić, 2016), but we have made appropriate preparations so that our approach may be implemented as designed the following academic year. Moreover, in the current, ongoing, implementation of our approach, we explicitly embrace an interdisciplinary dimension to our approach, by including the lecturers of the main courses of each department and their perspective about mathematics teaching effectiveness (Moutsios-Rentzos, Kritikos, & Kalavasis, 2017, 2019).

Through a process of systemic reflections, the protagonists observe, reflect and act upon a system that explicitly includes the protagonists themselves, thus being authentic for the system. Our approach supports the educational unit to develop an attitude "of mindful participation with a community around matters of shared concern" (Davis & Sumara, 2006, p. 101). Furthermore, we promote an increased level of leadership density in the educational system, referring to the level of leadership role exercised by the various educational protagonists (cf. Davis, Ellett, & Annunziata, 2002), which is essential factor for an educational unit to become a learning organisation.

The proposed approach accords with relatively recent attempts to address the complexity of the educational system (Begg, 2003; Kershner, 2021). Moreover, our approach added to existing research findings with respect to the aspects that are included; for example, about conceptions about mathematics or approaches to study (Maass & Engeln, 2019; Wood et al., 2012). On the other hand, it allows us to gain deeper understanding in the complex phenomenon of teaching mathematics in a tertiary educational system (e.g., ASPETE), thus adding to the related literature (FitzSimons, 2001, 2013; Engelbrecht, Bergsten, & Kågesten, 2012).

Consequently, we argue that the proposed approach may be implemented in diverse educational systems without losing the core element that characterises it: its authenticity. The fact that it essentially builds on reflective viewings of the relationships of the viewings that different perspectives offer allows it to be meaningful in different engineering education systems (cf. Aditya & Olds, 2014; Pohjolainen, Myllykoski, Mercat, & Sosnovsky, 2018), as it also explicitly incorporates the peculiarities of the specific educational system, its subsystems, and its environment.

Acknowledgements

This chapter draws upon a research project that has been co-financed by the Greek School of Pedagogical and Technological Education through the operational programme "Research strengthening in ASPETE" – Project 80147: "Mathematics Education and Educational Technology; MATHETE".

References

Aditya, J., & Olds, B. (Eds.). (2014). *Cambridge handbook of engineering education research*. Cambridge University Press.

Backes, B., Goldhaber, D., Cade, W., Sullivan, K., & Dodson, M. (2018). Can UTeach? Assessing the relative effectiveness of STEM teachers. *Economics of Education Review, 64*, 184–198.

Begg, A. (2003). Curriculum: Developing a systems theory perspective. In L. Bragg, C. Campbell, G. Herbert, & J. Mousley (Eds.), *Proceedings of the 26th annual conference of the Mathematics Education Research Group of Australasia*. Deakin University.

Begg, A., Davis, B., & Bramald, R. (2003). Obstacles to the dissemination of mathematics education research. In A. J. Bishop, M. A. Clements, C. Keitel, J. Kilpatrick, & F. K. S. Leung (Eds.), *Second international handbook of mathematics education* (pp. 593–634). Kluwer.

Bertalanffy, L. V. (1968). *General system theory: Foundations, development*. George Braziller.

Biggs, J. B. (2001). Enhancing learning: A matter of style or approach? In R. J. Sternberg & L. F. Zhang (Eds.), *Perspectives on thinking, learning, and cognitive styles* (pp. 73–102). Erlbaum.

Biggs, J. B., Kember, D., & Leung, D. Y. P. (2001). The revised two factor study process questionnaire: R-SPQ-2F. *British Journal of Educational Psychology, 71*, 133–149.

Bingolbali, E., Monaghan, J., & Roper, T. (2007). Engineering students' conceptions of the derivative and some implications for their mathematical education. *International Journal of Mathematical Education in Science and Technology, 38*(6), 763–777.

Boyatzis, R. E. (1998). *Transforming qualitative information: Thematic analysis and code development*. Sage.

Cai, J., Kaiser, G., Perry, B., & Wong, N. Y. (2009). *Effective mathematics teaching from teachers' perspectives*. Sense Publishers.

Chen, D., & Stroup, W. (1993). General system theory: Toward a conceptual framework for science and technology education for all. *Journal of Science Education and Technology, 2*(3), 447–459.

Creemers, B. P. M., & Kyriakides, L. (2008). *The dynamics of educational effectiveness: A contribution to policy, practice and theory in contemporary schools.* Routledge.

Davis, D. R., Ellett, C. D., & Annunziata, J. (2002). Teacher evaluation, leadership and learning organizations. *Journal of Personnel Evaluation in Education, 16*(4), 287–301.

Davis, B., & Simmt, E. (2003). Understanding learning systems: Mathematics education and complexity science. *Journal for Research in Mathematics Education, 34*(2), 137–167.

Davis, B., & Sumara, D. (2005). Complexity science and educational action research: Toward a pragmatics of transformation. *Educational Action Research, 13*(3), 453–466.

Davis, B., & Sumara, D. (2006). *Complexity and education.* Lawrence Erlbaum Associates.

Engelbrecht, J., Bergsten, C., & Kågesten, O. (2012). Conceptual and procedural approaches to mathematics in the engineering curriculum: Student conceptions and performance. *Journal of Engineering Education, 101*(1), 138–162.

Entwistle, N. J., McCune, V., & Walker, P. (2001). Conceptions, styles and approaches within higher education: analytic abstractions and everyday experience. In R. J. Sternberg & L. F. Zhang (Eds.), *Perspectives on cognitive, learning, and thinking styles* (pp. 103–136). Lawrence Erlbaum.

Fennema, E., & Sherman, J. A. (1976). Fennema-Sherman mathematics attitudes scales: Instruments designed to measure attitudes toward the learning of mathematics by females and males. *Journal for Research in Mathematics Education, 7*(5), 324–326.

Fereday, J., & Muir-Cochrane, E. (2006). Demonstrating rigor using thematic analysis: A hybrid approach of inductive and deductive coding and theme development. *International Journal of Qualitative Methods, 5,* 80–92.

FitzSimons, G. E. (2001). Integrating mathematics, statistics, and technology in vocational and workplace education. *International Journal of Mathematical Education in Science and Technology, 32*(3), 375–383.

FitzSimons, G. E. (2013). Doing mathematics in the workplace: A brief review of selected literature. *Adults Learning Mathematics, 8*(1), 7–19.

Garner, J. K., & Kaplan, A. (2019). A complex dynamic systems perspective on teacher learning and identity formation: An instrumental case. *Teachers and Teaching, 25*(1), 7–33.

Herrington, A., & Herrington, J. (Eds.). (2006). *Authentic learning environments in higher education.* Information Science Pub.

Husserl, E. (2001). *Logical investigations* (J. N. Findlay, Trans.). Routledge.

Jay, J. K., & Johnson, K. L. (2002). Capturing complexity: A typology of reflective practice for teacher education. *Teaching and Teacher Education, 18,* 73–85.

Kalavasis, F., & Kazadi, C. (2015). The learning and teaching of mathematics as an emergent property through interacting systems and interchanching roles: A commentary. In U. Gellert, J. Gimenez Rodriguez, C. Hahn, & S. Kafoussi (Eds.), *Educational paths to mathematics. A C.I.E.A.E.M. sourcebook* (pp. 425–429). Springer.

Kasimatis, K., Moutsios-Rentzos, A., Matzakos, N., Rozou, V., & Kouloumpis, D. (2021). Pre-service engineer educators learning mathematics: Mapping the lived complexity. In M. Carmo (Ed.), *Education applications & developments VI* (pp. 51–65). inSciencePress.

Kasimatis, K., Moutsios-Rentzos, A., Matzakos, N., Rozou, V., & Kouloumpis, D. (2020). Effective mathematics teaching in tertiary technological education: The case of ASPETE. *New Trends and Issues Proceedings on Humanities and Social Sciences, 7*(1), 158–168.

Kasimati, K., Moutsios-Rentzos, A., & Matzakos, N. (2016). Antilipsis yia to rolo ton mathimatikon stis spoudes kai stin ergasia kai prosengisis meletis: i periptosi tis A.S.PAI.TE. [Conceptions about the role of mathematics in studies and career and approaches to study: the case of ASPETE]. In *Proceedings of the 33rd Panhellenic conference of Mathematics education of the Hellenic Mathematical Society* (pp. 418–426). HMS.

Kershner, B. (2021). *Understanding educational complexity: Integrating practices and perspectives for 21st century leadership*. Brill.

Kump, B., Knipfer, K., Pammer, V., Schmidt, A., Maier, R., Kunzmann, C., & Lindstaedt, S. N. (2011). The role of reflection in maturing organizational know-how. In W. Reinhardt, T. D. Ullmann, P. Scott, V. Pammer, O. Conlan, & A. Berlange (Eds.), *Proceedings of the 1st workshop on awareness and reflection in technology-enhanced learning* (pp. 30 45). CEUR-WS.

Maass, K., & Engeln, K. (2019). Professional development on connections to the world of work in mathematics and science education. *ZDM, 51*(6), 967–978.

Marton, F., & Säljö, R. (1976). On qualitative differences in learning – I: outcome and process. *British Journal of Educational Psychology, 46*, 4–11.

Moutsios-Rentzos, A., Kalavasis, F., & Sofos, E. (2017). Learning paths and teaching bridges: The emergent mathematics classroom within the open system of a globalised virtual social network. In G. Aldon, F. Hitt, L. Bazzini, & U. Gellert (Eds.), *Mathematics and technology* (pp. 371–393). Springer.

Moutsios-Rentzos, A., & Kalavasis, F. A. (2021). *Systemic, interdisciplinary approach to educational planning about mathematics in the educational unit* [Manuscript in preparation].

Moutsios-Rentzos, A., & Kasimati, K. (2014). Mathimatika, spoudes, kariera: dierevnontas tis antilipsis phititon tis ASPAITE [Mathematics, studies, career: an investigation about the conceptions of ASPETE students]. In *Proceedings of the conference of the Greek Association for Research in Mathematics Education (5th GARME)*. GARME.

Moutsios-Rentzos, A., Kritikos, G., & Kalavasis, F. (2019). Co-constructing teaching and learning spaces in and between mathematics and physics at school. Proceedings of CIEAEM 70. *Quaderni di Ricerca in Didattica, 2*(3), 215–220.

Moutsios-Rentzos, A., Kritikos, G., & Kalavasis, F. (2017). Functions of operations and operands in school mathematics and physics: A complex interdisciplinary (de)mathematised phenomenology. Proceedings of CIEAEM 69. *Quaderni di Ricerca in Didattica (Mathematics), 27*(2), 297–299.

Muijs, D., & Reynolds, D. (2017). *Effective teaching: Evidence and practice*. Sage.

Nikitina, S., & Mansilla, V. B. (2003). *Three strategies for interdisciplinary math and science teaching: A case of the Illinois Mathematics and Science Academy*. Project Zero, Harvard University.

Nissilä, S. P. (2005). Individual and collective reflection: How to meet the needs of development in teaching. *European Journal of Teacher Education, 28*(2), 209–219.

Nowell, L. S., Norris, J. M., White, D. E., & Moules, N. J. (2017). Thematic analysis: Striving to meet the trustworthiness criteria. *International Journal of Qualitative Methods, 16*(1), 1–13.

Patrick, J., & Smart, R. M. (1998). An empirical evaluation of teacher effectiveness: The emergence of three critical factors. *Assessment & Evaluation in Higher Education, 23*(2), 165–178.

Pepin, B., & Roesken-Winter, B. (Eds.). (2014). *From beliefs to dynamic affect systems in mathematics education: Exploring a mosaic of relationships and interactions*. Springer.

Pohjolainen, S., Myllykoski, T., Mercat, C., & Sosnovsky, S. (Eds.). (2018). *Modern mathematics education for engineering curricula in Europe: A comparative analysis of EU, Russia, Georgia and Armenia*. Springer International Publishing.

Roth, W. M., & Tobin, K. (2001). The implications of coteaching/cogenerative dialogue for teacher evaluation: Learning from multiple perspectives of everyday practice. *Journal of Personnel Evaluation in Education, 15*(1), 7–29.

Senge, P. (1990). *The fifth discipline: The art and practice of the learning organization*. Doubleday Currency.

Senge, P., Roberts, C., Ross, R., Smith, B., & Kleiner, A. (1994). *The fifth discipline fieldbook: Strategies and tools for building a learning organization*. Doubleday Currency.

Teodorović, J., Stanković, D., Bodroža, B., Milin, V., & Đerić, I. (2016). Education policymaking in Serbia through the eyes of teachers, counselors, and principals. *Educational Assessment, Evaluation and Accountability, 28*(4), 347–375.

Wittmann, E. C. (2001). Developing mathematics education in a systemic process. *Educational Studies in Mathematics, 48*(1), 1–20.

Wood, L. N., Petocz, P., & Reid, A. (2012). *Becoming a mathematician*. Springer.

Zahavi, D. (2003). *Husserl's phenomenology*. Stanford University Press.

CHAPTER 16

Parents' Views on the Authentic Evaluation of Students in the Experimental Schools of Greece

Antonios Bouras and Anastasia Papadopoulou

Abstract

Studying the Greek and international literature indicates that there is agreement as to the need and value of authentic evaluation in school. This is a necessary process not only for the performance of students but also for the implementation of educational goals, as defined by the curricula. Besides, if we want to talk about a healthy educational system, it should be open and enable its review and improvement. Such an educational system contributes to monitoring of the development of children's knowledge and reflects the effectiveness of teaching and the skills of teachers (MacBeath, 2001). The authentic evaluation, which involves the teachers and the students, the parents and the educators in the process of evaluation, offers the above opportunity (Stiggins, 1994). In current chapter, therefore, we focused on the evaluation of the Pilot and Experimental Schools in Greece through the point of view of parents. Specifically, the aim of this chapter was to investigate, record and capture the views of parents whose children attend Pilot and Experimental schools, concerning the contribution and effectiveness of authentic evaluation as well as the achievement of educational goals, as they are formulated in the curricula. The research sample consisted of 240 parents. Regarding the results, the parents of students attending both Experimental and Pilot Schools have a positive view of their operation and their contribution in all aspects surveyed. They are also positive in terms of the evaluation of factors that affect the effectiveness of the educational process and the school unit in general.

Keywords

authentic evaluation of students – experimental schools in Greece – parents' views

1 Introduction

The experimental schools were internationally expressed in the appearance of the Labor School with main representatives G. Kerschensteiner and H. Gaudig in Germany, J. Dewey in America, M. Montessori in Italy, Decroly in Belgium. The first experimental school "The Laboratory School of the University of Chicago" was founded by the educator J. Dewey between 1896 and 1903. It was a laboratory school owned by the Department of Psychology and Pedagogy at the University of Chicago. Special laboratory training programmes were applied to it.

The first Experimental school in Greece (Experimental school of the University of Athens was founded by law 4376 in 1929 (Government Gazette 300/21.8.1929). It was founded on the initiative of Professor of Pedagogy Nikolaos Exarchopoulos. K. Gondikas was the Minister of Education. Then, the foundation of the Experimental schools of the University of Thessaloniki and Patras followed.

The Experimental Schools had a direct connection with the Pedagogical Schools of the university institutions in order to apply the new experimental methods.

Along with the Experimental ones, there were Model Schools for excellent students. The Institution of Model Gymnasiums was established in 1936 and under the Law 247 of 14th October 1936 (Government Gazette 460/17-10-1936, article 7). It is provided that Model Gymnasiums may be established and after a suggestion of the Board of Education and the approval of the Minister, the "by way of derogation of the programme implemented in other gymnasiums" is approved. It is unknown which schools were converted to Model ones. The Gymnasiums of Zosimea, Varvakio and Anargyrios-Korgialenios were named Model Gymnasiums in 1937 with (Government Gazette 263 / 13-07-1937) and Ionidios in 1946. The same year the High School of Honor Students "Anavrita" was named as Model, which was founded on the initiative of the then royal family, in 1972 the Evangelical School of N. Smyrni and in the same year the 2nd High School of Patras. After 1945 none of the 120 Model Gymnasiums operated. The 3 historical Model schools (the Zosimea School, the Varvakio and the Ionidios), as well as Anavryta, and the Evangelical School continued their operation. The Korgialenios-Anargyrios School in Spetses had ceased its operation. Until the Framework Law of 1985, Model Schools were distinct from Experimental schools. The historical Model Schools were abolished under the Law 1566/1985. Until then they operated in parallel with the other public schools and were transformed into Experimental.

For the first time under the law 3966/2011 the two terms "Model" and "Experimental" characterise a school unit. The concept of the Model Experimental is a new formation in the educational reality, which includes all the procedures and processes that existed in the Experimental and the Model schools until that time. Students were selected through examinations in order to study in the Model and Experimental Schools. For the first time in Greece, the evaluation of the teachers of the Model Experimental schools takes place (Papadopoulou, 2018). Law 3966/2011 was implemented until 2015. After the change of the government policy, the law 4327/2015 is passed, by which the Model Experimental schools were declassified and are defined as experimental schools, except for the school units that are defined as Model schools. The way of students' selection changed. For the Experimental and Model schools, the students were selected after examinations.

Authentic assessment is increasingly used in conjunction with the classic ways of assessment in the educational field having many positive results for everyone, learners, teachers and the school community

In general, the alternative forms emphasise not only the knowledge but also what the student can achieve through the effort he makes, the skills he cultivates and the attitudes he adopts while learning.

The tasks offered are in the form of a practical daily problem – they can be solved in many different correct ways, they are based on the interdisciplinary and holistic approach and are carried out in an individual or group context depending on the classroom conditions. Therefore the types / forms of this type of assessment are supportive in the learning process of the child and take into account the fact that everyone learns in a different way and rhythm (Papageorgiou, 2017).

It is aimed at parents and students as it provides detailed information on the results of learning efforts. In this way, a more complete information is offered to the parents and the students about the progress and the general/general image of the child in relation to the teaching objectives (Papageorgiou, 2017).

2   Research Goals

The aim of the research is to capture the views of parents, whose children attend Model and Experimental schools, regarding the operation of these schools. The research questions that specify the above aim are the following: 1. Parents' views on the importance of experimental schools. 2. Parents' views on the importance of model schools. 3. Parents' view on the separation of Model and Experimental schools. 4. Parents' view on teachers' evaluation. 5. Parents' view on the selection of students in the Model Schools after examinations or skill tests. 6. Parents' view on the selection of students in the Experimental Schools after a draw.

3 Research Methodology

The methodological approach of this study is the quantitative analysis using a structured questionnaire and statistical analysis of the data collected.

The target population is the parents of students of Model or Experimental schools. The questionnaire was implemented in physical form and distributed to all parents associations of the model and experimental schools. The target population numbers about 6,000 families of which 240 people responded to the survey. The processing was done using SPSS v.25 software. The questionnaires were collected, coded and entered into the database of the editing software. Basic descriptive statistical measures and graphs such as mean values, standard deviations, bar graphs and the cographs were derived. The independent samples T-test was done in order to test the difference between the means.

The research scales consist of questions that refer to characteristics of the experimental schools and are measured on a Likert scale from the value 1 to the value 5. As a result, the mean values of the scales also occur within this period. Regarding the evaluation of the scale, at the left edge, namely the negative values are in number 1, such as expressions of disagreement with the claim or non-agreement with the claim, while the neutral value is in number 3, which is expressed by "neither agree nor disagree", namely the correspondence with "not little", "not much" and the fully affirmant value, which depicts the expression of agreement is in number 5 and expresses the absolute identifying of the parent who answers through the claim of concerned question (cronbach alpha = 0.87). The research was conducted in 2020.

3.1 Sample

The sample consists of parents of children attending either model or experimental schools. The sample is composed of 240 people, of which 37.5% (n = 90) are men and 62.5% (n = 150) are women. Regarding the age, 1.7% (n = 4) are people up to 35 years old, 20.4% (n = 49) are people 36 to 45 years old, 71.3% (n = 171) are 46 to 55 years old and 6.7% (n = 16) are the parents over 56 years old.

Regarding their education, 0.4% (n = 1) declare that they are primary school graduates, 6.7% (n = 16) declare that they are high school graduates, 41.7% (n = 100) declare that they are graduates of an International Hellenic university (IHU) or of a Technological Educational Institute (TEI), 39.2% (n = 94) declare that they are holders of a postgraduate degree and 12.1% (n = 29) declare that they are holders of a doctoral degree. Regarding the type of their child's school, 29.2% (n = 70) stated that their child attends an experimental school, while 70.8% (n = 170) stated that their child attends a model school. Regarding the level of education, 10.8% (n = 26) stated that their child attends primary school, 37.9% (n = 91) stated that their child attends Gymnasium (Junion High School), while 51.2 % (n = 123) stated that their child attends Lyceum (High School).

3.2 Research Tool

A structured questionnaire was used for the answer of the research questions. In the first page of the questionnaire information is provided to parents whose children attend Model and Experimental schools and is related to the necessity of the research, the type and number of questions, the ensurement of the confidentiality of the answers and other instructions for completion. In addition to this introductory part of the questionnaire, the questionnaire consists of two parts:

Part I includes data that shape the personal/demographic profile of the respondent (questions A1 to A6). Part II includes questions that ask parents to express their views on the purpose and necessity of Model and Experimental schools as well as the institutional changes that took place in the period 2011–2019 (questions B1 to B9).

3.3 Results

3.3.1 Parents' Views on the Importance of Experimental Schools

Regarding the degree of importance of the experimental schools according to the parents' point of view, the table with the mean values and the standard deviations is given. As shown by the grouped thecogram and the table of mean values and standard deviations, the most intense agreement of the parents concerns the fact that the most important contribution of the experimental schools has to do with the support of innovative teaching practices and this is found with a mean value of 3.97, which means that parents believe that experimental schools contribute a lot in this area. The application of new teaching methods, the implementation of new teaching tools, the implementation of new course of studies and curricula are approximately at the same level regarding their mean value. The lowest contribution of the experimental schools is found at the level of the methods of experimentation in new ways of administration and operation of the school unit and in the implementation of the textbooks. According to the parents, these are considered as the two most residual, in relation to the other sectors, elements of the experimental schools. However, there are two features that need to be highlighted. The 1st characteristic is that all the elements and characteristics that are proposed for evaluation to the parents, as mean values mark values above the intermediate value 3, namely the neutral value of the scale, so the Model and Experimental schools are satisfactory on both of them, in the sense they are not evaluated as residual by parents in these fields, while the second element that emerges is that the model schools do not seem to have a very high mean value above the level 4, let alone to approach the level 5 in any of these fields. So, if we did an overview of this research question, that is, the degree of importance of the experimental schools in the various fields according to the parents will be above average with a lot of opportunities for improvement, since they do not get values above four, on a scale from 1 to 5.

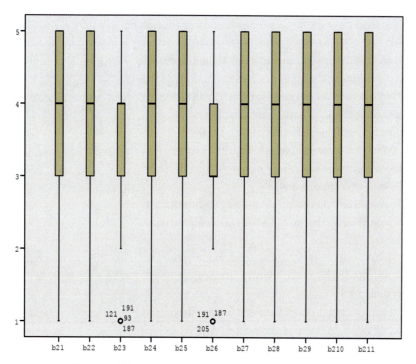

FIGURE 16.1   Box plot of B2 responses

In addition, the boxplot shows that there is a uniform distribution of 75% of the sample which takes values from 3 to 5, i.e. there are parents who rate the performance of the experimental schools with 5, the 75% of the parents rate them from 3 to 5. The above data is very clear, apart from the field of the experimental school regarding the claim that the experimental schools contribute to the implementation of new modes of administration and operation. In this

TABLE 16.1   Mean values and standards deviations of parents' answers

Question	Mean value	Standard deviation
B2.1. To what extent do you consider that EXPERIMENTAL schools contribute to the implementation of new course of study and curricula	3.88	1.085
B2.2. To what extent do you consider that EXPERIMENTAL schools contribute to the implementation of new teaching tools	3.94	1.031
B2.3. To what extent do you consider that EXPERIMENTAL schools contribute to the implementation of textbooks	3.57	1.076
B2.4. To what extent do you consider that EXPERIMENTAL schools contribute to the implementation of other educational material	3.84	1.028
B2.5. To what extent do you consider that EXPERIMENTAL schools contribute to the application of new teaching methods	3.94	1.075
B2.6. To what extent do you consider that EXPERIMENTAL schools contribute to the implementation of new ways of administration and operation of the school unit	3.44	1.141
B2.7. To what extent do you consider that EXPERIMENTAL schools contribute to the drawing of conclusions for the formulation of educational policy	3.71	1.195
B2.8. To what extent do you consider that EXPERIMENTAL schools contribute to the comprehensive development of students	3.88	1.083
B2.9. To what extent do you consider that EXPERIMENTAL schools contribute to education with practical training of undergraduate students	3.83	1.021
B2.10. To what extent do you consider that EXPERIMENTAL schools contribute to the support of curricula and teaching methods	3.84	1.040
B2.11. To what extent do you consider that EXPERIMENTAL schools contribute to the support of innovative teaching practices	3.97	1.072

case it seems that the distribution is much lower, at lower levels, while what is also observed is that extreme values (very low values) appear in almost all dimensions. The thecograms depict that 25% of the parents and this percentage remains constant for most variables, has a negative point of view of the model experimental in all areas. Regarding the dimension of the experimental that has to do with the implementation of new modes of administration and operation of the school unit, the smallest variation appears. In particular, while in all other variables the views of the parents are very heterogeneous, in the matter of whether the experimental ones are effective in the implementation of new modes of administration and operation in the school units, there is an agreement in the views which converges to slightly higher values from number 3. The conclusion that they are residual in terms of their operation is safe.

3.3.2 Parents' Views on the Importance of Model Schools

To investigate the view of parents regarding the degree of importance of the Model schools, the table with the mean values and standard deviations is given. As shown by the evaluation of mean values a phenomenon which is repeated is that all the mean values of the dimensions given for evaluation are to the right of the mean value 3. More specifically, the parents of students of Model schools have a positive view of the operation and contribution of the models in all the dimensions that were given to them to be evaluated. However, it seems that the mean values exceed in the vast majority of dimensions the value 4, speaking of the Model ones, while in the experimental schools none of the mean values exceeded the value 4.

This means that the parents of the children who attend a model school are much more satisfied with the performance of the model schools. In addition, the lowest performance value according to the parents concerns the operation of an exemplary organisational structure and the operation of exemplary conditions. The top contribution value of Model schools concerns the support of innovation and excellence by creating groups, the ensurement of public and free high-quality education for all, the creativity of students, the scientific competence of the teaching staff and then the exemplary operation compared to other public schools.

It turns out that all parents evaluate the Model schools above the value of 3, i.e. with a purely positive approach. Exceptions to this are two aspects, two variables of the Model schools, the operation of an exemplary organisational structure and the operation of exemplary conditions where simply one in four parents finds disagreements in this regard, while three out of four evaluate the model schools positively at this level as well.

3.3.3 Parents' Views on the Separation of Model and Experimental Schools

Parents are asked to what extent they consider that the model and experimental schools should be declassified, i.e., to be separated into model and experimental. In the whole sample, 30.8% disagree with the claim, 12.9% of

TABLE 16.2 Mean values and standard deviations of parents' responses

Question	Mean value	Standard deviation
B3.1. To what extent do you consider that MODEL schools contribute to the establishment and operation of exemplary conditions	3.92	1.019
B3.2. To what extent do you consider that MODEL schools contribute to the operation of an exemplary organisational structure	3.79	1.094
B3.3. To what extent do you consider that MODEL schools contribute to the scientific adequacy of the educational potential	4.13	0.933
B3.4. To what extent do you consider that MODEL schools contribute to the application of exemplary teaching practices	4.01	0.983
B3.5. To what extent do you consider that MODEL schools contribute to the exemplary operation compared to the other schools	4.11	0.968
B3.6. To what extent do you consider that MODEL schools contribute to the support of innovation and excellence by creating groups	4.39	0.856
B3.7. To what extent do you consider that MODEL schools contribute to the ensurement of public and free high quality education for all	4.32	0.994
B3.8. To what extent do you consider that MODEL schools contribute to the comprehensive development of the students	4.08	1
B3.9. To what extent do you consider that MODEL schools contribute to the support of the students' creativity, by creating groups	4.29	0.904
B3.10. To what extent do you consider that MODEL schools contribute to the support of innovation and excellence by creating groups	4.38	0.864

the sample agree slightly, 14.6% indicates moderate agreement, 15.4% of the sample indicates significant agreement, while 26.3% of the sample strongly agrees with the separation. As shown in the bar graph, it appears that the sample is symmetrically placed around the moderate value.

B4. To what extent do you consider that the Model Experimental Schools should be declassified into Standards and Experimental Schools?

EXPERIMENTAL SCHOOLS OF GREECE 359

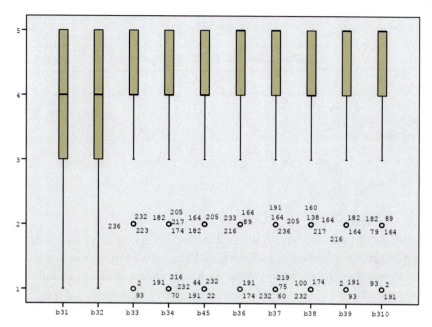

FIGURE 16.2 Box plot of B3 responses

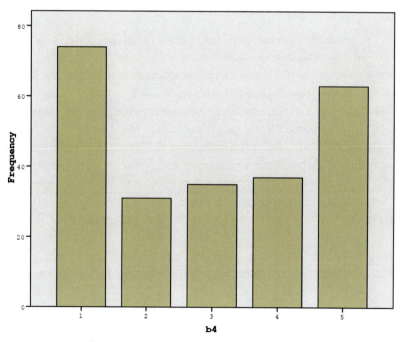

FIGURE 16.3 Bar chart of relative frequencies of parental responses

TABLE 16.3   Frequencies of parents' views on school segregation

		Not at all	Slightly	Moderately	Considerably	Extremely	Total
A4. Type of school your child attends	Experimental	28	11	13	4	14	70
	Model	46	20	22	33	49	170
Total		74	31	35	37	63	240

3.3.4   Parents' View on Teachers' Evaluation

Regarding the parents' view on the evaluation of teachers, the table with the mean values, the standard deviations and the cogram of the answers is given. It turns out that all the mean values are higher than 4, that is, not only the parents consider the evaluation of the teachers very important, but they consider it quite important. In addition, it seems that all mean values are in a very narrow range between 4.42 and 4.76, which means that all aspects are considered important by parents. Finally, it is important for parents to evaluate the personality of teachers.

3.3.5   Parents' View on the Selection of Students in the Model Schools after Examinations or Skills Test

B.6. To what extent do you consider the selection of students in the Model schools correct after examinations or skills test?

Continuing with the corresponding question concerning the degree of agreement of the parents on whether the selection of students in the Model schools should be made after examinations or skills tests, it is observed that 5% disagree, 1% slightly disagree, 7.9% moderately disagree, 16% considerably agree, 69.2% extremely agree. In total, about 87% considerably or extremely agree. This marks a universal agreement on the claim that the selection of students in the Model schools should be made after examinations or a test of skills.

3.3.6   The Parents' View on the Selection of Students in Experimental Schools after a Draw

B.6. To what extent do you consider that the selection of students in the Experimental schools is correct after a draw?

Regarding the view of parents in relation to question B6, ie the degree to which parents consider as correct the selection of students in experimental

TABLE 16.4   Mean values and standard deviations of parents' responses

Questions	Mean values	Standard deviations
B10.1. To what extent do you consider the evaluation of teachers in the Model and Experimental schools regarding the evaluation of studies important	4.52	0.696
B10.2. To what extent do you consider the evaluation of teachers in Model and Experimental schools regarding the evaluation of teaching experience important	4.6	0.658
B10.3. To what extent do you consider the evaluation of teachers in Model and Experimental schools regarding the evaluation of academic and other qualifications important	4.43	0.789
B10.4. To what extent do you consider the evaluation of teachers in Model and Experimental schools regarding the evaluation of professional development programmes important	4.47	0.786
B10.5. To what extent do you consider the evaluation of teachers in Model and Experimental schools regarding the evaluation of participation in pedagogical training activities important	4.58	0.727
B10.6. To what extent do you consider the evaluation of teachers in Model and Experimental schools regarding the evaluation of didactic and pedagogical competence important	4.72	0.608
B10.7. To what extent do you consider the evaluation of teachers in the Model and Experimental schools regarding the evaluation and development of innovative educational actions important	4.65	0.727
B10.8. To what extent do you consider the evaluation of teachers in Model and Experimental schools regarding the evaluation of their personality important	4.76	0.632

schools after a draw, it turns out that 31.7% do not agree at all with the methodology of the draw, 9.2% slightly agree, 18.3% moderately agree, 12.9% agree and 27.9% strongly agree with the draw. In total, about 40% considerably or extremely agree and also about 40% do not agree at all or slightly agree, ie there is also a symmetry and a balance between the positive and negative answers around the issue of the draw.

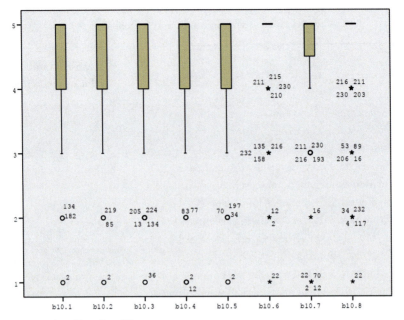

FIGURE 16.4   Box plot of B10 responses

TABLE 16.5   Distribution of frequencies and relevant frequencies of parents' responses

	Frequency	Percentage
Not at all	12	5
Slightly	4	1.7
Moderately	19	7.9
Considerably	39	16.3
Extremely	166	69.2
Total	240	100

The observed significance level of control has a value of 0.002 (dispersions unequal). Therefore, at a significance level of 5% the degree of satisfaction differs. Parents' satisfaction about the model school is higher than the satisfaction about the experimental schools.

4   Conclusions

The research shows that both the experimental and the model schools are evaluated positively. One in four parents in experimental schools do not have

TABLE 16.6   Distribution of frequencies and relevant frequencies of parents' responses

	Frequency	Percentage
Not at all	76	31.7
Slightly	22	9.2
Moderately	44	18.3
Considerably	31	12.9
Extremely	67	27.9
Total	240	100

a positive view of their operation. All the parents of the model schools have a positive view of the operation of their school. The degree of parental satisfaction with the Model schools is significantly higher than the degree of satisfaction of the Experimental schools.

Regarding the separation of the model schools from the experimental schools, the parents of the experimental schools are evenly divided between agreement and disagreement on the separation of the two types of schools. On the contrary, the parents of the experimental schools strongly agree with the separation of the two types of schools.

All parents strongly agree with the admission of students to the Model schools through the examination process. In contrast, regarding the admission of students by draw to the experimental schools, the parents are divided between agreement and disagreement.

Regarding the evaluation of teachers of both types of schools, parents strongly agree with the expediency of evaluation in all dimensions. However, the most important dimensions are the evaluation of the cognitive and didactic competence and the personality of the teachers.

Overall, the project of the model and experimental schools is evaluated as very positive, differences are identified in the impact of these schools on the parents and points for further improvement are highlighted. Therefore, both need to continue, points of improvement are identified and the need for further increase of school units is documented.

In a modern assessment system it would be good to propose the learning motivations of the children as the latter are the main protagonists of the pedagogical process. In addition, there is an insurmountable need to emphasise the individualisation of assessment and the avoidance of standard comparison procedures between children. In this way, the "learning identity" of each child will be highlighted, taking into account his individual way and pace of learning, the stage of his language development, but also the opportunities offered by his socio-economic environment (Papageorgiou, 2017).

We recognise at the same time the importance of proper and complete evaluation both for the organisation of society and the efficiency of the educational system and for the personal development and success of the child in all areas. At this point it would be good to refer to Neil's anti-authoritarian education, since some of its basic characteristics could, with the appropriate adaptation to the Greek reality, be integrated into the current educational system in general and in the way of evaluation in particular.

Metacognitive awareness is the basis of learning and requires a variety of skills such as: the person's reflection on what he knows, continuous assessment of his knowledge, identification of the nature of a problem and its analysis in the structural elements for devising an action plan in order to solve it. Finally it involves implementation of this plan, corrective interventions and final evaluation of the result of the organised intervention.

Therefore the learning that takes place under the control of the student is a consequence of cognition and motivation for learning. Therefore, students who self-regulate and become autonomous cognitively have a good knowledge of the subjects, the appropriate strategies to choose which one to apply each time, high educational goals, good self-assessment, active role in workgroups, high self-efficacy and self-confidence and can set realistic goals and act on their own to achieve them (Papageorgiou, 2017).

References

Antoniou, G. (2014). *Model experimental schools. Responding to today's challenges, tracing tomorrow's prospects*. Steering Committee of Model Experimental Schools.

Association of Secondary Education Officers of the Model Schools. (2015). *Experimental schools as a tool for upgrading public education. The experimental schools: The institutional framework and their role in the educational system*. http://docplayer.gr/3178951-Ta-peiramatika-sholeia-os-ergaleio-anavathmisis-tis-dimosias-ekpaideysis-ds-elme-protypn-papatsimpa-l-roympea-g.html on 5-6-2016

Australian Institute for Teaching and School Leadership. (2018). *Leading for impact: Australian guidelines for school leadership development*. AITSL, Melbourne.

Barkatsas, A., & Hunting, R. (1996). A review of recent research on cognitive, metacognitive and affective aspects of problem solving. *Nordic Studies in Mathematics Education, 4*(4), 7–30.

Barkatsas, A. (2019). *Theoretical approaches and the educational evaluation system of Australia in Greek educational evaluation company.* http://www.eletea.gr/wp-content/uploads/2019/09/EEEA-2019-2.pdf

Bird, J. J., Wang, C., Watson, J. R., & Murray, L. (2009). Relationships among principal authentic leadership and teacher trust and engagement levels. *Journal of School Leadership, 19*(2), 153–171. doi:10.1177/105268460901900202

Bouras, A. (2005). *Evaluation and mathematics in primary education.* PHD, Athens.

Cros, F. (2018). Les innovations pédagogiques et leur évaluation. In M. Kassotakis (Ed.), *Educational evaluation: Current trends & perspectives, 2nd Scientific Conference* (pp. 85–93). Hellenic Society for Educational Evaluation. http://www.eletea.gr/wp-content/uploads/2019/12/PRAKTIKA_TOMOS_2_TELIKO.pdf

Derrington, M. L., & Campell, J. W. (2018). High stakes teacher evaluation policy: US principals perspectives and variations in practice. *Journal Teachers and Teaching, Theory and Practice, 24,* 246–262.

Kassotakis, M. (2006). The experimental school of the University of Athens, the past, the present and the future. *Chronicles of the Experimental School of the University of Thessaloniki.*

Kassotakis, M. (2010). The role of the experimental schools of the universities in the modern era. In *The proceedings of conference of the Association of Secondary Education Officers of the Model Schools. The role and operation of the experimental schools in public education* (pp. 117–131). Ellinoekdotiki.

Kernis, M. H., & Goldman, B. M. (2006). A multicomponent conceptualization of authenticity: Theory and research. In M. P. Zanna (Ed.), *Advances in experimental social psychology* (Vol. 38, pp. 283—357). Academic Press. https://doi.org/10.1016/S0065-2601(06)38006-9

Mena, J., García, M., Clarke A., & Barkatsas, A. (2016). An analysis of three different approaches to student teacher mentoring and their impact on knowledge generation in practicum settings. *European Journal of Teacher Education, 39*(1), 53–76. doi:10.1080/02619768.2015.1011269

Papadopoulou, A. (2018). *The views of the teachers of the model experimental schools of the secondary education regarding their evaluation* [Doctoral thesis]. Department of Philosophy, Pedagogy and Psychology, National and Kapodistrian University of Athens

Papadopoulou, A. (2020). The model and experimental schools in Greece: A short chronicle. *Journal Themes of Educational History, Hellenic Society of Educational Historians.*

Papageorgiou, K. (2017, November). *Alternative evaluation proposals for primary education.* Paper presented at 9th International Conference in Open & Distance Learning.

Pierce, R., Stacey, K., & Barkatsas, A. (2007). A scale for monitoring students attitudes to learning mathematics with technology. *Computers & Education, 48,* 285–300.

Scriven, M. (2003). Evaluation theory and metatheory. In *International handbook of educational evaluation* (pp. 15–30). Kluwer Academic.

Scriven, M. (2012). The logic of valuing. In G. Julnes (Ed.), *Promoting valuation in the public interest: Informing policies for judging value in evaluation* (pp. 17–28).

Zouganeli, A., Kafetzopoulos, K., Sofou, E., & Tsafos, V. (2009). Evaluation of the educational work and the teachers. In Quality in Education (Ed.), *Research for the evaluation of qualitative characteristics of the primary and secondary education system*. Athens.

CHAPTER 17

Authentic Evaluation and Authentic Leadership in Education

Two Converging Concepts in the Case of School Principals

Chrysoula Arcoudis, Anastasia Papadopoulou and Athina Chalkiadaki

Abstract

Effective leadership skills of school principals are synonymous with quality of teaching and learning in schools. This has been an accepted concept in most educational outcomes research. In many countries around the world, performance evaluation of school principals as leaders forms an intricate component of ongoing school evaluation and improvement strategies. Although it is generally agreed that documenting and improving the quality and effectiveness of school principal leadership in an authentic setting should be central to any evaluation process, very little has been said and done regarding the use of authentic evaluation tools. In an increasingly demanding value-based society, school principals are faced with decisions of ethics and morality, in an authentic setting, especially as they relate to deciding what is right, what is important and what is a priority. There is continued pressure within new global workplace "realities" for authentic leadership.

This chapter will explore the paradigm of authentic assessment and evaluation in authentic leadership with regards to school principals.

Keywords

authentic evaluation – authentic leadership – education – school principals

1   Introduction

Schools, as gateways to authentic learning[1] expose students to real-world issues, problems, and applications and provide the opportunity to internalise a style of critical knowledge consumption in what Mayo (2010) defines as a Socratic Teaching Method approach, teaching towards an understanding of the world that is shaped by knowledge and morality. Students who are authentically engaged take responsibility for their own learning and are able to explore, discuss and meaningfully construct concepts and relationships in contexts that involve real-world problems that are relevant to the learner and their world (Donovan, Bransford, & Pellegrino, 1999).

School principals as leaders, play a critical role in school educational success. The push however for more autonomous school decision making, has meant that school leaders need to have more than just instructional leadership skills (OECD 2019a). Leadership in schools requires a sincere type of leadership and a hopeful, open, visionary and creative response to changing social situations.

Copeland (2016) describes the push for emerging theories of authentic and ethical leadership due largely in response to the tumultuous ethical leadership failures observed in the early 21st century, an era tainted by corporate meltdowns, worldwide terrorism, political upheaval, and international health issues such as the SARS epidemics. Schools, as organisational entities within societies, can only reflect this new surge for effective authentic leadership.

Authentic leadership is considered as one of the positive leadership styles and contributes to the formation of positive organisational culture.

George (2003) describes authentic leaders as genuine, moral and character-based leaders and often demonstrate five qualities such as, understanding their purpose; practicing solid values; leading with heart; establishing connected relationships and demonstrating self-discipline. They are usually "people of the highest integrity, committed to building enduring organisations ... who have a deep sense of purpose and are true to their core values and who recognise the importance of their service to society". Begley (2006) proposes three prerequisites to authentic leadership as applicable to school principals, that is, self-knowledge; a capacity for moral reasoning; and sensitivity to the orientations of others. He based these notions on research related to the valuation processes of school principals and their strategic responses to ethical dilemmas. He purports that the achievement of self-knowledge, capacity and sensitivity to others can be best achieved in professional settings including education, through strategies of personal reflective practice, and sustained dialogue on moral issues and the ethical dilemmas of educational practice.

A pivotal question still remains however, after three decades of research in authentic leadership: how can include authentic assessment constructs as part of an ongoing holistic school improvement reform policy?

This chapter examines the notions and parameters of authentic assessment in authentic school leadership. It aims to highlight the relationship between authentic leadership and authentic evaluation by outlining the characteristics of authentic leadership and describing some of the tools, methods and approaches of authentic assessment that could be incorporated in school principal selection and evaluation procedures when designing a policy for authentic leadership in education.

2   Methodology of Approach

A literature review was carried out regarding authentic assessment tools used in authentic leadership and authentic school leadership in order to identify key concepts, assumptions and the scope of tools in school principal evaluations. A critical analysis of the contents was carried out and, in some cases, the main conclusions were presented.

For the purposes of this research, on line research journals related to authentic evaluation, authentic leadership in education and school principal leadership were used. A literature review was carried out in the following journals: *Hellenic Review of Educational Assessment, Educational Administration Quarterly, Journal of Educational Administration, The Leadership Quarterly, Educational Management Administration & Leadership, European Journal of Teacher Education.*

3   The Notion of Authenticity

Authenticity has its roots in ancient Greek philosophy and is directly linked to the famous inscription "Γνῶθι Σαυτόν" (Knowing one's self) written above the main entrance of the Oracle of Delphi where by enticing those who passed through the gate to give thought to the discovery of who they really are and not who they think they are, that is to say, to gain self-awareness, an important state of being.

Authenticity comes from the ancient Greek word αὐθέντης, which means the absolute lord, the one who has universal power as reflected in the concept of being a master of their own situation – being in control of their own destiny (Liddell & Scott, 1996).

An early reference to authentic functioning is Socrates' focus on self-inquiry as he argued that an "unexamined" life is not worth living (Platon, Apology of Socrates 38a 1-6). Socrates (c470 BC–399 BC) sought a kind of moral and cognitive self-awareness, in the sense that, to know what one is doing and to be conscious of what one is doing to the point where knowledge of abilities, character and personality can be reached. The individual must know what he/she is doing, because knowledge gives value in practice, leading the individual to virtue, since virtue is knowledge.

Aristotle (c384–322 BC) set out virtues as personal characteristics that inform right judgement and decision-making. He argues that each true virtue discerns the right path by highlighting extremes to be avoided on either side. Virtues such as courage, temperance, generosity, greatness of soul, friendliness, trustfulness, wit, justice and friendship lend themselves to authenticity.

In its modern day application and according to Gardner et al. (2011, p. 1121), the concept of authenticity is defined by four components:(1) awareness (i.e. knowledge and confidence in thoughts, emotions, motivations and values), (2) impartial processing (i.e., objectivity and acceptance of one's positive and negative characteristics), (3) behaviour (i.e. the person acts on the basis of his true preferences, values and needs and not just to please others, or to ensure rewards or avoid punishments) and (4) orientation in relationships (i.e., achieving and assessing honesty and openness in one's close relationships (Kernis & Goldman, 2006) argue that people discover and construct a basic sense of themselves through four basic processes: (1) authentic function, (2) self-awareness, (3) openness (acceptance) for objective recognition of their reality and (4) actions and orientation towards interpersonal relationships.

4   Authentic Leadership

The concept of authenticity was used in leadership research for the first time by Avolio and Gibbons (1988) as mentioned in Bass and Steidlmeier (1999), who recognised the importance of transformative leadership.[2] This marked the movement from the notion of the construct of personal authenticity, as developed by the ancient Greek philosophers, to a theory of authentic leadership in organisational constructs. It is a type of leadership that promotes ethical and honest behaviour for long-term organisational outcomes. Ladkin and Taylor (2010) link authentic leadership to moral leadership. This explains why moral and ethics theories (Kegan, 1982), values (Schwartz, 1992) and leadership (Fry, 2003, 2005) have had a significant impact on the development of decision-making process. Luthans and Avolio (2003) defined authentic leadership as the process that draws on both psychological abilities and highly developed organisational contexts and leads to both high self-awareness and self-regulating positive behaviours, both in terms of the leading oneself and others and promoting self-improvement. Hence, authentic leaders are characterised as optimistic, resilient, ethical, transparent, confident and those who prioritise leadership and development. The authentic leader does not try to enforce his/her values on others, but rather, their own authentic values and actions act as a model for those that follow them. As May, Chan, Hodges, and Avolio (2003) indicated, authentic leaders show the moral ability to judge dilemmas from different perspectives and are able to take into account the different needs of stakeholders, with whom they interact.

Within the field of education, Begley (2001, 2006) and Bhindi and Duignan (1997), define authentic leadership as being composed of four components: authenticity, intentionality, spirituality, and sensibility. Begley (2001) further equates authentic leadership with effective and ethical leadership in the context of educational administration. He argues that "authentic leadership implies a genuine kind of leadership — a hopeful, open-ended, visionary and creative response to circumstances" (p. 354). He encompasses the notion of hopefulness (Luthans & Avolio, 2003) and self-knowledge (Begley, 2004), a quality central to most conceptions of authenticity (Kernis & Goldman, 2006) and authentic leadership (Gardner, Avolio, Luthans et al., 2005; George, 2003; Ilies et al., 2005; Ladkin & Taylor, 2010; Luthans & Avolio, 2003; Shamir & Eilam, 2005).

5 From Authentic Leadership to Authentic Evaluation Processes, Methods and Tools

Based on the characteristics of an authentic leaders in educational settings, it is perceived that the authentic leader differs from a traditional education executive. Therefore, the recognition and selection of those skills and competences, such as optimism, self-awareness, orientation of the collective good, self-awareness, ethical and moral decision making and responsibility, cannot be measured in a 'traditional way' of school principal evaluation.

It is therefore necessary to investigate the methods, tools and procedures of authentic evaluation and connect these to authentic school leaders.

6 Authentic Leadership Measurement

An essential facet within the theory development of authentic leadership is the construct of the validity measurements used by researchers such as Henderson and Hoy (1983), Jensen and Luthans (2006), George (2003), (Kernis & Goldman, 2006) and many more. Each quantitative empirical study on authentic leadership used a measurement tool for their conceptual definitions. Henderson and

Hoy (1983) for example used a Leader Authenticity Scale (LAS), Bass and Avolio (1993) developed a Multifactor Leadership Questionnaire (MLQ), Eigel and Kuhnert (2005) used semi-structured interview defining Leadership Development Levels (LDL). One of the most frequently used measurement tool is the one developed by Walumbwa et al. (2008) a 16 items questionnaire consisting of 4 subscales: (1) self-awareness (4 items), (2) relational transparency (5 items), (3) internalised moral perspective (4 items), and (4) balanced processing (3 items)) summed to form composite Authentic Leadership Score (ALQ).

Walumbwa et al. (2008) used the conceptual approaches of researchers such as Avolio and Gardner (2005), Ilies et al. (2005) and Gardner et al. (2005). Walumbwa et al. (2008) defined authentic leadership "as the archetype of authentic behaviour that builds and promotes both positive psychological abilities and a positive moral climate to develop a higher self-awareness, internal moral perspective, balanced information processing and transparency of relationships in leader-follower cooperation, thus leading to positive self-development".

The ALQ self-assessment questionnaire identifies different dimensions of authentic leadership such as self-awareness. That is, awareness of the world and of its effect on others; relationship transparency, as the manifestation of behaviours that promote trust; balanced treatment, the objective analysis before decision making and internal moral perspective, the internal, structured form of self-regulation. Through a score range, an individual can compare stronger and weaker components with regards to overall authentic leadership score. This self-regulation is driven by internal rules and values in the face of organisational and social pressures, resulting in decision-making and the manifestation of behaviours is consistent with these internal values of the individual.

The ALQ has been a tool used in a number of authentic leadership research studies in education: Shapira-Lishchinsky and Tsemach (2014), Pavlovic (2015), Feng (2016), Fraser (2014), Alazmi and Al-Mahdy (2020). Most of these later studies have to do with the relationship between principals' authentic leadership skills, school effectiveness and teacher efficacy.

7   Authentic Leadership and Measurement in Education

The concept of authentic leadership in educational settings is relatively new, although some earlier research has been noted in authentic behaviour of the school leader, the trust and commitment of teachers in school, their work performance, the school climate and the results of learning (Begley, 2001; Bird,

Wang, Watson, & Murray, 2009; Wang & Bird, 2011; Begley & Stefkovich, 2007; Starratt, 2007; Shapira-Lishchinsky & Tsemach, 2014). With the change towards more autonomous schools and the role of school principals taking on a greater accountability and ethical organisational significance, there has been a shift of interest towards authentic leadership in school leadership.

Effective principal leadership practices improve school organisation, teaching, and student achievement outcomes. These practices include framing and communicating a school's goals and mission, creating shared expectations of high performance, clarifying roles and objectives, and promoting professional development (Day, Gu, & Sammons, 2016; McCarley, Peters, & Decman, 2016; Gurley et al., 2016). The quality of principal leadership is the second-most influential school-based effect on student achievement, after classroom instruction (McCarley, Peters, & Decman, 2016).

The positive impact of effective school leaders on teachers' job satisfaction and school efficacy as regards to student outcomes (Bogler, 2001; Dipaola & Tschannen-Moran, 2001; Bird, 2009) and "for professionally effective, ethically sound, and consciously reflective practices in educational administration" (Begly, 2003), has been well researched and documented. This is due to the fact that decision-making and problem solving are pervasive in the school's management and involve multiple stakeholders such as teachers, students, collaboration with parents and the school's social and community environment.

This is also reflected in research where effective School Principal leadership is related to school efficacy (Andrews & Soder, 1987; Kythreotis, Pashiardis & Kyriakides, 2010) with regards to transformational, managerial and behaviour management skills (Richter, Lewis, & Hagar, 2012). The assumption here is that principals who are able to identify and sustain a vision of the school have conceptual skills and are able to intellectually stimulate other members of the school. This can only be done by individuals who know the educational processes of a school by using a combination of the technical and interpersonal skills; and individual consideration for others and the interpersonal or human skill (Ross & Gray 2006). Hence, authentic leadership in education acts as a chain reaction, with the effects reaching teachers through the school principal's relationship with the school staff, students through their relationship with teachers and to parents/guardians of students through wider relationships, ultimately creating a favorable school climate of personal development and learning.

The need to develop and include authentic constructs that are contextualised and closely linked to new authentic challenges in school leadership has been increasingly recognised in educational policies and practices internationally (OECD, 2013), where school leadership activities ranked third out of 29 activities in OECD countries (OECD, 2008). Advanced leadership skills and standard indicators have become a vital component of new Principal professional development programmes supporting Avolio's (2010) research "that leaders were more made than born" (p. 736). In turn, these standards are reflected in assessment and performance measurement practices for school principals' selection and appraisal.

8 Authentic Leadership Measurement in School Leadership Policies

This new language in performance measurement and standards setting is reflected in many school leadership policies as evidenced in Australia (AITSL, 2019a), the USA (AIR, 2012; Wallace Foundation, 2009) and New Zealand (KIWI Leadership for Principals, 2008; New Zealand Council for Educational Research, 2019). Currently, although the indicators and measurement tools in principal selection approaches focus mostly on instructional leadership and management skills assessment, there are elements of authentic leadership competencies. The key emphasis is on standards setting (Educational Leadership Policy Standards: ISLLC 2008; Leading for impact: Australian guidelines for school leadership development, 2019a) and they include notions of vision, values, knowledge, understanding and personal qualities within the School Principal leadership requirements. These standards and profiles of effective leaders can be used by school principals as leadership guides and can help the school community and those on interview panels understand the role of the principal in authentic settings and therefore design position descriptions, selection questions and interview exercises for leadership recruitment processes.

The Australian Institute for Teaching and School Leadership (AITSL) develops policies and resources and defines and maintains national standards for teachers and principals. The Leadership Profiles are presented as a set of leadership actions that effective principals implement as they progress to higher levels of proficiency. Principals and aspiring principals can use the Profiles to help them grow and develop as school leaders. The implementation of these reforms is left at the State level.

In 2017, the New South Wales Government of Australia (NSW) released a School Leadership Strategy in support of school leadership. From this, a Merit Selection procedure for principals in NSW public schools was developed which outlined the procedures and indicated six general selection criteria deemed essential for all principal positions in schools. These include skills to lead and manage a complex public school focused on the delivery of high-quality education; ability to lead and manage rigorous and inclusive whole school teaching and learning programmes and high level communication and interpersonal skills with the capacity to build positive relationships and engage all levels of the school and educational community.

The Merit Selection procedures of Principals in Victoria on the other hand, were designed to help make the most accurate match between the requirements of a school principal position and the skills of an applicant. Set criteria against the Standards such as strategic thinking, vision, action with shared values, focus on achievement and collective capacity, form the bases of the selection process which can be assessed through optional selection tools. It makes reference to capabilities in both instructional and human leadership. The Bastow Institute of Educational Leadership (Bastow) in cooperation with the Victorian Government and the Victorian Curriculum and Assessment Authority, provides transformative professional learning for educational leaders, teachers.

The Quality School Leadership (QSL) programme developed by the American Institute for Research (2012) goes further and defines a range of tools available for committees for the selection of School Principals. It based this practice on the assumption that "assessments are considered valid when they measure what they are intended to measure" and hence identified two fields of assessment with regards to school leader performance: content validity and construct validity. As an example of the content: "An education leader promotes the success of every student by acting with integrity, fairness, and in an ethical manner" (Council of Chief State School Officers, 2008, p. 15). The construct validity can include a multiple test for collecting evidence needed to determine the degree to which the standard is met. In this case, testing for construct validity would determine how well items and observations measure principals' abilities to act with integrity, fairness, and in an ethical manner. The QSL identified 20 possible school principal performance assessment measures, among them: the Diagnostic Assessment of School and Principal Effectiveness (Ebmeier, 1991, 1992),[3] Instructional Activity Questionnaire (Larsen, 1987),[4] Leadership Practices Inventory (Kouzes & Posner, 2003),[5] Principal Instructional Management Rating Scale (Hallinger & Murphy, 1985)[6] and Principal Profile Tool (Leithwood & Montgomery, 1986; Leadwood, 1987),[7] amongst the list, most of which were developed 20–30 years ago. Other measurements include self-assessment questionnaires or rubrics that provide an aggregate score and help principals to self-assess while some others include intensive 360-degree surveys from multiple constituents to create an aggregate profile, which can provide comparative information based on multiple perspectives to principals about their performance.

The Vanderbilt Assessment of Leadership in Education (VAL-ED) developed by developed at Vanderbilt University with Wallace Foundation support is an evaluation tool that could be integrated into school improvement systems. The VAL-ED is a paper and on-line assessment which utilises a multi-rater, evidence based approach to measure the effectiveness of school leadership behaviours known to influence teacher performance and student learning. It is a "360 degree" assessment, where teachers, the principal, and the principal's supervisor respond to a behaviour inventory. The instrument consists of 72 items that comprise six core component subscales and six process subscales. There are two parallel forms of the assessment to facilitate measuring growth over time. For each item, the respondent rates the effectiveness of a principal's behaviour on a five-point scale after having first indicated the sources of evidence on which the effectiveness is rated. The School Principal does not need to have performed the leadership behaviour directly but must have ensured that the behaviour was done by others. The reference period is the current school year. The instrument is constructed to have the following eight features: (a) work well in a variety of settings and circumstances, (b) be construct valid, (c) be reliable, (d) be unbiased, (e) provide accurate and useful reporting of results, (f) yield diagnostic profiles for formative purposes, (g) be used to measure progress over time in the development of leadership and (h) predict important outcomes. At each stage of the design and 25 development process, the properties of the instrument are investigated through empirical study and expert review. The process is guided by design imperatives based on the Standards for Educational and Psychological Testing (American Educational Research Association) and best test development practices (Murphy et al., 2021).

A different policy approach regarding school leadership standards was recently noted in the release of the "Navigating the Educational Moral Maze" by the Ethical Leadership Commission of the United Kingdom (2019). The commission was set up in 2017 by the Association of School and College Leaders to help school and college leaders consider the ethical foundation of their work, and to offer guidance for leaders at a time of great change and unprecedented pressure. The report contains a Framework for Ethical Leadership that resonates closely with the notion of authentic leadership. It defines the ethical standards regarding selflessness, integrity, objectivity, accountability, openness, honesty, trust, wisdom, justice, courage, service and optimism. It is designed to tackle the concerns around a lack of guiding principles for ethical leadership in education by embedding the Framework in leadership practice in education through strategic leadership (vision, ethos, strategy); accountability (standards and financial performance); people skills, compliance and evaluation. The Report makes recommendations to the National Professional

Qualification for Executive Leadership to incorporate the Framework into their standards so that prospective school leaders are provided with the opportunity to demonstrate that they are able to reflect on abstract concepts and make independent ethical decisions based on good practice.

The question remains whether measurement tools can tap into the currently changing ethical leadership requirements of school principals, taking into consideration the need for authenticity, accountability and precision decision making often needed in socially and morally complex situations. Goldring et al. (2009) suggest that many principal performance assessments to date seem inadequate to measure the complexity of the relationship of the principal to the school community as indicated in the weakness of research on school leadership evaluation. In their analysis of school principal assessment instruments, they conclude that more attention is given to school management and instruction than to the categories of leadership qualities, and to the school's authentic community environment. This is particularly important when one considers that autonomous schools need to work closely with and within a local community context.

An authentic leadership approach to school Principal leadership assessment can be an integral part of a standards-based accountability system and school improvement. When designed appropriately, executed proactively, and implemented properly, authentic principal leadership assessment can inform and can further enhance leadership quality and improve organisational performance at all levels. Millikan (2010) maintains that effective educational leadership in schools is authentic by nature as the school is embedded in an authentic context and teaching is a highly specialised profession which demands an ethical commitment which is significantly greater than any other profession. Hence, according to Millikan, fundamental elements of educational leadership are per se authentic educational leadership.

So, what are the paradigms of authentic assessment and measurements that can be incorporated in authentic school leadership evaluation policies?

According to Wiggins (1989a, p. 703), authentic assessment is "a true test" of intellectual achievement or ability because it requires learners to demonstrate their deep understanding, higher-order thinking, and complex problem solving through the performance of exemplary tasks. Authentic tasks replicate real-world challenges and "standards of performance" that experts or professionals typically face in the field (Wiggins, 1989a, p. 703). Authentic assessment is situated in real-life experiences or scenarios, is based on multiple forms of measurement, includes observation and documentation over a period of time and in multiple contexts, it includes opportunities for self-assessment and revision and has a clear goal to inform practice. Authentic assessment should be rooted in authentic achievement to ensure a close alignment between assessment and outcome.

Through authentic assessment, the individual has the opportunity to know their skills levels, which are developed within a context of authenticity, in the sense of applicability to real situations but also to internalisation of critical knowledge consumption, Wiggins (1993) and (Varsamidou, 2012, p.28). Self-assessment is an integral part of the authentic evaluation process (Wiggins, 1998a, 1998b; Varsamidou, 2012). The notion of authentic assessment has been used in educational and school reform and according to Gulikers et al. (2004) it is also appropriate for use with assessments in professional and training contexts. However, there is little in the way of measurement tools other than 'best authentic self' and 'case scenario' narratives, in assessment of authentic leadership identity and competencies from the perspective of the leader (Wiewiora & Kowalkiewicz, 2019).

When considering authentic leadership theory, it is important that there is a clear trajectory into practice. The extent to which authentic assessment practices can be incorporated in authentic leadership educational policies depends on the extent of the openness and decentralisation of the education system and to the scope of the autonomy of the school as an organisational and learning unit.

9 Conclusions and Recommendations

As recent educational reform policies have pushed towards more autonomous schools, the role of school principals has taken on greater significance as effective authentic leaders in changing learning organisations. Authentic leadership lends itself to a type of positive leadership "that is knowledge based, values informed ... as it influences on the actions of individuals and on administrative practice" (Begley, 2001). The changing school morphology requires not only effective administrative leaders but also ethical and moral leaders.

To what extent authentic leadership perspectives are integrated into leadership policies for school principals depends highly on the extent of the autonomy of decision-making at the school level. Principal selection seems a crucially important process and the standards and criteria include aspects that lend themselves for more moral and human leadership. The need to develop and include authentic constructs and measurements that are contextualised and closely linked to authentic leadership in schools has been increasingly recognised in educational policies and practices through the developing trends on school principal selection. What needs to be done is further qualitative empirical studies in authentic leadership in schools through authentic assessment measurement for clear and well defined links between and the benefits of authentic leadership and authentic assessment.

Notes

1 In education, *authentic learning* is an instructional approach that allows students to explore, discuss, and meaningfully construct concepts and relationships in contexts that involve real-world problems and projects that are relevant to the learner (Authentic Learning, n.d.).
2 Transformative leadership "begins with the question of justice and democracy; it critiques inequitable practices and offers not only greater individual achievement but of a better life in common with others" (Shields, 2010).
3 This measure to identify the strengths of schools and their leaders so that school improvement plans and principal professional development goals would be better informed. To complete the assessment separate surveys are completed by students, teachers, parents, principals, and principal supervisors. The measures indicate how these groups view themselves, school leadership, and school performance. Multiple measures are completed by multiple groups to identify matches between school leader traits and school characteristics
4 As a performance assessment tool that specifically addresses instructional leadership aspects of principals' work as cited in Heck et al. (1990).
5 Extensively interviewing and surveying leaders, including principals, to identify best leadership practices. Thus, LPI views leadership practices as transferrable across professional types. What works to inspire people in business settings also may work in educational settings. LPI's domains are as follows: (1) modeling the way, (2) inspiring a shared vision, (3) challenging the process, (4) enabling others to act, and encouraging the heart to include real life organisational changes.
6 Hallinger and Murphy (1985) developed the Principal Instructional Management Rating Scale (PIMRS) to determine the degree to which principals serve as instructional managers.
7 The Principal Profile Tool was developed through extensive interview and consultation with principals, teachers, superintendents, and department heads. Two key assumptions inform the tool: (1) student growth should be a benchmark for school leader effectiveness and a factor in performance evaluation and (2) school leader effectiveness is marked by consistency of actions, in that principals need a well-defined set of purposes and the skill and knowledge to achieve them on a consistent basis.

References

Alazmi, A. A., & Al-Mahdy, Y. F. H. (2020). Principal authentic leadership and teacher engagement in Kuwait's educational reform context. *Educational Management Administration & Leadership*. doi:10.1177/1741143220957339

American Institutes for Research. (2012). *Measuring principal performance. How rigorous are commonly used principal performance assessment instruments.*

Andrews, R. L., & Soder, R. (1987). Principal leadership and student achievement. *Educational Leadership, 44*(6), 9–11.

Australian Institute for Teaching and School Leadership (AITSL). (2018). *Australian charter for the professional learning of teachers and school leaders.* australian-charter-for-the-professional-learning-of-teachers-and-school-leaders.pdf

Australian Institute for Teaching and School Leadership (AITSL). (2019a). *Leading for impact: Australian guidelines for school leadership development.* leading-for-impact.pdf

Australian Institute for Teaching and School Leadership (AITSL). (2019b). *Australian professional standard for principals and leadership profiles.* australian-professional-standard-for-principals-and-the-leadership-profiles-(web).pdf

Australian Institute for Teaching and School Leadership (AITSL). (n.d.). *Interactive profiles.* aitsl.edu.au

Authentic Learning. (n.d.). *The glossary of education reform.* http://edglossary.org/authentic-learning

Authority for Quality Assurance in Primary and Secondary Education of Greece (A.DI.P.P.D.E). (2020). *The selection of training executives from 1982 until today: The institutional framework and cases of its implementation.* Report. [in Greek]

Avolio, B. J., & Gardner, W. L. (2005). Authentic leadership development: Getting to the root of positive forms of leadership. *The Leadership Quarterly, 16,* 315–338.

Avolio, B. J., & Gibbons, T. C. (1988). Developing transformational leaders: A life span approach. In J. A. Conger, R. N. Kanungo, & Associates (Eds.), *Charismatic leadership: The elusive factor in organizational effectiveness* (pp. 276–308). Jossey-Bass.

Barkatsas, A. (2019). *Theoretical approaches and the educational evaluation system of Australia in Greek educational evaluation company.* http://www.eletea.gr/wp-content/uploads/2019/09/EEEA-2019-2.pdf

Bass, B. M., Avolio, B.J., Jung, D. I., & Berson, Y. (2003). Predicting unit performance by assessing transformational and transactional leadership. *Journal of Applied Psychology, 88,* 207–218.

Bass, B. M., & Steidlmeier, P. (1999). Ethics, character, and authentic transformational leadership behavior. *Leadership Quarterly, 10,* 181–217.

Begley, P. T. (2001). In pursuit of authentic school leadership practices. *International Journal of Leadership in Education, 4,* 353–365. https://doi.org/10.1080/13603120110078043

Begley P. T. (2003). In pursuit of authentic school leadership practices. In P. T. Begley & O. Johansson (Eds.), *The ethical dimensions of school leadership* (Studies in Educational Leadership, Vol 1). Springer. https://doi.org/10.1007/0-306-48203-7_1

Begley, P. (2006). Self-knowledge, capacity and sensitivity: Prerequisites to authentic leadership by school principals. *Journal of Educational Administration, 44,* 570–589. http://dx.doi.org/10.1108/09578230610704792

Begley, P. T., & Johansson, O. (Eds.). (2003). *The ethical dimensions of school leadership*. Kluwer Academic Publishers.

Begley, P. T., & Stefkovich, J. (2004). Introduction: Education, ethics, and the "cult of efficiency": Implications for values and leadership. *Journal of Educational Administration, 42*, 132–136. doi:10.1108/09578230410525568

Begley, P. T., & Stefkovich, J. (2007). Integrating values and ethics into post secondary teaching for leadership development: Principles, concepts, and strategies. *Journal of Educational Administration, 45*(4), 398–412. http://doi.org/10.1108/09578230710762427

Bhindi, N., & Duignan, P. (1997) Leadership for a new century: Authenticity, intentionality, spirituality and sensibility. *Educational Management & Administration, 25*(2), 117–132. doi:10.1177/0263211X97252002

Bird, J. J., Wang, C., Watson, J. R., & Murray, L. (2009). Relationships among principal authentic leadership and teacher trust and engagement levels. *Journal of School Leadership, 19*(2), 153–171. doi:10.1177/105268460901900202

Bird, J. J., Wang, C., Watson, J., & Murray, L. (2012). Teacher and principal perceptions of authentic leadership: Implications for trust, engagement, and intention to return. *Journal of School Leadership, 22*(3), 425–461. doi.org/10.1177/105268461202200302

Bogler, R. (2001). The influence of leadership style on teacher job satisfaction. *Educational Administration Quarterly, 37*(5), 662–683. doi.org/10.1177/00131610121969460

Branson, C. (2007). Effects of structured self-reflection on the development of authentic leadership practices among Queensland Primary School principals. *Educational Management Administration & Leadership, 35*(2), 225–246. doi:10.1177/1741143207075390

Coen, l., Manion L., & Morrison, K. (2007). *Methodology of educational research*. Metaixmio.

Copeland, M. K. (2016). The impact of authentic, ethical, transformational leadership on leader effectiveness. *Journal of Leadership, Accountability and Ethics, 13*(3), 79–97.

Day, C., Gu, Q., & Sammons, P. (2016). The impact of leadership on student outcomes: How successful school leaders use transformational and instructional strategies to make a difference. *Educational Administration Quarterly, 52*(2), 221–258.

DiPaola, M., & Tschannen-Moran, M. (2001). Organizational citizenship behavior in schools and its relationship to school climate. *Journal of School Leadership, 11*(5), 424–447. doi:10.1016/j.leaqua.2011.09.007

Donovan, M. S., Bransford, J. D., & Pellegrino, J. W. (Eds.). (1999). *How people learn: Bridging research and practice*. National Academy Press.

Ebmeier, H. (1991). The development and field test of an instrument for client-based principal formative evaluation. *Journal of Personnel Evaluation in Education, 4*(3), 245–278.

Ebmeier, H. (1992). *Diagnostic assessment of school and principal effectiveness: A reference manual.* KanLEAD Educational Consortium Technical Assistance Center.

Eigel, K. M., & Kuhnert, K. W. (2005). Authentic development: Leadership development level and executive effectiveness. In W. L. Gardner, B. J. Avolio, & F. O. Walumbwa (Eds.), *Authentic leadership theory and practice* (pp. 357–385). Elsevier.

Eurydice. (2013). *Key data on teachers and school leaders in Eurydice report* (pp. 111–116). European Union.

Eurydice. (2015). *Assuring quality in education: Policies and approaches to school evaluation in Europe.* Eurydice Report. European Union.

Fraser, S. (2014). *Authentic leadership in higher education: Influencing the development of future leaders.* Education Doctoral. Paper 187.

Fry, L. W. (2003). Toward a theory of spiritual leadership. *The Leadership Quarterly, 14,* 693–727.

Fry, L. W. (2005). Introduction to the leadership quarterly special issue: Toward a paradigm of spiritual leadership. *The Leadership Quarterly, 16,* 619–622.

George, W. (2003). *Authentic leadership rediscovered. Authentic leadership rediscovered.* HBS Working Knowledge, Harvard Business School. https://hbswk.hbs.edu/item/authentic-leadership-rediscovered

Goldring, E., Cravens, X., Murphy, J., Porter, A., Elliott, S., & Carson, B. (2009). The evaluation of principals: What and how do states and urban districts assess leadership? *The Elementary School Journal, 110*(1), 19–39.

Gulikers, J. T., Bastiaens, T. J., & Kirschner, P. A. (2004). A five-dimensional framework for authentic assessment. *Educational Technology Research and Development, 52*(3), 67–86.

Gurley, D. K., Anast-May, L., O'Neal, M., & Dozier, R. (2016). Principal instructional leadership behaviors: Teacher Vs. self-perceptions. *NCPEA International Journal of Educational Leadership Preparation, 11*(1).

Hallinger, P., & Murphy, J. (1985). Assessing the instructional management behavior of principals. *The Elementary School Journal, 86*(2), 217–247. http://www.jstor.org/stable/1001205 10.1177/0013161X96032001002

Hannah, S. T., Walumbwa, F. O., & Fry, L. W. (2011). Leadership in action teams: Team leader and members' authenticity, authenticity strength and team outcomes. *Personnel Psychology, 64,* 771–802. doi:10.1111/j.1744-6570.2011.01225.x

Hargreaves, A., & Fullan, M. (2012). *Professional capital: Transforming teaching in every school.* Teachers College Press.

Heck, R. H., Larsen, T. J., & Marcoulides, G. A. (1990). Instructional leadership and school achievement: Validation of a causal model. *Educational Administration Quarterly, 26*(2), 94–125.

Henderson, J. E., & Hoy, W. K. (1983). Leader authenticity: The development and test of an operational measure. *Educational and Psychological Research, 3*(2), 63–75.

Ilies, R., Morgenson, F. P., & Nahrgang, J. D. (2005). Authentic leadership and eudaemonic well-being: Understanding leader-follower outcomes. *The Leadership Quarterly, 16*(3), 373–394. doi:10.1016/j.leaqua.2005.03.002

Jensen, S. M., & Luthans, F. (2006). Relationship between entrepreneurs' psychological capital and their authentic leadership. *Journal of Managerial Issues, 18*, 254–273.

Kegan, R. (1982). *The evolving self: Problem and process in human development.* Harvard University Press.

Kernis, M. H., & Goldman, B. M. (2006). A multicomponent conceptualization of authenticity: Theory and research. In M. P. Zanna (Ed.), *Advances in experimental social psychology* (Vol. 38, pp. 283–357). Academic Press. https://doi.org/10.1016/S0065-2601(06)38006-9

Kizlik, R. J. (2012). Measurement, assessment, and evaluation in education. Retrieved March 2020, from https://www.adprima.com/measurement.htm

Kouzes, J., & Posner, B. (2003). *Leadership practices inventory: Facilitator's guide.* Pfeiffer.

Kythreotis, A., Pashiardis, P., & Kyriakides, L. (2010). The influence of school leadership styles and culture on students' achievement in Cyprus primary schools. *Journal of Educational Administration, 48*(2), 218–240. http://dx.doi.org/10.1108/09578231011027860

Ladkin, D., & Taylor, S. S. (2010). Enacting the 'true self': Towards a theory of embodied authentic leadership. *The Leadership Quarterly, 21*(1), 64–74. https://doi.org/10.1016/j.leaqua.2009.10.005

Leithwood, K. (1987). Using the principal profile to assess performance. *Educational Leadership, 45*(1), 63–66.

Leithwood, K. A., & Montgomery, D. J. (1986). *Improving principal effectiveness: The principal profile.* OISE Press.

Liddell, H. G., & Scott, R. (1996). *Greek-English Lexicon.* Clarendon Press.

Luthans, F., & Avolio, B. J. (2003). Authentic leadership: A positive developmental approach. In K. S. Cameron, J. E. Dutton, & R. E. Quinn (Eds.), *Positive organizational scholarship* (pp. 241–261). Barrett-Koehler.

May, D. R., Chan, A. Y. I., Hodges, T. D., & Avolio, B. J. (2003). Developing the moral component of authentic leadership. *Organizational Dynamics, 32*, 247–260.

Mayo, J. A. (2010). *Constructing undergraduate psychology curricula: Promoting authentic learning and assessment in the teaching of psychology.* American Psychological Association.

McCarley, T. A., Peters, M. L., & Decman, J. M. (2016). Transformational leadership related to school climate: A multi-level analysis. *Educational Management Administration and Leadership, 44*(2), 322–342.

Mena, J., García, M., Clarke A., & Barkatsas, A. (2016). An analysis of three different approaches to student teacher mentoring and their impact on knowledge generation in practicum settings. *European Journal of Teacher Education, 39*(1), 53–76. doi:10.1080/02619768.2015.1011269

Millikan, R. (2010). *Authentic leadership in schools*. Xlibris.

Murphy, J., Goldring, E., Cravens, X., Elliott, S., & Porter, A. (2021). *The vanderbilt assessment of leadership in education: Measuring learning-centered leadership*. Vanderbilt University.

New Zealand Council for Educational Research. (2019). *Teaching, school and principal practices survey*. New Zealand Ministry of Education. www.nzcer.org.nz/research/teaching-and-school-practices-survey-tool-tsp

New Zealand Ministry of Education. (2008). *KIWI leadership for principals*. Wellington NZ.

NSW Government. (2016). *Merit selection procedure for principals in NSW public schools*. sel_panelproc2.pdf (teach.nsw.edu.au).

OECD. (2004). *Education at a glance: OECD indicators 2004*. OECD Publishing.

OECD. (2008). *Improving school leadership*.

OECD. (2013). *Leadership for 21st century learning*. oecd-ilibrary.org

OECD. (2016). *Education at a glance. OECD indicators Australia*.

OECD. (2018). *Education for a bright future in Greece, reviews of national policies in education*. OECD Publishing.

OECD. (2019a). *Working together to help students achieve their potential*. OECD Publishing.

OEDC. (2019b). Greece. In *Education policy outlook: Working together to help students achieve their potential*. OECD Publishing.

Papadopoulou, A., Chalkiadaki, A., & Kolybari, T. (2021). The democratic profile of the school principal in Greece and the evaluation. In *Proceedings of the 16th conference of the Pedagogical Society of Greece and the University of Thessaly*.

Pavlovic, N. (2015). Authentic leadership in educational institutions. International. *Journal for Quality Research, 9*, 309–322.

Richter, M. M., Lewis, T. J., & Haggar, J. (2012). The relationship between principal leadership skills and school wide positive behavior support: An exploratory study. *Journal of Positive Behavior Interventions, 14*(2), 69–77. http://dx.doi.org/10.1177/1098300711399097

Robinson, V. M. J., Hohepa, M., & Lloyd, C. (2009). *School leadership and student outcomes: Identifying what works and why, best evidence synthesis*. Ministry of Education.

Ross, J. A., & Gray, P. (2006). School leadership and student achievement: The meditating effects of teacher belief. *Canadian Journal of Education, 29*(3), 789–822. http://dx.doi.org/10.2307/20054196

Schwartz, S. (1992). Universals in the content and structures of values: Theoretical advances and empirical tests in 20 countries. *Advances in Experimental Social Psychology, 25*, 1–65.

Shapira-Lishchinsky, O., & Tsemach, S. (2014). Psychological empowerment as a mediator between teachers' perceptions of authentic leadership and their withdrawal and citizenship behaviors. *Educational Administration Quarterly, 50*(4), 675–712.

Shamir, B., & Eilam, G. (2005). "What's your story?" To life-stories approach to authentic leadership development. *The Leadership Quarterly, 16*, 395–417. https://doi.org/10.1016/j.leaqua.2005.03.005

Shields, C. M. (2010). Transformative leadership: Working for equity in diverse contexts. *Educational Administration Quarterly, 46*(4), 558–589. doi:10.1177/0013161X10375609

Starratt, R. J. (2007). Leading a community of learners: Learning to be moral by engaging the morality of learning. *Educational Management Administration & Leadership, 35*(2), 165–183. doi:10.1177/1741143207075387

Wallace Foundation. (2009). *Assessing the effectiveness of school leaders: New directions and new processes.* Washington.

Walumbwa, F. O., Avolio, B. J., Gardner, W. L., Wernsing, T. S., & Peterson, S. J. (2008). Authentic leadership: Development and validation of a theory-based measure. *Journal of Management, 34*(1), 89–126. doi 10.1177/0149206307308913

Wiewiora, A., & Kowalkiewicz, A. (2019). The role of authentic assessment in developing authentic leadership identity and competencies. *Assessment & Evaluation in Higher Education, 44*(3), 415–430. https://doi.org/10.1080/02602938.2018.1516730

Wiggins, G. (1998a). *Educational assessment: Designing assessments to inform and improve student performance.* John Wiley.

Wiggins, G. (1998b). A true test: Toward more authentic and equitable assessment. *Phi Delta Kappan, 70*(9), 703–713.

Index

3D objects   240, 245, 246, 248, 250–253, 256

assessment   IX–XII, 4–10, 13, 16, 19–21, 24–31, 35, 37, 44–46, 53–57, 60–64, 69, 73, 95–110, 116, 117, 119–122, 124, 132–136, 142–153, 155–157, 162–166, 168, 170, 172, 176, 177, 180, 188, 212, 240–243, 256, 262–266, 269, 280, 352, 368, 369, 377–379
authentic assessment   IX–XII, 4–10, 13, 16, 19–21, 24–31, 35, 37, 44–46, 53–57, 60–64, 69, 73, 95–110, 116, 117, 119–122, 124, 132–136, 142–153, 155–157, 162–166, 168, 170, 172, 176, 177, 180, 188, 212, 240–243, 256, 262–266, 269, 280, 352, 368, 369, 377–379
authentic assessment for learning   162, 170, 241, 243, 256
authentic evaluation   XII, 329–333, 335, 336, 344, 345, 350, 367–369, 371, 378
authentic evaluation of students   350, 367–369, 371, 378
authentic leadership   XII, 367–374, 376–379
authenticity   X, XI, 4, 5, 7, 8, 10, 11, 13–17, 19, 21, 27, 29, 54, 56, 57, 62, 63, 97, 100, 102, 103, 105, 107–109, 151, 156, 157, 163, 165–168, 170, 179, 181, 255, 263–269, 277–281, 345, 369–372, 377, 378

capstone   XI, 143–151, 157, 163–166, 168–174
capstone-authentic conversations   143, 163
classroom management   5, 9, 14, 19, 26, 27, 34, 41, 46, 55, 59, 71, 75, 117, 121, 125, 189, 190, 205, 206, 222, 223, 247, 287
collaboration   30, 32, 34, 43, 57, 62, 71–77, 80, 89, 110, 143, 145, 150, 153, 156, 170, 289, 297, 373
complexity of task   30, 31, 37, 44
critical reflection   30, 69, 77, 83, 84, 86, 88, 164, 169, 170, 180

diagnostic formative assessment   188, 193, 213, 303, 304, 307
distance education   116, 117, 119, 120, 122, 124, 135

education   X, XI, 3, 4, 6, 9, 54, 55, 57, 61, 63 70, 72, 73, 77, 80, 81, 95–98, 100–103, 108, 110, 119, 243, 262, 264, 265, 268, 276, 277, 279, 280, 330
engineering education   XI, 345
English as additional language (EAL)   287, 290, 291, 294, 295, 297, 298
experiencial learning   10, 18, 58, 60, 63, 72, 74, 79, 96, 108, 109, 152, 163, 164, 168, 171, 179, 180, 255, 256, 264, 268, 269, 280, 289, 294, 299, 303–308, 336
experimental schools in Greece   XI, 350–358, 360–363

geometric reasoning   76, 244, 246, 249, 254–256
graduate standards   4

humanising mathematics education   X, 262, 264, 265, 267, 268, 276, 277, 280

initial teacher education   X, 3, 4, 6, 9, 54, 55, 57, 61, 63
integrative review   X, 27, 28, 31, 39, 46

learner questioning   272, 298, 302, 307
learner-centred instruction   187–190, 197, 205, 209, 210, 213
learning trajectories   187–190, 210, 212
lifelong learning   IX, 108, 109, 154
linguistic diversity   286, 287
literature review   XI, 6, 27, 28, 219, 287, 288, 294, 315, 325, 326, 369

mathematical language skills   116, 117, 119, 122, 125, 127, 129, 132–136
mathematics education   X, XI, 70, 72, 73, 77, 80, 81, 95–98, 100–103, 108, 110, 119, 243, 262, 264, 265, 277, 279, 280, 330
mathematics learning   XI, 101, 103, 110, 119, 245, 247, 263, 264, 268, 280, 332, 335, 339–342
mathematics teaching effectiveness   329–338, 340, 344, 345
multilingual learners   285–287, 292, 294, 299–301, 308

online assessment   71–74, 77, 80, 88, 218, 228, 230, 234, 376

parents' views   350, 352, 354, 357, 360
peer interaction   70, 72, 73, 76, 88, 205
performance assessment   IX, 4, 9, 25, 27, 29, 32, 33, 35–37, 55, 56, 63, 96, 145, 375, 377, 379
phenomenological inquiry   269
place value   IX, 217–220, 223, 229
preservice mathematics teacher   72, 88, 105, 116, 119
preservice mathematics teacher education   72, 88

ratio reasoning   188, 193, 198, 201
real world   IX, X, 6, 7, 10, 15, 17, 26, 30, 31, 37–39, 42, 56, 58, 63, 87, 100, 105–108, 143–146, 156, 164, 165, 169–172, 174, 176, 177, 180, 188, 248, 265, 367, 368, 377, 379

school principal   XII, 368, 369 371, 373–378
social learning   31, 38, 41–45, 58, 72, 165, 172, 174, 176–178
STEM education   X, 24–30, 33–38, 41, 42, 44–46, 107, 108, 240
systemic approach   XI, 329, 330, 336, 344

teacher education   X, 4, 6–9, 12, 28, 54, 55, 57–59, 61, 63, 88, 142, 143, 145–149, 157, 316, 321, 369
teacher evaluation   316–321, 323–326
teaching performance assessment   4, 7, 25, 27, 29, 32, 33, 35–37, 55, 56, 63, 96, 145, 315, 325, 375, 377, 379
translanguaging   285, 287–295, 298, 302–308

virtual simulation   X, 53–55, 57, 60–64

Printed in the United States
by Baker & Taylor Publisher Services